20p.

ONCE AN AUSTRALIAN

Adieu, adieu! my native shore
Fades o'er the water blue;
The night-winds sigh, the breakers roar,
And shrieks the wild sea mew.
Yon sun that sets upon the sea
We follow in his flight;
Farewell awhile to him and thee,
My native Land — Good Night!

Lord Byron

Leaving the narrow world of childhood,
we're inclined to think we've landed in
the big wide world, but usually we've got
it the wrong way round.

Jenny Diski

When you leave home it travels with you.

Peter Conrad

Some of us feel at home nowhere …

Peter Porter

ONCE AN AUSTRALIAN

Journeys with Barry Humphries, Clive James,
Germaine Greer and Robert Hughes

Ian Britain

Melbourne
OXFORD UNIVERSITY PRESS
Oxford   Auckland   New York

OXFORD UNIVERSITY PRESS AUSTRALIA

Oxford   New York
Athens   Auckland   Bangkok   Bombay
Calcutta   Cape Town   Dar es Salaam   Delhi
Florence   Hong Kong   Istanbul   Karachi
Kuala Lumpur   Madras   Madrid   Melbourne
Mexico City   Nairobi   Paris   Port Moresby
Singapore   Taipei   Tokyo   Toronto

and associated companies in
Berlin   Ibadan

OXFORD is a trade mark of Oxford University Press

© Ian Britain 1997
First published 1997

National Library of Australia
Cataloguing-in-Publication data:

Britain, Ian, 1948– .
   Once an Australian: journeys with
   Barry Humphries, Clive James, Germaine Greer
   and Robert Hughes.

   Includes index.
   ISBN 0 19 553742 4.

   1. Greer, Germaine, 1939– . 2. James, Clive, 1939– .
   3. Humphries, Barry, 1934– . 4. Hughes, Robert,
   1938– . 5. Authors, Australian — 20th century —
   Biography. I. Title.

A828.3009

Text design by Steve Randles
Cover design by Steve Randles
Typeset by Steve Randles
Printed through South Wind, Singapore
Published by Oxford University Press,
253 Normanby Road, South Melbourne, Australia

Contents

To

Ian Campbell

John Foster

Michael Howard

Malcolm Wild

Johann Wolfram

Wish you were here

Preface

'Writers want things to be over, so that they can write the elegy', remarks Clive James, one of the writers whose careers form the subject of this book. But the careers of writers don't have to be over for some kind of assessment of them to be possible. Elsewhere, referring to Germaine Greer, another of the subjects of this book, James compares a television programme of hers to the 'despised genre' of the magazine profile, but argues that this genre 'can have its uses, especially as an introduction'. What I have attempted in the following pages are 'profiles' of four Australians whose careers appear to be far from over: Barry Humphries and Robert Hughes, as well as Clive James and Germaine Greer. There is a common theme, provided by the decision of these four figures to leave their native land and pursue their careers abroad; but the profiles are largely independent of each other and may be read in any order.

In a sense, these figures have become so prominent as to make introductions unnecessary. One of the things which unites them, apart from their expatriatism, is their aptitude for self-publicity. It is highly selective publicity, however, and even at its most searching and confessional, as in the form of personal reflection on various facets of their earlier lives, it suggests as much a talent or a taste for privacy and self-effacement, if not self-concealment.

Of the four figures concerned, Robert Hughes has published least in the way of autobiographical recollection. It is only recently, when he has sensed that others may be interested in writing about his life, that he has begun to show some promptings to produce his own version. Generous to correspondents who have requested further information about the subjects of his art reviews in *Time* magazine ('I always reply to those letters', he has said), he has proved less easily accessible when approached by reviewers or critics of his own career, let alone by suspected snoops and gossips.

Germaine Greer has movingly combined biography with autobiography in the memoir of her father, *Daddy, we hardly knew you,* as well as making extensive use of each of these modes in her critical and polemical writings. She has signalled contempt, however, for what she sees as the invasiveness and parasitism of biographers in general, especially for those who have shown any interest in chronicling *her* life. One of them she recently dubbed 'wretched flesh-eating bacterium'.

Clive James was just past fifty when he produced a third volume of his memoirs, but he has delighted in calling them 'unreliable' and tantalising us with the possibility that they might be little more than novels in disguise. A well-known interviewer of other prominent figures on matters regarding their private as well as their professional lives, he has declared that he himself is 'not a good interviewee' — 'the world's worst', in fact. He will still grant interviews to promote his work, but has said of his customary manner in them: 'Evasive's the word'.

Barry Humphries has already been the subject of one biography, as well as of a monograph on his style as a performer which includes much incidental biographical detail. He has written one volume of autobiography and a novel that appears to have a strong autobiographical element. There is a note at the beginning of the novel, however, cautioning readers not to be deceived by 'personages which you perceive you know, or think you recognise … ' He claims that 'they have no existence beyond these pages'. He has also granted many interviews with journalists and others down the years, but has affected a similar posture in them to Clive James'. After an address at the National Press Club in Canberra in 1978, he told his audience: 'I'm happy to provide an evasive answer to any question you care to put to me'.

I have perhaps been too easily deterred by these walls of reserve to attempt to break them down by conventional means. From a combination of respect for these figures, shyness in the face of their formidable reputations, and a certain reticence bred in me from years of scholarly introversion, I decided at an early stage to have as little direct contact with them as possible. Any fresh profiles of them had to be more than just an introduction, given that they had already achieved such prominence in the public eye; but if the time was not right for an elegy — too *early* in the case of this genre — the same objection seemed to apply to a comprehensive biography. It still does. How can a biography be truly comprehensive when the subjects are (by ordinary standards) far from the end of their lives or careers, and when their private papers remain largely, and quite properly, in private hands? One might seek 'authorisation' from them to begin on such an enterprise, though the experiences of those who have tried to do this have hardly been very encouraging; and, even if successful in gaining authorisation, one would have no guarantee of complete independence.

The so-called 'in depth' interview (assuming one could arrange such a thing) has some related drawbacks. There have been so many interviews with the figures concerned already, and they provide some good sources of incidental information; but it is debatable whether further exercises of this kind would be very helpful in uncovering more substantial depths when the subjects concerned have proved increasingly — and quite understandably — wary of such attempts at exposure.

I have had to keep thinking, therefore, about what sort of profiles might be viable that were more than introductory sketches but less than complete portraits, and that didn't rely on direct encounters or 'sittings' with their subjects. The result of these thoughts, reflected in the following pages, is a hybrid, but one, I trust, that is not without some use, pleasure, stimulus and legitimacy. While I have tried to retain a biographical focus, my research methods and narrative techniques also draw on the practices of the social historian and cultural critic (reflecting my own early professional training). Although I have had hardly any access to the private correspondence of my subjects, I have managed to mine considerable detail of biographical interest from their public pronouncements and writings. I am partly beholden here to the model of one of the reigning princes of biography, Richard Holmes, who has shown so deftly and so sensitively in his own work how much may be gathered of 'the personal life that is hidden in, and below, the printed page' (see *Footsteps. Adventures of a Romantic Biographer,* London, 1985, p. 31).

If some of my more speculative biographical deductions seem insensitive to my subjects, make them wince with embarrassment, not at their own but at *my* deficiencies of perception, I hope that they will also understand that the attempt to engage in such speculation has sometimes been a necessary, even unavoidable, part of recounting the course of their careers, explaining the motivating impulses of their work, and elaborating its full context. There can be no doubt that the four figures who form the subject of this book remain most important to us for the nature and impact of their work, not for the detail of their personal lives, however interesting. But it is impossible to separate these things completely, especially when their work has been partly about their life or has grown out of some of its central facets and preoccupations. The integral relationship between the life and the work has been most obvious in the case of Barry Humphries and of Germaine Greer, and openly acknowledged by them on various occasions, even if they have fudged or forgotten the precise details. It has not been quite so obvious, perhaps, with Clive James and Robert Hughes, or not so loudly trumpeted by them. That doesn't mean it can't be traced or isn't of comparable significance. One should consider their own example here when they address the work of some of their own subjects — poets, mainly, in James' case, and painters in Hughes'. Each has emphasised the significance to this work (and to our appreciation of it) of such intensely personal matters as the sexual and emotional lives of the individual artists concerned. Both have also often invoked, as a part of their interpretation, their subjects' national or racial identity, family and domestic circumstances, social origins, religious beliefs, and political positions. There seems no logical reason why such aspects and considerations should be any less relevant to the work of James or Hughes, and where some evidence for these things has been available, I have readily employed it in my interpretation, though not, I trust, without due discrimination.

I have taken extra heart in this whole enterprise from some recently reported statements of Germaine Greer, who has been the most vocal in her opposition to any biographical perspectives on her work. In a lecture she delivered to the annual Hay-on-Wye Literary Festival in June 1996, she argued that the original meaning of publication was to become public, adding that: 'All authors are one way or another obliged to invade the privacy of people they know'. On being quizzed subsequently as to the implications of this statement for herself, she is quoted as replying: 'the point about me being treated as public property is true. I have to take what's coming ... '

In getting this enterprise off the ground, I owe most to the encouragement and energy of my publisher, Peter Rose, at Oxford University Press, Melbourne. He spotted the potential of the subject in an early piece I wrote on Barry Humphries for the journal, *Voices,* and he has been of invaluable assistance at every subsequent stage, not least in the gentle but firm prodding which he had to apply to get me over the finishing line.

To the editors of *Voices,* and of various other journals (*Meanjin, 24 Hours, Thesis Eleven, Australian Historical Studies*), I owe thanks for permission to republish or re-work sections of material which appears in their pages.

There are numerous institutions, and individuals within those institutions, to whom I wish to express my gratitude for easing the tasks of, and providing the services for, the various kinds of research involved in the production of this book: the Baillieu Library and the Educational Resource Centre at the University of Melbourne (where I received particular help from Juliet Flesch and Lesley Skinner); the Fisher Library at the University of Sydney; the State Library of Victoria and the State Library of New South Wales; the Performing Arts Museum in Melbourne; the Chifley Library and the Menzies Library at the Australian National University in Canberra; the National Library of Australia (where I received special assistance from Graeme Powell, Richard Stone, Bill Tully, and Leonie Voorhoeve, not to mention John Thompson, of whom more anon); the New York Public Library; the British Library in London; Simon Rooks at the BBC Sound Archive; and Keith Phillips of BBC 'Program Access' at the TV Centre, Shepherds Bush, London — the most marvellous resource for media buffs and scholars of television history and performance.

One of the great librarians of the world, and a great personal friend, is John Thompson, whose enthusiasm for this project often outpaced my own and was always backed up by his assiduous attention to my every bibliographic need. He also read every word of every draft, and helped save me from numerous mistakes and solecisms.

One of the great research assistants of the world, and another great friend, is Ann Brothers. I never had much faith in the uses of research assistants until she began to help me out on a casual basis at what turned out to be the half-way mark of the project. Without her subsequent help and support, this would have been the quarter-way mark at most. To her uncanny empathy with my own ideas for the project she added an independent initiative which helped extend and enrich those ideas.

I have been very lucky in all of my friends and colleagues, worldwide, who provided hospitality to an inveterate scholar-gypsy and boosted the morale of a natural panic-merchant while also dispensing a wealth of advice (professional or, even more useful, non-professional) on a wide range of scholarly, technical and stylistic matters. I often chafed at this advice when first given, but I have ended up following it in nearly all instances. There are numerous others I met in my travels while completing this book who have improved it and enriched it in ways they now mightn't even recognise or remember. It seems so unfair simply to lump all these advisers and assistants together in one long undiscriminating list, but it would take another chapter to single out their respective contributions. So here is the list, in alphabetical order: William Abrahams, Jane Adamson, Michael Adcock, Brett Bailey, Cally Baxter, Paul Baxter, Peter Beilharz, Frank Bongiorno, Caroline Brothers, Nicholas Brown, John Buckley, Verona Burgess, Janet Chimonyo, Carolyn Cliff, Bill Cobbett, Peter Conrad, Jim Davidson, Juan Davila, Graeme Davison, Cheryl Delalande, Ian Donaldson, Mark Downing, Fraser Fair, Barbara Falk, Antonia Finnane, Bill Granville, Giulia Guiffrè, Simon Haines, Jennie Hazelgrove, Rosanna Heal, Tony Heal, Katie Holmes, Ken Inglis, Nick Jose, Al Knight, John Knight, Jeremy Kruse, John Lack, Marilyn Lake, Susan Lever, Graham Little, Jennie Little, Alan McBriar, Marilyn McBriar, Heather McCalman, Iain McCalman, Janet McCalman, Tammy McCarthy, Brian McFarlane, Gerie McFarlane, Norman MacKenzie, Dave McLachlan, Humphrey

McQueen, Bill Mandle, Anne Murch, Brian Nelson, Evie Nelson, Brenda Niall, Philip Olander, Helen O'Shea, Courtney Pederson, Ros Pesman, Lily Petkovska, Stuart Piggin, Peter Porter, John Rickard, Sue Rickard, Ian Robertson, Geoffrey Rogers, Geoffrey Serle, Ann Smith, Barry Smith, Bernard Smith, Max Smith, Mary Spongberg, Peter Stansky, Peter Stewart, Lachlan Strahan, Jackie Templeton, Greg Terrill, Scott Thornbury, Jock Tomlinson, David Tredinnick, Chris Wallace-Crabbe, Robin Wallace-Crabbe, Cynthia Wild, Jocelyn Wogan-Browne, Iain Wright, Margaret Wu. (My apologies to any I have missed.)

To my parents I owe an enormous debt of gratitude for their continuing faith in my work at times when I was losing my own faith in it, and for their continuing support in all sorts of other ways, from reining in my stylistic excesses to videotaping pertinent television programmes at the shortest notice or providing innumerable dinners at times of great pressure.

For indispensable financial and/or institutional support during the course of the project, I wish to thank the Departments of English and History at the Australian National University, which elected me to a research fellowship in the second semester of 1992, the Department of History at the University of Melbourne, which kept on renewing my Research Associateship year after year, and the Humanities Research Centre at the Australian National University, which awarded me a fellowship for the early months of 1996 and provided me with the most conducive environment I can imagine for the finishing stages of a book like this. During 1995, when the bulk of the research and the preliminary drafting of chapters was carried out, I was kept afloat by a generous grant from the Literature Board of the Australia Council. (This may only confirm my subjects' well-publicised doubts about the wisdom of arts grants.)

I am grateful to Harry M. Miller for permission to consult material relating to Barry Humphries in the Miller Papers at the National Library of Australia. I should like to thank Gerard Windsor for permission to consult the manuscript of his history of St Ignatius' College, Sydney, held at the National Library of Australia. For permission to reprint from copyright material not covered by 'fair dealing' provisions for works of research, criticism and current reportage, such as represented by this book, I am grateful to the following: Oxford University Press, for Peter Porter;

Punch and Bilarm Music Pty Ltd, for Barry Humphries, and Mr
Humphries himself for the lyrics to Edna Everage's song, 'Australian
Vitality'; Peters Fraser & Dunlop Ltd and *London Review of Books*, for Clive
James.

This project has been assisted by the Commonwealth Government
through the Australia Council, its arts funding and advisory body.

Ian Britain
Melbourne, December 1996

Chapter One

Word Children

Barry Humphries, Clive James, Germaine Greer, Robert Hughes: there are few individuals of greater lustre or notoriety on the roll-call of expatriate Australians since the Second World War, and none that are more commonly talked about in the same breath. They all talk about each other, too; yet they never meet as a group, and they have managed to resist the more incestuous intimacies of metropolitan coteries like the Bloomsbury Group or the Algonquin Round Table. They have never even been particularly close friends at any stage of their lives.[1] What do they share, then, apart from their status as expatriates and popular celebrities?

One of their marks of collective identity has been their dependence on words in forging their individual identities. They are all writers, and not just writers of books, but verbal performers in various media, most notably television. It is their compulsive use of words, their addiction to public articulation, which has helped make them celebrities, and determined the kinds of celebrity they are. Though they have often made a point of praising direct, ordinary, everyday English, or of setting themselves up as scourges of mystification, academic verbiage, jargon, or 'fancy' speech, they have shown a lingering attachment to more arcane words in their own discourse.[2] The following lists provide a random sample:

1

HUMPHRIES anaglyptic, fuliginous, gramineous, grumous-kneed, hircine, hispid, impetiginous, lacunose, muscareous, psittacine, stercoraceous, teratalogically.

JAMES acromegalic, armigerous, asymptotic, autoschediastic, catabasis, echolalia, eidetic, haplography, kludge, ogival, pelagic, tede.

GREER algolagnia, anophobia, auscultated, caracoled, chorionic, emmena-gogic, gadrooned, kurtosis, phatic, purulent, sacroiliac, sparagamos.

HUGHES autophagy, chthonic, emulgent, fulgid, haptic, hunker, roiled, oneirically, rachitic, steatopygous, telluric.

This is hardly a representative sample of their general diction or modes of speech (if it were, their fates might have been as obscure as the words themselves), but it can supply some clues to the intersecting patterns in their lives. It lends an insight into the whys and wherefores of their career paths, makes sense of the where-froms and where-tos in their trajectories as well. It is a symptom — perhaps the most telling one — of whatever distinctiveness or unity they can be said to have as an expatriate group.

There are some significant parallels in their personal backgrounds and circumstances, but they are neither very precise nor particularly distinctive ones. They were all born in the same decade into middle-class, Christian homes situated in the suburbs of either Melbourne or Sydney, Australia's two most populous cities. Hughes, James and Greer made their first appearance in the world within a few months of each other, towards the end of the 1930s; but Humphries preceded them by four or five years. Except for James, who was an only child, each of them had siblings of both sexes, although their respective positions in the family, *vis-à-vis* their brothers and sisters, were varied. Their families also represented varying levels, from the upper to the lower extremes, of Australia's delicately stratified middle class, and different religious denominations (two were Catholic families, the other two Protestant).

There are some coincidences in the patterns of their expatriatism, but rough ones; and the variations in these patterns are as striking. Humphries, James, Greer and Hughes all left Australia within a five-year span (1959–64) when they were in their early to mid-twenties. Their first destination and overseas base was England, and for three of them this has remained the case, although all of them were to spend spells of differing lengths in Europe or America, and one of them (Hughes) has long been settled in New York. All of them have retained their Australian passports, and continued to revisit their native land, but there has been little consistency in their respective toings and froings.[3]

Humphries first left Australia in 1959 and made his first return visit in 1962. This was a long gap for him, if we are to judge by the frequency of his subsequent trips back to Australia. The length of his stays has often been months at a time, even when he has not been involved in one of his stage shows.

Clive James left on New Years Eve 1961. He has claimed subsequently that he only intended to stay away from Australia for about five years, but some ten years on he had still not returned, even on a visit, and he could be found declaring that 'I'm never going back to Australia to live'. It was not till 1976 that he made his first return trip. He has revisited with increasing frequency in subsequent years — comfortable air travel is now no financial obstacle for him — but these visits have been brief compared to Humphries'.[4]

Germaine Greer left in 1964, and returned for the first time some eight years later, in order to promote her book, *The Female Eunuch*. She has intimated that when she first departed her antipodean 'home' she had imagined it would be for ever. From childhood, she claims, she had formed an ambition to be 'a citizen of Europe'. She has, in the event, made further trips back to Australia, though they have been as infrequent as they have been brief. Her longest return visits were in the Australian summer months of 1986 and 1987, when she was doing research for the book about her father, *Daddy, we hardly knew you*.[5]

Robert Hughes also left Australia in 1964, and with a similar burning resolve to put Australia behind him once and for all. His appetite for the northern hemisphere had already been whetted by a brief trip he had made to England in 1959. He had also caught his first glimpse of New York in that year, going there on a flying visit — literally so, according to Clive James, who recalls how Hughes ventured forth on one of the new jet airliners which have since become a standard mode of travel for everybody.[6]

His second and more permanent departure five years later was not to rule out return visits. The first of these, as in Greer's case, was in 1972, a short while after he had moved from England to America. Since then, they have become more regular than hers, if not much longer in duration.

These variations, complications and innovations in the patterns of their journeyings may prompt us to wonder how far the term 'expatriate' is still applicable to them as a general label. 'Any reality associated with the expression has long vanished', Clyde Packer protested in 1984, introducing a book of interviews with various Australians abroad (including Germaine Greer and Robert Hughes).[7] The fact remains, however, that Hughes, Greer, James and Humphries have all shifted and then retained the main base of their personal and working lives outside Australia; and in this there is an underlying conformity among them to a very old pattern of response to their country, by whatever name we call it.

From the time Australia was first established as a British colony at the end of the eighteenth century, it has not been unusual for a proportion of its population to seek to depart its shores and settle elsewhere, most commonly in the United Kingdom. It has been estimated that over half of those who came out to Australia with the First Fleet found a way of returning. Up to nearly a third of this number may have been former convicts, who had been forced to come in the first place. They can hardly be accounted expatriates in any modern sense, though there was an older meaning of the word which meant 'banished from one's native land', and in this sense, they may be regarded as expatriates of Great Britain who succeeded in *re*patriating themselves. We would now call them returned exiles.[8]

Colonial Australia's British origins, and its continuing legal, political, economic and cultural ties with Britain, made the 'mother country' an obvious source of fascination and deference (as well as of varying degrees of resentment) for native-born Australians in subsequent generations. From the earliest years of the nineteenth century, some of the native-born from the better-off families were being sent to Britain to receive at least a part of their education, and while they would still have been children at the time, with little choice in the matter, there were those among them who ended up electing to stay there. By the middle of the nineteenth century, with the introduction of a steamship run, and then the opening of the Suez

Canal in 1869, Britain was already becoming a standard travel destination for adult Australians who could afford the fare, and both fares and journey times were to be considerably reduced over the following decades. As the ancestral 'home' of most white Australians, as the fount of their language and the main focus of what they learned at school about literature and history, Britain merited at least a visit; and in the eyes of some, the trip itself came to assume the form of a 'rite of passage' to full maturity.[9]

It is impossible to calculate, from the skimpy records of the nineteenth century, precisely how many Australians made this trip from year to year, and what percentage of these stayed on in Britain to become more or less permanent expatriates, but in 1911 British census statistics revealed that there were some 23 000 Australians temporarily or permanently resident in England and Wales. Just over half a century later, roughly coinciding with the journeys of Humphries, James, Greer and Hughes, some unofficial figures were quoted in an article by Jack Lindsay in the Melbourne literary quarterly, *Meanjin,* which placed the total number of Australians travelling to Britain at around 32 000 *each year.* Of these, Lindsay reported, 'about half are persons planning to stay'. (He himself had left Australia for Britain nearly four decades earlier, 'planning to stay' only a few years but in the event never returning.) He gave no source or authority for his figures. Official Australian statistics of 'permanent departures' to the United Kingdom in the year this article was published (1963) give the much lower number of 1791; though the respective categories are not strictly comparable. Many may have indeed planned to stay in Britain once they got there — or even before they got there — without having registered themselves as permanent departures.[10]

Whatever the case, when they left Australia in the late 1950s and early 1960s, Humphries and James and Greer and Hughes were clearly part of a long and substantial lineage among their countrymen. It was a richly varied lineage, too. The official statistics of 'permanent movement' from Australia in those years singled out twelve broad occupational categories, including 'professional, technical and related workers', 'administrative, executive and managerial workers', 'clerical workers', 'sales workers', 'craftsmen and production-process workers', 'labourers', 'service ... , sport and recreation workers', and 'persons not in work force — children and

students'. (By far the highest number, of either sex, belonged to the last category — which was swollen, perhaps, by the multiple number of
dependants of those in the other categories.)[11]

How would our 'famous four', in the days before they acquired their
fame, fit into this schema? Not very easily then, and not enough to make
them readily or specifically identifiable now. Each of them, on the basis of
early dabblings in the worlds of journalism, the stage or television, might
be incorporated under one or both of the headings, 'recreation workers'
and 'professional' — though their earliest dabblings in such fields had been
as students, and they had only just started to earn any kind of living from
these endeavours. It is not certain, either, that all of them would have been
entirely happy about the pairing of their endeavours with 'sport'. Only one
of them, Germaine Greer, remained officially a student, and was to go to
England on a scholarship, but it was a high-powered, advance-level, relatively well-paying scholarship that assured her considerable material and
creative independence for a few years at least.

Jack Lindsay, in presenting his figures of Australians in England in the
early 1960s, had speculated that 'a large proportion ... are members of the
arts or professions', and that over the last decade an 'exodus of intellectuals' had become 'large-scale and significant'. The title of his article was 'The
Alienated Australian Intellectual'. (The cultural critic, P.R. Stephensen, had
already noted in the 1930s a 'formidable batch' of Australian writers and
intellectuals who had emigrated to London — partly driven out, he said,
by 'the smugness, the intolerable hegemony of the Second-rate in positions
of authority ... ') The very fact that there was no specific slot for 'artists'
or 'intellectuals' in the official figures might be taken as a measure of the
alienation of these groups from Australian society at large, or at least of
their inability to fit recognised categories of social significance. Certainly,
even among members of these groups who elected to stay in Australia, it is
hard to find any testimony around this time to a sense of integration on
their part with the rest of society. If there were those who didn't feel themselves to be misfits or marginals, their voices have been well and truly
drowned out by those who did.[12]

Three well-known diatribes against Australian mediocrity, produced
by intellectuals resident in Australia, date from the very period in which

Humphries, James, Greer and Hughes were all leaving, or planning to leave. In 1958 Patrick White, who had returned from England about a decade earlier to continue his novel-writing career, discoursed in an article commissioned by an Australian literary journal on

> the Great Australian Emptiness, in which the mind is the least of possessions, in which the rich man is the important man, in which the schoolmaster and the journalist rule what intellectual roost there is, in which beautiful youths and girls stare at life through blind blue eyes, in which … food means cake and steak, muscles prevail, and the march of material ugliness does not raise a quiver from the average nerves.

In 1960 the Melbourne architect, Robin Boyd, discoursed at book length on *The Australian Ugliness*, focusing his attention on urban and suburban architecture. His critique had implications far beyond his professional field of concern. 'The basis of the Australian ugliness', he declared, 'is an unwillingness to be committed on the level of ideas. In all the arts of living, … Australia shuffles about vigorously in the middle … of the road, picking up disconnected ideas wherever she finds them'. In 1964 the maverick journalist and editor, Donald Horne, who had returned to his homeland in 1954 after a five-year spell in England, discoursed on Australia's material good fortune and social stability in his book, *The Lucky Country*, although the title was at least partly ironic and his diagnosis of the national condition in non-material senses was as unpropitious as White's or Boyd's: 'Australia is a lucky country run mainly by second-rate people who share its luck', he had concluded. Earlier in the book he claimed that 'in a sense' Australia 'has not got a mind. Intellectual life exists but it is still fugitive. Emergent and uncomfortable, it has no established relation to practical life'.[13]

Neither Boyd nor White, any more than Horne, depicts Australia in the 1950s and 1960s as completely anti-intellectual, as actively inimical to all creative thought and endeavour. They would hardly have been able to function as critics, let alone as practitioners of their respective arts, if it had been so. For them, the general sense of emptiness, ugliness, second-rateness, are a result not of any passionate hostility to art or intellect but of qualities that lack passion: indifference, neglect, complacency, ignorance, unadventurousness. Such qualities are not exclusively Australian, Horne acknowledges in the second edition of his book. White clearly suggests at another point in his diatribe that Australia, for all of its pervasive mediocrity, was not the worst of environments for the likes of himself; he had originally returned from England, he said, because he didn't want to turn 'into that most sterile of human beings, a London intellectual'. Boyd recognised qualities in the Australian climate and diet (including the surfeit of steak derided by White) that were positively conducive to the early nurturing of artistic gifts, even if — as he went on to imply — the professional development of those gifts demanded the challenges and stimuli of other environments, older, colder, less evenly affluent but more aesthetically receptive:

> Many talented and potentially-creative Australians ... do not starve. They make a good living at something else and practice [sic] their art as a hobby. Others leave the country. A list of successful Australians in creative fields in London and New York suggests that there is something about the Australian sun and the meaty diet that produces a high proportion of talented people.[14]

Humphries, James, Greer and Hughes were still too young, or were not sufficiently established, to appear among the particular names that Boyd invoked here to support his point. Untested as yet by sustained exposure to other countries (James and Greer still hadn't set foot outside Australia at the time Boyd's book was first published) they were inclined to sense their alienation from their native land all the more acutely, and they were less inclined to notice or to appreciate what its physical and material advantages had afforded them.

Their passionate attraction to words, their urge and capacity to articulate — all a part of what made them feel alien to start with — has continued to tempt them into neat epigrammatic generalisations about the frustrations of Australian cultural and intellectual life around the time they were growing up or thereafter. Just at the time he was cutting his ties with Australia, in 1964, Robert Hughes could be found pronouncing, in an article he wrote on 'The Intellectual in Australia': 'there is no tradition of intellect in Australia. There are only intelligent men'. He meant by this that there was no 'habit of enquiry' for its own sake, and that what intellectuals there were had to 'cloak their role behind their "job", as if embarrassed ...

['l']he intellectual as such has never found a place in Australian society'. In 1971, nearly a decade after he had left Australia, Clive James was declaring, with specific reference to his own line of work as a writer: 'The penalty for staying home is to accept provincial standards'. He echoed Hughes in judging his homeland as 'not a good place to be interested in ideas for their own sake', and he was to echo Hughes again five years later, when, following his first return visit to Australia, he stated that it 'was the critical journalism which finally got me down, making me realise that my birthplace would probably have no place for me'.[15]

As late as 1984, Barry Humphries was suggesting that while Australia produced an enormous number of artists, the only genuine ones had had to 'pursue careers abroad'. In the same breath he roundly declared that Australia 'has no Intelligentsia whatsoever'. The capital 'I' here, as well as the context (an introduction to an anthology of writings on Australia from *Punch*), might suggest an impish irony behind these observations; but there is a more earnest, more dogmatic imp at work in the sub-conscious of Germaine Greer ('the Fury', as she describes it, or 'my worse self') which was to remind her, when she was writing the book on her father in 1987, that 'No Australian likes a clever child'. When, a few years earlier, she had written an introduction to a famous Australian novel about the travails of a clever child, *The Getting of Wisdom* by Henry Handel Richardson, she sought to remind readers in her own voice of the 'utter philistinism' of her and the author's native land.[16]

Humphries, at the head of the *Punch* piece, quoted his own 'Fury' or alter ego, Edna Everage, on Australia:

> It's the land of milk and honey,
> It's so rich and safe and … funny.

In retrospect, the funniness of Australia could go some way to redeeming its philistinism, its indifference to the intellect, its provinciality — the qualities Edna herself personified to a T. But the milk and honey, much as they had helped to nurture the bodies and minds of Edna's creator and his compeers, were to be among the very ingredients which turned them off their native land in the first place, made malcontents and tearaways out of them. At the time they left, Australia was too rich and too safe to be bearable for them.

The reign of Robert Menzies and the Liberal–Country Party Coalition from 1949 to 1966 had coincided with, if not served to initiate, an era of rapid job expansion (for women as well as for men), substantial industrial growth, steadily rising wages, and rapid increases in the ownership of houses, cars, and domestic appliances among the population in general. That a succession of governments led by one man was in power for so long gave Australia a veneer of extraordinary stability, for all of the cracks along political, social and religious lines which often peeped through (Cold War tensions between right and left, friction between employers and unions, the sectarian conflicts of the Protestant majority with a sizeable Catholic minority), and despite remaining inequities in the status of women and of the country's indigenous population.[17]

The two decades preceding this era were notable neither for being 'rich' nor for being 'safe', having witnessed a world depression and then a world war. Our 'famous four' were all born into this era, but were too young at the time to be as conscious of its upheavals, or as fully caught up in them, as their parents' generation. Having lived through this era (if managing to survive it, that is; Clive James' father was one who didn't), this older generation doubtless thought it was doing the right thing in trying to rebuild a secure and comfortable world for its children. But it was those securities and comforts which some of its more precocious progeny claimed to find *most* oppressive. They had been over-protected. The playwright, poet and fiction-writer, Ray Mathew, who came to settle in London in the early 1960s, suggested that the only real effect of '*The War* and *The Depression* — the shibboleths of my generation's childhood' was an intensification of the protective, inward-turning urges among the older generation. 'Nothing', he stated in 1962, 'has happened to force Australians to reconsider themselves and their values'.[18] A land where nothing happened was to be a familiar refrain of the expatriate chorus when its members chose to look back at what they had left.

'There's the sun and the wealth', said Clive James of Australia in 1971, ' … and it really is a wonderful country to be young in. The trouble, as far as I'm concerned, is that it's also a wonderful country to *stay* young in'. If the climate and the affluence were not in themselves responsible for this perpetual state of immaturity, they were not a sufficient counter-force against it either. Germaine Greer admits to little that was wonderful about her Australian youth — wonder was precisely the ingredient that was missing from the daily round. 'We were perfectly secure', she told the psychiatrist, Anthony Clare, who interviewed her on BBC radio in 1989: 'The sun shone most days, and it was bloody lethal'. Writing a memoir for Barry Humphries on his sixtieth birthday, she recollects her own experiences of their shared home town:

> My parents … ate meat and veggies in the evening except on Sundays when they ate them at midday, owned only the books given away free by the newspaper group my father worked for, no records, no record-player until I was in my teens, and much admired Frank Sinatra and Robert Menzies. Not only these behaviours but every aspect of Melbourne suburban life I found boring.[19]

Humphries' own first book, *Bizarre,* an anthology of the grotesque in literature and photography, published when he was just twenty-six, was 'frankly addressed' to 'those who find a literary diet of steak and eggs curiously insufficient'. In a radio talk he broadcast a few years later, he said that his native land had 'not always' been a funny place for him, and that 'there was a time when Australian life, or Australian suburban life seemed an oppressive and terrible thing'. He specifically located the source of this oppression, of the 'terrible boredom and vacuum' which was its chief symptom, 'somewhere at the heart of all that suburban coziness and upholstered security'.[20]

There were more obvious, more brutal forms of oppression facing 'Australians in the 1950s', according to Robert Hughes: 'all manner of censorship, Grundyism and excessive police power'. The sun and the sea and the hedonistic appetites they encouraged were a beguiling smokescreen for such iniquities, he intimated — just as they had been when the country was still a penal colony a century or more earlier. Not long before he left Australia in the mid-1960s, Hughes took a visiting American writer to lunch at a fish restaurant on Sydney Harbour, the Ozone. There was no denying its bountiful pleasures, but they were those of a numbing drug:

> You sit all afternoon, glutted with sun and sweating with food, and sink into that agreeable torpor where talk … becomes a pastime … The Ozone is a

microcosm of Australia, a place where nothing that happens beyond the terrace seems altogether real and where all things conspire to be comforting.

'All things' included much of the art that was on offer as well as what passed for intellectual discourse. Reporting on the festival of the arts in Adelaide earlier the same year, Hughes noted: 'The choice of plays, concerts and operas was kept safe by the official committee: it was a soothing, unchallenging fortnight ... Except in painting and ballet, Adelaide was not a showcase for the avant-garde'.[21]

Robert Menzies' visions for Australia, sketched out long before his extended reign in the 1950s and 1960s, had certainly not excluded a place for intellect or the creative spirit, but it was an orthodox, highly respectable sort of place that he had in mind. Nothing sums it up more succinctly than his hymn to the middle class (the group in Australia which came to provide the main basis of his support) in a famous radio broadcast he made in 1942: 'The middle class provides more than perhaps any other the intellectual life which marks us off from the beast; the life which finds room for literature, for the arts, for science, for medicine and the law'. This was bound to be too restrictive for restless young lions in any of these fields, especially in literature and the arts.[22]

Donald Horne claimed of Menzies in *The Lucky Country*: 'insofar as he does have intellectual or artistic interests, they are extremely provincial and old hat'. These interests were also too closely focused on institutions. From 1932, when he had been Attorney-General in the Victorian state government, Menzies had been hatching plans for an Australian Academy of Art. The Academy was officially launched in 1937, but Menzies' ill-guarded sneers at the modernist avant-garde were bound to divide practising artists about the merit of the institution, and it soon foundered on those divisions, as well as on various personal, institutional, and regional jealousies. He was to have much greater success in his efforts to expand university education in the 1950s. All of our famous four were to attend Australian universities in this period, but two of them (Humphries and Hughes) abandoned their courses long before they were due to complete them. In his valedictory pronouncement on the Australian intellectual, Hughes was to raise a cry of concern at 'the inexorable process by which intellectuals are institutionalized'.[23]

Both Hughes and Humphries had found a good initial base for their wider cultural interests on their respective university campuses, but they soon outgrew this and had no real need of it. While James and Greer did complete their first degrees, and went on to further academic studies of various sorts and at different levels, they too were eventually to make their names outside university walls. The famousness of the famous four has stemmed from their intellectual insouciance and outrageousness rather than from scholarly introversion — though their scholarly promptings should not be overlooked; these continue to underpin their bravura, lend solidity to their dazzle. They are the sustaining source of their verbal athleticism, the covert steroid that continues to empower them.

The world of words, books, languages and literature was the first world to which this group had gravitated in order to escape the conformities and gentilities of middle-class Australia of the 1940s and 1950s. It might have compounded their sense of alienation, but it also provided them with a way of coping while waiting to escape to places in the 'real world' where they imagined they would be less alien. It allowed them to imagine the possibilities of such an escape. 'The pages of a book', recalls James in the third volume of his autobiography, were 'always, since my earliest childhood, my favourite place to hide'. The only interesting thing in her whole childhood, according to Greer, was 'the world of my books'. The syndrome, if that is what it is, has been best described by the novelist, David Malouf, who has contrived to divide his time between Australia and Europe for most of his writing career:

> Australians of a certain turn of mind are literary beyond the imagination of most Europeans. We live out of books. Isolation breeds in us, or used to, a particular intensity of imagination, and a kind of contempt for everyday experience, that makes the *idea,* for some of us, quite resistant to even the strongest assaults of the actual. Real life happens elsewhere.[24]

The books to which Australians of any turn of mind were exposed in the 1940s and 1950s — whether at school, university, or the local library — were not exclusively from elsewhere. The days when English authors and English subjects, together with those of classical Greece and Rome, all but monopolised what reading was done had already begun to pass by the closing decades of the nineteenth century. Australian history and geography had long entered the set textbooks, and Australian poetry commonly figured in locally-produced anthologies. There was a rich trove of Australian fiction available, including children's fiction. Yet non-Australian, and particularly English, writing was still the staple fare of the literary market at all levels, and still provided a powerful standard for literary judgment, however much the so-called 'cultural nationalists' and certain other local pundits protested against this situation.[25]

Speaking of nineteenth-century Americans, Robert Hughes might well have been speaking for his generation of twentieth-century Australians when he stated recently: 'One's own experience endowed the English or European work with a stupendous authority'. For those of 'a certain turn of mind', in Malouf's phrase, this experience started very early, as if by some innate instinct, and regardless of class. Peter Conrad, the prodigious Oxford don who lived out his first twenty years in a humble Hobart suburb where his father was a builder, recalls that 'once I began to read, I discovered somewhere else to live: the Noddyland or Neverland or wonderland or secret garden of English books ... Thus I became unassuageably homesick for a place I had never seen'. Barry Humphries, raised in the more salubrious suburb of Camberwell, Melbourne (where his father was of that slightly higher species, a *designer*-builder), would have us believe that he was dreaming of England from his bassinette, inspired by the illustrations in English books. Conrad's fellow-Tasmanian, the novelist Christopher Koch, who first left for Europe in 1955 but has since returned to Australia to live, recalls being brought up on A.A. Milne's stories of Christopher Robin (after whom he was named), as well as on Dickens, Lewis Carroll, Conan Doyle, Kipling, and the boys' paper, *Chums*, among numerous other British popular classics. 'No English man or woman', he says,

> will ever be able to experience what a colonial Australian ... felt about England. What no native of the 'mother country' could ever understand ... was the unique emotion summoned up by the first sight of a country known at one remove from birth, and waited for as an adolescent waits for love.[26]

It was from writers like Dickens and Conan Doyle that Koch was able to conjure up his visions of London in particular — 'the distant centre of our universe', 'capital of the world', 'city of cities', 'the great web' for 'a global empire', 'centre of civilisation', 'that centre 12 000 miles away for which we yearned'. But for their fellow-writers who happened to have been born at such a distance from that centre, vicarious visions were usually not enough to appease the yearning. They had to be there in the flesh. 'Forty years on' from the time of his first arrival in London, the Brisbane-born poet, Peter Porter, reflected in 1991:

> It was notation of the English air
> which brought me here
> that blood not words in books might share
> with me this working atmosphere.

There were undoubtedly some Australian writers of the period who never felt much of this yearning to start with; but they appear to have been the exceptions that proved the rule. The novelist, Thomas Keneally, has said of the poet, Judith Wright: 'At a time when it was every writer's sacred duty to be alienated by Australia — to be a European soul descended into this terrible place — she was unaffected. Instead she made her myths out of this place'. This was not because of her sex. The Sydney-born novelist, Shirley Hazzard, may have been equally unusual in finding 'nothing mythic' about her birthplace (or in allowing the narrator of one of her books to articulate this sense of nullity so unequivocally); but she is one of many Australian women authors down the years who have surrendered to the siren call of foreign shores and felt no urgency to return on a permanent basis.[27]

England's particular magnetism for colonial writers and intellectuals not only resulted from the dominance of English literature in their early reading and education. There have always been some very practical reasons for it, too. For centuries the country has offered a superabundance of facilities catering to the special needs of these professions and a wealth of opportunities in their line of work. Outsiders, not used to such riches at home, have often appreciated them more than the locals. Many English writers, from the time of Lord Byron on, have sought to flee England, bid their native land goodnight, for some of the same reasons that their Australian counterparts left Australia: the oppressions of middle-class morality or 'suburban' respectability combined with a hedonistic indifference — even in some of the more educated circles — to any rigorous or challenging artistic and intellectual endeavour.[28] The Australian expatriates, not least the ones that form the subject of this book, were themselves soon awakened to such drawbacks in the older societies they were entering — if they ever had any illusions to start with. But for them the compensations more than made up for the drawbacks.

From medieval times England had boasted two of the world's great scholarly powerhouses: the universities of Oxford and Cambridge. Since they first went to study there after their departure from Australia, Greer and James have both retained a strong if irregular presence in Cambridge (James through a family house he has always kept there, Greer through more academic links, formalised in recent years by a part-time appointment to her old college). For the past two centuries or so, several of the world's great commercial publishing houses, major literary periodicals, and most influential newspapers have been based in London; and all of our famous four have found outlets for their work with these enterprises. London has been a theatrical capital over an even longer period — and, since the 1960s, the main theatrical home for Barry Humphries when he has not been performing in Australia. For verbal performers who seek to project their voices to as wide an audience as possible, London has had the additional attraction in the present century of being the headquarters of BBC radio and television, as well as of its commercial counterpart, ITV. Even with his departure for New York, the BBC has continued to take a major role in the production of Robert Hughes' television work, while Humphries, Greer and most notably James have glided between both broadcasting networks.[29]

The magical lure of London for Australians, despite or because of the mix of feelings it could engender, is best evoked perhaps in the words of an expatriate who eventually did return to her native land. In one of the newspaper 'pieces' — her phrase — which she penned on her return, the novelist, Charmian Clift, reflected:

> I used to think that the most desirable state of being that could be imagined was to be a young and talented Australian in London. Weren't we healthier, more vital, more buoyant? And didn't we have so much enthusiasm, so much

talent that it was frustrating to the point of actual discomfort to keep ourselves within decent British bounds? We kept bursting out all over the place ...
We were enchanted, amused, excited, indignant, frustrated, discouraged, and
sometimes contemptuous.[30]

In a broadcast he made in 1971, Clive James declared that 'unless he's
a talent of truly enormous robustness, a writer is bound to head for the
language centre — and for the English-speaking world the language centre is still England'. He was not unaware, however, of the comparable
magnetism of New York. His broadcast was published as part of his first
book, a collection of essays entitled *The Metropolitan Critic,* and the title
essay in this book was about one of his favourite critics, Edmund Wilson
(a favourite of Robert Hughes, too) who had spent most of his working life
in New York. Hughes himself had gone to live and work in New York in
1970: only the latest in a long line of Australian writers (including Shirley
Hazzard as well as her fellow-novelists, Christina Stead and Sumner Locke
Elliott) to have chosen the American over the English option. It was not
long before Peter Conrad, the youngest of this crop of expatriates, would
find a way of dividing his working life *between* England and America.[31]

It was only by committing oneself to a truly metropolitan centre,
James suggested, that Australian writers could hope to transcend those
'provincial standards' that dogged them at home. Among the attractions of
England in particular — what had helped foster, perhaps, its metropolitan
atmosphere, the sense of 'centrality' there — was its receptiveness to talent,
wherever in the world this might have originated. Christopher Koch spoke
of the 'amused tolerance and even good will' with which the English greet-
ed him and his fellow-Australian pilgrims to 'the cultural blessed isles' in
the 1950s. James, reflecting on the number of Australians who had done
well in British journalism in the 1960s, guessed that this was due to the fact
that it was impossible to place them in the class system: 'English society
was ready to be shaken up. Authentic barbarians were welcome in the
drawing room'. Not that this meant they had secured anything like parity
or had attained to those mystical metropolitan standards. If such things
were ever fully achievable, they required a great deal of extra effort. Only
after a decade or so of exposure to English intellectual and literary life did

James feel, as he put it in *The Metropolitan Critic,* that he had 'caught up with the Englishmen of my generation'. A seal of their recognition of this achievement lay in the imprint of the book:

> First published in 1974
> by Faber and Faber Limited
> 3 Queen Square London WC1[32]

Such an imprint would serve as a reassuring symbol in his own eyes that he had been admitted to the metropolitan, even cosmopolitan, pantheon. It is not entirely coincidental, perhaps, that he felt able to make his first return visit to Australia a couple of years after the book was published. The other expatriates featured in the following pages had all secured their admission to this pantheon somewhat earlier: Barry Humphries as far back as 1965, when his bizarre *Bizarre* was published by Paul Elek in New York (it was indicative of the vestigial Grundyism still existent in England that one of the major bookstore chains there, W.H. Smith, refused to stock this work);[33] Robert Hughes in 1968, when his first book on a non-Australian subject, *Heaven and Hell in Western Art,* was brought out by the great London publishing firm of Weidenfeld and Nicolson; and Germaine Greer in 1970, when MacGibbon and Kee published the hardback edition of her trailblazer, *The Female Eunuch,* in Great Britain, soon to be followed by the paperback edition from Paladin, London, and a string of foreign-language editions.

Words in other people's books had provided a private fantasy world — or the only reality — for these four expatriates when they had still been living in Australia, waiting for the chance to escape their provincial home. The words in their own books, published outside Australia, were a way of effecting their arrival on the metropolitan scene and then consolidating their position there. Yet some of those words, in their very striving to hit the metropolitan note, have also been a giveaway of their provincial origins. Our expatriates have not been oblivious of the process, as it relates to others at least. Introducing his autobiography, Barry Humphries promises to avoid the literary indulgences of 'the provincial opsimath' or such 'high-falutin'' mannerisms as are 'beloved of Australian and American authors keen to parade their multi-lingual skills and sophistication in the face of strong suspicions to the contrary'. Clive James, commenting in the *New Yorker* on the Brooklyn-born wit, and former columnist in that journal, S.J. Perelman, notes how his 'macaronic vocabulary seems bent on superseding provincialism as its first impulse'.[34]

'Opsimath'? 'Macaronic'? The first of these words, according to the *Concise Oxford Dictionary*, is a 'rare' one, meaning a person who 'learns late in life'. The second, used in the sense of a stylistic 'medley', is hardly as obscure; though when referring to Perelman's vocabulary in an earlier essay, James was prepared to use the simpler epithet, 'mixed'. At least one can find both 'opsimath' and 'macaronic' in a regular dictionary, which can't be said for several of the words listed earlier in this chapter. There is a strong similarity between these and the words with which the hero of Hanif Kureishi's recent novel, *The Buddha of Suburbia,* tests his old father, a Pakistani living in London: 'analeptic, frutescent, polycephalus and orgulous'. One has to wonder whether their function isn't similar, too. Kureishi's narrator continues: 'He'd look at me and say, "You never know when you might need a heavyweight word to impress an Englishman."'[35]

'Oh yes, he had the long words,' noted the interviewer, 'N.V. Rampant', when he contemplated his latest subject in 1984: the formidably precocious English novelist, Martin Amis. This interview, first published in the *London Review of Books,* was later reprinted in Clive James' collected essays for the years 1980–87. Yet as the Japanese hero of James' novel, *Brmm! Brmm!* came to observe, it was one of the puzzling characteristics of the English that 'they never used such words'. They might be found in an English dictionary, but it was usually only the non-English who bothered with them.[36]

If not the only collective signature of the four Australian expatriates dealt with in this book, the recourse to long or ornate or recondite locutions is one of their most distinctive and revealing characteristics in common. The narrator of an earlier James novel, *The Remake,* expressly conjures up the 'Australian expatriate extravaganza style' at one point. 'They all write like that', he notes, and proceeds to cite the most telling examples: 'Jennings' (the name James uses in his memoirs for Barry Humphries); Huggins (his name for Hughes); Bartelski ('Peter C. Bartelski', as he is called in James' first novel, *Brilliant Creatures*: at least partly related to Peter Conrad, may we surmise?); 'Walter Waiter' (Peter Porter?); and 'even that bastard James'. 'Romaine Rand', he continues (there's no need for surmises about her identity), *talks* like that ... They all pile it on. Kangarococo'.[37]

It is time now to throw up the curtain on the first-named performer in this extravaganza, and attend to the words of his own tales of travel.

Chapter Two

The Camberwell Tales

The Strangeness of Barry Humphries

Dame, Dame, the watch is set;
Quickly come, we all are met.

A chorus of witches await their doyenne for the start of their nocturnal rites in *The Masque of Queens*. This was a spectacle devised by Ben Jonson for the delectation of the royal court in London in 1609; but it might well be the start of one of Barry Humphries' theatrical spectacles anywhere in the world today, or of his television show with the spookily resonant title, *Dame Edna's Neighbourhood Watch*.[1]

In Barry Humphries we are dealing with one of the most erudite comic performers of our century. The parallels with seventeenth-century masque in his writing and performances are hardly exact, and even at their closest they don't provide sufficient evidence of the direct influence of these older theatrical forms on his work. They are instructive, however, in suggesting the breadth of the artistic traditions to which his art is related, and the range of sources informing it.[2]

True to the democratic temper of the twentieth century, Dame Edna's rites are performed before a mass audience, and involve it directly in the action. The audience itself becomes her coven, eagerly if apprehensively willing her presence. There can be no doubt, however, as to who dominates and controls the action once she appears. Starting out her stage life in the mid-1950s as a modest housewife from Melbourne, Australia, the character of Edna — just plain Mrs Everage in those far-off days — has evolved into a diabolonian woman-of-the-world. She will brook no interference or competition from her assembled followers. At one of her stage shows in London in recent years, a voice-over grimly announced before the proceedings began: 'Should a particularly malign manifestation occur near you, kindly desist from drawing attention to yourself. Fully qualified exorcists are stationed throughout the auditorium'.[3]

'*A curtain flying up, a horrid scene appeared … as if darkness, confusion, and deformity had possessed the world.*' Amidst this benighted landscape we find a figure of fury, '*her hair upright, mixed with snakes, … and … tawny skirts down to her feet. In her hand she brandished a sable torch, and looking askance with hollow envious eyes came down in to the room*'. She proceeds to complain how

> … *the world should everywhere*
> *Be vexed into a storm save only here!*
> *Thou over-lucky, too-much-happy isle …*

We are back in the world of seventeenth-century court masque — in this instance William Davenant's *Salmacida Spolia*, performed in 1640. But it could be Dame Edna sounding off at the latest follies either of her colonial birthplace or of its former suzerain, England, where she first rose to her international celebrity. The antipodean virago's style of dress and head-dress is equally outlandish, and she also bears a torch, training its more merciless electric gleam on any who should dare to arrive late for her own nocturnal rites.[4]

> *But first relate me what you have sought,*
> *Where you have been, and what you have brought.*

So the Dame in the Ben Jonson masque proceeds to address her retinue. One of her followers has brought back human carrion snatched from the beak of a raven. Another has made a specialty of 'plucking plants'.[5] The

Dame matches these offerings with her own bizarre array of charms, including 'Horned poppy' and 'cypress boughs'. Don't we catch an echo here of Dame Edna's stage shows when she intently quizzes some of her captive fans on the contents of their handbags? Or when, at the end of the shows, she contrives to produce a seemingly inexhaustible supply of gladioli to throw at her coven? The same flower serves as a magic wand which uncannily leads her to her victims on *Neighbourhood Watch.*

> *The scene changed into a calm, the sky serene; afar off Zephyrus appeared, breathing a gentle gale; in the landscape were cornfields and pleasant trees sustaining vines fraught with grapes, and in some of the furthest parts villages, with all such things as might express a country in peace, rich and fruitful. There came breaking out of the heavens a silver chariot, in which sat two persons, the one ... representing Concord; somewhat below her sat the Good Genius of Great Britain. Being arrived and descended from the chariot, they ... departed several ways to incite the beloved people to honest pleasures and recreations which have ever been peculiar to this nation.*

This is the second scene of Davenant's masque, preparatory to the arrival of the King, called 'Philogenes, or "Lover of his People"'. He has the power to dispel the dark, malicious forces of Fury, and remind the people of their 'blessings' and their 'comforts', for all that these are under constant threat of renewed disruption and may be 'too great to last'.[6] The precariously idyllic prospects evoked here might easily be those of the 'villages' or suburbs which comprise Dame Edna's home-base some twelve thousand miles away and three centuries later. Edna's autobiography, *My Gorgeous Life,* evokes the scene of her return home from her first trip abroad in remarkably similar detail to Davenant: 'It was a glorious Melbourne autumn day, the sky a lavender blue and the plane trees in Humouresque Street chafing their big yellow leaves in a soft breeze'. There is even a version of the silver chariot: 'I had run to the front door', Edna continues, 'while the Silvertop taxi driver unloaded the car'.[7]

Edna herself, however, is no figure of Concord, and the serenity of this setting is soon punctured by her angry denunciations of her family, neighbours and friends. But she has her more benign moments when she at least poses as 'Lover of her People'. Three of her early songs remorselessly catalogue the blessings and comforts of her homeland: the 'Highett Waltz' of 1959, named after the 'beautifully quiet' Melbourne suburb of Highett where her daughter and son-in-law live; 'Australian Vitality' in 1962, a celebration of what she now sees, having travelled overseas, as a peculiarly antipodean virtue; and 'Edna's Hymn' of 1968 to the pleasures and recreations of Australians, which borrows its tune and its reprise from the traditional English hymn, 'All Things Bright and Beautiful'.[8]

You won't find Edna's 'Humouresque Street' in any Melbourne street directory, but Moonee Ponds, the 'village' or suburb where it is supposed to be situated, is as real as Highett, despite the improbable name. It is situated on Melbourne's less fashionable west side, though it has had its share of 'comfortable citizens' among a largely working-class or lower middle-class population. Humphries has maintained that it was for the 'euphony' of the name, aside from any amusement-value it might have, that he chose Moonee Ponds as Edna's home base. Even if, as he also acknowledges, this suburb was not solidly middle-class enough in social composition to chime with Edna's youthful pretensions to gentility, the name does have a quirkily pastoral or idyllic ring to it. One might also detect in it a gothicky undertone portending her darker incarnations of later years.[9]

The Silvertop taxi which returns Edna to Moonee Ponds is also an actual brand of cab in Melbourne. Back in 1959, in a sketch which Humphries devised for Australian television just before his own first trip away, we find another modern equivalent of Davenant's chariot: an 'air-conditioned twin-diesel-powered … Parlour-coach'. It is transporting its passengers to a yet more 'villagey' part of Melbourne on the other side of the city. The setting is every bit as serene. The driver of the coach, Jeff Pritchard, a character which Humphries also played in the sketch, informs his passengers: 'Your coach will shortly be … entering the garden suburbs of Hawthorn and Camberwell. Here are to be found many stately and historic home units in the idyllic setting of lawn and flowering shrub … Soon after we have bidden farewell to Camberwell it will be noticed that the terrain assumes a semi-rural character'.[10]

The whole of Camberwell, on its city side also, had once prided itself on its 'natural' landscapes. These could be the height of artifice, however. Some of the men who first opened up the area for settlement — rich politicians and merchants from Melbourne, seeking a rural retreat — did not scruple to eradicate much of the native bushland in order to cultivate large estates in the manner of English country gentlemen. 'The Good Genius of Great Britain' is as apt a phrase as any to sum up their abiding model. Surrounding the great houses they erected were large areas of parkland, meadow and orchard, complete with vines in some instances, as well as a range of 'pleasant trees' introduced from the northern hemisphere. The coming of the railway to the Camberwell area in the 1880s was to occasion the gradual breaking-up of these estates into smaller blocks sought after by Melbourne's expanding middle class. More modest in their means, they were no less romantic and Anglophile in their ideals of architecture and landscape. It was this area of Melbourne, this class, this milieu, with which Humphries himself was most intimately acquainted.[11]

Born at a hospital in the neighbouring suburb of Kew in 1934, he was to spend his childhood in a succession of houses designed by his father, a professional builder, in Christowel Street, Camberwell. Dubbed the 'Golf Links Estate', after an earlier incarnation, this area had only begun to be opened up to residential housing development in the 1930s. The rather poignant pretensions of the houses are neatly captured in Jeff Pritchard's phrase, 'historic home units'. They were all free-standing, solid brick structures, set sufficiently well back from the street to allow for a stretch of lawn, the odd large tree, a bed or two for shrubs and flowers, and (in one instance) an ornamental birdbath; but the grounds were hardly expansive. Each was built in a particular 'period' style, named after various English monarchs or dynasties of centuries past. Number 38, the first of them, was dubbed 'Tudor', number 30 'Elizabethan', and number 36 'neo-Georgian'. The largest of these, number 36, became the permanent family home, and for official purposes Humphries was still citing it as his home address during his earliest years abroad.[12]

It can be no coincidence that 36 is the number of Edna's house in Humouresque Street; 'Edna is more a Camberwell character than a Moonee Ponds character', Humphries later maintained. His most enduring character after Edna, Sandy Stone, has lived at '36 Gallipoli Crescent', Glen Iris, for all of his stage life and, until very recently, has continued to haunt the place as a ghost. Again, the street name is an invention, but the suburb is not, and from the turn of the century until recent years Glen Iris fell within the official boundaries of the municipality of Camberwell, along with a string of other neighbouring suburbs like Canterbury, Chatham and Surrey Hills. The choice of such place-names is sufficient testimony in itself to the promptings of Melbourne's earliest developers to emulate and spread the 'Genius of Great Britain' at the opposite ends of the earth.[13]

'Real names', Sandy Stone says of the denizens of these suburbs in his younger days: 'the Dunns, the Greys, the Clarks, the Whittles, the Longs, the Braggs'. Real because British, like the place-names. The place-names haven't changed, but they remain only as a wry vestige of British cultural dominance in Australia, while the names of the local inhabitants have turned increasingly unreal, by Sandy's criteria, with successive waves of immigration from Europe and Asia. 'The first real foreigner' to move into Sandy's Glen Iris 'was a little Israelite called Eckstein'. Among the latest is a 'couple called Ng from Vietnam. That's their name. N.G. they spell it', Sandy informs us incredulously. Those idyllic prospects in the 'natural' landscape, transplanted from Britain by the first white settlers of the district, and sustained in more modest fashion by the likes of Sandy and his generation, are bound to fall victim to the barbarian invaders' unnatural practices. Sandy notes, for instance, how at number 28 Gallipoli Crescent, once the proud demesne of 'Doug and Thelma Littlejohn',

> a Sicilian chappie has put plastic and pebbles down over what was left of the garden after they'd added the rumpus room and treble garage. But for a few years afterwards, the old bulbs kept trying to come up through the plastic; snowdrops, grape hyacinths and a few jonquils. Even the odd freesia tried squeezing up … But Reno kept on mowing them until they all finally gave up. I remember how Doug used to have lily of the valley thick down the south side of that home, but when a bit of that showed up beside the pebblecrete, they had to have a couple of goes with the Zero to get rid of it.[14]

The court masques of the seventeenth century did not spare their audiences reminders of the vulnerability of British order, British beauty, British blessings and comforts; but they usually ended on an up-beat note. The scenes of dark discord over which Jonson's malicious Dame presides in *The Masque of Queens* are replaced early on by the spectacle of 'a glorious and magnificent building, figuring the House of Fame'. This mythical building, as Jonson acknowledges, had provided the title and setting for a poem of Chaucer nearly three centuries earlier. It was to figure again in Jonson's last scene. Into this setting descend the forces of Heroic Virtue and Good Fame to celebrate their victory over 'poor and envious witchcraft' in a succession of elaborate songs and dances. Davenant's *Salmacida Spolia* ends with a joyous ascension. Though performed in the year that civil war was to break out in England, there is an insistence on the harmony of the final spectacle, as assembled 'deities' ride up into the heavens above a scene of 'magnificent buildings' and a more distant prospect of 'the suburbs of a great city'. This genre of theatre often made use of elaborate stage machinery by which the characters could be elevated and lowered at the appropriate moments. Some further parallels may be found here, *mutatis mutandis,* with Barry Humphries' theatrical and television spectacles in our own day.[15]

Following the damehood 'officially' bestowed on her by Australia's Prime Minister, Gough Whitlam, at the end of the film, *Barry McKenzie Holds His Own* (1974), Edna has resolutely created a 'house of fame' around herself, complete with the requisite mechanical trappings. There were 'Audiences with Dame Edna' televised nation-wide in England and Australia during the 1980s, but only hand-picked celebrities, from the worlds of show business, the arts and politics, were ever admitted to the studios for these occasions. For her chat-show series of 1987, *The Dame Edna Experience,* and its American equivalent a few years later, *Dame Edna's Hollywood,* the studio itself was tricked out in the guise of a glitzy penthouse, fit only for the most illustrious guests. They would first have to ascend by lift to a precipitously perched gallery-floor before descending a staircase to commune with their hostess in the salon below. Less welcome callers — discredited celebrities or pretenders to fame — would arrive at the top of her stairs only to be flung downwards through a trapdoor controlled by a button from Edna's seat.[16]

In the stage show, *Back with a Vengeance,* which opened in London the same year as *The Dame Edna Experience,* our hostess would bring the evening's performance to a close by having herself hauled up by a crane to the top of the stage and then swung outwards by the same device into the uppermost tiers of the audience, known traditionally as the gods. Not content with damehood, she now aspired to saintly or divine status. Or so it might have looked. In practice, this ascension allowed the old she-devil to spread her 'vengeance' the more effectively. By an ironic convention of theatre design, 'the gods' have been the lowliest or lowest-paying members of the audience. Affecting to commune with them, on their own level, Edna now proceeded to queen it over them in her most intimidating manner, rubbing in their status as 'paupers'. This was a barb she had hurled at them from below. Now they were in the direct line of fire, and from her floral as well as her verbal missiles. Along with the masochistic throngs below, they could only be grateful for being included in these rituals. If she was bringing her audiences closer together in this way, it was harmony with a savage twist. The democratic beneficence of the aspiring goddess proved to be but a confirmation of her sinister powers.

There are quite conscious links here with older artistic traditions, and not just theatrical ones. In conversation with John Lahr, the most exhaustive chronicler of his work to date, Humphries remarked of Edna's climactic ascent in *Back with a Vengeance:* 'It's a parody of the Assumption as though painted by Murillo or perhaps a late Venetian master'. The Spanish master, Bartolomé Murillo, lived from 1617 to 1682, the heyday of masque.[17]

Elsewhere in his conversation with Lahr, Humphries reminds us that artistic influence does not always operate or manifest itself in the most obvious and direct fashion. He notes at one point: 'Just as religious traditions become subterranean and re-emerge in other forms, the theatre has some traditions as old as religions and certain persistent themes have traditionally touched people'. He is specifically referring here to another of his best-known characters, the raucously randy Australian diplomat and 'cultural attaché', Sir Les Patterson. 'There are literary allusions in Les', he told another interviewer, 'but you're not really meant to get them. He is a music hall character, very much a vaudeville figure ... ' The priapic obsessions for which he has become so notorious, however, may be traced back nearly two and a half thousand years, to ancient Greek comedy and 'the spirit of Aristophanes'.[18]

By this token, tracing Dame Edna's provenance back to the age of Jonson, Davenant and Murillo might be to sell her short. If we look more closely at her personality, her style of narration, her very title, we can find suggestions of a rather longer literary lineage. This may be so 'subterranean' at times that even her creator may not entirely be conscious of it — may not 'get' all of the allusions. One cannot readily assume this, however. Humphries' nose for the more recherché specimens of all artistic genres and forms was already highly developed by the time of his adolescence. A schoolfriend of his, Ian Donaldson, who has gone on to become a distinguished literary scholar — and a specialist in the works of Jonson — recalls the Barry Humphries from those years as 'neither prankster nor clown, but a formidably learned, prodigiously clever young man, serious, ironical, allusive, intense. How, as a teenager, had he already acquired that astonishing stock of knowledge?'[19]

If Sir Les' more obvious inheritance is from the world of music hall and vaudeville, Dame Edna's is from a slightly earlier, but still enduring, form of British popular culture: the pantomime. The 'Dame' in her name, we need to remember, was not of her own devising; the honour was playfully conferred on her by a Labor Prime Minister who had made it his business to scrap all such titles for any real-life Australians. It was more than just local political parody, however. It was appropriate recognition of Edna's kinship with the termagant or the scold who had become the dominating figure of English pantomime, was traditionally called a 'Dame', and had always been played by a man.[20]

Humphries has expressly acknowledged that the earliest conception of Edna as a stage character to be performed by himself consciously drew on the panto-dame tradition; though again this was not his own conception, as he recalls, but that of a friend and early mentor, the playwright Ray Lawler. Humphries originally envisaged an actress in the part. He has maintained more recently that his own way of approaching this part never really conformed with the rather 'sturdier' conventions of the panto-dame model, yet was not simply a 'drag act' either. 'The joke of the dame', he explains,

> is the tension between the female clothes and the stocky footballer's legs and boots. The drag queen is the other extreme, really a man who is mocking a woman and at the same time trying to titillate the audience. Edna is really somewhere in between, closer really to character acting, a man playing a woman and making points about life.[21]

Edna was destined to be dame, however, through a train of other connotations and associations stretching back at least as far as the middle ages.
By the seventeenth century in England, the word 'dame' was being applied
specifically to the mistress of a local private school catering usually for
younger children. She was often of very modest means. Edna, we know, had
very modest roots — Moonee Ponds was something of a step up from
Thornbury, the largely working-class suburb from which her parents hailed
— though she was never reduced to looking after any but her own brood of
youngsters. There were yet older meanings of 'dame' which fitted her position more exactly, or captured its ambiguities as she ascended the social
scale. Since the fourteenth century at least, a dame might be a humble
though not indigent housewife, or a matriarch of rather grander stature, up
to noble or even royal rank. Several of the grandest variety wend their way
through Chaucer's *The House of Fame;* though none is actually called dame
in that poem. (The House itself is presided over by Lady Fame.) The best
known literary version of the species is another creation of Chaucer's, the
Wife of Bath, whom he specifically names 'dame Alis'.[22] Chaucer's Wife of
Bath is no noblewoman, queen or goddess of the sort we find in *The House
of Fame,* but she has become a prosperous businesswoman through her
skills in clothmaking, and has managed to outlive five husbands.
Humphries' housewife of Moonee Ponds can claim no comparable occupational skills, and has so far been married and widowed only once.
(Humphries' own marital record of four wives corresponds more closely to
Dame Alis', all of them remain alive to tell their own tale.) Dame Edna and
Dame Alis still have much in common, and beyond the coincidence of their
titles: a penchant for 'making points about life', especially about the tribu-
lations of love and marriage; a compulsive jollity and solicitude that is little
more than a facade for a brutally domineering nature, capable of intimidating other women as well as hobbling men; a taste for ostentatious
dresses and hats, bordering on the ludicrous; and an insatiable urge to
travel. 'And thryes had she been at Jerusalem', we learn of the Wife of Bath,
as well as 'At Rome ... and at Boloigne,/ In Galice ... and at Coloigne'.

These were all important sites on the pilgrim routes of the middle ages.
The avowed motives for Dame Edna's expeditions abroad, some six centuries
later, are more secular: her 'special mission' is to spread the news of Australia's
'wondrous way of life' and to reassure her compatriots about this on her

rcturn. But there is a similar ring of deep personal restlessness to her list of destinations, as she reels them off herself in her song, 'Australian Vitality':

> I've been to England and to Scotland and to th'Isle of Man,
> I've been to Wales and to Holland and to France and Japan,
> China, Carolina, and Cambodia too,
> I've been to Burma and to Germany, Brazil and Peru,
> I've been to Italy and Sicily and New Mexico,
> To Pakistan, Afghanistan and wild Borneo,
> I've been to the Malayan Archipelago and
> I've been to Ireland and to Thailand and to Heligoland,
> Silesia, Rhodesia, and Portugal, Spain,
> To Malta and Gibraltar, Yukatan, The Ukraine.
> Siberia, Liberia, Estonia, Greece,
> Albania, Romania, the Peloponnese.
> Scandinavia, Gallipoli, Moravia and Tripoli
> And to the Argentine...
> And from everywhere I've been,
> In three short roving years
> I've brought back souvenirs
> And something else besides:
> One million
> Four thousand
> Two hundred and eight-six
> Coloured slides![23]

The echoes in Edna of medieval poetry may be no more precise, and no less of a coincidence, than those of seventeenth-century masque. A link of some substance, however — at least to the period in question — is suggested in Edna's own revelation that 'Barry plucked me out of a passion play'. According to one recent scholar, who includes Dame Edna in his survey, the whole tradition of the pantomime dame can be traced back as far as the character of Mrs Noah in the Chester cycle of mystery plays, a related genre to the passion play in Chaucer's day. In listing his literary models, moreover, Humphries has invoked Chaucer's own poetic portraits.[24]

It is in one of these poetic portraits that the Wife of Bath is unveiled. The narrator of the general Prologue to Chaucer's best-known work, *The*

Canterbury Tales, provides an introductory sketch of her, and of a motley assortment of other characters, before they each take up the narrative in turn with a prologue and tale of their own. These characters are all pilgrims, wending their way to one of the great sacred sites of England, the shrine of St Thomas, situated at the hub of the country's ecclesiastical life.

Chaucer's title for this work may have had an added resonance for the young Barry Humphries — and a slightly eerie one. Canterbury was the name of one of those suburbs that bordered on his childhood home at Camberwell, but this whole neighbourhood was on the other side of the world and part of a region with very different climatic patterns, mixes of population, and historical traditions. He claims to have had a disturbing sense of such incongruities from boyhood. A friend from Sunday school invited him over once to listen to some recordings of Delius at 'a dark house in an old section of the suburb', and he recalls: 'It was strange sitting in that dim house on a still night in a city of South-east Asia, as this most English of music floated out the window into the heavy English foliage of Canterbury Road'. The tensions, the ironies, and the sense of strangeness arising from such incongruities have provided a distinctive theme of many of his own 'portraits' or 'tales'.[25]

The very adaptability of the characters in these tales to distant literary, theatrical and artistic models only confirmed their strangeness. 'I was brought up with Sandy Stone standing on one side of me and Edna Everage on the other', Humphries once told an interviewer. But what were they doing there so far from their cultural and racial roots? And what was he doing there in their midst? These were mysteries he started to puzzle over from his cradle, he makes out; and they have continued to unsettle him — in a quite physical sense — for much of his life. He was to tell another interviewer how, as a young child in Melbourne, he had been given 'a very good illustrated edition of Robin Hood', from which he had first 'got a glimpse of another landscape'. This other landscape had been

> hinted at slightly, in some of the gardens of Camberwell, Balwyn and Kew ... but it was the English landscape, I knew it to be strange, to be foreign, but to be richly inviting, and because of my English grandfather, my father's father, I knew that somewhere I belonged there too. I was therefore interested

in forests, in woods and in gardens, my earliest childhood memories are of gazing out of a bassinet at the flowers and honeysuckle in a suburban garden in Melbourne and, I knew one day I'd be going to England. But it wasn't for quite a few years.[26]

We can't rely on these recollections as an exact rendition of his feelings at the time; but, as an adult gloss on childhood experience, they serve to highlight some of the recurrent tensions, impulses, motifs, preoccupations, which are to be found in his own life's tale. There is the pervasive sense of strangeness, which attracts him as much as it disturbs him. The strangeness of England enhances his sense of belonging there rather than diminishing it. The strangeness of Camberwell and its environs is somehow fainter, perhaps because it has been transplanted, superimposed, and is in that respect inauthentic. Yet as part of the same process these environs contrive to furnish some quite genuine, tangible tokens of English culture, in the shape of books or plants, that prepare him for the greater riches ahead and heighten their enticements for him. For all its pallid fakeness, the milieu of his youth is not without its nurturing capacities and an idyllic quality of its own.

It is easy to overlook the stimuli of his birthplace, because of the success with which he cultivated the myths of its barrenness and of his own alienation from it. His resistances to his upbringing have been far more obvious than its beguilements for him. 'He is an extraordinary artist to have sprung unheralded and fully-armed from the subsoil of Australian culture', concedes one of his sternest critics, the Sydney journalist Craig McGregor. The Melbourne journalist and broadcaster, Phillip Adams, who was an active promoter of Humphries' film career before a falling-out with him, has remarked: 'You'd never deduce that he came from a normal Melbourne suburb'. Ian Donaldson was all the more awed by Humphries' precocity at school because 'No learned mentors or twinkling models seem to have lurked in Christowel Street, Camberwell, and none most certainly were at that time to be found at our expensive yet impoverished school. The cleverest person I'd ever met seemed to have come from absolutely nowhere'.[27]

The cultural subsoil from which he emerged, the normal suburb of his childhood home, *was* a complete nowhere-land, a part of Humphries would have us believe. The nullity of their condition is an explicit theme of his earliest characters, Edna Everage and Sandy Stone; and when he says that he was brought up with these two on either side of him, he tempts us to identify them directly with the Christowel Street neighbourhood or his own parents. The house number they share with his family's own number further suggests some disturbing parallels in the patterns of all of their lives. Sandy Stone (could there be a name more emblematic of aridity and desiccation?) expressly recalls from his grave how he used to study the tiles on the bathroom floor of his house 'to take my mind off the fact that nothing was happening'. He might only consciously be referring to the state of his bowels, but Edna Everage is unambiguously referring to the state of the nation when she sings of 'the land where nothing happens' in her version of 'All Things Bright and Beautiful'. Her tone here is as exultant as when she celebrates 'Australian Vitality', though her global gallivantings from early on — leaving her children behind with her husband in Melbourne — make you wonder whether she isn't seeking an escape from home at any opportunity. She never fails to return, however. Sandy, all the while, has barely budged from his local neighbourhood all his life, or even in death, unless it has been to commute to work on the same railway line — the Camberwell line — every day. He seems content enough to mind the domestic hearth while his wife, Beryl, does the gallivanting.[28]

From other evidence supplied by Humphries — inadvertently in some instances — a somewhat more complicated picture emerges. To start with, the provenance of Edna and Sandy as characters is broader, more muddled. Edna shared a name, he has revealed elsewhere, with his 'first and favourite nanny' (his mother's name was Louisa). Some of Edna's external characteristics — vocal intonations, mode of dress and so on — derived from a 'lot of aunts', and not just his own but those of his friends. She was 'made up', he recounts, 'from various acquaintances and observations around Camberwell'. All of these models were still close enough to home, but Sandy's origins were more wide-ranging, geographically speaking, for all of the character's own strictly circumscribed horizons. There had been a conductor on the Camberwell tram who asked for fares in a breathy, light, slightly hissing voice; there was a 'dessicated cicada of a man' on the commuter train which took Humphries to school every day; and there was a childless old neighbour down his street, Mr Whittle. Here were some of the seeds of Sandy as we now know him; but they didn't germinate, by Humphries' account, until he went on a visit to Sydney in 1956. Strolling along Bondi Beach, he came across 'a wiry old fellow ... with thin sandy hair', who addressed him in the extraordinary circumlocutory manner which has since become a trademark of the character. The shoreline setting as well as the man's hair clinched the name.[29]

There can still be no doubt that Edna and Sandy embody certain facets of Louisa or of Eric Humphries, as their eldest son came to view them in his formative years. He told John Lahr bluntly:

> I invented Edna because I hated her ... I suppose one grows up with a desire to murder one's parents, but you can't really go and do that. So I suppose I tried to murder them symbolically onstage. I poured out my hatred of the standards of the little people of their generation.

Lahr, while recognising that there is a range of models and motives behind Humphries' characterisations, doesn't question the antagonistic tenor of this explanation. It certainly tends to bear out a more general impression among Humphries' interpreters that he has been *anti*-suburban, even *anti*-Australian, in his earlier work at least, as well as engaged in a war against his particular upbringing. There are slight notes of reservation in this statement, however — the repeated 'I suppose' — which should caution us against categorising his attitudes too readily in this fashion. Glimpses that he allows us elsewhere of his parents and their milieux are more variegated. They attest to some riches in his childhood experience on which he has been able to capitalise in his creative work, and they suggest the persistence in him of a more ambivalent view of that experience. They provide evidence and some explanation of his lingering attachment to the world of Camberwell as he has explored much wider worlds beyond in his adult years. They alert us to the hazards of placing Barry Humphries' work, sensibility and attitudes in any sort of category.[30]

Humphries' mother, like Edna Everage, was from a Thornbury family. She had worked as a milliner at Melbourne's main department store, the Myer Emporium, before she married and moved to Camberwell. As this was in the early 1930s, when Melbourne with the rest of the world remained in the grip of the Great Depression, she could be considered very lucky; but there were losses as well as gains entailed in her elevation to middle-class wife. 'She had artistic qualities that were *all* suppressed', her son has emphasised. This suggests a strain of puritanism in her that is not the same as Edna's 'philistine denial' (Lahr's phrase) and weakness for kitsch. Humphries' mother would not countenance his having a D.H. Lawrence novel in the house, though he was not otherwise discouraged in his reading; and she actively tried to encourage him when he developed an interest in painting, arranging for him to be sent to classes at one of Melbourne's best known private art schools, George Bell's, and footing the bill.[31]

Her puritanism was at least as much imposed on her as it was ingrained. She had to enjoin her son not to tell his father about the art lessons, which led him to suspect that 'she might even be my secret ally against the strictures of my father' and was concealing her own 'great love of beauty … in order to be a respectable housewife and mother'. Both she and her husband were practising Anglicans, though he had been brought up in a strict Methodist family and retained something of its 'fundamentalist attitude', in the early years of their marriage at least. She appeared to go along with this, but according to her son 'found religious observation boring and incomprehensible'.[32]

Family obligations, too, may have been a source of frustration for her, although, unlike Edna, she did not try to escape them; we know of only one overseas trip she made, and this was with her husband, following Barry's own first marriage. Up to then he had always been amply provided for in the way of accommodation and nutritious food — to an extent where he even wished he had been 'just slightly neglected' in such matters. What he appears to have suffered from was emotional neglect, or 'emotional evasiveness', as the main character in his recent novel, *Women in the Background,* puts it, when recalling relations with *his* mother. A surfeit of caring, in the material sense, could well be a form or tactic of emotional evasiveness. In various recent reflections on his own life, Humphries has declared that his mother was 'not a particularly warm woman', and that 'her expressions of love for me were sometimes evasive or ambiguous'. 'She was impossible to read and I was never quite certain if I was loved.' He has recalled the general 'lack of intimacy' at home and 'the mysterious lack of rapport which seemed to have grown up between parents and child'. On the other hand, when dedicating his autobiography to his sister and brothers, he concedes that they 'would probably tell you a very different story'.[33]

It is clear that, for all the encouragement she might have given to his early ventures into painting, his mother never really supported him in his eventual choice of artistic career. By his account, she would revel in the unfavourable comments that theatre critics or others directed at his shows or his characters. She never remarked on the good reviews he scored. As a rule, it seems, she kept away from the shows herself, unlike his father who made occasional efforts to sneak into them when she didn't actively deter him. Humphries wryly observes at one point: 'I could understand my mother's absence from a widely advertised evening of relentless vulgarity'.[34]

It would be all the more understandable if his work in general represented nothing but a hateful, murderous attack on his parents and their world. His father's gestures of support would then be a puzzle, however. Why should either of them willingly submit to such an act of vengeance against them? But his work has never been just that. At its most remorselessly confronting, it has been an act of homage, too — if not an expression of love. Humphries remarked to John Lahr: 'There aren't many books which describe the parent realistically and lovingly as well. That element of love has to be there somehow. It's impossible to write truthfully about any human being without love'. It is clearly not easy to see the love or the realism in Edna, and Lahr imagines that in this role Humphries must have struck his parents as 'a freak of comic excess calling attention and humiliation on himself by dressing up as a woman'. Yet it is possible that they (and his mother in particular) might also have divined something more disturbing here: a bid for intimacy beyond the bounds of social convention or manageability.[35]

Humphries and his mother had clearly enjoyed some moments of intimacy together when he was a very young child. There is nothing unconventional about these, unless it is the vivid intensity with which he recalls them decades later. In his memories such moments are often connected with clothes — sources of great sensuous pleasure for him even as they represented a tantalising barrier to full physical intimacy. His pyjamas he recalls as 'the cosiest and most secure caress of all, next to the embrace of a parent'. Luxuriating in his mother's clothes produced a special thrill, if the luxuriance of his language in evoking this experience is any guide. Early on in his autobiography, we find him recalling, with an almost sinister fondness, his mother's silver-fox fur: 'With my nose buried in that musky pelt, I gabbled my vespers in my mother's perfumed embrace. The longer I protracted my prayers the longer I could bask in Evening in Paris, Charmosan face powder and the faint vulpine odour of her wrap'.[36]

It is not clear when these moments came to an end, but they would have started to tail off when Humphries' baby sister arrived on the scene, near to his third birthday, followed by the births of his two brothers. The silver-fox vignette in his autobiography immediately leads into a recollection of the day when 'there was suddenly and unexpectedly another focus of attention in our house'. The competition was not serious for a time, but Humphries' recollections of the next few years register subtle shifts in his relationship with his mother. These are also associated partly with clothes. We learn how the young boy used to accompany his mother to her dressmaker's. Her favourite fabric was taffeta, Humphries tells us. He extols it, too: 'Taffeta was cool and it rustled and chafed upon itself, and … it was … the nicest textile to say your prayers against'. But the choice of words here ('cool', 'chafed', 'nicest', 'against' compared to 'basked in') also suggests something of the diminishing intimacies between mother and son, of her growing irritation with his demands for closeness, and of his dawning resentment at the rituals of respectability. 'Nice', in particular, is an ambiguous epithet in Humphries' lexicon; it has been a part of his whole creative endeavour to expose what he has termed 'the tyranny of niceness and order' in the Australia of his youth.[37]

Much as they were to represent what he found hateful or ridiculous in Australian society, his mother's favoured accoutrements have also provided a poignant reminder of what he once shared with her. They have become the only tangible means of remaining close to her or of reproducing that proximity. 'Lovely … It was all hats and glads', he reports her as saying of an official luncheon she attended at the Melbourne Town Hall, and then he elaborates on this with impish suggestiveness: 'Gladioli, especially flesh-pink ones, were the floral symbols of respectability, success and thrusting, unquestioning optimism'. He would eventually choose to put a much greater physical distance between himself and this world, yet the very remorselessness with which he has gone on satirising it shows how inextricably tied to its fetishes he has remained. He wittily crystallised this paradox in a title he once gave to an article he wrote: 'My Love Hat Relationships'. In tacit recognition of a hereditary trait, he billed himself there 'a noted millinery addict'. Hats have been a feature of his performances from the start, as well as of his own attire when not publicly performing. He wore one of his mother's hats for Edna's first stage appearance, together with some other discarded clothes of hers. The gladioli came a bit later, but now there is no show of his that is complete without them.[38]

In a television interview which Melvyn Bragg conducted with 'both' Barry Humphries and Edna Everage in 1989, Edna described her creator as 'a touching paradigm of the Australian intellectual of the 80s … rooted in the 50s' and 'still exploring his own childhood'. In his continuing yearnings for the intimate moments he had enjoyed with her as an infant, Humphries' mother may have sensed such regressive fixations in him from early on. She could hardly have been expected to indulge these with any equanimity, and especially when her other children arrived on the scene, with their own needs and demands. Emotional evasiveness was the obvious, if not the only, defence. Humphries has always had a fine sense of his own unnervingness. 'When they looked at me', he has said of both his parents, 'they saw someone who was interested in things that seemed very strange. They had a permanent anxiety about what the boy would be'. Talking elsewhere about his general fascination with the suburban world of Edna and Sandy, 'despite my original scorn', he refers to 'the incredible strangeness of the overfamiliar'. It is tempting to imagine, in the absence of their own testimony, that this was what struck his own parents about him. Nothing was stranger — nothing more disconcerting — than the unremitting intensity of his interest in them.[39]

In conjunction, the scorn, the yearnings for intimacy, and the intellectual prodigiousness, would be a challenge to any parent. The magnitude of this challenge can be felt behind Louisa Humphries' recurrent protestation about their eldest son: 'Eric and I don't know *where Barry comes from*'. This was hardly the most reassuring thing to repeat before him, and it is understandable that it should have added to anxieties of his own that he might have been adopted. There were some grounds for genuine bemusement on her part, however; and a need, if only out of self-protection from his demands, to preserve some sense of distance from the child. Her refrain is not dissimilar from Ian Donaldson's expressions of wonderment at the intellectually brilliant schoolboy who appeared to have sprung out of 'absolutely nowhere'. And it was only the brilliance that Donaldson ever had to puzzle over.[40]

'We sometimes wondered where Derek came from', echoes the mother of Humphries' hero in his recent novel. Derek Pettyfer has also made a part of his career out of performing in women's clothes. It is precisely this penchant for 'dressing up' which has prompted his mother's bemusement at his origins. If this was partly the case with Mrs Humphries' puzzlement, too, she need have looked no further for a clue than her own consuming interest in clothes. There were to be other fetishes of his suburban upbringing that Humphries made into a key subject of his creative work — the gladioli, of course, but flowers more generally, and all the paraphernalia of the domestic garden and the family home. Interest in these things was not peculiar to 36 Christowel Street, of course; Humphries could hardly have won and sustained a wide audience for his work if it were. In his family, however, there was a particular combination or concentration of such interests, and this provides further clues to his evolution as an artist. It helps illuminate the mix of passions in his own life and work.[41]

For Sandy Stone, as we noted earlier, everything in the gardens of Glen Iris was lovely before the social and demographic changes occasioned by the Second World War. From the confines of his Genoa velvet armchair, he revels *ad nauseam* in this lost Eden, and treasures its every remnant. He is also a punctilious recorder of every sign of foreign incursion or trendy depredation since the beginning of the Fall — inside the houses of his neighbourhood as well as outside. His daily scrutiny of all those little chips of marble around the lavatory bowl — 'one like a shoe and another like a map of New Zealand and another looking a bit like a Scottie dog upside down' — has clearly perfected his eye for domestic minutiae. Death has not been allowed to dim that eye, nor still his tongue. Those faculties may even be getting sharper. His nostalgia has begun to yield to a dispassionate, almost clinical antiquarianism. 'So much gone now you stop missing things', he declares in 'A Letter from Limbo', written in the late 1980s. But Humphries cannot let Sandy go; his shade has now quitted 36 Gallipoli Crescent 'for an indefinite period of time', but up until one of the latest shows *(Look at Me When I'm Talking to You!)* it has retained its vigil over his old suburb. In his own inert way, Sandy has proven to be as resilient as Edna.[42]

Humphries recalls that Edna, at her inception, 'described in exact detail the house of the early 1950s ... everything was described'. He was scarcely exaggerating. In the Union Theatre Repertory Company revue sketch which launched her stage career, towards the end of 1955, we learn of her own Genoa velvet couch (a close relation, no doubt, of Sandy's chair), of the double doors with sand-blasted reindeers on the glass, of the burgundy Axminster squares on her floors, of her duck-egg blue bedroom walls, her bird's eye blonde three piece suite and her new chenille bed-spread 'in a sort of pinky colouring' — all within the space of about twenty lines. 'They'd never heard their own houses described in the theatre', Humphries went on to recall of his first audiences. 'No one had served them up suburban Melbourne before.' Again, he was not exaggerating. Some three years after Edna's first appearance on stage, and the year after Sandy's inauguration on a record, an architect writing in the 'Small Homes Section' of the Melbourne *Age* noted the 'pleasure and relief' which Humphries' catalogues of seeming trivia had brought to his home-town following. 'In a nation of avid homebuilders', he wrote, ' ... it is now strange to think that our entertainers took so long to wake up to the inher-ent humor of our homes'. It was as if Humphries had lifted some ancient taboo, dispelled a mysterious inhibition.[43]

It didn't take long for him to start playing up the sexual suggestiveness of the domestic objects he described (Sandy and Beryl's thermos flask; Edna's 'slot' of a letterbox). Over thirty years on, in her television series *Neighbourhood Watch*, we find Edna on the other side of the world escort-ing us through people's actual houses with the same obsessive attention to detail as in the original sketches and a rather more knowing eye for the erotic promise in everyday paraphernalia. The houses are not like the opu-lent pleasure domes you might routinely catch on *Great Castles of Europe* or *Lives of the Rich and Famous;* they are nothing like her own fancifully extravagant House of Fame on *The Dame Edna Experience;* they offer none of the conventional titillations of a house of *ill*-fame. They are stunningly ordinary bourgeois nests, masterpieces of pebbledash or redbrick mediocrity, shrines to the salubrious, private museums of the middlebrow. As in the earliest sketches of Humouresque Street or Gallipoli Crescent, the frisson of these places is their normality, combined with the rarity of their public exposure. But now we *see* their assembled objects, rather than just having them described to us, and they are in a real setting, even if their arrangement (two rolling pins beside a jar of vaseline, for instance) can sometimes seem a touch contrived. Voyeurism's pleasures consort with those of fetishism in a straight-to-air domestic striptease. Nothing affirms more clearly the erotic undercurrent of the 'overfamiliar' than Dame Edna's confession in the first show of the series: 'I've always been interested in homes. Homes get my juices going. Homes touch my spot. Homes turn me on. Homes arouse me. You know I once thought I might even be a home-o-sexual'.[44]

It is always difficult to sort out Humphries' own feelings and attitudes from those of his characters. Keeping us in a state of uncertainty on this matter lends a persistent tension to his work that is a part of its vitality and a key to its wide appeal. Yet this is not always a result of conscious control on his part. The tension is persistent because he has never been completely certain himself. The effect of his characters on his audience has sometimes taken him by surprise, led him to see unsuspected complexities in his creations and in his own relation to them and their world.

There was clearly never a time when he was not preoccupied by the subject of the home, and especially the suburban home. 'I was aware of the growth of suburbia at first hand', he told an interviewer in 1968, 'because my father was — is — a builder'. There was some pressure on him when a boy to make it his own occupation. The Humphries family had been employed in various aspects of the building business for three generations now; and Eric Humphries, thanks to his acumen and his special talents as a designer, had managed to make a go of it even during the Depression and the Second World War when the building industry was in the doldrums. One of his younger sons was eventually to become an architect. The preoccupation with houses that his eldest son developed, however, was to be disturbingly different. If the term had been around, it might well have looked at times like a case of 'home-o-phobia'.[45]

In his autobiography Humphries recalls how his parents used to take him on Sunday drives around Melbourne's suburbs when he was a schoolboy. 'For my father, the builder, it was a professional excursion', he notes; but 'the lovely homes bored me. As we glided along ... past the raw new houses, admiring the azaleas and the "crazy" stone work, the "feature" chimneys and the names of the houses ... in duck-egg blue wrought-iron, I hankered for hovels'. Another critic of the suburbs, Robin Boyd, had singled out 'Featurism' as an abiding vice of domestic architecture in his book, *The Australian Ugliness,* published in 1960. By this he meant 'the subordination of the essential whole' in the structure of a house, and 'the accentuation of selected separate features', such as the chimneys of Humphries' recollection. Though Boyd was fifteen years older than Humphries and had trained as an architect while Humphries was still at school, the two men clearly came to recognise some strong affinities with each other. Boyd was a resident of Camberwell when *The Australian Ugliness* appeared, and two years earlier he had written 'a complimentary blurb' for the first recording of Humphries' material, *Wild Life in Suburbia,* which contained the earliest sketches involving Edna and Sandy. Back in 1952, when Humphries had just left school, Boyd had published his first critique of the suburbs, *Australia's Home.* His main target here was what he called 'Stylism'. This was a more general vice than 'Featurism', though not unrelated. What Boyd meant by it was precisely the kind of historical eclecticism in architectural design that Humphries' father had been perpetrating in suburban Camberwell from the 1930s. Though he didn't mention Eric Humphries by name, he did list several of the styles most favoured by the builder, including two that had been chosen for the Humphries' own family homes, 'Neo-Tudor' and 'Modern Georgian'.[46]

Far from wincing with embarrassment at this put-down of his father's favourite designs, the young Humphries was likelier to have exulted in its vindication of his own precocious reactions. We don't know if he read through either of Boyd's books; though it is interesting, in *Australia's Home,* to find both Genoa velvet upholstery and pink gladioli included on the list of domestic atrocities. Humphries might well have borrowed these details from Boyd when planning his theatrical exposés of suburbia in the Edna and Sandy sketches a few years later, though his own memories of items just like this were rich enough, as we'll see, and required no more than a nudge from someone else. Boyd, in turn, was possibly borrowing from Humphries when he added 'the lusty pink chenille' to his hit-list in *The Australian Ugliness*.[47]

Sandy probably bore even less resemblance to Eric Humphries than Edna did to Louisa Humphries, but it was in the Sandy sketches, with their 'sterile and obsessive details of his appallingly monotonous life', that Humphries vented much of his own distaste for the suburbs his father had helped to build. Yet the grounds for that distaste were rather different from Robin Boyd's: more complicated, less sure. *Australia's Home,* its author announced in his preface, was 'the story of a material triumph and an aesthetic calamity'. The calamity was an aesthetic one, it turns out, because the builders of the Australian home had been, if anything, *too* aesthetic; they had striven so hard, so self-consciously, for a beautiful effect that they had sacrificed those essentials in a building of 'integrity, wholeness and devotion to its own idea'. Humphries' objections were rooted in no such ideological principles. His were stories of material triumph and *emotional* calamity, and they were intensely personal stories with himself at their centre. The Camberwell of burgeoning housing estates was at once 'hideous' and 'heartbreaking' for him, as he announced in an 'Ode' he composed for his sister in 1968. At the same time, the telling of these stories offered him a means of rescue from the calamity — led him to see that it was not such a calamity after all. The same poem evokes a string of vignettes of 'sweet far-off childhood days'.[48]

In his relations with his father, as in those with his mother, the calamity took the form of a loss of intimacy. Its tokens, in his father's case, were provided by an obsession with houses, as it had been in his mother's by an obsession with frocks and hats and floral arrangements. As Humphries recollects them, the moments of intimacy with his father, and the signs of its abatement, were both connected with his father's occupation as a builder. Talking of his days as a toddler, he has recalled in a number of places how his father used to take him out for various treats and trips. There would be excurions to the Museum or the Aquarium and shopping expeditions to Camberwell market, or he would be driven into town when his father had some business there, or he would be taken out on his father's supervisory tours of the sites for Melbourne's ever-spawning housing estates. In recounting these tours of inspection over forty years afterwards, he speaks of 'sitting on joists eating lunch and watching the construction of these edifices which have since fascinated me'. There is no reference here to his boredom with houses on the Sunday drives in his later childhood.[49]

Unalloyed boredom appears to have been only a temporary phase, though it roughly coincided with a time of growing distance from his father. This came a bit later than it did with his mother. The arrival of his first sibling had done 'little to spoil' his excursions with his father. 'On the contrary', Humphries says in his autobiography, 'so that my mother could devote herself to this squealing, coconut-faced intruder, we spent more time together than before'. It was with the 'material triumph' of his father's business, to borrow Boyd's term, that the change came. 'My father became very successful', he declared in his conversation with John Lahr. 'I didn't see a great deal of him. He was always very, very busy.' He pictured his father at this stage as 'surrounded by drawing boards, set squares, drawing pins, which were the tools of his building trade and the source of the increasing wealth ... '[50]

It is significant that Sandy Stone should have been gazing at floor tiles when he sensed 'nothing was happening'. Another early Humphries character, the successful businessman but aggrieved paterfamilias, Colin Cartwright, charts the wastefulness of his eldest son by listing all the gifts to him that have been discarded or spurned over the years: 'a lathe, a bandsaw, an electric drill, the works!' These items, all associated with the building trade, are as trivial-seeming in their way as Edna's gewgaws, and in their very functionality they are even more boring, perhaps. Cartwright doesn't stop to consider how they may be tools of his own emotional evasiveness. Yet does his son stop to consider the weight of emotion they still bear, for all its concealment? Is 'nothing' happening in these lives and relationships? Or is all that is happening a calamity? It was partly the response of his audiences, Humphries has maintained, which helped alert him to unexpected ambiguities in his own characters' personalities and lives: riches where there seemed to be impoverishment — and vice versa.[51]

His very first audience, he claimed, 'recognised' Edna, but 'seemed to loathe her less than I did. It was the same with Sandy Stone. To my fury, people liked him; even as they laughed at him'. With Sandy, at least, his fury has turned to an almost serene acceptance — a serenity he has caught from the character itself. In 1968, the same year as his 'Ode to the City of Camberwell', Humphries reflected on Sandy: 'as I developed him I began to realise he was a damn sight happier than what I thought were the swingers'. There has been a long line of 'swingers' in Humphries' gallery of characters: Morrie Tate, the beatnik, from the early 1960s; the Kafka-spouting 'intellectual', Neil Singleton, from the mid-1960s; the folk-singer, Big Sonya, at the end of the 1960s — a monument to political correctness, *avant la lettre*; Martin Agrippa, pillar of the cinematic avant-garde, from the same period; Craig Steppenwolf, the progressive schoolteacher, Father Rod Nunn, the trendy gay vicar, and Lance Boyle, the wife-cheating, wheeler-dealing trade unionist, all in the 1970s; and Phil Philby, a version of Martin Agrippa for the 1980s. They might all have taken their motto from Morrie Tate's parting shot of 1962 — 'suburban conformity gives me the shits' — and yet that is precisely the measure of their own underlying conformity. Their rantings, collectively considered, are hardly less monot-onous than Sandy's dronings; and their worldly ambitions offer them far fewer consolations than Sandy's very circumscriptions can offer him. All that he needs in order to soothe his own disappointments and discontents is the memory of his wife's roast dinners or 'famous passion sponge'. On his characters in general, Humphries has recently reflected:

> It was a way of finding out — in retrospect I see this, more than at the time — I made them up in order to find out about my own life. Sandy represented the most exasperating type of person I would see going to catch the same train every morning … Then I discovered, of course, that even though I thought his seemed to be the dullest life that could be conceived, it was far from dull to him. And so in impersonating the character of Sandy I began to see it had its own nuances, this life — its own rewards, even its own richness.[52]

The savour of the Sunday roast, the spectacle of 'huge quantities of cake and scones' at afternoon tea, have remained among the treasured con-solations of Humphries' own season in the suburban bland-lands. In all their cornucopian plenty, of course, they might only add to the impression of a household starved of any but material sustenance. As much as

Humphries has tried to abet this impression, he has also let slip some other details which bring it into question.[53]

His mother's encouragement of his interest in painting might have been part of a battle against the austerities of her husband's regime, but Eric Humphries' own sensibilities were not unremittingly puritanical. The young Barry had clearly found some enchantment in his father's work before he became disenchanted; he later described how he had watched the suburbs grow 'under the spell of my father's theodolite'. Building implements did not *have* to be boring. And in all their cute, derivative whimsy there was some sense of aesthetic playfulness about his father's architectural designs. Robin Boyd's modernist exercises surely derived from a much sterner kind of rigour.[54]

While Humphries' father put some pressure on him to take up this most 'utilitarian' of artistic occupations, he did not try to discourage him from literary pursuits and fancies. Humphries can still plead that he had 'no literary origins' in the sense of parents who were avid readers (or writers) themselves. But someone had clearly started to nurture his own enthusiasm for books by giving him that sumptuously-illustrated edition of *Robin Hood* which first awoke him to the delights of England. He was to claim in later years that 'my father bought me whatever books I wanted'. And not just books; one has to wonder about the need for keeping his art lessons a secret when he tells us how his 'very generous father' would give him 'anything' he wanted, including oil-paints and easels. There was also the radiogram his father bought him, which allowed him to start exploring from home the obscurer corners of European music — another lifelong passion. He was plied with more gifts by his favourite uncle, Wilf, who had collected 'a lot of books' himself. Among the books he gave his nephew, Humphries remembers in particular 'a handsome leather bound copy of William Orpen's "Outline of Art"'. Wilf also introduced him to a new card game, with mouth-watering scenes of British landscapes emblazoned on each card. However unwittingly, the warders who ran the suburban prison in which Humphries felt entrapped provided him with a vision, if not the means, of escape.[55]

He confesses to developing 'very early a kind of snobbishness about books, a kind of bibliomania'. It was another of those 'strange' interests or passions which far exceeded those of his family but did not emerge out of 'nowhere'. He is conscious in himself of a more general 'sense of intellectual superiority', and acknowledges that this could be inherited from a socially snobbish vein in his mother. It is a tendency that has made him even more scornful of his formal education than of his family home and its environs. Once again, however, the scorn is not entirely unmixed with affection or nostalgia, and some positive stimuli to his later creative work can be detected in the bleakest of his student experiences.[56]

His first school was a kindergarten just around the corner from home, run single-handedly by a Mrs Flint. In various recollections he has dubbed it a 'dame school'. This is both an exact and a mischievously loaded use of the term. From his description, Mrs Flint's establishment technically fits the classic (indeed, now archaic) sense of 'dame school' explained above. More to the point, however, the figure of Mrs Flint provided his first education away from home in those combined qualities of ingratiation and intimidation which have been the hallmark of Dame Edna. Fawningly attentive to their parents and nannies, she became a terror to her charges: a living embodiment, in their young imaginations, of the witch in *Hansel and Gretel*. 'No great reader' herself — as the budding bibliomaniac in her care could already intuit by scanning her bookshelves — she had made this fairytale the staple of her own classes. Humphries' accounts of her classroom may be almost too precise at times to be entirely credible. It is significant all the same that among its other trappings he should record those early favourites of Edna and Sandy: 'a Genoa velvet couch' and 'Genoa velvet lounge chairs'.[57]

At other times, Humphries' recollections of his days at Mrs Flint's can be curiously blurred, if not evasive. An earlier version of them rehearses an incident in which his tricycle was involved in a collision with that of a friend, resulting in the friend's being taken to hospital with a broken arm. The arm was never to set properly. In this rendition of the story, Humphries acknowledges the guilt that came to haunt him when he saw his former friend in later life with his withered arm. The guilt was too great to bear, perhaps, when Humphries came to retell the story in his autobiography, or else he now felt he had mis-remembered. Whatever the reason, he effectively disowns his previously-confessed role in the incident, beginning the story: 'One day two bikes rammed into each other just in front of me … ' If he wasn't directly implicated, it is the more remarkable that this incident has stayed with him. Its impact on him is a symptom of a lingering fascination with human deformity and grotesquerie. He had a spastic cousin, the son of his uncle Wilf; and witnessing this boy at close quarters might have further helped to fuel this fascination. Symptoms of it are to be found in his creative work from childhood.[58]

Among his drawings that have survived from his schooldays there is a caricature of a witch-like dowager proffering a claw-like hand from her muff, and another of an animal skeleton (possibly a wolf's) decked out in clerical gear. We have various anecdotes of his schoolboy or undergraduate pranks in which he would imitate cripples and blind men in public places, or get his friends to do so while he staged a violent assault on them. It was while still at school that he had first become interested in Dadaism — 'that thrilling poetic movement', as he later described it, 'which had spilt with such fortuitous bad taste into the visual arts'. By his first year at university, in 1952, he had produced his own 'Dada Manifesto', somewhat in the manner of the original 'Collective Dada Manifesto' drawn up by Richard Huelsenbeck in 1920. Humphries' manifesto proclaimed, among other things, 'DADA is working with all its might to introduce the idiot and the cretin everywhere'. This manifesto accompanied an exhibition on campus of 'Dada-Surrealist' works which Humphries helped organise, and to which he contributed some of his own paintings and sculptures. There were to be other exhibitions in subsequent years of his works in this vein. He gave these works some telling and teasing titles: 'Exquisite Corpse', 'Siamese Shoes', 'Creche Bang' (the last involving a pram, not bikes or trikes). Some of his earliest revue sketches were to feature cretins, blind piano tuners, broken limbs and protruding cancers. One of these sketches formed the basis of a mini-novel, *Tid*, published in literary periodicals in Australia and Britain, and featuring as its eponymous hero an 'androgynous and eldritch child' with 'toasting-fork sharp' arms. Humphries' first book, *Bizarre*, published in 1965, was a sumptuously-produced anthology of forgotten gems in the literature and art of 'teratology', representations of the monstrous, the freakish, the weirdly abnormal, complete with deeply learned notes by himself on each of the contributors to this arcane genre. The cast of characters in his script for the film, *Barry McKenzie Holds His Own* (1974), includes Hugo Cretin, Modeste Imbecile, and Dorothy, 'a hideously deformed hunchback dwarf'.[59]

'Strange, even alarming images' in art have continued to be among its chief attractions for Humphries, as he intimated in an introduction he wrote to the work of Melbourne-based painter, Dominic Ryan, in 1984. Ryan's images are nearly all of bodily parts, fastened to or strung from weirdly elaborate mechanical devices, and variously distorted or distended. Humphries' own performance art has continued to strike observers as more or less subtle exercises in 'teratology'. In Edna Everage and Sir Les Patterson, John Lahr contends, 'Humphries has created a credible form of the monstrous'. (It is significant in this regard that Humphries should have named an earlier version of the Australian cultural supremo 'Ken Frankenstein'.) Clive James sees Lance Boyle and Neil Singleton, in addition to Sir Les, as 'perfect monsters'. Only Sandy Stone, among the major characters, is exempt from these lists of *adultes terribles*.[60]

The grotesqueries which Humphries has observed or represented over the years have taken so many different forms, offered such a variety of facets, that it would be idle to reduce his preoccupation with them to any one impulse. An early, hostile critic of his work, Ian Syme, detected in Humphries 'a deep sense of inadequacy comforting itself by the sight of other, more obviously inadequate, human wrecks and accidents'. Syme contrasted Humphries with a long line of artists — from Shakespeare to Schoenberg — who 'were strongly committed to the elucidation and expression of love and humanity'. A typical defence of Humphries has been that he 'forced you to look at the ugly and monstrous' as a way of entrapping 'bogus emotion, denial, what we all do' when we avert our gaze or merely mouth compassion. Either of these interpretations is eminently arguable, and they are not entirely at odds. (Confronting the world with what it generally evades does not necessarily rule out comforting oneself, and vice versa.) But both in their way underestimate the degree of Humphries' personal identification with the bizarre and the strange, and the positive view he could take of that identification. It was to be among the chief lessons of his education.[61]

Reviewing Patrick White's novel, *The Vivisector* (1970), Humphries was to remark: 'one turns to a new book by Patrick White fearfully ... The events he chronicles are so strange but so compellingly, repulsively familiar. We discover his freaks within ourselves … ' It is difficult to tell how far Humphries is speaking about everybody here, how far about himself. But an intuition of his own strangeness may be traced in him from his early schooldays and has persisted ever since. The remarks on White suggest it is hardly a comforting feeling for him, but becoming aware of it has not been an entirely fearful process either. Humphries has made of his strangeness a badge of pride and defiance, a shield, a weapon of provocation, the stuff of a self-defining and self-distinguishing legend — and the means of a not inconsiderable livelihood. It has had so many uses for him that he has been inclined to exaggerate it, where not inventing it.[62]

Of his life at school immediately after his departure from the dreaded Mrs Flint's, he recalls: 'I felt set apart a little, already'. The reference is specifically to his social position as a privileged child filling in time at a state primary school while awaiting entry to a posher one, but it is symptomatic of his more general feelings of apartness as a schoolboy. In his recollections these feelings begin to mount, become the more explicit, as the schools he describes become posher. Another 'gorgon' of a schoolteacher, Miss Jensen, had (he believed) unjustly stigmatised him as a bully when he was at the state school. In fact, he claims, it had been the other boys who had started bullying him and then deftly shifted the blame when he had tried to defend himself. Eventually he was able to take up a place at the local private school, Camberwell Grammar. Originally founded in 1886, it had been taken over by the Anglican Church some forty years later. During the period Humphries was there — the last years and immediate aftermath of the Second World War — the school occupied the site of a large Victorian house with much of the original garden still intact. It was at this establishment that he completed his preparatory education and began his secondary schooling. As he recounts them, his experiences of the place were his happiest ever at a school; though on first arriving, he recalls, 'I found the strangeness a bit terrifying', and there was still bullying and the boredom of compulsory games to contend with. The antidote was to find and cherish the strangeness in himself.[63]

Nothing could have been more calculated to feed misogynistic feelings in him than his successive exposure to Mrs Flint and Miss Jensen; but at

Camberwell Grammar he was to come across 'lots of nice teachers, mostly female, because the chaps were mostly at the War ... ' He was even able to persuade them to call him by his Christian name, a rare form of intimacy in private boys' schools of the day which may have done something to compensate for the waning intimacy with his parents. If niceness was a quality he was already a bit equivocal about, he was to find more solidly reassuring qualities, true pedagogic inspiration, in the shape of two teachers in the senior part of the school. One of these, Stan Brown, was to take a lifelong interest in Humphries' literary pursuits. The other, Ian Bow, was to encourage his early ventures in painting. Both proved so inspiring to him, not because they helped diminish the sensations of strangeness produced by the school but because they relished and actively nurtured his own kinds of strangeness. It was through Bow's example in particular, Humphries recalls, that he was 'introduced to the exhilaration of eccentricity'. Into the 1950s, when he had quitted schoolteaching for adult education, Bow was still passionately preaching against the 'strangling clutches of mediocrity' and declaring that 'it is the modern artist who is doing the most in the fight' against such forces.[64]

Suddenly, arbitrarily, around the time of his thirteenth birthday, Humphries was to find himself removed from this bohemian Eden. It was through no misdemeanour on his part. The local vicar (perhaps a model for that drawing of the skeletal wolf in pastoral clothing) had advised Humphries' parents that it would be for the best if their gifted son should complete his education at the elite Anglican school, Melbourne Grammar. The fact that it was 'the poshest school in town', attracting pupils from top business and professional families as well as a few sprigs of an older landed class, would have pandered to Louisa Humphries' social snobberies. Nothing could have been less attractive at the time to her son. The commercial success of 'the *nouveau-riche* middle classes' was particularly repugnant to him. After all, it was what effectively had taken his father away from him. It also represented for him the antithesis of those aesthetic and anti-establishment values he had thrilled to in the teachings of Ian Bow. It was 'The Enemy', whose reincarnation was visible in the captain of the school. 'There were several of them, of course', he acknowledged in later years, ' ... but prefects and captains merge, in my memory, into one odious type: a bully with the face of a stillborn stockbroker'. Dame Edna was to pick up this theme, describing Melbourne Grammar on one occasion as 'the elitist school that has turned out some of Australia's top insurance brokers and upmarket motor dealers'.[65]

Humphries' own intellectual snobberies further fuelled his resentment of his new school. 'By the time I got to Melbourne Grammar', we find him recalling nearly forty years on, 'I was quite arty underneath. I had read more books than most of the schoolmasters, which wasn't hard, and I painted in oils'. The tone of contempt in his autobiography a few years later was even greater. Here he depicts his schoolmasters as pretty well all 'ignorant dotards' who 'made no effort to communicate knowledge since they had no store of this article on which to draw'. All that they and most of their pupils had seemed to value, he has recalled elsewhere, was sporting success: 'the great god was athletics'. He has judged as odious 'the absurd lengths to which they went to parody a British public school system'. It is not the original model he is denigrating, note, so much as the limp attempts to emulate it. A house system had been introduced, for instance, even though most of the pupils at Melbourne Grammar commuted to school from their family homes on a daily basis. What boarders there were formed an elite of sorts but one that was 'uniformly dull of wit, loud-mouthed and ferociously conformist'. His recollections of the 'dreadful conformity' of the place have led him to assert that he 'received perhaps the worst education that anyone could ever get'.[66]

These are considered retrospective verdicts on his schooldays. There are more impish asides such as we find in the 'biographickal noats' he has dashed off for the programmes of his stage shows ('Educated during the holidays from Melbourne Grammar', reads one from 1971). The underlying themes are similar: the mutual estrangement of the school and himself, proceeding from his determined nonconformity and lofty oddity. It is not that the others around him don't have their kinds of freakishness, with their stillborn or dotard looks and their stunted brains. But his own kind is both rarer and more rarefied. It is the deformity of an over-developed brain that cannot fit regular confines or engage with the quotidian. At least, that is how he represents it.[67]

There were, for instance, what he calls his 'rather freakish results' in the

Matriculation examinations of 1951, which marked the end of his school-days. These results were no doubt outstandingly good if judged by the general standard in the whole state of Victoria (he was placed within the top thirty candidates overall, having gained first-class honours in English Literature and British History, and been placed equal top in the latter). Judged by the standards of his year at Melbourne Grammar, however, they were not so exceptional: another six boys also made the top thirty, and one of them came top of two of his individual subjects. However unstimulating Humphries and others found the teaching at the school, and however dull-witted its general run of students, it has somehow always contrived to harvest some extraordinary academic results.[68]

There are other senses in which his examination performance might be considered freakish. Thanks to the examiners' caprices as well as his own, the results could well have been very different. They were certainly not predictable. Bearing out other testimonies, like Ian Donaldson's, to his compulsive precocity at Melbourne Grammar, Humphries has acknowledged the 'rather unappetising characteristic of mine, to have read specifically in areas which had been neglected by the master'. He relished spouting Scott Fitzgerald (not yet returned to fashion), various writers of the decadent and aesthetic movements of the 1890s and their successors (from Ernest Dowson to Ronald Firbank), and the Gothic authors and 'curdled late romantics' of the eighteenth and early nineteenth centuries. In the heyday of F.R. Leavis, nearly all these authors would have been accounted freaks of literature in themselves. (In *The Great Tradition,* published in 1948, Leavis had even deemed *Wuthering Heights* 'a kind of sport'.) In Matriculation English Literature, Humphries could not have entirely avoided more mainstream classics — it was here he would have had his first sustained exposure to Chaucer, as sections of *The Canterbury Tales* were always prescribed — but he chose to devote a good deal of his paper to a discussion of one of the most *outré* of Gothic fictions, William Beckford's *Vathek.* This was 'a work that had certainly not been set for study', recalls one of Humphries' examiners. How were they to respond to answers that 'bore little direct relation to the set questions' yet were 'dazzlingly sharp and intelligent'? They considered failing the paper before awarding it a first.[69]

In the end, therefore, 'impartial' examiners from outside his school had recognised Humphries' talents, even indulged them. He describes how this kind of recognition suddenly made him realise what a 'strangely insulated life' he had been leading at Melbourne Grammar, where in the internal examinations directly preceding the external ones some of his teachers had failed him. In making it a basis for judgment on his whole school career, he sets too much store by this anomaly. If his life was insulated there, it was because of the extraordinary facilities, opportunities and privileges which an elite school could offer all of its clientele, even in the austere aftermath of the war years. Some of these (particularly in the sports department) he obviously didn't relish; but for all that he says of the tyranny of games, there were several other activities on offer which he clearly made the most of, and which helped shape his later career in various respects.[70]

There were Debating Societies (Junior and Senior), a Dramatic Society and an Art Club at Melbourne Grammar; and it is remarkable with what consistency Humphries' name crops up in the notes on these groups published each term in the school's magazine, the *Melburnian*. He was clearly a galvanising force in all of them. It was not only with a Dada and Surrealist exhibition in his final year (a dress rehearsal of sorts for his more comprehensive exhibitions at the university) that he made a splash. Two years earlier he had delivered a 'lecturette' to the Junior Debating Society on 'Modern Art' which, according to the *Melburnian,* 'stimulated a discussion that promised to last indefinitely'. In the same year he had taken the role of Mrs Pengard in a satirical comedy by Walter Hackett, and was so convincing in the part that 'for moments at a time', the reviewer noted, 'his true sex was forgotten'. The reviewer remembered that the previous year Humphries had already revealed himself in another play as 'a talented female impersonator'.[71]

These notices in the *Melburnian* were unsigned, and it is not inconceivable that Humphries wrote some of them himself. The magazine's so-called 'Original' section was certainly hospitable to his writing talents, carrying many signed poems by him in various issues, as well as a version of his talk on modern art, with its astonishing cascade of allusions to 'fin-de-siècle aestheticism', the Fauves, Cubism, Le Corbusier, Freudian psychology, Walt Disney, 'le Jazz hot', Schiaparelli, Sartre, Christian Dior, Gertrude Stein, and much else of like interest. All of this knowledge cannot have come out of the books given him by his father and uncle. Some of it he had already begun ferreting out for himself in exhaustive raids on Melbourne's secondhand bookstores and 'curiosity shops'; but there was also a trove nearer by. 'At the disposal of the whole school', noted the *Melburnian* in the same issue in which it printed Humphries' talk, 'is a very comprehensive art library containing volumes on Art and artists, past and present'.[72]

Reflecting something of his own life's journeyings, Clive James has observed: 'As so often happens with the Australian expatriates, ... Humphries discovered his Europe before he got there'. Books were probably the most potent agents of this process for both men; though James, as we shall see, did not have anything like the same access to them at his state technical school in Sydney as Humphries did at Melbourne Grammar. There were other special features of Humphries' school which helped facilitate the process, most notably (and noticeably) the way it *looked*. Not only in its organisational structure — the 'house system' — or in its deification of sport did it contrive to emulate the British Public School. Its buildings, grounds and surrounding landscapes were also something of a 'parody' of British models. Even when opened in the 1850s, it could not enjoy the same sense of spaciousness and seclusion as some country schools (whether in England or Australia), and its founders chose to use the distinctive local bluestone for its central core of buildings. But its close proximity to public parks and gardens have continued to lend it something of a pastoral ambience to this day, while the most prominent architectural features of the buildings (castellated towers, a spire, rows of pointed arches) were typical of the so-called Gothic style through which many of the English public schools of the nineteenth century attempted to assert their kinship with the great medieval foundations of Winchester and Eton. For all of his deep discontent at school, Humphries couldn't help being impressed with these 'architecturally interesting', 'very beautiful' survivals of an older culture, and beguiled by their setting. Of the move from Camberwell to Melbourne Grammar, he claims at one point in his recollections: 'Slowly, in spite of myself, I began to enjoy the new school with its

old buildings and the nearby Royal Botanic Gardens to which we sometimes escaped during lunch hour'.[73]

When his 'freakish' brilliance in the Matriculation examinations won
him a scholarship to the University of Melbourne at the beginning of 1952,
he would happen upon more grand gothic confectionery. The Law Faculty
to which he was first admitted, and the main library at that time, were both
parts of a set of buildings connected by an arched cloister in the manner
of some of the colleges at Oxford and Cambridge. At the south-east corner
of the cloister there had stood the old Wilson Hall built in the manner of
a medieval cathedral. A fire had reduced it to a heap of ruins just a month
or so before Humphries was due to begin his course. By his accounts, he
spent hardly any time at the law school; he had only enrolled in that faculty because he lacked the foreign language prerequisite for entry into Arts.
Of the old Wilson Hall, however, he affected to recall in later years how it
was 'my home ... which I subsequently destroyed by fire; and it became,
quite naturally, the cultural mecca of Melbourne'. He goes on to quote
from a purported diary of the time:

> 31st September, 1952 ... Arrived Wilson Hall ... I opened at random a volume
> entitled 'The Dada Painters and Poets' ... I had found a new word; inaugurat-
> ed a revolutionary movement. The word I had miraculously discovered was
> ... 'Dadaism' ... [74]

Humphries the irreverent incendiary? The revolutionary subversive?
Such images comport with a part of him that has always represented himself as some kind of monstrous malcontent. The talk here of destroying his
'home' echoes those murderous feelings he entertained about his parents.
Yet it is fantasy-talk, and his feelings are as always mixed, unamenable to
easy labelling. While he may not have immediately confessed to his soft
spot for old buildings, dating back to his schooldays, it was already becoming a recurrent theme of his public pronouncements from the early 1960s.
His more common posture before such buildings has been a reverential
one; his dominant impulse a conserving one. (The modern replacement of
the Wilson Hall was to be included in his *Treasury of Australian Kitsch*.)
The only real irreverence in these recollections is for chronology. He post-
dates not just the Wilson Hall fire, but also his introduction to Dadaism,

which we know from his recollections elsewhere, and from independent records, goes back at least a year earlier to the end of his schooldays. Robert Motherwell, the editor of the volume to which he refers, points out how confusion or inaccuracy over dates was something that the earliest exponents of the movement shruggingly justified as 'being Dada'. This was far from being their sole form of subversiveness, of course, but they too are not so easily categorised as 'revolutionary' or even as a movement, in the sense of having any cohesive political or cultural programmes.[75]

An updated Dada manifesto produced by Richard Huelsenbeck in 1949 — three years before Humphries' own version — was blatantly anticommunist, and led to bitter squabbles and divisions among his fellow-Dadaists of old. Humphries himself, still in school at that stage, was only just deciding 'to become a communist', partly out of a desire to shock his teachers and also, perhaps, as a way of clearly distinguishing himself from his stockbroker-like peers. According to his autobiography, however, this stage was momentary. When he procured a copy of *The Communist Manifesto,* he relates, he found it 'practically unreadable'. 'The next best thing' then 'was to *appear* to be a communist … My political period — the only one in my life — was short-lived'.[76]

Whether this was as conscious a process as suggested here is difficult to fathom, but we are alerted again to the hazards of summing up Humphries' opinions on anything under conventional categories. It has *appeared* to various commentators that his sensibilities, political or otherwise, have inclined to the reactionary since his youth, and that he has become more assertively 'right-wing'. There are certainly some weighty bits of evidence to support this impression. But can we ever be certain that they too have not been contrived principally to shock, to trick, to bait those who would order individual opinion according to such divisions? The evidence is usually more complicated than it looks at first. Far from conforming with any neat ideological or party lines, it challenges their validity, upsets regular understandings of how they operate or affect to operate. Humphries' 'political periods' continued long after his schooldays, in spite of what he says — but ultimately in the service of being anti-political. Even that last epithet is too strong, if it suggests anything like an anarchist's subversiveness. Humphries' challenge to conventional political divisions and categories is more in the nature of instructive mischief, of a needling *jeu d'esprit*. 'Far from wishing to change society', he said as early as 1965, 'I can only hope that my audience will pause, reflect for a moment, and pass on their immutable way; not forgetting, perhaps, to drop a coin in my hat'.[77]

The succession of 'swingers' he has satirised in his gallery of Chauceresque portraits from the 1960s on are all of leftish or progressive or libertarian complexion — or that is how they would like to see themselves. But their behaviour or tone of address reveal them on the whole as pious authoritarians of a kind that would ordinarily be associated with the religious or political right. Lance Boyle the unionist, his creator has intimated, has all the brutality and corruptness of a classic 'fascist'. Erich Count Plasma, the ghoulish leader of the communist state of Transylvania in *Barry McKenzie Holds His Own,* used to be a personal friend of Hitler's before he conveniently defected to the Eastern Bloc. Humphries, the schoolboy anti-capitalist, has continued to include businessmen and entrepreneurs in his gallery of ghouls and monsters. His lampooning of such figures is much more in the tradition of old-style Tory disdain for the *nouveaux riches* than of any principled socialist objections. Socialism, or what now passes for socialism, is likely to be all too complicit with capitalism. The latest and most monstrous of Humphries' businessmen-types, Daryl Dalkeith, is notable for having been 'too close' to the leadership of the Federal *Labor* Party in Australia. That other prize monster, Sir Les, was supposedly an appointee of an earlier Labor leader, Gough Whitlam, and can still be found harking back to the 'golden age' of 'the Socialist Revolution of the 70's'. But he has cannily remained a 'bi-partisan' survivor. Back in the 1950s, at her advent, Edna Everage had been a fervent admirer of Mr Menzies, leader of Australia's long-reigning conservative party, the Liberals; but it was only a short time after Whitlam made her a Dame that she confessed she had 'become a *teeny bit* Left Wing'. Mr Menzies' 'lovely speaking voice' had been a prime attraction in earlier days, and it helped in her conversion to the new regime that Whitlam and his wife were not 'coarsely-spoken like the laborites used to be'. Edna's conversion was so far-reaching that she even went on a pilgrimage, not (like the Wife of Bath) to the tomb of St Thomas in Canterbury, but to the tomb of Karl Marx at Highgate Cemetery in London. We have vivid photographic evidence of this. Now she 'claims to be as left as they come'. Some recent critics of Humphries have liked to point out that both in her career path, and in her style of bossy 'caring', the political figure with whom Edna has most in common is Margaret Thatcher; but Humphries has explicitly dwelt on these parallels himself. Edna, too, has recounted how the former *grande dame* of the British Conservative Party would ring her for advice at three in the morning, wailing: 'How do I pretend to like the environment?'[78]

While declaring himself to be 'a staunch supporter' of the Whitlam government in early 1974 — near the middle of its term of office — Humphries was already voicing reservations in the press about its foreign policy. 'He is certainly not, he says with a smile, right wing', reported one journalist who interviewed Humphries a fortnight later; but in the same interview, and elsewhere, Humphries gave vent to his exasperation with a kind of puritanism — or 'wowserism' — which he associated with the left in particular. By June the following year, before the Whitlam administration fell, he had already joined the editorial board of the Sydney literary periodical, *Quadrant,* which was assertively anti-communist in its editorial line, and generally considered (however justifiably) as a house magazine of the Australian intellectual right. He was to contribute sketches and articles to the magazine over several years, remaining on its board till 1987. In defending *Quadrant* (and himself) a year earlier against automatic ascriptions of right-wing views, he pointed out that 'some very good and liberal people write for it'. More devilishly, in a 'birthday' letter he wrote to its editors on the occasion of its twentieth-fifth year of publication in 1982, he had declared: 'Long may the radicals of the right bash, baffle and bewilder the poor old pinko conservatives'.[79]

There is a typically mischievous scrambling of categories in the wording of this declaration which complicates its exultant blimpish tone. It artfully confuses and conflates traditional political labels in a way that gives us 'pause', makes us 'reflect' a little, before we go on bandying them around — or it would have done so in the years before the legacies of Thatcherism and the eclipse of the Soviet Union made the scrambled associations of right-wing with radical, communist with conservative, into commonplaces themselves. There have been further complications in Humphries' political position more recently which clearly dissociate him from any of the current varieties and conceptions of radicalism. What surfaces here are further symptoms of that old-style Toryism traceable to his schooldays. Yet it remains difficult to call this a political position, tinged as it is with an impish contempt for any brand of politics — or for any political figures at least. With the proviso that he can duck every kind of labelling, it is best summed up as a form of *cultural* conservatism, rooted in a selective Anglophilia.

Tories were traditionally the champions and protectors of the British monarchy. There has been a growing movement in recent years to make Australia a republic, entirely independent of constitutional or legal ties with Britain. Not a new movement by any means, it gained an added dynamism through the support of the Labor Prime Minister, Paul Keating, before his fall from power. Humphries has made no secret of his scorn for Keating or the other republicans. Yet his main objection, as expressed in his autobiography, stems not from any principled or passionate attachment to monarchy on his own part, but rather from a suspicion of the republican movement's rhetoric — what he calls 'its cant about patriotism'. The prominence of Irish names among its champions, including Keating's, was enough to persuade Humphries that the movement was 'just another form of pommy-bashing'. That he turns the name of another republican exponent, Donald Horne, into 'O'Horne', to clinch his point, reveals the ubiquitous sprite of mischief behind the political jeremiah.[80]

Just a couple of weeks before the Federal Labor Government's fall in March 1996, Humphries could be found pillorying Keating and his political colleagues in the press. He was aiming to expose official complicity in the damage done to Australia's rural and urban environments by technology, popular culture, and a brand of patriotism that was less hypocritical than 'loony'. More elaborate telephone wires, new styles of tram, the waft of 'Big Macs', the opening of casinos, the spread of carparks and shopping malls, and the replacement of the elm by the gum in parks and gardens were all symptoms for him of the rapid effacement of a golden age: 'the great reign of Queen Victoria'. These symptoms have proliferated unchecked — or positively encouraged — by government policy; and what was once in his eyes 'the land where nothing happens' has now been turned into something far more threatening: 'The road to Eventville'.[81]

Humphries can't hold Labor wholly responsible for such atrocities, however — and he doesn't. In his home state of Victoria, the continuing focus of his anxieties, it has been the Liberal Party who has held the reins of office for some years. Traditionally a bastion of old-style conservatism, its image is being transformed — as the British Conservative Party's was, under Margaret Thatcher — through the aggressive dynamism of its leader, Jeff Kennett. If by nothing else, its growing affinity with radical right-wing Thatcherism has been signified, in Edna's terms, by its 'pretending to like the environment'; and in letters to the press, as well as in articles, Humphries has voiced his outrage at the Kennett government's 'devastation' of Melboune's Albert Park for the purposes of constructing a motor-racing track, and at the continuing endorsement of 'dual-occupancy laws' facilitating the construction of 'gimcrack units and townhouses on the front lawn'. Quizzed on her attitude to Kennett, Edna herself has been roused to say: 'the sooner someone builds a brick veneer on his front garden the better ... Ambition can sometimes be an attractive characteristic but not necessarily in his case, if it is at the expense of a city'. In his own voice, Humphries has been particularly exercised about the threat of dual occupancy to his childhood environment of Camberwell, and the 'nobler dwellings' of the sort his father built on the Golf Links Estate, 'that comfortable and leafy monument to pre-war Melbourne decency'.[82]

Whether in the matter of politics or suburban architecture, it is still risky to talk of any transformations in Humphries' opinions, or even of shifts, when we have no idea how far his tongue remains in his cheek. It's never likely to be dislodged entirely, whatever the issue. From university days on, his main aim has not been to take political sides but, rather, to 'goad the humourless' regardless of sides. His Dada manifesto of 1952 declared: 'We are incapable of treating seriously any subject whatsoever ... ' In 1996 we find Dame Edna declaring: 'I don't think you should take anything too seriously'. (She is attending the opening of a casino in Cairns, just the sort of enterprise her creator has recently been berating as part of the modern blight.)[83]

Universities themselves, Humphries has suggested on various occasions, are the breeding grounds of the most puritanically earnest, humourless, and conformist people anywhere, and particularly of that species of so-called swinger whose very mode of rebellion is just another form of regimentation. As he recalls it, his own experience of the University of Melbourne was a great disappointment to him after the oppressiveness of school, because

> everybody was wearing another uniform — an undergraduate uniform — suede shoes, knitted ties, all smoking pipes and drinking beer … They were already set on the inexorable path to middle age. What was almost the most offensive thing was their new-found liberalism. Their tolerance for foreigners. They were reading Hopkins and Eliot. I'd been there. I'd gone beyond all that. I wanted somehow to scratch the surface of this liberalism a bit.[84]

What may have been a disappointment in one sense was an opportunity in another, however. If the bulk of his fellow-undergraduates were really all so grey, they afforded him an even greater lustre in contrast — or a yet deeper demonic darkness. One of his contemporaries notes how Humphries' 'strange career in this University' was 'the more striking against the staid character of the times … There were other dominant people, with a personal style, about the place; but none so eccentric-seeming (and being)'. Freed from the regimes of an ultra-respectable school, Humphries cultivated and flaunted his freakishness with impunity. Except during a brief period of compulsory national service at an army camp towards the end of his first year at university, he was now able to start growing his lank, black hair and to sport a forelock. In combination with his favoured apparel (striped trousers, dark coat, occasionally a wide-brimmed hat), the effect was not of a hippy ten years before his time, but of a throwback to some more aristocratic or decadent or romantic incarnation from much earlier decades. Contemporaries have variously likened him in their memories to 'an illustration depicting a sixth-former in an English school story' — the Hon. Arthur Augustus D'Arcy in the St Jim's yarns of the Edwardian period, perhaps — or to some Beardsleyesque aesthete or to 'Chopin, Liszt, the young Brahms'.[85]

He failed his law course at the end of his first year, but had been studying German at a crammers which enabled him to fulfil the language requirement for entry into the Arts Faculty the following year. He was supposedly enrolled for majors in English and Fine Arts, though his approach

to his formal studies was resolutely dilettantish, in keeping with his languid *fin-de-siècle* appearance. 'I practiced [*sic*] the role Undergraduate', he
later wrote; but his attendance at lectures and classes dwindled rapidly as
he turned his attentions almost exclusively to extra-curricular roles and
activities in the worlds of student theatre, the film society, and ever more
outrageous Dadaist 'happenings'.[86]

Part of the point of the Dadaist stunts, exhibitions and performances
was that there was no point to them. They were deliberate challenges to
rational ways of apprehending and operating the world, concerted 'attacks
on student conformity', passionate assertions of Humphries' resistance to
the regimentations of workaday adult life. They connived at re-enacting a
childhood world of irresponsibility and naughtiness, with the audience cast
in the role of punishing or indulgent parents. Years later Humphries reflected that he was 'happy to say that the exhibitions produced a great deal of
hostile reaction amongst university students, also a great deal of amused
curiosity'. Negative responses meant at least as much to him as positive ones.
Rejection might even have been preferable to acceptance, as it served to confirm what he imagined had happened in his relation with his own parents.[87]

In other recollections we find Humphries revelling in the 'sublime
infantilism' of his campus lunchtime revue of 1953, *Call Me Madman!* The
title punned on the name of the currently-touring American musical, *Call
Me Madam!* The figure of the madman, like the figure of the child, allowed
an escape from the world of conforming adults, while commanding attention from that world. Humphries' title has at once a defiant and an
importunate note. It was as if he had become addicted to the idea of his
strangeness. He had learned to exult in the distinctive identity which it
afforded him, and now needed or craved situations which would go on con-
firming it. There was an experimental film made around this time, *Le Bain
Vorace,* which featured him as a mad scientific genius who disposes of those
around him with acid, relishing 'the last laugh' at their expense. The bath of
the title is the scene of these grisly crimes. Many of the scenes were shot,
Humphries recollects, 'on location at my parents' home in Camberwell'.[88]

Call Me Madman! was so provocative, he has claimed in various recollections, that it eventually led the audience to stampede, and 'Mr John
Sumner, who was in charge of the Union Theatre then, forebade the Dada

group to ever hire it again'. Humphries' accounts differ, however, as to which sketch in particular proved to be the last straw for the audience; and there are accounts of the show by others that have no memories of a stampede and suggest nothing more than some faint registrations of boredom or irritation. John Sumner's version is that he 'first heard of Barry Humphries when … I received a deputation of ladies complaining about his act … and asking me to ban it. I had not seen the act, but when I did I offered Barry a job'. The job was as a regular actor with Sumner's university-based repertory company.[89]

Humphries dropped out of his university courses altogether at the end of 1953, never taking a degree. One lecture which he had managed to attend while still formally enrolled as a student was given by Stephen Spender, the visiting British poet who had been closely connected in the 1930s with the group of so-called Marxist writers revolving around W.H. Auden. The lustre of Spender's name and associations was a sufficient attraction for a young Anglophile who had flirted with communism himself; though it was as if by some benign premonitory instinct that Humphries was also drawn to Spender's talk. In 1991, nearly forty years later, he took it upon himself to compile an anthology of verse written by Spender's friends in celebration of the poet's eightieth birthday. He included a poem of his own, recollecting Spender's lecture. There was to be a much more personal link with the poet. The progeny of British writers as much as their works has had a lingering attraction for Humphries. When he was living in Britain during the 1960s he was to have a long-standing extramarital affair with Georgina Barker, the daughter of the poet, George Barker; and since 1990 he has been married to Spender's daughter, Lizzie, an actress, playwright and cookery writer.[90]

His attraction to, and for, strongly assertive women of a creative bent — the kind that his mother might have blossomed into if she had had the background and the opportunities — can be traced back to his schooldays, and the sparrings he enjoyed with the 'beautiful, fierce and witty debating opponents' from Melbourne Grammar's sister schools. At that stage they had seemed 'unattainable', but not because they didn't reciprocate his adulation. (His schoolfellow Ian Donaldson recalls their bedazzlement by Humphries and the envy this induced in the other boys.) School rules and prevailing moral conventions of the day would have been the main obstacle. One of the releases of university life, and particularly of the avant-garde and bohemian circles in which he started to move, was into a world of freer sexual experimentation. Sustained emotional attachments to women have not proved easy for him, but he started falling in love with them from his first year at university. Not quite two years after abandoning his course, when he was still only twenty-one, he made his first foray into marriage. It was also to be the briefest, lasting less than a couple of years in effect. He met his first wife, Brenda, when they were acting together in one of the Union Theatre Repertory Company's Shakespearean productions. (The play, with some prophetic irony, was *Love's Labours Lost.*) She was a ballerina as well as an actress; and while there can be no doubting her creative bent it is possible that she wasn't assertive enough for him — nor for her own sake. She was still in her teens when they met, as dewy-eyed about him as the girls at school had been. It was to be an extraordinarily testing period for both of them in several respects.[91]

She claims to have suspected him from early on of casual infidelities with various women in their theatrical circles; but there was to be another, older woman who presented more sustained and more unusual competition for her husband's attentions. On 13 December 1955, only a few weeks after their marriage, Edna Everage arrived on the scene. She had been growing in Humphries' mind over the previous year, with the encouragement of Ray Lawler and other fellow-thespians as they travelled around Victoria's country towns with their shows; but from being a disembodied voice at the back of a touring-bus, she now emerged on stage in full regalia and emphatically up-front. Here was a sort of live-in mother-in-law no young bride could have anticipated.[92]

There was another incipient demon with claims on her husband. While he was still an undergraduate he had been introduced to the pleasures and consolations of alcohol. Prohibited in any public place by the locality he was brought up in — the whole of Camberwell had been legally declared a 'dry' area from the beginning of the 1920s — drinking was frowned on by his mother even in the privacy of their home. It could be a gesture of defiance in itself, therefore, against the regimentations of suburban life. It also provided him with a fitting weapon of protest against his mother — and not just her values in general but what he saw as her with-drawal of favours from him, personally, when he was a child. He hinted at the connection when, at the height of one of his binges in later years, he told Patrick White: 'I've already been weaned off one or two toxic breasts'; White felt at the time that 'he must have got on to at least one of them again'. Humphries had made a spectacle of bingeing from the start. As he tells it, his first fatal tipple had been the purple liqueur, Parfait d'Amour — nothing as 'conformist' as beer — which he had 'quaffed by the tumbler' at a student party. It had made him 'volcanically sick'. The bingeing was to continue, albeit with 'more conventional beverages', for nearly another two decades. His 'increasingly abnormal drinking' over those years served to feed his other addiction — became a part of it: his addiction to the idea of his strangeness, to his vision of himself as a freak *extraordinaire*. He used to imagine, he says, that he was part of some 'aristocracy of self-destruction', in the tradition of his schoolboy hero, Scott Fitzgerald, and other drunken artistic geniuses of the century. The very way he has continued to charac-terise his delusions of that time — as '*monstrous* self-justifications' or '*grotesque* alibis' — retains an air of Grand Guignol.[93]

The drinking was rarely allowed to compete with his stage work, but together with the womanising it certainly took a toll on his marital rela-tionships. The itinerant nature of theatrical life was an added pressure on his first youthful marriage. A few months after their wedding, both Humphries and his wife found work in Sydney with the Phillip Street Theatre, which specialised in revue. His stint there was to last nearly a year and a half. With its reputation for a certain dissolute hedonism, encouraged by generous doses of sun, the city of Sydney promised him his first sus-tained taste of liberation from the oppressive proprieties of his home town. He was to find considerable creative stimulation there, and a whole new group of bohemian friends. But there were accompanying setbacks and rejections as well, which only accentuated his usual feelings of marginality; and even the acceptances, as he recalls them, could not be depended on to palliate those feelings, but at times even compounded them:

> in this strange, new raffish city, I began to feel a little more at home …
> However in Sydney people seemed to sit through my tirades with an amused

indulgence. I needed to draw attention to myself, for I was in a strange city, missing my Melbourne friends, scared of my marriage and worried that I might disappear forever ... Despite the convivial atmosphere at Phillip Street, I still felt like an exile in Sydney.[94]

Humphries took Edna to Phillip Street with him. If perceived as 'a little foreign' by Sydney audiences, she upset the dire predictions of Humphries' Melbourne advisers by transplanting easily and well in the new environment. It was in Sydney, too, as we have seen, that the seeds of the character of Sandy Stone finally germinated; though it is significant that Sandy himself, as he emerged, proved so Melbourne-obsessed and Melbourne-rooted. He helped offset, if not relieve, his creator's own feelings of disorientation while away from his home base. The first seed of another of Humphries' major characters, Sir Les Patterson, was also to be planted in his mind while he was in Sydney, but in distinctly unpleasant circumstances. On trying out his sketch about the 'eldritch child', Tid, before an unappreciative lunchtime audience of boozy war veterans at a suburban club, he was unceremoniously shown the door by the manager of the establishment, who was scarcely more sober than his clientele. Never one to forget or easily forgive rejection of any kind, Humphries states in his autobiography that the creation of the monstrous Les 'was, perhaps, an oblique and long-delayed revenge on the Club Secretary ... ' He was to be let loose upon the world some eighteen years later, in 1974, in the not dissimilar milieu of a Sydney football club. This was but a couple of years after Humphries had finally managed to give up drinking himself, so that there is a measure of self-expiation in the character of Sir Les as well as of revenge. In the longer term, as other commentators have suspected, the character may also have come to provide some of the thrills and outlets of drinking in surrogate form.[95]

'He's from Sydney ... He could *not* have originated from Melbourne, my home town', Humphries avers of Sir Les. For all of Sir Les' grossness, this is no automatic recommendation of Melbourne, which Humphries has continued to belabour for its pervasive dullness. But belabour *and* cherish. It is a dullness raised to such religious and artistic heights ('transcendentally dull', 'exhilaratingly dull', 'exhilaratingly depressing', 'exquisite boredom' are typical of the phrases he uses to capture this quality) that it has provided the perfect place to repair to in a crisis. Towards the end of 1957, Humphries recalls in his autobiography, he had 'hastened back to my hometown at the first opportunity' when his chances of continued employment in Sydney started to wear thin and his marriage was crumbling. The offer of a fresh acting job in Melbourne allowed him to make the break with his wife, who did not return with him. The city was certainly not devoid of genuine artistic opportunity and inventiveness, for all its circumambient dullness. Peter O'Shaughnessy, a friend and mentor from Humphries' days with the university repertory company, was planning to stage the first Australian production of Samuel Beckett's *Waiting for Godot,* and asked Humphries to take the part of the gloomy tramp, Estragon. It would have suited his image of himself at the time. 'Madness, badness, suffering and cruelty' were Beckett's 'chief themes', the revisiting expatriate actor, Leo McKern, had announced in the Melbourne *Age* when organising a rehearsed reading of the play a few months earlier. Estragon himself is given to declare at one point: 'We are all born mad. Some remain so'.[96]

The part of another forlorn and marginalised character came Humphries' way in the New Year when O'Shaughnessy invited him to appear in a children's play, *The Bunyip and the Satellite.* Humphries was to be the Bunyip, and with something of a free hand in devising a persona for this mythological creature he elected to play it as a bird-like clown in search of an identity. The clown's traditional white face poked out from a costume of painted-on feathers, designed by one of Australia's leading artists, Arthur Boyd, and it was surmounted by a crown of twigs and gum leaves. There could be no more suggestive emblem of Humphries' European sensibilities tangled up in antipodean trappings.[97]

The cast of *The Bunyip* also included the New Zealand dancer and actress, Rosalind Tong, who was to become Humphries' second wife as soon as his divorce was finalised with his first. While this was in process during the course of 1958, she appeared with him again in *Rock 'n Reel,* an 'intimate Revue' which he had devised with Peter O'Shaughnessy. It was staged, as *The Bunyip* had been, at the New Theatre, a favoured haunt of Melbourne's left-wing literati. Sandy Stone made his stage debut in one of the sketches in this show, while Edna, portending her later pushiness, featured in no less than three of them. There is no doubt of Humphries' burgeoning success at this time. *The Bunyip* took off to Sydney for a few weeks, together with *Godot;* and there was a demand for a return season of *Rock 'n Reel* at the New Theatre. At O'Shaughnessy's instigation, he made those initial recordings of his Edna and Sandy material for which Robin Boyd provided the sleeve notes. He staged another of his Dada art exhibitions, this time at the Victorian Artists' Society, 'a revered forum for more traditional art', as one commentator has recently noted. Humphries' show attracted some good sales and even better publicity. A commercial television network persuaded him to adapt the Bunyip character for a children's show to be screened every week. The national broadcasting network, the ABC, commissioned him to write and perform his own material for a couple of television 'specials'. But for one who had come to depend on his 'strangeness' as a mark of identity, these tokens of worldly success and acceptance were to be a source of tension within him, a tension that has never been entirely resolved.[98]

Humphries has certainly not disdained what he thought of as due remuneration for his busking talents — the 'coin in my hat', as he was to put it in 1965. From the time the coins started mounting, however, he has had to devise ways of keeping himself strange, sustaining the myth of his inveterate marginality to the workaday world of conforming capitalists. In part this has been a shrewd business manoeuvre in itself. As he was to acknowledge in 1973, following the success of the first film version of his comic-strip series about the gauche Australian globetrotter, Barry McKenzie: 'somehow I … felt in my buffoon's bones that the public likes a good laugh and frequently pays good money for the privilege'. But there has remained a counter-impulse behind his studious buffoonery: a deep suspicion of the more conventional kinds of commercial success exemplified by his father's building business and associated in his mind with the erosion of intimacies within his childhood home. It was in the context of discussing some of his favourite old buildings in Melbourne, and the possible threat to them from urban developers, that he claimed on one occasion: 'Their protection from the ravages of prosperity lies in their eccentricity'. It is a maxim which he seems to have thought applicable to human beings as well, and which has been an abiding determinant of his own life's course.[99]

He saw the human ravages of prosperity not only in his home but almost everywhere else. To him, his schoolfellows and even most of the students at university had already become fossilised by submitting to various forms of regimentation: social, political, sartorial, linguistic, and so on. His youthful Dadaist pranks had been one way of preserving himself from the same trap. 'Shocking people', he told John Lahr many years later, ' … gave me a sense of identity. I guess it gave me a sense of power, too, because I felt rather powerless and swamped by — well, the dullness of Melbourne'. When Melbourne proved itself so dull as to start absorbing these shocks, enjoying them, even paying him for them, new ways of avoiding the perils of conformity and regimentation had to be found. One obvious way, especially now that he had the means, was to escape to those 'strange', 'foreign', 'richly inviting' shores on the other side of the world which he had known about from his childhood picture-books but had never personally experienced. He explained to another interviewer:

> I knew I had to go to England … because I was becoming quite popular. That delighted me, but at the same time it filled me with fear that I would become possessed by my audience; I might end up with my own TV show or something of the kind. And then I would become too prosperous to ever want to leave. So I knew that I had to go out on a limb again: it was just instinct more than anything.[100]

This is as persuasive a summing up of his reasons for leaving Australia at this time as we shall find anywhere in his writings, though there are other accounts he gives which serve to complicate this question in certain ways. As we learn from his autobiography, he did already have his own television shows in a fashion; and they were partly what helped to make him popular. At the same time, he was still perfectly capable of shocking some sections of his audience. He started to lace his Bunyip scripts with Australian slang which brought complaints from parents; and then, to cap it all, when the creature's beak accidentally dropped off on camera during one episode, he tried to 'save' the situation by having it confess to leprosy. This was too much for the stomachs of his producers at least, and he had no alternative now but to retire, 'disgraced'. 'I recalled', he says, 'that references to this malady cropped up rather often in the Bible', but if this was ever intended as a defence, it was hardly a judicious one. In addition to its repellent physical symptoms, leprosy carried symbolic associations with evil in the Judaeo-Christian tradition, and in Australia had long been identified in the popular imagination with the 'heathen' Chinese and fears of invasion by the 'yellow hordes'. These might have been accounted superstitions and blatantly racialist stigmata by more enlightened liberal opinion, but Humphries hardly endeared himself in such quarters either when, a few months later, on a satirical show he was asked to do for the ABC, he took off one of their darlings of the day, the political pundit, Myra Roper, who had just returned from China flushed with enthusiasm for Mao Tse-tung's ten-year-old communist regime.[101]

'I decided that the time had come at last to go to England', he comments immediately after relating the Bunyip scandal in his autobiography. The juxtaposition here might suggest that a sense of rejection still played a part in prompting his departure from his homeland, though (in combination with the Roper affair, which took place on the eve of his departure) it looks like a kind of rejection that he deliberately courted, as he had done with his Dada antics. It was quite consistent with his ambivalent feelings about popular acceptance and success in his homeland, with the fears about those things which mingled with his delight in them. More recently still, he has recalled: 'Australia in the late 1950s and early 1960s was terribly small and afflicted by the most stifling intellectual torpor. If you did anything at all you had to get away and prove yourself where the competition was intense'. As he intimated in a song of his from this period, nothing could be more oppressive than being 'a great big fish in a tiny little pond'.[102]

On 14 March 1959 he and his new wife quitted their tiny antipodean pond and set off for the Mediterranean. It was in the late 1950s, too, if we can trust the internal evidence in her autobiography, that Edna first quitted Moonee Ponds, making her way to London. After disembarking in Venice ('I always longed to live in a city where you couldn't drink the water'), the Humphries spent a few weeks travelling in Italy and Greece before getting to London at the beginning of June. They had exhausted all their funds and had no assured prospects of employment. In his autobiography, he makes out that arriving in England 'as an obscure actor after a taste of hometown fame' was as disconcerting as his shift of schools from Camberwell to Melbourne Grammar had been. To John Lahr he suggested that the experience was 'like the Big Table at which he was not allowed to sit. "People are talking, and you're outside"'. Nearer the time concerned, we find him planning a film or television series on these early experiences, to be called *In Quest of a Stranger:* 'a lightly satirical comic-documentary', as he described it, 'about a stranger as he discovers the habits, institutions and peculiarities of people living in ... London'. The lonely or excluded child, the stranger among the strange: these were more comforting images for him than that of the big fish. Here in England he would at last feel he belonged, not despite but because of its strangeness. It complemented his own strangeness; and there were his ancestral affinities with the place, as well as his prior immersion in its literature, painting, music, architecture and landscape.[103]

This sense of belonging to a foreign place had been a fantasy of his from his bassinet, or so he liked to recall. Has the fantasy ever been realised? Did he want it to be realised, once the opportunity arose? There is no question that in certain ways he managed to adapt to his larger pond with remarkable speed and ease, using his strangeness to do so. A school report from his second year at Melbourne Grammar, reproduced in his autobiography, had presciently spotted this facility: 'Despite his preoccupation with his particular interests, and a tendency to exhibitionism, he has shown a pleasing capacity to adjust himself to the full life of the School'. Ian Donaldson, who had arrived in England a little earlier, remembers being struck at how Humphries 'fitted in immediately. He knew London. He knew about various writers and artists who we thought were dead ... He established this extraordinary network — still not getting employment — but becoming known and being seen as someone of extraordinary knowledge who was also entertaining'. Adjusting, fitting in, are not the same as belonging, however — or feeling you belong or that you want to belong.[104]

For an 'obscure actor' from half a world away, it did not even take very long for Humphries to find creative employment. Thanks to a letter of introduction from an English television producer who had caught his act in Australia, he was presenting one of his Sandy Stone monologues as a filler on a television talk show within a few months of arrival. By his account, the occasion was as ignominious as it was brief, but the spot brought him his first attention in the British press. 'A Star Here?' mused one London newspaper critic, who had also managed to see Humphries' work on a visit to Australia. He had a more convinced, and more prominent, fan in the poet, John Betjeman, who had heard some of his Sandy Stone recordings while on a British Council reading tour of Australia, and his talents were beginning to be known and talked about among a small coterie of British humorists, including Peter Cook, Dudley Moore, Spike Milligan, Ned Sherrin and Caryl Brahms. The Melbourne-bound Sandy, of all Humphries' characters, was probably too recherché to bring about any overnight mass following in Britain. Before Humphries left Australia, the reporter in the 'Small Homes Section' of the Melbourne *Age* who had raved about his comic breakthrough with local, domestic material, was certain that Humphries' brand of humour 'would not cross an ocean'. Through his London contacts, however, there were other roles to be found in other people's works. He was cast as a madhouse keeper in the short run of a musical version of *The Demon Barber* and then as the undertaker, Sowerberry, in the much longer-running season of Lionel Bart's *Oliver!* Here was a classic pair of English grotesques, even more suited to his morbid sense of himself than Beckett's Estragon. Yet such parts clearly didn't satisfy his creative instincts, which kept on drawing their sustenance from the small pond he had left behind.[105]

'Barry was writing scripts all the time', Ian Donaldson recalls of Humphries in London in the early 1960s: 'He was working on his characters. He was thinking of Australia a lot'. All of these characters remained Australian, if not based in Australia. There was a whole breed of new ones who had recently travelled to London like their creator: the prize-winning tenor, Eric Ballarate, called Dudley Ballarate or Mervyn Arrowsmith in the earliest drafts for the character; the ex-public school boy, Buster Thompson, 'on a pubcrawl through our Western heritage'; 'nice upper-middle-class' Debbie Thwaite, a compulsive monitor of the toings and froings of other nice upper-middle-class Australian girls in Europe; and the dealer in Australian painting, Lantana Holman, whose promotion of her country's art does nothing to mitigate her general contempt for the place. ('If the world needs an enema, Melbourne is the place.') None of these, except perhaps the last, ever contemplates *not* returning home. Buster and Debbie were to be immortalised, together with Sandy in his most elaborate of exercises in nostalgic free-association, on the disc, *Sandy Agonistes,* recorded in London in 1960. In the same year the ABC (having, presumably, forgiven if not forgotten his Myra Roper send-up) commissioned Humphries to write and record a series of 'travel sketches' featuring Edna on her first foray abroad. Humphries' contractual obligations to *Oliver!* kept him in London for another couple of years, but when he was released from these, he took up an offer of the Australian impresario, Cliff Hocking (the first of a string of managers to whom Humphries has entrusted the business side of his work), to take Edna and some of his other characters back to Australia for the first of his one-man shows. Called *A Nice Night's Entertainment,* it toured in three states, and was generally accounted a great success.[106]

'I was not surprised', said John Betjeman, who first got to know Humphries when he was still playing in the London run of *Oliver!,* 'to find he was longing to return to his own country for his inspiration is local and derives from Melbourne in particular'. There had been an early sign of this yearning on Humphries' first trip to Sydney, before he had ever left Australia. In England the yearning had been deeper from the start, accentuated by the strange landscape which he had thought to find so accommodating. Amidst this he suddenly felt the tug, not of the bush territory surrounding the Bunyip, but of the domestic interiors of suburban Camberwell. When preparing for the Hocking show he had taken a pile of Australian magazines with him down to a Cornish farm: 'I felt instantly transported back home', he claims in his autobiography, 'to a world of cosy certainties; a land of sponge cakes and pavlovas, ... seersucker and Thai silk. It was hard to believe that I was actually living in that mysterious unattainable place, which Australians call "Overseas"'. He was soon rather brutally confronted with this fact when he slipped on the ice on the Cornish cliffs, injuring his shoulder and arm. The Australian trip had to be postponed for a couple of months.[107]

When his stint back home in *A Nice Night's Entertainment* was coming to its close, towards the end of 1962, Humphries was offered his old part

of the undertaker in the Broadway production of *Oliver!* He accepted, as
the season was to be a limited one, the contract was lucrative, his wife was
expecting their first child, and it would be an economical way of eventually returning to England. Peter Cook was sufficiently taken with what he
knew of Humphries' Australian material to offer him a three-week season
at a cult comedy venue in London, the Establishment Club. Edna and
Sandy made their English stage debut there in May 1963; but it turned out
to be a débâcle. Judging from the polite indifference of the audience, and
the less than polite response of most of the critics, it looked as if the
Melbourne Cassandras had been right in declaring that Humphries' creations would not survive world travel. The season at the Establishment had
to be cut short. Edna records in her autobiography that she went back to
Melbourne at this point. Her creator could not yet contemplate such a
retreat. He now had his own family responsibilities in London, following
the birth of his daughter. This event helped alleviate the humiliations of
his failure at the Establishment Club, though not so much as to curb his
drinking. The urge to 'prove yourself' in a foreign place also remained
strong within him, even if the urge to belong to that place, or the likeli-
hood of ever doing so, was clearly diminishing.[108]

'In London', Humphries later remarked of this period, 'it was a question of finding a voice that people could actually hear and wish to listen to'.
One obvious approach would have been to attempt to compose material
of his own for English voices; and in 1968, on his third trip back to
Australia in nine years, he told an interviewer: 'I've been there [in England]
long enough to have an ear for English idiom and character'. Save for a
handful of sketches he contributed to some satirical programmes made by
the BBC at the end of the 1960s, there has been no sign of this ear's ever
being put to use in his own creative work as a performer. All of the characters he has played in his own work for the stage have been Australians.[109]

It was to be a '"stage" Australian' in another sense, as Humphries
termed a character invented after the Establishment Club débâcle, which
provided the breakthrough voice he was seeking. The character never
appeared on the stage as such, and was not even his own invention, strictly speaking. As he explained in an article he wrote in the *Times Literary
Supplement* of September 1965:

From the time some nine months ago, when the artist Nicholas Garland first suggested that I might like to write the balloons for a character called Barry McKenzie in a new *Private Eye* comic strip, we had thought of presenting the adventures of an Australian Innocent Abroad who spoke in the 'fair dinkum sport' jargon which would be most familiar and comprehensible to English readers. It is sufficient that he is now recognisable to English readers — to whom the strip is addressed — as a familiar expatriate figure; *someone they know*. Needless to say, if such a figure walked down Collins Street, Melbourne, now, not a few heads would turn.[110]

The relative unfamiliarity of this sort of character in present-day Australia, its conformity with old-hat stereotypes of the oafish ocker, was to cause a few ripples of protest among some of Humphries' more sensitive compatriots; but he affected, at least, to delight in this reaction. It served to protect him from appearing as a conformist in his own art. In an interview he gave after the first film version of the McKenzie strip, he suggested that audiences in Australia had become too accustomed to the idea of him, or his characters, as somehow 'realistic'. They 'at last had got me into a pigeon hole as an accurate chronicler of the dialect of certain groups and classes'. The form of the comic-strip, the brazen crudity of its characterisation, meant that he could 'enjoy subverting these ideas'. It was another case of that resolute resistance to easy categorisation which has shaped his attitudes and career.[111]

The McKenzie strip was to remain a more or less regular feature of *Private Eye* for almost ten years. Garland continued to do the drawings, but Humphries soon became the dominant partner in the enterprise, determining the story-line and dictating most of the jokes. As one English reviewer suggested at the time, part of the piquancy of the humour derived from the clash in sensibilities 'between the two Barrys: the frightful, clodhopping McKenzie and the highbrow Humphries, his creator'. The BBC interviewer, Joan Bakewell, was to observe a few years later: 'Behind the outrageous smile of Edna Everage and the vulgar innocence of her nephew Barry McKenzie stands the gentle, cultured figure of their creator and alter ego Barry Humphries'. The most conspicuous thing the two Barrys had in common was an inclination to excessive drinking; but while McKenzie remained a relentless drinker for the duration of the strip, Humphries finally gave up alcohol a few years earlier (around New Year 1971) following extensive treatment in a hospital back in Melbourne. A broader, more enduring parallel is to be found in some of the inner tensions of the character. McKenzie's sense of being 'strangely drawn to England' while feeling none the less that he has 'always been outa place in Pommyland' is a reflection of a dilemma which has continued to face his creator even to the present. Humphries told Bakewell that McKenzie was 'one of the kind of Australians … who make me feel uneasy about my own provincialism in London'.[112]

Humphries was to enjoy no real breakthrough in England with his other antipodean characters until 1972, when his compatriot, Bruce Beresford, made the first of his two hugely popular films based on the McKenzie strip. Edna, never seen in the strip itself, was now imported into the story as McKenzie's aunt. Beresford's *The Adventures of Barry McKenzie* allowed her unprecedented exposure to British audiences. Humphries had successfully toured Australia for months at a time in 1965 and 1968 with one-man shows featuring both Edna and Sandy; but when he had tried to launch the second of these at a small theatre in London's West End during 1969, the response (though not nearly as disastrous as that at the Establishment Club six years earlier) had been far from encouraging. One sympathetic observer noted at the time that: 'His fans rallied, he made some conversions, while the rest of the critics registered shades of disapproval ranging from terse bemusement to open hostility'. The season had been lucky to last six weeks. Edna was to reappear in the second Beresford film of 1974, *Barry McKenzie Holds His Own,* and she had by now sufficiently established herself in the popular imagination to encourage her creator to put her on stage again in London in the show, *Housewife-Superstar!* in 1976. On this occasion the critics came to the party; and the show met with almost unanimous and unstinting plaudits from them. Nearly half a million people went to see it during its four-month season. It was in this show that Sir Les Patterson was also unleashed on London audiences, and there was an 'adagio' interlude with Sandy.[113]

Dame Edna, Sir Les, and Sandy still proved too strange for American audiences when an attempt was made to transfer them to New York at the end of 1977. 'I'll either last a day or a year', Humphries predicted. He lasted four weeks. As in his early days in Australia and Britain, he found an immediate cult following among an intellectual and artistic avant-garde, even winning favour with Andy Warhol; but a sour review in the *New York Times* was enough to kill the show's appeal to any more general audience. There were perhaps more intractable cultural problems. John Lahr, one of Humphries' most stalwart American fans, notes that there is 'no pantomime tradition' in his country, and 'generally not much appetite for irony'. Unfamiliarity with Australian accents may have been an added difficulty. Whether from a determined thirst for conquest, or a lingering taste for rejection, Humphries has continued to seek ways to strut his stuff in America — or at least Dame Edna's stuff. She has managed on occasion to barge her way on to major American television networks with versions of her celebrity chat-shows and 'audiences', slightly adapted to suit imagined ideas of mass American taste. But these ingratiations make her look stranger and more awkward than ever, and she has never caught on there in the way of some other Australian entertainers, such as the late Peter Allen.[114]

There has been no question, on the other hand, of Humphries huge continuing commercial success in England over the past two decades. Three years after *Housewife-Superstar!*, his *A Night with Dame Edna*, staged at the Piccadilly Theatre, won him the Society of West End Managements Award for Comedy Performance of the Year; and a further three years on (1982) saw him filling one of London's largest and most illustrious theatres, Drury Lane, for ten weeks of *An Evening's Intercourse with Barry Humphries*. Dame Edna had already started to appear on her own television shows at the beginning of the 1980s. By the end of that decade one English critic was to note how even Sandy Stone, 'though less successful on television, is a great success in provincial and suburban theatres'. Humphries was also regularly publishing books based on his work in other media. The anthologist of 'teratological' literature in the 1960s, and also of what he had titled *Innocent Austral Verse* (neglected gems of the poetaster's art from a bygone Australia), was now putting his own monsters and naifs between covers, in various collections of the sayings or doings of Edna, Sir Les, Sandy, Bazza McKenzie, and the less renowned of his mythological folk. His most recent literary foray — into the genre of the comic novel — has met with a mixed critical response; but his autobiography of 1992, *More Please,* won him almost universal acclaim and a major literary award in England, the J.R. Ackerley Prize.[115]

He is still prepared, or driven, to shock. The reviewer in the *Guardian* of his latest London show — an evening devoted entirely to Sir Les Patterson's priapic pyrotechnics — noted that it is 'a measure of his achievement that at least 75 per cent of the material cannot be relayed even to readers as liberal and broadminded as the Guardian's'. What better drawcard for his show could Humphries hope for than this? Yet it involves the opposite of any relaxation in his efforts to eschew the more conventional sorts of commercial success. In his jokes about Princess Diana and her bulimia (which the *Guardian* critic feels it just safe enough to quote), or, less repeatable, his child-abuse jokes and his enema jokes, he is still testing, challenging, contriving to push back the general boundaries of what might be considered acceptable on the stage. But as with the leprositic bunyip incident on Australian television nearly four decades earlier, these are also a personal test, a form of self-subversion, an attempt to keep himself clean of too much popular favour.[116]

At the end of *More Please,* we find Humphries reflecting how his successes of the past two decades have done nothing to settle him physically or emotionally: 'Throughout the seventies and eighties I continued to work in the same vein, commuting between England and my homeland, without ever being sure where I really belonged … I am never quite sure what is abroad'. At one point in the early 1970s, he explained to his manager of the time, Harry M. Miller, that he was setting off for Europe once again partly 'to satisfy my great public who prefer to think of me as a compulsive globetrotter'. He told an interviewer from an Australian newspaper a couple of years later: 'I always like to have a ticket to somewhere'. 'Eastbourne, 13 May 1968', 'Transylvania, June 1972', 'Ritz Hotel, Lisbon, 1977', 'Auckland, July 1984', 'Cintra, 1990', 'Beverly Hills, November 1991', 'Gstaad, Switzerland': the by-lines to his writings, or the addresses he gives in his public correspondence, flaunt exotic locales like so many labels on a Louis Vuitton valise. These are no less accurate a guide to his actual where-abouts for being a mischievous goad to his 'friends in the Australian media', with their 'lovingly ambivalent attitude … towards their expatriate ambassadors'. Humphries has travelled and stayed in all these places, as well as his main 'overseas' base of London. Yet, as applied to himself, the category 'expatriate' is as problematic as any other that we may be tempted to file him under. For the ticket in his pocket is often likely to be a return one — and not just to anywhere in Australia, but specifically to his home town in Melbourne, even on occasion to his old home suburb.[117]

Following the three return visits in the 1960s with his one-man shows, he was to be bundled back from London to Melbourne in 1970, along with most of his possessions, in order to 'dry out' after one of his most destructive drinking binges ever. It was to be in abstemious Camberwell, of all places — just 'a stone's throw from my parents' house' — where he suffered a relapse, which led to his arrest by the local police, followed by the first of two long spells of hospitalisation in his home town. It was during the second of these that he was finally 'cured' of his drinking problem. Over the following decade there was hardly a year when he did not return to Australia for at least a short spell. There were always family commitments in Melbourne: to his ill father (who died in 1974), to his mother (who lived on for another eleven years), to his siblings, and, most important of all to him, his two daughters from his second wife, Rosalind. She had proven to be much more resilient than his first wife, but was finally worn out by his drinking and his affairs, and elected to stay on in Melbourne permanently with the children from 1968. It was to be in Melbourne in the mid-1970s that Humphries met Diane Millstead, the painter, who was to become his third wife in 1979, and who bore him two sons prior to the emotional and business altercations which brought this marriage to an end nearly a decade later. In addition to all these family links with his home town, there were his various shows, which toured more widely in Australia, and for extended seasons, in both the 1970s and 1980s. The acquisition of an English wife from the beginning of the 1990s does not appear to have altered this 'commuting' pattern. If anything, he seems to be popping back and forth between the two hemispheres more regularly than ever now. This has been an easier feat to achieve since the increased opportunities for jet travel from the late 1960s, but among the expatriates featured in this book, none has taken more advantage of this opportunity than Humphries.[118]

Humphries has continued down the years to voice explicit criticisms of what he sees as the 'regimentation of Australian life' and of the ways in which some of his interpreters in Australia have been keen to regiment him, personally ('trying to place me in some ideological pigeon-hole'). But his sense of frustration with his homeland, far from keeping him permanently away, has been a crucial factor in bringing him back to it, both in the physical sense of a frequently returning visitor and, moreover, in his professional activities and social concerns as an artist — wherever in the world those have happened to be exercised. The very limitations, crudities and oppressions in Australian culture, as he has experienced or witnessed them, are its main fascination for him, its distinctive and abiding source of interest. He observed on a return visit in 1968: 'Pressures on people to make them conform are greater than they ever were ... This is what concerns me ... I try to see what is human and funny in it, and I try to perhaps show my audience the same thing'. To two student reporters who interviewed him in Melbourne in 1974, he said: 'I think that as Australia becomes more and more regimented and humourless that if it's only the pose of the buffoon and dilettante it's important that there should be a few around'. In 1983 he told a journalist in the Melbourne *Age:* 'Most of my jokes are about Melbourne ... Melbourne is something that never leaves you. It stays in your blood like herpes'. And on one of his latest trips back, towards the end of 1995, he professed in another interview in the press: 'Trying to understand Australia is my life's work'. 'Any closer to it?' his interviewer quizzed him. 'Not much', he replied.[119]

Whatever the deficiencies or distortions in his understanding of Australia since he first went away, the attempt to make it the basis of his work is unparalleled by any of the other expatriates studied in this book. Edna Everage, in one of her poems, mentioned both Germaine Greer and Clive James in her list of 'Famous Names' who 'Have all been taken to Old England's Bosom'; but she did not cite her own creator for once. Like herself, she may have deduced, her creator still cleaved to what she had called, in an earlier poem, 'the bosom of my home'. Weaning from this breast, however 'toxic' Humphries has imagined it to be at times, has never taken place in his case. On one of her *Neighbourhood Watch* shows in England, Edna's own breasts are accommodated in a frock that looks just like one of Humphries' father's attempts at a 'historic home unit' in suburban Camberwell, complete with a 'feature' chimney pertly protruding from the shoulder.[120]

'The essential doesn't change', reflects Vladimir, Estragon's fellow-tramp in *Waiting for Godot*. The slave-driver, Pozzo, complains to Estragon a little later: 'I don't seem to be able … to depart'. 'Such is life', replies Estragon. And such is the life of the Melbourne actor who portrayed him in 1957: a compulsive itinerant rooted to one spot. It remains the strangest thing about him.[121]

Chapter Three

The Awkward Sage

The Dislocations of Clive James

'I wanted to be an opera star', Clive James has recalled of one period in his life, not long after he left Australia for England. Is there any field of creative endeavour in which he has not wanted to be a star? The fact that he has lacked the physical or technical requisites for certain of his fancied professions has proved an enduring obstacle for him; but it has also been a goad to his learning as much *about* them as possible, communicating that knowledge and enthusiasm to others, and arranging encounters with as many 'stars' in as varied firmaments as he could contrive.[1]

Frustrated yearnings are something we all share, he tells us in the closing pages of his novel, *The Silver Castle*. They make up what he calls there 'a democracy of longing'. Less common, we might add, is the knack which he has exhibited in his career for turning frustration into opportunity. He has developed this into something of an art-form in its own right, with its own supporting philosophy. That obstacles themselves can provide a crucial incentive in creative careers, 'the departure point for inspiration', has become something of a mantra for him. Coming from a distant place, where the odd star appeared but rarely lingered, was an example of an obstacle-turned-incentive, entailing in James' case a literal departure, from one hemisphere to the other. It has provided him with a privileged if idiosyncratic

84

perspective on both hemispheres. 'An outsider looking in' is his motto for Marcel Proust, one of his all-time stars, though only able to be encountered now in the pages of his monumental novel. While James' background, career and sensibility share nothing with this 'homosexual, part-Jewish' Parisian, apart from the urge to take up novel-writing in later life, that motto is as applicable in its way to its coiner: an obsessive voyager-voyeur.[2]

Reviewing some new poems by Peter Porter, James states that his fellow-expatriate's 'unembarrassed admiration for the historic over-achievers in all artistic fields is one of the driving forces of his poetry'.[3] It is a form of idolatry shared by all the individuals featured in this book, if not a common driving force behind their expatriatism. Not all of them are poets; although this is one of the fields in which James himself has been an active practitioner, as well as critic, long before he took up novel-writing or ever came to England. His own admiration for over-achievers extends very much into the present as well, and to fields far outside the conventionally defined limits of the arts: to the sciences and to all forms of popular entertainment, including sport.

He has interviewed well-known scientists on radio or television, such as the naturalist, Jane Goodall, or the palaeontologist, Stephen Jay Gould. A star Australian scientist, whose field *is* the stars — radio-astronomer, 'Joel Court', is made the narrator of James' second novel, *The Remake,* published in 1987. This could be a fanciful vestige or extension of his own ambitions as a teenager to become an aeronautical engineer. (That the character's initials are his in reverse supports the hunch.) In the years since the appearance of his first novel, *Brilliant Creatures* (1983), which centred on the stars of the London literary and television worlds, James had also been extending the skills he gained as television critic and travel-writer for the *Observer* during the 1970s into the area of sports-reporting for the same newspaper. Starting with an account of the epic battle between Niki Lauder and Alain Prost in the Portuguese Formula One Grand Prix of 1984, at least four of these articles have been devoted to motor racing. It is ironic that James turns out to have written less substantially on Proust ('my idol of idols to this day') than on Prost.[4]

The authoritative detail and fanatic brio that characterise his sporting articles are not dissimilar to the qualities of his earlier journalism, dating back to his student days in Australia and devoted largely to various European or American writers. Not surprisingly, the car-race pieces are collected under the sub-title, 'The *Art* of Sport'. More surprisingly, perhaps, they come from someone who has confessed elsewhere that he didn't know how to drive any sort of car at the time he left Australia for Europe. One is put in mind here of another of James' great literary idols, the Italian literary and philological scholar Gianfranco Contini, to whom he has attributed the 'habit of revealing whole new ranges of erudition at a few seconds' warning'.[5]

If he has not done everything, it seems that James has written on everything and interviewed everybody who is anybody who is still alive. One of his early idols was the American novelist, John dos Passos, who he claimed had not just 'done everything', but had also 'been everywhere' and 'met the big fish and the little fish'. Anything or anybody that has managed to slip through James' own net is bound to be caught in it one day, especially now that its capacity has been so enlarged through the medium of television. Even doing everything he has admired or desired is not beyond the realms of possibility now. His early forays into the genre of travel-writing, collected in the volume *Flying Visits*, still cast him in the voyeuristic roles of witness and recorder. The television version, *Postcards*, allows and encourages him to become an actor, in the sense of doer as well as performer — and one for all the world to see. In *Postcard from Miami*, for instance, he has the opportunity to try a spot of big-game fishing off the Florida coast, as well as catch the local celebrities and socialites back on shore. In *Postcard from Bombay*, he scores a bit-part in a 'Bollywood' movie, giving him an affinity of sorts with the central character in *The Silver Castle*, young Sanjay. In *Postcard from Cairo*, he meets the city's biggest local (and international) star, Omar Sharif; he is also able to do something of a star-turn himself, as a dancer in a downtown dive. It's belly, not ballet, dancing. But who is to say, should he send us a *Postcard from Milan* one day, we may not see him on the stage of La Scala, finally achieving the operatic fame of his youthful dreaming, at least for the allotted fifteen minutes or so?[6]

In his television retrospect on *Fame in the Twentieth Century*, it's back to a more vicarious role, though the subject matter and his control of it as writer and presenter offer him similar opportunities. Viewers as well as himself are given the chance of a brush with some of the famous dead whom he cannot interview and a few of the living whom he has not yet got round to; but any reflected glory from their lustre is his alone, as he sits there delivering his judgment on them under the halo of a carefully trained studio spotlight. It is more tempting than ever here to turn back on himself his pronouncements on others, most notably his verdict on Madonna — not the haloed original of a much earlier century, but her thoroughly postmodern simulacrum. Charting this Madonna's career, in the final episode of the series, James observes that

> transforming herself into a new self was only one more beginning in a career
> that saw every end as a new start. Madonna wasn't content to be famous for
> what she could do. She wanted to be famous for what other people had done
> as well.[7]

The transformations in James' own 'self' are more complicated than this, however; the beginnings and ends in his career are rather less clear-cut; and the pursuit of fame, celebrity and publicity continually mixed up with a retreat into modesty, a passion for privacy, a yearning for self-effacement and oblivion. So we are led to believe from his own statements about himself, though whether these are any more trustworthy as a guide to this self than his statements about others is one of the complications in charting and assessing his career. The collective title he chooses for his three volumes of autobiography, *Unreliable Memoirs,* does nothing to simplify the matter. It positively invites distrust, asserts self-distrust; yet how far might this be another affectation or disguise?

At the conclusion to the third volume of these memoirs, published in 1990, James presents us with the vision of a new project for himself which he claims will take him more than a decade to bring to fruition. One of the intended results of such long self-absorption will be complete self-effacement:

> if I am granted life, I will write a book about what happened in the Pacific
> when two nations, Australia and Japan, met and fought, and about what has
> happened since, in the long, blessed peace which by some extraordinary

stroke of good fortune has coincided with my own life. If I have an important book in me, that will be the one, but I will have no warrant to take pride in it, because it will be the book into which I finally disappear, having overcome an inordinate need for attention … I will be invisible at last. There is not much time left, though. Already I have lived half as long again as my father did …[8]

It is a curious and tantalising declaration in many ways. James the historian? This may not be such a fanciful prospect as James the opera singer: his literary criticism has always revealed an impressive historical perspective; he has been contributing trenchant and substantial reviews of recent works in Australian or European history to distinguished periodicals both in England and America; and his own chronicling instincts, if overwhelmed at times by his comic ones, have already revealed themselves in his retrospect on *Fame,* or in the 'Review of the Year' which he has presented annually on television since the early 1980s.[9] As a creative exercise, therefore, his projected book could hardly be claimed to involve anything as radical as a 'transformation' into a 'new self'. The claim that there will be *no* self visible in this book is, however, more difficult to accept. Whatever his methods or emphases, one cannot imagine a subject *less* likely to facilitate his hoped-for vanishing trick than that of the Pacific War and its aftermath. By his own account, the war has had a fundamental and continuing personal significance for him, even though he was far too young to be a direct participant in it.

In the passage quoted, the personal significance for James of the Pacific War is signalled in the last sentence when he alludes to his father's premature death. For this death was directly occasioned by the war — or, in an especially cruel twist of fate, by the war's end. James was about to turn six, having been born in October 1939 just after England and Australia declared war on Germany. His father, who had been interned in Japanese prisoner-of-war camps since 1942, was released after Japan surrendered in August 1945 but was put on a plane home that crashed into the sea during a typhoon. Trying to come to terms with this fatality in later life, James has reasoned with himself that it didn't weigh as heavy in the scale of human horrors as the sufferings and losses of so many other victims of war or ideological battles in our century. Neither did it cause the same intensity of grief in him as it induced in his mother.[10] The particular freakishness of the circumstances, however — the elements of pure acci- dent and bad luck in his father's death, the fact that this should have coincided with the very beginning of his own life, cheating him even of the poignancy of a detailed memory — have meant perhaps that they are not finally amenable to reasoning. Coming to terms with these circumstances would remain something of a Sisyphean task for him. It is hard to see how in making a whole book out of the wider circumstances of the war he could avoid haunting the subject as much as it has haunted him. Appearing to disappear proves to be as characteristic of him as the urge to flaunt his appearance everywhere.

The ship that first took the young James to England, when he was in his early twenties, happened to call in at Singapore on the way, and he made a pilgrimage to Changi gaol, his father's first place of internment by the Japanese. Any palpable trace of the man was gone. He realised then, as he recorded later in his first volume of memoirs, that 'I would never find my father as he had been ... One day, in my imagination, he would return of his own accord'. The first of his books to appear, a collection of criticism compiled in his mid-thirties from the articles and reviews he had pub- lished in English magazines, was dedicated 'to my mother, and to my father's memory'. A couple of years later, in 1976, he was to make his first return trip to Australia in a decade and a half, and it occasioned the first of his substantial travel articles for the *Observer*. A further two years after this, he added to the series with articles from Japan, written on one of the ear- liest of several trips which he has made there since. As it had been his father's last place of internment before the fatal plane crash, it provided another obvious pilgrimage site. In winding up his impressions of the country, James could not resist a reference to his father's failure to return from there: 'I still feel that my whole life is taking place in the light of that one event'. Appearing as a guest on Roy Plomley's BBC radio programme, *Desert Island Discs,* not long afterwards, James reiterated that 'someone not being there' was 'probably still the central experience of my life even though I am now forty years old'. In a long poem reviewing the year 1982 — a genre that might have helped inspire his television 'Reviews' of each year's events — he included a personal note recording another pilgrimage he had made, this time to the cemetery in Hong Kong where his father lies buried. At the end of this decade, and on the brink of his fifties, James was to be found musing again on his father's death and on what it has meant to him over the years. When he was first old enough to reflect, he says, he had thought this event 'the epitome of dislocation'. On revisiting Hong Kong in 1995, to compile one of his television postcards, he spent the concluding section of the programme walking around the war graves cemetery and discoursing yet again on his father's beliefs and fate.[11]

What he means by dislocation in this particular context is not certain, but the word provides an important clue to understanding his whole career and sensibility. In the sense of a part of the body out of joint with the rest, it might be less apt than some other anatomical or medical terms — amputation, say — as a metaphor for the loss of a father to a family; but it does capture something of James' own feelings of detachment from the experience of more 'normal', fully intact families. He has averred elsewhere: 'I was, am, and will continue to be to the grave, incurably envious of all families'. The afflictions of the 'fatherless child' can take more or less extreme forms, but there is a recognisable pattern of 'self-love and the unassuageable need to have it confirmed'.[12]

Removal from one's natural habitat is another meaning of dislocation; and James has suffered from an acute sense of this all his life. His endless travels on leaving Australia are just *re*locations: symptoms of a more chronic condition. It has been difficult for him ever to know quite what his natural habitat is or to feel completely attached anywhere. The symptoms can even show up in his body and general appearance. There have been no actual dislocations in this respect; throughout all his travels, he has remained sound of limb, effectively retained all his faculties into late middle age (including twenty-twenty vision till very recently). But a general impression emerges of some congenital awkwardness in him, whatever his surroundings: of someone never quite fitting together in his own skin as well as never quite fitting in with the world around him. Hair loss and weight gain, increasing self-preoccupations of his, might add to this impression, but it goes rather deeper. Portrait painters have caught the various kinds of misfit in him most readily and graphically.[13]

The image of him in a recent portrait painted by his fellow-expatriate, Jeffrey Smart, is reduced to minuscule size, out of all proportion to the looming iron fence that provides the background. Smart later expounded on James' 'terribly strange face': 'His eyes are slits, … his cheekbones are not on the same level, one ear is tremendously higher than the other, his nose is bent, his mouth is contorted, he has an enormously thick neck'. There is a touch of mischievous caricature, of course, in both the visual and verbal images here; but James takes delight in this. Of the painting he remarks, 'It is so wonderfully ego-deflating'; and certainly it seems to conform with, if not pander to, his own impulses to shrink the self 'to vanishing point'. Smart's words, too, conform with a self-deprecating impulse in his subject. James blithely cites another of the painter's darts, directed at him during one of the sittings: 'I'm trying to get those hairs between your eyebrows — they echo your deformed teeth'. If we are to credit the recollections in his memoirs, James had been collecting evidence from his schooldays 'bolstering the case for my physical abnormality'.[14]

He can at least play at being susceptible to the counter-evidence also, as when he comments on another recent portrait of him, by the English painter, Sarah Raphael: 'I rather like the immediate message of macho power, reinforced by those Iron John forearms'. While the work is not so flattering as to disguise his thinning hair or over-extended waistline — or the slit eyes for that matter — at least the James-figure in it is the centre of attention and is kept in proportion to the whole. Within the gaze of the figure, however, James himself picks up on a suggestion of solitariness or apartness: 'If only I didn't look so very isolated and inward-turning, as if self-sufficiency had been bought at the cost of losing contact with the world. That can't be right, but what if it is?'[15]

Elsewhere in his writings, James is almost profligate with testimonies to his sense of apartness from the world and of awkwardness within himself. And these states of mind, he suggests, were manifested from early childhood. The earliest manifestation is associated with his name, and would have surfaced, one imagines, even if his father had lived and he had grown up as part of a 'normal' family.

A poem he wrote in 1980, commemorating the fiftieth birthday of fellow-poet and critic, Anthony Thwaite, ends with the lines:

> And that's a fact as certain as my name's
> (This line I'll have to pad a bit) Clive James.

But we learn from the first volume of his memoirs, published in the same year, that this had not always been so certain. His parents, he tells us here, had originally called him Vivian, after a tennis star of the 1930s; but this had become a source of great confusion when he started going to school. By that time the name (in spite of a different spelling) had become ineluctably linked with the film star, Vivien Leigh, after she played the lead in *Gone With the Wind*, produced in the same year James was born. The association with a girl became such an irritant for him that his mother allowed him to choose a new first name, and he picked Clive, because it happened to be the name of a character played by another film star of the period, Tyrone Power. He does not specify the film concerned, but it is likely to have been Anatole Litvak's *This Above All* (1942), in which Power played the character of Clive Briggs, a brave soldier of humble origins in the British Army during the Second World War. In a moment of disenchantment with his country and its ruling class, he becomes a deserter, but is put back on the track of true patriotic virtue by a young aristocratic girl, who reminds him in a long speech of all the great treasures and traditions of England's landscape and literature still worth fighting for. It might have been more than the name Clive in this film that registered itself on the nascent impressions of the future expatriate.[16]

Less sexually ambiguous than Vivian, Clive still 'wasn't an Australian name' in the 1940s, according to James. Whether or not this was the case, it would have carried a touch of exoticism from its echo of Clive of India, also a soldier of humble origins (though a real-life one, of course) who two centuries earlier had become an all-conquering hero in the cause of British Imperialism, and was mythologised in a film of 1935. Our Clive may have relished this extra glamour about the name. His preference for it was not just — perhaps not even — an early flexing of macho muscles; 'Vivian' had caused general bureaucratic bother, and not (or so he makes out) any personal crisis of identity over his gender. 'I just got sick of ending up on the wrong lists', he tells us in his memoirs. This is not to say there were not deeper problems over his sense of identity. His slightly exotic choice of

name presaged other feelings and assertions of dislocation from his immediate surroundings. That it appealed to him as the name of a character
from the movies was another such portent. 'I know now', he claims a few
pages earlier in his memoirs, 'that until very recent years I *was never quite
all there* — that I was playacting instead of living'.[17]

The phrase 'never quite all there' is close to the one applied to his dead
father when talking to Roy Plomley about his memoirs ('Someone not
being there') — except that his father's absence from the world of the living was complete, permanent, and no performance. Although, maybe
because, there was nothing else very remarkable about the young James'
early upbringing, the inexplicable fact of his father's death was sufficient to
foster his own feelings of detachment and provide a continuous cue for
their enactment. Judging from the details he gives, there could be no more
conventional a setting for its time than the one in which he was reared.

The family house was in Kogarah, Sydney, a lower middle-class suburb
of the sort where most Australians lived: neither slummy nor swanky.
Before going off to the war, his father had been a motor mechanic (perhaps
a stimulus to James' studious passion for racing cars, though making his
failure to learn to drive until long after he left Australia the more curious).
The religious beliefs of the family were nominally Anglican; though he was
not discouraged from attending the local Presbyterian Sunday school and
fellowship group meetings, while his ordinary schooling was at a series of
state-run, secular, co-educational establishments such as the majority of
the population attended. There were some early signs of his detachment
from this environment, but it was far from a complete detachment.

James has spoken of his 'terrific incapacity for paying attention' in the
classroom — except to one particularly good English teacher who taught
him how to parse a sentence. He still managed to become a class captain
and 'teacher's representative' at the so-called opportunity school which he
attended between the years of his primary and final secondary education;
and he also happened to obtain good enough marks in his examinations
there to win a bursary to one of the most prominent high schools in the
state system. It boasted some social prestige as well as a proven record of
academic excellence, at least in the more traditional subjects of the curriculum. This was the time, however, when it was James' ambition to

become an aeronautical engineer — an upmarket version of his father's trade, though (as he managed to persuade himself) too downmarket a pursuit for the august establishment concerned. From a variety of motives he finally opted for a technical school instead. This proved wholly misguided. 'I just didn't connect with it', he recalls in a symptomatic phrase. Some poor teaching of the subjects in which it specialised perhaps only reinforced a more definite shift in his focus of interests towards English and foreign languages; but the provision for such subjects was sufficient at least to let him scrape through the examinations qualifying him for entry to Sydney University's Arts Faculty. Not that he had 'connected' much with the prescribed books even on the courses he proved best at; as he relates it, he spent much more of his time poring over comics, boys' adventure magazines, detective stories, popular mechanics periodicals devoted to cars or planes, and other kinds of downmarket literature.[18]

There is an impression of almost miraculous luck in his accounts of his educational progress — almost, because he has never avowed any faith in miracles. Personally, he disavowed all attachment to religious faith from early on while retaining, or coming to learn, a certain respect for certain forms of it in others. His mother went on 'believing in something' but James was already, by his teenage years, the unshakeable 'ex-Christian' and atheist he has since gone on declaring himself. If not 'immunized from birth against religion of any kind', as he has declared elsewhere, it is quite likely that his resistance to the beliefs of his family in God the Father and all the rest stemmed from the time that his own father was so arbitrarily removed from their midst. He still maintained formal attachments to church groups in his locality right up until his first year at university, when, under the influence of Bernard Shaw, one of the first of those cultural 'over-achievers' that he has proceeded to worship instead of a god, he came out as an atheist in the Presbyterian Fellowship's own newspaper. There were already some warning signs of irreverence and subversive literary influence in the Fellowship revue which he organised earlier that year; but these had been sufficiently concealed in the past by his prowess in bible class which had won him all the available prizes and eventually led to his appointment as a Sunday School teacher. Only his pupils knew that he had spent far less time on bible instruction than on regaling them with stories of rather more recent, less holy interest, such as the Japanese attack on Pearl Harbor or the Western Desert campaign. If this is not an entirely 'unreliable' story in itself, it suggests how far back we may trace his preoccupation with chronicling the war which led to his father's death and to his primal experience of dislocation.[19]

Consciously or unconsciously, other forms, circumstances and meanings of dislocation in his life are suggested in the recollections of his teenage activities. Not least there is his continuing sense of acting out 'characters', at least some of whom bear his own name, and to whom the relationship of his 'real' or 'essential' self (so long as we or he can continue to believe in any such concepts) remains ambiguous, never wholly distinct nor wholly at one. 'At school and church', he notes, 'I got by as an entertainer, but it was a solitary's way of being gregarious. I was never really at ease in company'. Prior to his performing on stage in revue shows which he also scripted and directed, the sorts of entertainment he had organised were a form of street theatre, featuring schoolboy gangs who would dress up in masks and capes to haunt the local neighbourhood at nightfall. The young James established the original model for these characters, known as the 'Flash of Lightning', but 'there was no fruitless speculation about my real identity'. Fully conversant from his comic-strip reading with 'dual-identity' figures like Superman disguised as Clark Kent, James had perceived that the trouble with these was that 'no one thought much of them when they were in mufti'. He was determined that this wouldn't happen to him. 'Discreetly informing people one by one, I made sure everybody in the district knew that when the dusk descended it was I, and nobody else, who became the Flash of Lightning'.[20]

By his account, the masks he adopted in his church activities were altogether more subtle and devious. Only he knew that his principal reason for continuing with his roles in this sphere as long as he did was that 'there were girls involved', either as fellow-worshippers or fellow-participants in the recreational and social pursuits. Religion in these respects provided a cover for his developing sexual interests, or a convenient displacement of them while he hopefully — at times also fearfully — awaited more direct opportunities in the adult world. Sexual activity with girls at this stage was very limited as well as furtive, confined to clumsy gropings and hesitant fumblings: an inhibition occasioned by social and moral codes in the days before the contraceptive pill but a reflex, too, of personal anxieties or uncertainties. From such tentative experiments as these, in his late teenage years, James grew confident that it was exclusively with females that his sexual future would lie.[21]

Up to that time there had been 'rampant sexuality', but it was directed towards other boys and, in practice, centred only on one, whom he calls Gary. 'I was as queer as a coot', James recalls of this period, or at least 'queer for him'. What detail he records of such experiences suggests that they went no further than mutual masturbation. 'Nevertheless the emotions were real', he says in general of his attractions to males at this stage. But of the nature or basis of these emotions it is hard to be certain. In spite of a growing flirtatiousness with women in the years since his late adolescence, so overt now as to prompt plausible charges of sleazy sexism, there remains an uncertainty about his attractions in this direction as well. He suggests a link when he says at one point of his *tendresse* for Gary that it was but 'the outward expression of an inward yearning for the feminine'. But what kind of yearning is that?[22]

In his television series on *Fame in the Twentieth Century,* he refers to a 'feminine quality' in James Dean, teen idol of the period in which he (James, Clive) was growing up, and he goes on to quip that this might suggest the young actor 'had acquired some of his initial training ... by dressing up in his mom's clothes when she wasn't home'. More recently, in one of the episodes of *The Clive James Show,* he adverts to having done the same himself as a child. It's a casual remark tossed into an interview with Boy George, just one of many gags in the polite, teasing banter that develops between him and his sartorially ambiguous guest. Yet diplomacy with guests, putting them at their ease, containing their egos, strikes Joel Court, narrator of James' *The Remake,* as a 'feminine' quality in itself. Observing his poet-, novelist- and performer-friend, 'Chance Jenolan' (whose initials need no reversing to guess at his provenance), Joel expressly commends 'the hostess in him'. There may be a small cry here for recognition of this quality in the creator of these characters. It is a quality that doesn't easily fit the usual outward impressions of him.[23]

When 'hostessing' any of his own television shows, James has so far resisted the urge to dress accordingly, unlike another expatriate performer featured earlier in these pages; but in the early to mid-1980s he made a number of television documentaries that at least skirted around the theme of women's clothes, where not focusing on the subject precisely: *The Clive James Paris Fashion Show, Clive James and the Calendar Girls* and *The Clive James Great American Beauty Pageant.* The titles alone emit a rather more insistent cry for a connection to be made between subject and host. James' writing from early on contains many incidental signals — just as insistent as they start to accumulate — of a preoccupation with what women wear. These passages provide no firmer ground than his much fuller treatment of motor racing, say, for any conclusions about his sexual yearnings. What is at least as striking, however, in the haunter of catwalks as in the haunter of the race track is the degree of his *aesthetic* engagement with the milieu, its personnel and artefacts. This is a strong and recurrent component in his 'yearning for the feminine', if not entirely separable from the sexual.

In his occasional fashion-house reporting for the press, it is the designers whose names James knows and drops. If he has taken the phone numbers of the models as well, he is not telling here; though the Japanese hero of his third novel, *Brmm! Brmm!* keeps a private dossier on the 'top-flight' ones. In all his novels, and especially the first, designer labels are not just attached to the characters' clothes; they are sewn in to the characterisation. Here, in *Brilliant Creatures*, grand society hostess Elena is sizing up smart, up-and-coming young television presenter, Sally, and recognises

> her suit immediately as being from the 1978 Chloe *prêt-à-porter* collection, not very expensive, especially when you allowed for how often it could be worn, but well-chosen for someone of her height, colouring, and unfussy knack with the accessories. Already … she had assessed the girl as having a good eye but here the fact was confirmed. Meanwhile Sally had spotted Elena's 1980 YSL pant suit as a couture original.

This is not just name-dropping. There is evidence throughout his writings that with the subject of women's fashion James has been building up yet another of his 'ranges of erudition', developing a good eye of his own for details of fabrics, stitching and cut. It can reveal itself in the most unexpected places, as when he is describing the original designs for the Sydney Opera House, and notes in passing how 'the roof shells had a sexily complex curve rather like a Mucha négligé'. This suggests just how far his 'yearning for the feminine' can extend, and how inextricable its aesthetic and erotic components can become.[24]

As for his own clothes, James has shown a resistance to fashion that goes beyond indifference. His customary garb for his television appearances — pale blue shirt, dark suit of the plainest cut — would not look out of place on a provincial bank manager of the 1960s. On him, it suggests a deliberate anti-style. He told one interviewer recently: 'I was very, very careful when I started out on television never to have an image'. His sartorial drabness (Australians would call it a 'daggy' look) is certainly not for want of knowledge about menswear designers. In his autobiographical writings, his fiction and some of his television commentary we can find precise references to such things as Turnbull and Asser shirts, Armani suits, and the distinctions between English and Italian tailoring.[25]

James doesn't dwell over the detail of men's clothes as much as he does over women's, and there is a moment in *Brilliant Creatures* when he seems to be sending up his own reliance on sartorial signifiers as a device of his art. One of the male characters in the novel observes of another: 'The soul of this man was in his clothes. There was an idea for the novel he was writing'.[26] Men's bodies, however, have had an abiding fascination for him, and are another focus of his aesthetic yearning.

He provides a particularly vivid example of this when he takes us back nearly thirty years in his memories to a meeting with some young Nauruans at a physical fitness camp he attended while at Sydney Tech. 'So black they looked blue, these were some of the best-looking boys in creation', is his judgment still; and he recalls in particular the son of their chief, called Detudame, or 'Det' for short, whose bulky body was 'all dark muscle, subtly catching tangential light like polished hardwood'. The noble Nauruan was an exotic, real-life version, perhaps, of the gorgeous fantasy-figure which James had already found (and has kept on idealising too) in Johnny Weismuller's impersonation of Tarzan, 'king of the jungle', in the movies of his childhood and early adolescence. Weismuller, who 'would have provided Hitler with a stunning example of what the master race looked like with its clothes off', had the added attraction of 'a face off the front porch of the Parthenon'.[27]

Part of the yearning here is for 'The Ideal' in a general aesthetic sense informed by classical canons of beauty. The reference to the Parthenon makes the aesthetic component more pronounced, more pure even, than is generally the case with James' attraction to women; though the links between the two sorts of attraction are suggested in his paean to the face of another movie pin-up, Greta Garbo: 'an edifice, which, as Bernard Berenson said of Raphael, reflects back on us the classicism of our yearnings'. James is fond of this quotation from the American art historian and connoisseur. A character he bases on the English art critic, Kenneth Clark, in his long poem of the mid-1970s, *The Fate of Felicity Fark,* is reminded by the eponymous heroine's head 'of what Berenson once said — that Raphael is the Classic of our yearning'.[28]

Confident, as an adult, of his own heterosexuality, and vigorously protesting against such views as Gore Vidal's that 'any heterosexual man is a culturally repressed bisexual', James flaunts his aesthetic appreciation of strong and handsome men as brazenly as he bathes in the radiance of the women he fancies. These types have continued to pop up at all stages of his life, and in a variety of texts and contexts. There is the circle he moved in after leaving school when he went on to study at Sydney University (including 'Huggins' — Robert Hughes — with 'a face so handsome it was like a cartoon'). There are the friends and acquaintances he made in England at his second alma mater, Cambridge. (Here, as well as the American postgraduate student, 'Marenko', who looked 'so magnificent with his shirt off' he was known to drive young women off the road, James came across 'two of the most beautiful people I had ever seen in my life': an Indian couple, not unlike the charismatic charmers in a Ruth Prawer Jhabvala novel, as he depicts them. The young man, James notes, was 'if possible even more beautiful' than the girl). There are his friends and associates in the London literary world (like Proust's translator, the late Terence Kilmartin, a 'Truly Strong Man' in the tradition of 'some bare-chested Horst model' as idolised by W.H. Auden, or the young Martin Amis, with his 'stubby Jaggerish appearance'). There are just the passers-by that James has remembered from his travels to other places ('those young Hasidic devotees' he spots in Jerusalem, for instance, whose 'unblemished oval faces … glow like Modigliani odalisques': perfect aesthetic icons as he represents them here, though he slyly suggests a more profane kind of attractiveness when he adds: 'Have they got sisters?'). There are the guests on his television chat shows whom he makes a point of flattering about their looks (not just Greta Scacchi, Joanna Lumley and Kylie Minogue, but also Richard E. Grant and that 'bronzed god', George Hamilton). There are the scantily-clad, perfectly-proportioned young things that flit across his television *Postcards* (in addition to lingering shots of female 'angels', as James calls them, sunning themselves on tropic beaches in Latin America, Florida or Australia, the cameras pause over bare-chested male rap-dancers in London's Hyde Park or a muscle-clad black gymnast performing athletic miracles in the open air at the height of a New York summer). There are the characters in his novels (the tautly muscular young Japanese hero of *Brmm! Brmm!,* Suzuki, adrift in London, and much in demand from most of the women and some of the men, or the similarly sought-after Sanjay, from *The Silver Castle,* whose 'entire genital apparatus' — like young Detudame's entire body — 'conveyed the impression that it had been carved from hardwood by a master craftsman and lovingly polished over a period of years'). And there are further obvious pin-ups from his gallery of twentieth-century fame. 'Marlon Brando', James has commented, 'is rivalled only by Elvis Presley as the possessor of the most classically beautiful male face of modern times'; an earlier comment on these stars leaves the gender divisions undrawn, ascribing to them 'the two supreme classic faces of the twentieth century'.[29]

Classical canons of beauty can be so strict as to leave most people feeling irremediably inadequate about their physical features. The narrator of James' *Felicity Fark* notes of the heroine that she has

> the face that leaves us rooted to the spot —
> Benumbed by what it is and we are not.

This is a subtext of all James' rhapsodisings on male beauty as well, going back to his vision of Detudame and the other young Nauruans at the school camp. These boys were in such stark contrast to the 'freaks and wastrels' sent from Australian schools, among whom James forlornly enrols himself. Some of the yearning detectable in his re-creation of this experience is simply for the possession of a body like Det's. It represents for him an intensely personal as well as a general aesthetic ideal. 'Most men', James says elsewhere, have 'dreamed of being more attractive' than they are: 'We dream about our ideal selves'. Over the years he has sustained the dream with memories and fantasies of many others. What is so singular about his association of this ideal with the Nauruan chieftain's son is the way it evokes the sense of James' own physical ungainliness together with a sense of his emotional or psychological dislocations, as a fatherless only child: 'It will be apparent that I am talking about the kind of brother I would have liked to have, and I suppose I miss even now'.[30]

Here is a form of longing which is not only incapable of fulfilment but which no amount of achievement in later life is able to assuage. The poignancy of the yearning here is that it can never be fulfilled, and its associated dreams and ideals never attained. 'Beauty and ugliness are both accidents', James has reflected elsewhere — suggesting another connection with his fatherless state. An added irony was that his late father just happened to have been a good-looking young man. James was cheated, therefore, not only of his father's presence but of his father's looks as well. 'Stocky was the word for me. Handsome was the word for him', he observes of an early photograph of the two; the basis perhaps of endless other such comparisons to his detriment.[31]

The mother with whom he was left happened to have been a pretty girl. Whether or not he attempted to emulate her when a child by dressing up in her clothes, an especially intense identification with his mother was inevitable in the early years because of their shared deprivation. 'I'm a mother's boy', he still acknowledges — not entirely solemnly: 'I think it was W.H. Auden who said it was remarkable how many mother's boys became prominent. You become accustomed to getting what you want'. While there can be no arguing with accidents, their aftermath is to a degree controllable by those who survive them. For all the poignancy that may attend them, they don't have to be an occasion for inertia, let alone tragedy. In James' case they appear to have been the opposite of disabling. The sense of dislocation in the family caused by his father's death, and by the special intimacy with his mother that followed, may have been the first of those 'obstacles' in his life to provide a 'departure point for inspiration'. He would defy the odds of his situation (including the oddities of his physique) by making them his opportunity. Yet it remains the case that none of his successes in this direction has helped put the Humpty in him together again. Those successes have themselves been partly dependent on further dislocations.[32]

In James' case, 'getting what you want' out of life has meant as much as anything a studious detachment from his mother's skirts, putting on a show at least of getting out from under them. 'Being a mother's boy', he remarks in his first volume of memoirs, 'is a condition that can be fully cured only by saying goodbye to mother'. But it is not a condition of which he has ever claimed to be fully cured, even in leaving Australia for England. When he went up to Sydney University as a student in the late 1950s he continued to stay with her out in the suburbs, accepting all too easily the home comforts she kept on providing. The campus and its environs, however, were to offer him his first sustained exposure to an alternative world of political radicalism, cultural adventure, sexual experimentation, and religious heterodoxy. There had been clashes with his mother before over his lack of application at school; they were now bound to increase. With a shrewder instinct than his own at that stage for how his interests might best be served, she was evidently pleased that he had taken up the opportunity to go to the university and not another technical institution. Her pleasure may have been too evident for a young man seeking some release from the extraordinary bond between them. Any sense that she was getting what *she* wanted would have to be resisted. 'Night after night', he reports of this time, 'I reduced my mother to tears with my intellectual arrogance'. The ostensible issue in these tensions with her was religion, and her stubborn resolve to go on 'believing in something'. They reflected much deeper tensions within himself at the time.[33]

It was at the end of an era at Sydney University associated with the libertarian influence of one particularly charismatic teacher, the Professor of Philosophy, John Anderson. A free-thinking Marxist in the 1930s, he had by now long turned against communism, or any form of state socialism, though without losing his radical-secularist edge, rooted in the ideas of syndicalism and the Guild Movement. It was still the heyday of 'The Push', the collective name for a range of intersecting bohemian groups drawn

from students and ex-students of the university and involved conspicuously in various anti-establishment political, journalistic, or artistic
ventures when not, even more conspicuously, carousing in pubs. James
never studied philosophy and didn't read any of Anderson's writings till
after he left Sydney; but he threw himself frenetically into various activities of The Push or its fringes, not least the marathon drinking sessions.
Cultivating its tastes for modernist literature as well as for alcohol, he
became literary editor of the main student newspaper, *honi soit,* and
remained sufficiently sober to be made chief scriptwriter and director of
the annual student revue. He also finally lost his virginity to a woman from
within the Push, whom he calls 'Lilith' — a mysterious mythological cock-
tail, as he represents her, bearing the name of a Talmudic temptress,
vulgarly associated with Satan's wife, yet possessed of qualities closer to
those of some benign Greek goddess: 'classically beautiful ... softly spoken
and always elegantly dressed'. Lilith was a similarly ambiguous figure — at
once seductress and muse — in the work of the Australian poet,
Christopher Brennan, about whom James has written at length. James tan-
talises us with the notion at one point that the Lilith who seduced him may
even be 'a figment of my imagination'.[34]

Probably anything resembling a 'real' relationship — let alone the
responsibility of a marriage or family — was quite beyond the imagination of the freewheeling youthful circle in which he moved at the time;
but it was through one of the courses which he took in the English
Department of the University, around the same time, that he began to
consolidate a friendship with another woman of poise and refinement —
of the highest intellectual stature, too — who would eventually become
his wife and the mother of his two daughters. Her name was Prue Shaw,
and she appears as 'Françoise', a diplomat's daughter, in his memoirs.
Their marriage was quite a few years in the future, when James and she
had both left Australia; and he has adverted to various affairs with other
women in the interim, including a briefly resumed one with the mysterious Lilith. For most of the 1960s, he claims, 'freedom from convention
was my religion'. There are indications, however, that he did not entirely
throw off the moral standards and imperatives of more conventional
religious teaching.[35]

For the years following his marriage, at the end of the 1960s, he provides abundant evidence of the continuing allure that other women have held for him, but no specific documentation of further sexual involvements with them. Much of his writing slavers over their physical charms; a whole poem is rapturously devoted to 'the sweat of Gabriela Sabatini', for instance. He ogles, or openly flirts with, the female guests who appear on his television shows; in one notorious instance, at the end of an interview with Jane Fonda, he even proposes that he and the star should elope. He ends his interview of Boy George with the words: 'You're very nice to chat to even if it doesn't lead to other things'. Whatever we might believe about the actual outcome of the temptations which have come his way — whether or not they have ever led to 'other things' — the fact remains that he has stayed married for nearly three decades. Rather earlier in the marriage, he wrote another long poem, addressed to his wife, which celebrated this feat of longevity. It has nothing necessarily to do with a principled belief in fidelity or chastity on his part; nor with any consistent practice of these virtues. James doesn't view them as virtues, automatically — and especially not in men of plainer stamp, who, he suggests, cannot gain moral credit for resisting sexual opportunities which are less available to them anyway than to the hunk or the spunk. 'A lasting marriage isn't dreamland: it is reality', he asserted more recently, when commenting on the growing difficulties in the marriage of Prince Charles and Princess Diana, before their divorce. 'All marriages are difficult', he argued. If, in supporting this claim, he was alluding to difficulties in his own marriage, he also managed to suggest, in the tough-mindedness of his tone, the sense of reality which had helped keep it afloat for so long:

> Every marriage has something wrong with it. Marriage has something wrong with it. What it has wrong with it is people. The more individual they are, the less they are designed to live together. If people were meant to live together easily they would have half a personality each ... Most people who love once love again, and have even been known to fall for the person they once married, after realising that the person they let go was in a trap, and the trap was in themselves.[36]

There is even a case for arguing that the outrageous flirt and ogler we see on some of his television shows is another figment of James' imagination —

another artfully contrived character who happens to be called by his own name here. Characters and their creators cannot be entirely divorced, of course; what creators imagine has at least as deep a root in their sensibilities as any of their more mundane outward activities. But that doesn't mean there are not some practical discriminations to be made between these things. James has recently reflected on this subject in a discussion of the sexual fantasies in the films of Fellini, and of the effect of these fantasies on the director's relationship with his actress-wife, Giulietta Masina. A measure of self-reflection or self-identification might be detectable here, too. 'Masina', James says,

> was no doubt fully aware of Fellini's belief that a man can't help what goes on in his own mind, and so had better be judged on his conduct. What she thought of that belief is one of the many secrets of their long marriage'.[37]

'Judged on his conduct' has an echo of school, if not Sunday school; and in areas of life apart from sexual morality there are further signs in James of a continuing obeisance to the rules and rituals of his upbringing, along with the displays of resistance. He is not often very explicit about this tension within himself — he likes to stress the resistances, especially in talking about his early years — but there is one eloquent acknowledgment of it in his first volume of memoirs: 'On the one hand, I was a petty bourgeois student, on the other a libertarian bohemian. I could feel my own personality coming apart like the original continental plates'. This suggests the kind of dislocation in his sensibility that might develop into a split; it didn't, and couldn't, because the two components involved are not as opposed as he makes out. The tension was real enough, however; and, as with so much else in his life, its stresses and strains in him can be traced to the original dislocation resulting from the loss of his father.[38]

James was an inordinately energetic student, even if his energies were never exclusively channelled into the formal studies of a school or university curriculum. Taking control of the most creative part of a student newspaper, running the sort of theatrical show that must succeed or fail on the basis of its own fresh scripts and not those of some established author, must have demanded extraordinarily hard work. James recollects these activities in some detail, but is inclined to make light of them, as he does of his academic progress. He likes parading his laurels from the past, but could never conceive of resting on them. His is a work ethic which might have been confirmed by the homilies of the Kogarah Presbyterian Fellowship but is rooted in a more deeply personal compulsion. There is a moving allusion to this in a passage from one of his most recent poems, produced almost fifty years after the accident that devastated his childhood:

> … your life is on loan from those before you
> Who had no chance …[39]

Writing poetry has itself been a way — but only one among the many ways — by which James has sought to pay off his own loan. It can be no accident that his frenetic polymath expatriate hero in *The Remake* should be called 'Chance'.

One begins to wonder how far James was irresponsible even in his academic endeavours. Given his native talents, his record at Sydney University was certainly not as brilliant as the legendary Chance's is reported to have been;[40] but given, too, all the distractions of his other activities, James performed creditably enough from year to year, and it is hard to see how this could have gone on being purely the result of luck, or of the clever 'faking' to which he attributes his progress. His inclination is to minimise the extent of his mental labours and engagements; but a rather different impression emerges if you read between the lines or pause to consider some of the incidental detail he provides.

At the end of his first year, we learn, it was only his ability to regurgitate the lecturers' notes that got him through the exams; yet (if only because he must have been a regular attender of lectures in the first place) he ended up doing better in that one year than nearly all the other bohemians or aesthetes had managed to do over a much longer period. Later, having kicked the lecture habit, 'it was only my ability to conjure a fluent essay out of thin air that got me to the third year of the honours school. That, and the *benefit of reading Shakespeare morning, noon and night*'. But the fluency surely had something to do with his keen observance of the rules of English grammar, first drummed into him, as he tells us elsewhere, by one of his teachers at school. (He has continued to be a stickler for correct grammar, quick to pounce on any lapse he finds in the work of his fellow-writers or broadcasters, in political slogans, even in supermarket signs, and sharp to react against any attempts by insensitive or ignorant editors to 'correct' his own style.) Brushing up his Shakespeare with such feverish intensity was hardly a slacker's indulgence, especially not for someone who was also raiding the shelves of his friends for anything by the likes of Camus, Pound, MacNeice, Fitzgerald, Hemingway, Cummings, Mencken, Salinger, Auden and Isherwood. None of these modern authors' works was on the curriculum, but each was as enriching for him as any of the set texts, and no less demanding. He just casually reels off their names in his memoirs of this period, but several of them figure rather more substantially in his critical essays of later years — some as a main subject. His defence of the technical austerities of Auden's later work against more orthodox critical reservations had to await the English poet's full maturing as well as the ripening of James' own confidence as a critic, but the seeds of his authoritative enthusiasm for the subject were clearly sown during his early undergraduate years.[41]

James was also starting to acquaint himself during these years with various kinds of critical writing that would form the model for his own style, in journalistic reportage as well as the literary essay. This was a studiously non-academic (if not anti-academic) style, but it is important to stress the studiousness with which it was cultivated and refined as much as its resistances to high specialisation or any form of jargon. James recounts that 'when majoring in extracurricular activities at Sydney University' he once committed to memory a whole collection of the reviews and profiles of the *New Yorker* columnist, Wolcott Gibbs. Readers who relish James' own reviews and profiles in the *New Yorker* today, or who bought the *Observer* all through the 1970s just to keep up with his incorrigibly irreverent television column, have reason to be grateful for the early lessons he learned from Gibbs, as well as from other wags and pundits on the Anglo-American literary scene such as Shaw, H.L. Mencken, George Jean Nathan, S.J. Perelman, A.J. Liebling, Paul Dehn, C.A. Lejeune and Kenneth Tynan. The prime lesson was that 'a serious note can be struck in casual journalism, and struck most truly when the touch is light'. Among literary critics, the young James' chief idol was the 'metropolitan' maverick, Edmund Wilson. Avoiding the narrowness (and, in James' view, needlessness) of textual explication, as practised by the drones of academe, Wilson had devoted himself to 'the steady work of reporting, judging, sorting out, encouraging, reproving and re-estimating'. James seems to have devoured everything Wilson wrote, and his own critical procedures, as demonstrated in the 'revisionist' pieces on Auden, for example, were very similar. He was eventually to apply these procedures to Wilson's own creative forays into the realms of the novel and poetry, tempering his undergraduate enthusiasms with more discriminating (if still largely favourable) criticism.[42]

As part of his third-year honours course at Sydney, James had to attend a class in Anglo-Saxon, taught by one of Australia's most distinguished medievalists, George Russell. This was also the class James shared with his future wife. Prue Shaw was a dream pupil, he recalls, and Russell was 'a great teacher' (probably one of 'the two or three … English lecturers … of world class' at Sydney that he refers to in his memoirs). Typically he accounts himself 'the worst student' Russell ever had. As a critic of his fiction has observed, James has a nice line in 'self-deprecating vanities'; but this isn't necessarily one of them. Apart from some rudimentary German he had been taught in school, Anglo-Saxon was effectively the first 'foreign' tongue to which he had been exposed, and he had yet to develop the passion for language-learning which has now given him a reading knowledge at least of Latin, Italian, French, Russian, and Japanese, as well as German. There is no evidence that his brief initiation in Anglo-Saxon sowed even the smallest seed for this enthusiasm. What he did imbibe from Russell's teaching, however, was a deep admiration for great literary scholarship, of the kind represented by Ernst Robert Curtius' magisterial study, *European Literature and the Latin Middle Ages*. When Russell, addressing his class, gravely pronounced this work 'a great book', James records that 'the moment stayed with me'.[43]

The moment stayed to inspire his admiration of comparable scholars in other or wider fields, most notably the Olympian Contini. (Prue Shaw was to study under the great philologist when she first went to Europe to pursue her scholarly interests in Dante and medieval Italian literature.) The moment also stayed, perhaps, to fuel further his scorn for lesser academic fry obsessively involved in their business of textual explication, yet without anything of Curtius' or Contini's or Russell's cultural and linguistic range. For all James' own linguistic deficiencies at the time, the range of interests and enthusiasms that he had started to build up were evidently impressive enough for the memory of him to 'stay' with George Russell. It was to be Russell who two or three years later wrote James the reference that gained him admission to Cambridge.[44]

As well as teaching James and his future wife, Russell dispensed regular hospitality to the couple, entertaining them to dinner at home with his family and making sure they were well plied with good music as well as good wine. It was here, James recalls, that he was 'gently but firmly' introduced to the classical composers, another source of great enthusiasm for him in his maturer years. It was here also that the idea of his going to Cambridge University was first mooted. There is a sense that Russell became for a while a benevolent father-figure for James — one that the young man could rebel against in certain ways as well as revere. James wouldn't restrain his own interest at the time in more popular contemporary music, and insisted on playing his jazz records for the Russells; he also remained indifferent to, if not contemptuous of, the Cambridge scheme. The ancient university, he thought — when he thought on the matter at all — would be no place for the budding modernist poet he fancied himself to be; and as a citadel of establishment values and privileges its appeal was only as a target for the revolutionary iconoclasm he had started to pick up from his bohemian friends in The Push and in the Sydney University Journalists' Club.[45]

It was through the Journalists' Club that James met the woman he was to call his 'second mother': the visiting English comedian, Joyce Grenfell. On the surface, she was an unlikely choice of guest for such a hotbed of radicalism as the Club liked to imagine itself. In her film roles, solo stage performances, and occasional columns, she poked fun at a whole range of middle-class manners and attitudes; but her material, without being 'irredeemably genteel', as James first thought, was in no sense subversive either. 'Regal' in her own personal bearing and demeanour, she supported the monarchy and also adhered unwaveringly to her belief in God — positions similar to those of James' real mother as it happens. It may simply have been her lustre and rarity value as a star in faraway Australia that first attracted him and the Club, though it was a very discreet lustre. As a choice of alternative parent for James she was as unlikely-seeming as George Russell; yet he was to pursue her avidly for several years, first through letters when she returned to England, then through visits to her house when he went to England himself. Being able to claim her friendship was useful, of course, for someone planning a career in comedy, and James admits to 'ruthlessly exploiting' her in this way. By her own account, he spared her nothing (as with his real mother) of his 'anti-establishment, anti-authority' views; yet she remained unfazed, well disposed to him throughout. That was a good part of her attraction for him: her quality of imperturbable refinement. He found in it both a challenge and a comfort. The bourgeois-bohemian make-up requires a continuing anchor in the securities of the world it seeks to undermine and escape. It is significant that this mother-figure should have been English and that James should have begun to cultivate her not long before he was to pull up anchor from Australia.[46]

Part of his motive in leaving Australia was that he had exhausted what challenges and comforts it could offer him as a budding writer and performer. While still attached to Sydney University he was given his first opportunity to appear on television, but it was in a game show with some other journalists — just a slightly upmarket-sounding version of the kind of fare that tended to dominate locally-made programmes in the early days of the medium. He was also asked to review books for the *Sydney Morning Herald* and *Nation,* which gave him his first experience of mainstream journalism. When he graduated, the *Herald* offered him a full-time job on the paper as an assistant editor. This enabled him to make a living out of correcting other people's sentences (which, as we have seen, has remained one of his preoccupations) but there was no further call on him to contribute his own. Even if he had been asked to do more reviewing, it would probably not have satisfied him in the long run. Not only did a daily newspaper like the *Herald* offer little scope for anything beyond a brief puff or quick demolition job; it also appealed to a fairly small regional audience by the standards of dailies in London or New York. It was the oldest paper in Sydney, and while not so fusty as to baulk at the prospect of employing someone like James in its literary pages, it tended to tread a fairly conservative political line, and endorse the values of a culture he found stifling in its general social, racial and moral conformity.

Twenty, twenty-five, thirty years later, he has kept on recalling this 'monotone dominion' of his youth, this place where (in a phrase reminiscent of Edna Everage's Austral hymn) 'nothing happened' — or, making a slight concession, 'hardly anything'.[47]

In a more substantial concession, he has acknowledged that, from the late 1940s, an 'Australian literary community' had begun to form itself, thanks to the dedication and talent of a few individual writers (mainly poets, of the order of A.D. Hope and Judith Wright). The problem was that nothing in the Anglocentric literary education of Australian universities at the time, nor in the American and European enthusiasms of his closest friends, prepared him to be interested in this indigenous community or even to know of its existence. Some of its leading poets were also beginning to write good criticism, but there was no larger 'literary world', in the shape of a wide range of well-subscribed magazines, to promote, engage with, and judge their work, whether critical or creative. This, James claims, has remained a deficiency up till today, and not just of Australia, but of any place outside those twin metropolitan meccas of London and New York.[48]

In 1976, on his first return visit to Australia, he rhapsodised over the physical 'Paradise on Earth' that he had left behind a decade and a half earlier, but remained highly critical of the political, intellectual and artistic climate. There had been a brief 'revolution' of sorts with the return of the Labor Party to office in 1972, but this new regime had already vanished, to be replaced by 'the same conservative forces … as had ruled the country so suffocatingly when I left'. There were advances on the cultural front, most conspicuously in the 'scores of feature films … made … since the Whitlam Government introduced subsidies'; but the quality of the products fell far below the quantity, in James' judgment, and certainly didn't live up to the fanfares of publicity that accompanied them. James might have acknowledged, if he had known, that it was a 'conservative' administration, prior to Whitlam's regime, that had first put into place some of the bureaucratic structures for funding the new film industry. A few years later he was to acknowledge that his sweeping judgment on the cinema revival had obscured some its finer specimens, but that 'the general point remains true: the average Australian film is not *The Getting of Wisdom* but *Goodbye Paradise*'.[49]

What is interesting here is not so much his particular taste in movies as the choice of titles by which he represents it. Together they form a kind of fairytale epitome of the expatriate's career. A bright youth farewells the raw paradise of his birthplace in order to imbibe the wisdom of the old world. The paradise has plied him with some of the fruits of knowledge as well as more material sustenance, but neither he (nor it) appreciates the true value of this bounty or knows how to use that knowledge for his own growth. Only by expelling himself from this self-indulgent enclosure into the wider world can he begin to grow. As a result of this quest, *l'enfant du paradis* will turn eventually into a sage.[50]

James is realistic enough about his own, more desolate 'epitomes of dislocation' not to buy this sort of tale outright, nor to peddle it neat. The statement that we find in his first volume of memoirs, reiterated in various forms elsewhere, that he has 'never ceased to feel orphaned', movingly suggests the vestiges of the child in him that will always remain, however old he is, and however far removed from his place of origin. The child remains on the wild side, too; the rawness of youth is not entirely rubbed off. James told a Sydney journalist who interviewed him in 1989: 'I'm a bit of a larrikin. You don't ever get over that early vision of yourself'. Yet there are other occasions when he can suggest that the journey away from his birthplace has been the route to full maturity, personal and creative — and, moreover, the only possible route of that kind. These positions are not necessarily self-contradictory.[51]

In a 'Broadcast' he made in 1971, he declared that

Intellectually, Australians tend to mature late, if at all: for example, the country as a whole still hasn't woken up to the fact that the arts are not commodities. This slowness to mature goes on affecting you long after you've come away: when I went up to Cambridge I was about seven years older than most of the freshmen but felt about two years younger, and it's only now that I feel I have caught up with the Englishmen of my generation.

At the time of this pronouncement he was in his early thirties, yet in the first volume of his memoirs, published almost a decade later, he was to suggest that his 'tiresomely protracted adolescence' was drawn out a bit longer: 'Eventually, in my middle thirties, I got a grip on myself'. It would be absurd to expect complete precision over dates in this matter; the anomaly here is slight. It is on the question of what he thinks marks maturity, and his own in particular, that one might welcome more precision from him. The course of his career provides no obvious clue to any fundamental difference between his youthful and mature incarnations, and as to why being in England should have made that difference. But precision is inappropriate here, too. Judging from his statements on the careers of other writers and artists, maturation is not just a straightforward advance from earlier to later mental stages. Its secret lies not so much in outgrowing the gaucheries of one's younger selves as in recognising, and working to realise, the creative potential in these.[52]

'Here it is easier to just get on with your work', he says of England in his 1971 broadcast; and that degree of accommodation may be all that writers or artists need for their development, even if the work they are getting on with involves nothing but a replay of childhood themes. England's cultural climate appears to be particularly conducive to this sort of work; its distinctiveness may even lie in its infantilising effects. James is not always uncritical about the resulting fruits. In one of his most recent articles he rather sneers at what he deems 'the Henry James option — to go abroad and set up shop where artists were *more coddled*' (my emphasis). A momentarily guilty reflection on the Clive James option, perhaps. It is certainly a bit hard on his near-namesake, who before proceeding to his own mature phase with his great studies in childhood, *What Maisie Knew* and *The Awkward Age,* had to endure the far from 'coddling' boos of a London audience at his play, *Guy Domville,* in 1895. Elsewhere, and earlier, Clive James sounds rather more appreciative of the infantilising effects of English culture. In 1974 — the very middle of his 'middle thirties' — he approvingly noted the 'co-existence of sage and toddler' in one of English culture's choicest fruits, the reigning poet-laureate, John Betjeman. A native-born specimen, raised from the start in the hothouse conditions of England's elite educational institutions, Betjeman did not have to get wisdom by getting out, growing up, turning himself into anything: he was 'born old ... or else is still infantile ... or both'. In another home-grown English poet, Philip Larkin, James detected (in an article he published in 1981) 'a level of maturity which only those capable of childishness can reach … He did not put away childish things, and it made him more of a man'.[53]

Except on this level, it is difficult to find much obvious evidence of maturity in James' own work, right up to the present day, when he is getting past his middle fifties. He is conscious of, and has expressed admiration for, an alternative and rather more straightforward kind of maturity — that which involves 'a steady ripening of the faculties', such as might be found, he argues, in the work of a painter like Degas. 'I like the old hand who grows wise in his profession.' He contrasts Degas with Picasso, whose 'endless inventiveness', he says, is 'surely' that of 'a titanically gifted child rather than a grown man'. He is not shy — perhaps a little too keen — to identify himself with Picasso (another expatriate): 'Perhaps it is a reflection on oneself to find him babyish', he blithely hazards. But is this estimation of himself to be entirely trusted? James' penchant for character-playing should not be forgotten, and the child in him may partly be a role he has chosen for public performance. His memoirs suggest that going to England did nothing to discourage the child in him for years after he arrived there; if anything, it offered him the temptation and the facilities to prolong this condition. The record of his subsequent career in England, for all its undoubted successes, shows no marked change, unless it has been to intensify the condition further. It is arguable, however, that his most popular and most visible successes there, in the medium of television, have been dependent on a conscious flaunting of the childish or adolescent Australian self that he arrived with, and a studious putting away of adult things. It pays him to *appear* as though he's never got beyond his own awkward age. Part of the wisdom he has acquired has been in learning to obscure it. To a select audience, he can be quite open about such tactics. In a review article on some recent trends in Australian poetry, published in the *Times Literary Supplement* towards the end of 1987, he raised the 'consideration that the Australian expatriate, once the secret is all the way out, will lose his privileged status as a barbarian', then adding (as if drawing on personal experience): 'It has always been a rewarding role to play'.[54]

In the second and third volumes of his memoirs James has tirelessly documented his gaucheries on first coming to England. The titles are apt in this respect. *Falling Towards England* suggests that 'The Kid from

Kogarah' (the title he originally gave his first volume) is still finding his feet having finally escaped his antipodean kindergarten. If he has left mother, it is still towards a motherland that he is awkwardly reaching out; and in the rather aimless-seeming, desultory succession of tasks that he finds himself involved in during his first years in England — copy-editing here, clipping hedges there, then filing followed by filming, with lots of playtime and sleepybyes and drinkies in between — there remains an air of the more chaotic or liberated nursery school. (One attraction to Joyce Grenfell as his choice of adopted mother in England might have been her famous sketch of the nursery-school teacher battling serenely to tame her wayward charges.) A resolve 'not to take on anything which could not be successfully tackled by a ten-year-old child' coexists with a sense of listlessness that almost has him packing up to go back to Australia. Attempting to study again is the only other option, so that he is finally prompted to take up George Russell's offer of getting him into Cambridge. He is still convinced in theory of its anti-egalitarian influence in society, but a frightening encounter with some active student terrorists in London persuades him 'to abandon the revolution then and there'.[55]

He arrived at Cambridge in 1964. His years there are chronicled in *May Week was in June,* named after a 'dislocation' of the ordinary calendar in the University's own schedule of events. It was just one of many eccentric and confusing conventions of the place to which he had to adjust; but this was hardly a fresh challenge to one so experienced from infancy in dislocations of various sorts. 'Where else in the world would I ever fit in except here, where I had never felt the least urge to fit in?' he wonders half way through the volume. The facilities and ambience of the University offered him another 'personal playground', and he took to it with alacrity, expending his energies as feverishly and in at least as many directions as he had at Sydney University.[56]

Over a period of five years or so, he directed more than twenty revues, also writing many of the sketches for them and performing in them 'rather clumsily, many times'. Already he thrived on being an awkward misfit. His labours were to be rewarded by his election to the presidency of Footlights, the University's illustrious revue company, in 1966. He continued to write and publish poetry in various literary magazines. A newer line for him (though one clearly drawing on his verse- and sketch-writing talents) was the penning of song lyrics to the music of budding composer, fellow-student, and fellow-Footlights member, Pete Atkin. These songs were to attract something of a cult following and form the basis for a number of recordings in subsequent years. All the while James continued his omnivorous reading in English Literature — only a small part of it featuring on any curriculum — and began his travels on the Continent, especially in Italy, which planted an urge in him to master foreign literatures as well. He claims to have largely ignored the regular work set by his tutors, and yet ended up with a respectable enough degree to be allowed to proceed to postgraduate study. He was to start research for a thesis on Shelley and his relation to Italian poetry; but he didn't proceed very long or intently with this. The sustained, lonely rigours of research were not so easily combined with all his other pursuits, which included not only his presidency of Footlights, but also some reviewing and editing stints for prominent university magazines and a spot of debating at the Cambridge Union.[57]

Such activities brought him to the attention of Nicholas Tomalin, literary editor of the *New Statesman,* who had come up to Cambridge from London to participate in one of the debates. He invited James to write for his paper on an occasional basis. James' first contribution, published in the first week of July 1967, happened to be on a topic connected with his homeland (it was a review of Elspeth Huxley's account of her journey through Australia), though subsequent contributions ranged more widely, including a report on an exhibition of eighteenth-century Venetian painters, an Italian and a Cambridge 'Diary' column, and various other book reviews. The *New Statesman,* having been founded by the leading light of Fabian Socialism, Sidney Webb, in the Edwardian years, had built up a broad, solid readership among the left-liberal intelligentsia in Britain. Its general tone perfectly suited James' now-modulated version of social democracy, which (as he later summed it up) 'while still hospitable to the idea of universal popular enfranchisement, was concerned about the milk being delivered on time to the doorstep'.[58]

In one light this new pragmatism might betoken a mature Fabianish awareness about the art of the possible; in another, it tends to reduce

politics to the comforts of home. On the verge of marriage and father-
hood, he seeks a return to the securities of his suburban boyhood:
something to go with the cornflakes. Over subsequent years there have
been further 'modulations'. He has eschewed (at times trenchantly criti-
cised) the extremes of the Thatcherite right, but he has also directed some
of his most merciless satiric barbs at the British trade union and Labour
Party establishments. Michael Foot has even credited James with helping
to lose Labour the general election of 1983. Along with many other intellectuals disenchanted with Labour, James imagined he had found a
political home for a while with the Social Democratic Party at the height
of its short vogue in the early 1980s; though when its vogue had passed, so
did his own enthusiasm, and by the end of the decade he was pillorying its
leaders and their attempts to salvage the operation through 'a doomed
relationship' with the Liberal Party.[59]

Yielding finally to the values of his 'two' mothers, he is now a confirmed believer in the British monarchy, without becoming entirely
reverential towards it. In 1981, commenting on James' long satirical poem
chronicling the career of the Prince of Wales, *Charles Charming's
Challenges on the Pathway to the Throne*, Philip Larkin rebuked 'the corni-
ness of his mocking the royals'; and to this day individual members of the
royal family remain an all-too-easy butt for jokes in his television shows.
From his student days at Cambridge, however, there was already a counter-
impulse in him to protect them from the worst excesses of satire. When
elected President of Footlights, James put an embargo on any revue sketches about Prince Charles, who was then an undergraduate at Cambridge. He
also put a ban on jokes 'which had the appearance of being dirty purely for
the sake of being dirty'. Was this another vestige of the Sunday school
monitor in James? Perhaps there is a touch of irony in the very peremp-
toriness of his injunction: 'Smut was to be stamped on'.[60]

James' monarchist principles now extend to a vocal — if not particularly vociferous — opposition to the Australian republican movement. His
basic reasoning is that a constitutional system which has generally served
Australia well should not be tampered with; there is no virtue, and some
danger, in change for change's sake. He stresses the 'benefits of retaining an
off-shore, cost-free head of state who is out of politics and sets a limit to

ambition'. Something of the influence of his wife's long academic labours at Sydney, then in Italy, Cambridge and London, may be detectable here. The chief fruit of these labours has been her edition, recently published by Cambridge University Press, of the *Monarchia,* the political treatise by Dante in which he advances the idea of a world monarch as the best guarantor of personal liberties and individual self-fulfilment for all citizens.[61]

While continuing to support the monarchy, as the most reliable form of government for Britain and Australia, James has remained a dedicated fan of Princess Diana following her separation and divorce from Prince Charles. More than that, he appears to have become one of her unofficial advisers and — if newspaper and magazine gossip is to be believed — something of a personal friend, to be spotted with her at tête-à-tête lunches in Mayfair restaurants. What shrewder forecast of these trends in him could we find — what crisper explanation of their roots in the 'coddling' effect of English institutions — than this report he published in the *New Statesman,* as far back as 1968, on the dilutions of student radicalism at Oxford and Cambridge? Those admitted within their walls, he noted then, are inevitably exposed to 'the massive injections of gradualist compromise that shrivel the fine dreams of the generations. For who would seek death like Che Guevara once he had tasted the life of Riley?'[62]

Following this piece, James had continued writing for the *New Statesman* for a few more months of 1968 (with spasmodic reappearances over the following decade). Other London periodicals, most notably the *Times Literary Supplement,* soon began to court him. He was finally to realise his dreams of becoming a 'Metropolitan Critic' in the tradition of Edmund Wilson. He continued, however, to keep a base in Cambridge, partly for family reasons, and partly out of an enduring affection which (as he put it in 1980) 'anybody feels for a place where they read a lot, thought a lot, and wasted a lot of time'. The competing tugs — or complementary attractions — of London and Cambridge represented another kind of dislocation in his life, and one that has persisted into the 1990s; though over the years, as his 'metropolitan' commitments mounted, he found time only to spend his weekends in Cambridge, and in a recent radio interview back in Australia he identified his 'home' with his 'little apartment in London'.[63]

1968 had been an important year for James in other ways. It was the year he married his fellow-student from George Russell's classes in Sydney. Prue Shaw was now making her own career in academic life at Cambridge, which provided a good practical incentive for staying on in the town, though she was later to take up an academic position at the University of London. 1968 was also the year that James made his first appearance on British television, leading his college's team on the Granada network's quiz show, *University Challenge:* modest enough beginnings (especially as the team lost after a second round), but of more lustre than the game show he had appeared on in Sydney, and with a much larger viewing audience. There have been other contestants on that show (like Stephen Fry) who have gone on to make part of their careers as television performers, but none has done so quite as speedily as James.[64]

In the following year Granada invited him to write and present thirty-nine editions of their movie programme, *Cinema* — probably on the basis of the film criticism he had been writing for the *Cambridge Review* rather than his appearance on *University Challenge.* He had already made something of a distinctive name for himself in preferring to concentrate his critical attention on popular commercial films rather than the 'art-house' masterpieces that generally dominated the repertoires of university film societies. This may have had something to do with his democratic senti-ments, for all that their radical tinge had now faded. But it was also a profitable way of tapping back into a childhood obsession: the fantasy worlds of the great Hollywood and British studios which had been a staple of his cultural diet in suburban Kogarah, which had fed his penchant for playing characters, and which had helped supply his very name.[65]

Work in television and radio, or work about them in the shape of regular reviewing and criticism, came to be his main mode of employment in the 1970s. London Weekend Television made a song-show series out of his collaborations with Pete Atkin. He appeared in the BBC satirical programme, *Up Sunday,* in the early 1970s. The first time James himself ever 'walked *and* talked' on television, as he put it, was in 1979, when he was paired with Anna Raeburn to host a series called *A Question of Sex,* 'a "participative formula" exploration of the differences and similarities between men and women, social stereotypes and physiological realities'. In his previous television appearances, he had done little more than speak lines to a camera; now he was expected to interview, to chat to the studio audience, and to play games with props.[66]

Since 1971 he had conducted interviews on BBC radio with celebrities in various fields, and over the next few years he appeared as a guest himself on a number of panel games and quizzes revolving around literature or current affairs, as well as writing various scripts for broadcast on radio. The sense in which both television and radio acted together as a kind of alternative family for someone deprived of a real one is suggested in a recent recollection of his experiences in the 1970s. 'Compared to radio', he remarks, 'TV often strikes me as a more flamboyant but tongue-tied bigger sibling'. He adds: 'But it's the medium I know most about'.[67]

His knowledge of television comes partly from having spent so much time watching it when employed as the *Observer*'s regular critic. He was to write a weekly column on the subject for nearly a decade; whereas his earlier stint as a radio critic for the *Listener* had been once a month and lasted only briefly. His writings on television are probably more voluminous than any other critic's to date, and they were to bring as much attention to him as to the medium. He became something of a household name in England for the first time, or at least in households with any pretensions to cultural sophistication. Yet the secret of his attention-getting lay in his insouciant rawness of manner and address; he made this look sophisticated itself. Reflecting on his style, the literary editor of the *Observer* at the time James started there, Terence Kilmartin, was to note: 'he seemed so fresh, so different — a unique combination of elegance and modern verve, and a marvellous use of slang in a totally unvulgar way.'[68]

James' position as an antipodean up-tipped in another hemisphere, and his persistent consciousness of himself as a bereft child, could both have been impediments for him if he had allowed them to be. Typically, he turned these things to advantage by playing up facets of both the Australian and the child in him so as to provide a sustaining public identity for himself. The so-called orphan of the first volume of his memoirs evolved into 'that smart bastard in the *Observer*', the epithet first applied to him when being introduced as a character in his own novel, *The Remake*. Only later was this character expressly identified as 'Clive James'.

Because he had become such a household name, however, he could expect his readers to pick up on this clue immediately.[69]

'As for making a business of being Australian, I don't think I've ever really done that', he told Roy Plomley in his appearance on *Desert Island Discs,* not long before he gave up his *Observer* column. Yet the Australianness of his tone in that column was unmistakable to fellow-expatriate, Peter Conrad, when Conrad reviewed one of the collections James made of his television writings. It was manifest not just in 'the admixture of antipodean inflections' contributing to their overall style. Conrad shrewdly noted how James had 'devised a persona of bluff (yet often preachy) plain speaking — the voice of the man on the Bondi omnibus'. What also needs to be noted in these reviews, however — because it is the source of their exhilaration for readers as well as of occasional irritation — is the alternative persona of the street-smart child, or the voice of the schoolboy at the back of the class. These are what characterise the humour of the pieces: their cruelly keen observation of absurdity and excess in the passing parade of images (as when Barbara Cartland's eyes, 'twin miracles of mascara', are compared to 'the corpses of two small crows that had crashed into a chalk cliff'); their deadly accurate mimicry of pompous tones of voice or outlandish accents ('It is inneresting to try zis climb whizzout oxychen … what is important to explore is myself', a German mountaineer intones in James' rendering, while *Dallas*' oily oil-man, J.R., is reported as beseeching his wife: 'If we trah, really trah … we can solve all our prarlms').[70]

Being only a limited household name was bound not to satisfy James in the end, so insatiable was his need for attention. He finally signed off from his regular *Observer* column in 1982, and has since continued with his literary journalism and poetry-writing — finding new and impressive outlets for these activities in periodicals like the *London Review of Books* or the *New Yorker* — as well as completing his memoirs and embarking on a series of novels. His television work has absorbed more and more of his time, however, and become ever more ramifying in its search for wider and wider audiences. 'What I am after', he announced in 1991, is 'the whole audience, or as much of it as I can pull into the tent'.

You might think you were eavesdropping on Rupert Murdoch here if James was not at the same moment belabouring his 'erstwhile compatriot' for his own brand of omniverousness as a media mogul. What repels James is not so much the scale of Murdoch's ambitions as the way they are covered up by his much-vaunted crusade to rescue mass audiences from the mandarin paternalism of the standard television networks. James remains a champion of these networks, in England at least, and he passionately defends the combination of their elite staffing structures with their avowed 'vocation to enlighten the people'. These sentiments are hardly surprising in one who has been an accepted part of that elite for over twenty years. Oscillating between the two major networks in Britain, he has managed to satisfy at least part of his ambitions; though just recently he has formed (with a couple of partners) his own television company, Watchmaker Productions, so as to give himself greater scope and independence. There remain some questions, however, about just how 'enlightening' his own programmes have been, or how he defines that word and seeks to act upon it in the future.[71]

It is too early to pronounce on the fruits of Watchmaker Productions, but if the tendencies of his contract work for the BBC or ITV are anything to judge by, his populist urges appear if anything to be diminishing the range of his work as its volume increases, and homogenising its contents. The format of his annual New Year's Eve 'Review of the Year' — more like revues from his Sydney or Cambridge days in their relentlessly pillorying tone — has remained unchanged over a decade, apart from their extended duration and grander settings in recent years. His Saturday night chat-shows have been nominally focused on the theme of television itself, but their formulaic nature and even part of their content — a jokes corner, a celebrity guest spot, a comic video clip of some egregious television kitsch, a zany band number or spectacularly mutilated song — are reminiscent, in spite of the technology, of an old bill of fare from a palace of varieties or the contents of the weekly adventure magazines he used to devour as a schoolboy in Australia. There is still something of the cheeky wisecracking schoolboy in his style of hosting — though a rather more blandly genial one than was to be found in his television column, and with less inclination to show off his smartness. There is also perhaps something of the 'continuing provincialism' he diagnosed in Australian authors many years before in reviewing Hal Porter's *The Paper Chase* for the *New Statesman*. Its chief symptom, as he perceived it then, was their effort perhaps not consciously, to get on an emotional level with their audience because they can't be sure of being on an intellectual one. Mr Porter is surely a much brighter, more cultivated man than he allows his book to make out. But he isn't being modest. He is also protecting himself.

James himself had always, when it suited him, 'soft-pedalled the brainy stuff', as he once put it (hiding his degrees, for example, when applying for low-key jobs during his first years in London), but he has raised this to an art in itself now. When he affects to puzzle over the pronunciation of his guest, Greta Scacchi's, name, she has to point out protestingly that 'this man speaks perfect Italian'. It's just possible, of course, that this has been set up beforehand so that she shows his smartness for him.[72]

James still remains endearingly defensive about the kind of criticism that types him as 'some calculating poseur who will do anything to display his erudition, while simultaneously plunging ruthlessly down-market in search of viewers'. No one is saying 'simultaneously' (though the Scacchi exchange, if not spontaneous, would be a case in point). There has been until recently, however, a quite striking, and not uncreative, dislocation in James' television personae. The irrepressibly vulgar jester of the New Year's Eve and Saturday Night shows doesn't quite fit with the judicious, soft-spoken moderator we find on another sort of chat programme, which began in 1988: *The Late Show* or (as it was rechristened) *The Talk Show*. Here the chat, focused on a particular issue of contemporary culture, politics or morality each session, can be highly intellectual in its content and style, though laced with great urbanity, and the guests are among the most prominent and eloquent in their particular professions. The format and flavour of this show are prefigured in James' own description of one of Chance Jenolan's dinner parties in *The Remake*, published in the year before *The Late Show* first went to air: 'the participants have to be well cast, of course ... This was one of the rare occasions when four monologists in world class [there are three in the show, apart from James] were all able to bang away at once without the whole system overheating'.[73]

As its first title suggests, however, this scintillating *pas de quatre* was consigned to the very end of the evening's viewing; it was also broadcast on BBC 2, the minority viewing channel, and it lasted for only three series over a period of about eighteen months in all. Clive James' cover would not be blown with the wider audiences he craved. Even before the select audience for this show, he could make a game of hiding his intellectual light under a bushel. To discuss the topic 'Culture in the Twentieth Century', he chose as his three guests the American writer and critic, Helen McNeil, the English television dramatist, Dennis Potter, and his old friend from Sydney University days, 'Huggins', now the famous art critic of *Time* magazine, Robert Hughes, whose own story will be unfolded later in these pages. The topic of honours, titles and academic qualifications for artists and writers came up, and when Helen McNeil asked James to come clean about the letters after his own name, he brazenly admitted to 'only a BA failed'. 'Oh, you mean an Australian BA', Dennis Potter chipped in with gleeful relish. Australian mateship being what it is, 'Huggins' could be relied on not to spoil the game. 'That makes two of us', he crisply confirmed.[74]

Chapter Four

The Return of the Captive

The Equivocations of Germaine Greer

'It is not womanly to thrust yourself before the world.' In 1887, some five years before she formed her famous marital and professional partnership with Sidney Webb, Beatrice Potter pronounced this judgment in her diary after attending a public lecture by Annie Besant, the seasoned campaigner for birth control and various other radical causes of the day. It was to be almost a century before Germaine Greer thrust herself before the world with the publication of her book, *The Female Eunuch;* but it is interesting to ponder how 'the high priestess' of women's liberation and sexual equality, as journalists of the 1970s routinely called her, might have struck the young Beatrice, and vice versa. An instinctive recoil from each other would seem to be the most likely response. At the same time, there are more grounds of sympathy between them than one might at first suspect.

Beatrice Potter was soon to be converted to at least mildly socialist and feminist causes herself. What disturbed her about Mrs Besant's rhetoric was less its substance than its style, and what this style revealed (or served to conceal) of the famous orator's motives: 'her blighted wifehood and motherhood' resulting from the fact that 'the law had robbed her of her child'; 'her thirst for power and defiance of the world'; 'the impression … of acting a part'. There were to be strong echoes of just these sorts of apprehension in Germaine Greer's third major book, *Sex and Destiny,* published in 1984, almost a decade and a half after *The Female Eunuch.*[1]

Surveying birth-control campaigns from the time of Mrs Besant, *Sex and Destiny* mounted a sustained philippic against their ethics and their effectiveness. More provokingly, it challenged their central *raison d'être:* the notion of a so-called 'population explosion' and the widely-assumed need for the organised proliferation of chemical or surgical methods of birth control. Successive leaders of the birth-control campaigns were inevitably caught in Greer's fire. These attacks revealed a pervasive distrust for individuals who had thrust themselves before the world through the adoption and promotion of such causes. Greer repeatedly urged that this behaviour was something of a guise for self-promotion — a kind of act or performance — and was driven as likely as not by some thwarting of sexual or reproductive urges.

The Besant campaign, Greer observed, was to 'set the precedent for future promotions of birth-control', and Mrs Besant herself became a prime object of press attention at the time, 'being attractive, atheist, separated from her husband, and suspected of an improper relationship' with her co-campaigner, Charles Bradlaugh. The two most famous birth-control campaigners of the early twentieth century, Margaret Sanger and Marie Stopes, were even 'greater performers', according to Greer — 'tireless self-promoters'. Sanger aspired to 'the role of Lady Bountiful, like any other prima donna' and Stopes had a 'strong streak of exhibitionism in her nature'. Greer endorsed Sanger's own conviction about Stopes, that her sensational best-seller of the 1920s, *Married Love,* was the direct result of her 'unconsummated union with her first husband'; when she wrote it she 'knew nothing of the sufferings of women compelled to bear a child every year'.

Greer's suspicion about public campaigners of this kind went beyond Beatrice Potter's in making no distinction between them on grounds of their sex. Charles Bradlaugh was arraigned for his methods of promotion along with Annie Besant. He was not excused on the grounds that it was more 'manly' to thrust yourself before the world. And a thwarted sexual urge or reproductive instinct was at least hinted at in the case of male propagandists. Of Francis Galton, the chief driving force of the Victorian eugenics movement, Greer wrote bitingly that his faith in selective breeding is touching in a man who, after choosing a wife with a distinguished pedigree, failed to father a child. Such inconsistency might have been after all expected from such a pedigree, for he was the grandson of a Quaker who made a large fortune from the sale of fire-arms.[2]

The issue of consistency that Greer raises here presents a number of puzzles for any observer of her career. She seems to desire if not 'expect' consistency in others. In her latest book, *Slip-Shod Sibyls,* a chronicle and critique of women poets down the ages, she commends the vivid insights of fellow-critic, Camille Paglia, but finds them 'unfortunately inconsistent and largely incompatible with each other'. Yet the extent to which she herself has been consistent, or has valued consistency, in her own life, work, ideas and public image, is far from clear.[3]

Some of her most articulate readers and reviewers in recent years have seen little but inconsistency in these things. One of the most substantial reviews of her work on women poets has contrasted it directly to an earlier book, *The Obstacle Race. The Fortunes of Women Painters and Their Work,* which Greer published in 1979, between *The Female Eunuch* and *Sex and Destiny.* The main concerns of these works are clearly related, but, says this reviewer,

> In *The Obstacle Race* Greer was, by and large, sympathetic to the efforts of female painters. In *Slip-Shod Sibyls* she can see no art in her artists. She largely … withholds sympathy. True, she acknowledges special obstacles and obstructions, but these have tended to make the poetry worse.[4]

Greer herself was aware — but whether painfully or with a certain pride and pleasure is one of the abiding puzzles — that *Sex and Destiny* appeared in some lights to be a direct contradiction of *The Female Eunuch.* 'Such an attack upon the ideology of sexual freedom', she says at one point in the later book, ' … must seem shocking coming from a sexual radical, as the present writer professes to be'. When this work was launched at the Frankfurt Book Fair in October 1984, there was talk of the 'sensational turnabout' which it represented in Greer's views. Seven years on, the American journalist, Susan Faludi, could be found lamenting the appearance of this 'dour and deterministic' work, whose author, 'formerly the media's favourite as a flamboyant advocate of sexual emancipation', now 'championed arranged marriages, chastity, and the chador, and named as her new role model the old-fashioned peasant wife, happily confined to kitchen and nursery'. There is a sense of betrayal here if not of hypocrisy. Faludi didn't mention how this same work had also turned on previous sexual radicals for their very flamboyance, as well as for their lack of any practical experience of marriage or child-rearing. Exhibitionism or brazen self-promotion are accusations which Greer has also levelled at a number of the women poets she discusses in *Slip-Shod Sibyls*.[5] Such imputations and charges sit uneasily not just with her early writings but with much of what we know of her own life. Are there further grounds for suspecting hypocrisy here as well as inconsistency?

Greer's direct experience of marriage has been much more limited, in time at any rate, than Besant's or Stopes' or Galton's. In 1968, just before she turned thirty, she went through with a registry-office wedding in London to Englishman, Paul Du Feu, but she left him about three weeks later. Before that there had been a string of more or less temporary lovers going back over ten years to her days as a student at Melbourne and Sydney universities. (While at school in Melbourne in the mid-1950s, she had even had a passionate fling with another girl of her age, who in later life wrote about the affair in a novel, *Beyond Redemption,* in which Greer was called 'Michaela Martin'. It was Greer who ended this relationship, too — pressured by her mother, according to Greer, though not according to the novel.) She was to have several other relationships after she left Du Feu, but she never married again, and for whatever reason (it was certainly not by choice, according to her own account) she has never had any offspring. One former friend, the English novelist David Plante, has claimed that she advertised for a sire. Her compatriot, Richard Neville, alluded to her having an early hysterectomy — a false rumour given wide attention in the press, and which she was quick to scotch. On various occasions she has openly charted the more unfortunate aspects of her biological history: defective contraception, messy abortions, the unsuccessful attempts at remedial surgery to enable her to have a child. She has known the pain, she says, of losing a wanted child; but she has never experienced either the sufferings or the joys of raising any child of her own.[6]

Conversely, her experience as a public performer is long and richly varied, and the sorts of performance involved have rarely been less than flamboyant. After appearing with her in a chat-show at a London theatre in 1984, the comedian Kenneth Williams noted in his diary that while she was 'a beautiful woman with a charming presence & full of good humour, … she's *not* a performer', but his insistence on this goes against the grain of most impressions of her, and was based purely on what he saw as her deficiencies in vocal projection. Other observers have seen the beauty, the charm, the good humour, as all a part of her consummate theatricality, and noted how these theatrical inclinations have spilled over into the conduct of her private life and relationships, including her marriage. Her notorious and arbitrary-seeming descents into *ill*-humour have been seen as a part of the same quality. She is 'a great performer' who 'has got grander', David Malouf recently remarked, in the wake of a falling-out with her.[7]

When she chooses, she can also make a performance out of her private life by drawing on it in the arguments of her books, articles and other public pronouncements. This is not an unusual inclination in writers and pundits of any kind, but few have followed it, displayed it, capitalised on it, in such a big and brazen fashion as she has done. In 1989, when introducing her as the latest guest on his BBC radio series, *In the Psychiatrist's Chair*, Anthony Clare said to her: 'More than anyone I have interviewed, you have discussed your private intimacy'.[8]

Greer's own relentless 'thrust … before the world' seems to have originated in a need that the world of her childhood in Melbourne, Australia, could never fulfil. It was not that this world was devoid of opportunities and encouragements for a performer — in whatever sense of the word — but it was too circumscribed a stage to contain such a high-octane performer as herself. 'I'm a bolter', she told Clare. She was referring to her inability to sustain passionate relationships with other people, but she could have been referring to her relationships with places as well, and particularly her place of origin. To a recent Australian interviewer she reiterated that she didn't 'persevere in any relationship that is not working. I bolt … When I sense hostility or waning interest [she doesn't stipulate on whose part], I'm off'. To another interviewer, she claimed: 'Ever since I was a little girl I wanted to escape from where I was. I dreamed of a different place where people were interested in different things, and where I wouldn't feel such a freak, and where I couldn't be spoken of with such contempt'.[9]

Something of the constrictions of her birthplace, as she perceived them, is suggested in this comment she made when introducing a new edition of Henry Handel Richardson's novel, *The Getting of Wisdom*. The novel is set partly in Melbourne — though a Melbourne of half a century earlier than the time of Greer's birth in 1939 — and it deals with the travails of its heroine, Laura Ramsbotham, when she is sent to school there. Greer observes:

> The brashness of the provincial capital strikes as harshly upon the reader as it does upon Laura, and so we are committed to her from the outset. [S]he expects to find opportunities for further ranging; instead, she learns the hard way, that she has to compress herself into a smaller compass, to mitigate the brilliance of her effects and to ingratiate where she intends to astonish … Laura's intensity is the cause of most of her suffering, and it will also be the cause of her transcending it. However fervent her wish to cram herself into the common mould, she is too volatile to stay in it.

So often does Greer enact her own feelings and dilemmas in talking of the experiences of others that we can be misled into identifying these things with each other too closely. She calls Laura's school at one point, which was based on the Presbyterian Ladies College in Melbourne, a 'dreary suburban seminary'.[10] The term 'seminary' has retained more associations with Catholicism than with Protestantism in the twentieth century, and Greer was to have her schooling at various Catholic convents in Melbourne, all of them near to her successive family homes in the bayside suburbs of Sandringham and Mentone. By her own account, however, her experiences of these establishments, especially at the last of them, Star of the Sea, Gardenvale, were far from being unrelievedly 'dreary', and were certainly less so than her home life. Her fellow-pupils and her teachers provided her with her first mass audience.

For much of her infancy her father, Reg, had been away in Egypt and Malta on war service, and at the end of the war he 'came home a stranger'. It was more than his time away at the war that made him such a distant and mysterious figure; as his daughter was only to discover many years later, he had been hiding his origins and his real name (Greeney) from long before the time of his marriage. Greer was the only child of the marriage up to the time of her father's return from the war, and she spent nearly all her time with her mother, Peg, in those early years. She has insisted that she was an unwanted child from the start, and that during her father's absence her mother distracted herself by having an affair with an American (possibly a GI), to which Greer was an unintended witness. If this is not childhood fantasy (akin to Barry Humphries' belief that he was adopted), or a retrospective invention, it might help explain her own precocious interest in sexual matters. 'There is nothing innocent about childhood', she remarks darkly in *Slip-Shod Sibyls,* when reflecting on the infantile voyeurism she discerns in the poetry of Christina Rossetti. After Greer's father returned from the war, her mother gave birth to another daughter, and Greer remembers feeling more than ever that 'nobody wanted me'. Sibling rivalries intensified when, four years on, a brother was born, and proceeded to monopolise her father's affections for many years afterwards. In such circumstances, she makes out, going to school came as a 'tremendous release. I was a different personality there, quite mad and bursting with vitality. There was a library at school, and music, and a chance to act that's always been an enormous satisfaction to me. Learning was fun, and I ate it up.'[11]

It is clear from the recollections of her classmates and teachers that by her early teenage years she was already possessed of a sure theatrical instinct combined with a commanding physical and vocal presence. There were early signals of the urge to parade her knowledge of biological and sexual information generally kept discreet by the conventions of the day. A fellow-pupil of Greer's, at one of her junior convents, recalls her being 'the first person I ever heard say the word "period" out loud'. According to her own account, Greer went on to entertain the nuns at Star of the Sea with her classroom repertoire of precocious wisecracks. It was at this institution, too, that she seems to have acquired a taste — and some of the disciplines — for more formal and conventional kinds of performance. She joined the choir which, drilled by one of the nuns, 'sang everything' — masses, madrigals, musicals — up to four times a week. One of her school-friends recalls Greer's striking appearance as the Major General in *The Pirates of Penzance;* though the character based on Greer in the novel, *Beyond Redemption,* turns up her nose at Gilbert and Sullivan when she fails to win a major part in *The Gondoliers.* Greer also directed a play in her final year, and one of the nuns — a future Mother Superior at Star of the Sea — was to recall more than a decade and a half later 'the brilliance and the maturity of the production, quite amazing in a school girl.'[12]

If not so absorbed in academic disciplines — nearly the whole of her formal education seems to have been subsidised by a succession of hard-to-win scholarships — it is conceivable she might have enjoyed a full-time professional career as a performing artist of some sort. As it is, the two interests have been far from incompatible for her. Her entry to Melbourne University in 1956 gave her an opportunity to develop her burgeoning passion for literature (she claims to have been conversant with four European languages by the time she was twelve); but there was also a thriving student-theatre culture on the campus at the time. Already six feet tall by the time she had left school, she may have been almost too imposing for the run of conventional female roles, but she was a natural for over-the-top comedy and farce. In her first year as an undergraduate she won the part of the prickly spinster, Aunt Sylvia, in the Student Theatre Company production of Noël Coward's *This Happy Breed.* In her final year, 1959, the rigorous demands of her combined honours course in English and French did not deter her from taking on the part of Mrs Antrobus in the Melbourne University Drama Company's production of Thornton Wilder's *The Skin of our Teeth,* as well as all manner of roles and guises in the annual student revue. One critic of the revue, in the student newspaper, *Farrago,* was particularly impressed with her 'strong, musical torch-song-type voice'. She herself turned her hand to theatre criticism in the same newspaper. Reviewing a local production of *King Lear,* she can be found advising the producers that Shakespeare might be better served 'if Australian actors could be educated in the more rhetorical style of acting'. She continued to write theatre criticism for student newspapers when she embarked on her graduate studies at Sydney University in the early 1960s and at Cambridge in the mid-1960s. It is fitting that much of her apprenticeship as a writer and journalist should have been in a theatrical context.[13]

Live stage work, however, was likelier to bring her greater prominence. 'Her Mother Courage at Sydney University was great', the actor, Graeme Blundell, was to recall three and a half decades later. She found her real *métier* in revue. This form of theatre provided a simultaneous showcase for each of those attributes that struck the young Clive James when he over-lapped with Greer both at Sydney and Cambridge: her towering frame (like that of some 'Homeric goddess', as he recalls it) and her 'brilliantly foul tongue'. One of her self-devised sketches that he remembers in partic-ular from their Sydney days was her 'strip-tease nun routine'. It was to be an act he invited her to repeat when they were up at Cambridge together and he was producing the 'smoker' for his (all-male) college there. In a more momentous early blow for women's rights, she became, in 1964, one of the first female members of the university's illustrious revue company, the Footlights. The President of the Footlights at that time, Eric Idle, who had been determined to secure the admission of women during his term of office, observed that there was now 'no need for drag' (one of the com-pany's great traditions): 'Germaine did all that'.[14]

Resolutely thrusting herself on to ever larger stages, it is hardly sur-prising that she should have been attracted to the opportunities for public exposure offered by British television and journalism. She had left Cambridge when a friend from there with connections in the world of the media arranged an audition for her with Granada television in Manchester. On the strength of this she was given a regular spot in an early Kenny Everett series, *Nice Time:* 'a quirky alternative comedy show', as Richard Neville has called it. Neville was making his own idiosyncratic splashes in the world of the British media at the time with his under-ground magazine, *Oz*, and this magazine was to give Greer another arena for exposing her body as well as her mind to public audiences. In the photo session for one of its covers, on which she had been invited to appear, she bared her breasts before a pop star of the day and proceeded to unzip his fly. She made more regular, though hardly less insouciant, appearances inside the magazine's covers, with a series of squibs on a range of contem-porary radical themes: sexuality, drugs, pop music, Women's Lib. The issues were serious, and her tone of address rarely trivialising for all of her cheeky iconoclastic barbs and mischievous titles: 'In Bed with the English',

'The Universal Tonguebath', 'Flip-top legal pot', 'The slag-heap erupts', 'Welcome the shit-storm'. The cheekiness showed a keen sense of how to get an audience engaged with the issues, whether by delighting them or infuriating them. Greer once remarked in *Oz* of this up-front underground world: 'almost everybody has spent a season there'. There are echoes of Rimbaud's 'season in hell' here, but she was perhaps also alluding to the theatrical qualities of this milieu: its zany, exuberant posturings and the largely ephemeral nature of its achievements.[15]

The world of theatre-proper continued to beckon. In 1970, Kenneth Tynan, in his capacity as Literary Manager of London's National Theatre, invited Greer to contribute a programme note for a forthcoming production of *Mrs Warren's Profession,* Bernard Shaw's play about a respectable prostitute and brothel-owner. For the dazzle of his prose when reviewing theatre for the London *Observer* in earlier years, if not for his dandyish clothes and demeanour, Tynan had been something of a legend and model to many young Australian expatriates even before they left their native land. (Barry Humphries, Clive James and Robert Hughes all came under his sway in various ways.) He was also famous for being the first person to say 'fuck' on British television, as early as 1965, and for devising the erotic revue, *Oh! Calcutta!,* which was first staged in the early months of 1970. Now he found himself in the position of having to persuade Greer to cut the four-letter words she had included in her programme note lest they offend some of the National's more conservative patrons. (This was on the instructions of his boss at the theatre, Laurence Olivier.) She fought him on the issue but eventually gave in; and the note duly appeared, under the title, 'A Whore in Every Home'. Less euphemistic than Shaw's own title (Greer roundly chastised the dramatist for his evasiveness about the themes he had raised), it built on the image of the home-as-harem which she had just conjured up in her book title, *The Female Eunuch.* Something of her intuitions about the sexual activities of her own mother, when her father was away from home during the Second World War, might also have been reflected here. It is a trope she still employs, playfully at least; in a recent travel essay she published in *Granta,* she describes the household pets kept by Westerners — including herself — as 'concubines for emotionally inadequate humans'.[16]

In 1973 it was planned that Greer should make an adaptation for the National Theatre of Aristophanes' classic comedy of female revolt, *Lysistrata,* but the venture fell through, reportedly because of casting difficulties. Greer had become quite a close friend of Tynan's by now, though it would be hard for two such prima donnas to sustain a relationship without some friction and sparks. A couple of years later, she was to be among the luminaries whom he invited to contribute sketches to his projected sequel to *Oh! Calcutta!,* but the tensions in their relationship led to a falling-out when she allowed a newspaper to publicise her unfavourable comments on the production.[17]

It must have been difficult to resist more offers from the worlds of show-biz and the showier journalism, but Greer had so far always managed to keep these sorts of activity from impinging on her academic commitments. She had completed both her MA thesis at Sydney (for which she was awarded first class honours) and her doctorate at Cambridge in better-than-average time. She also took on considerable teaching responsibilities. She had been a tutor in the English Department at Sydney University up to the time of her departure from Australia in 1964; and on completing her Cambridge degree in 1967 she was appointed to a lectureship in English at the University of Warwick.[18]

Of the time he had shared digs with her in Cambridge, when she was in the last stages of her doctorate, Clive James remembers the incessant clatter of her typewriter resounding through the thin walls, and the failure of his efforts to distract her with offers of another part in a Footlights revue. Her academic cocoon at this time had its own theatrical qualities, however. By James' account, she worked wonders in transforming these damp, dingy quarters into an Aladdin's cave of plush exotica or the semblance of an eighteenth-century aristocratic salon. Her very name was reminiscent for him of the illustrious *mondaine* of the Napoleonic era, Germaine de Staël.[19]

Teaching necessarily draws on a range of performing skills; though it is doubtful whether many university lecturers have had the 'natural' theatrical attributes of a Germaine Greer or the flair and the bravado to dress them up as daringly as her legend at Warwick suggests. The Afro frizz that occasionally took the place of her customary mane of tresses and the bright green clogs that she was rumoured to sport were hardly means for playing down her imposing height. Her theatrical sense of dress was manifested not just in easy outrageousness; she knew when sobriety was more appropriate for particular settings, yet could make both a poignant and comic effect of it, as when she dropped in on Richard Neville's anarchic habitat in London, while still grinding away at her doctoral labours in libraries, 'wearing a cashmere twinset, a string of pearls, a tartan skirt and a beehive hairdo'. Barry Humphries' Sir Les Patterson has said of himself: 'I'm generally as busy as Germaine Greer's hairdresser, and he'd *have* to be busy'.[20]

It was on a visit to London the year after she submitted her thesis that she was to meet her husband through a mutual friend. The myth (still per-petrated by the likes of Neville) is that Paul Du Feu was a builder's labourer. He was so at the time of their meeting, but if we can trust the tes-timony of his own (now generally forgotten) book of memoirs, he was also awarded a scholarship to study architecture, he had a good degree in English Literature, he could talk with the 'best Oxford accent' and speak French, and he had worked intermittently as a teacher, comic-strip writer, ad-man, gardener, brothel-owner, property speculator, and journalist (writing occasionally and sympathetically on feminist issues). He is rather better known for his agreement — following the break-up of his marriage to Greer — to pose as the first full-frontal male nude in the pages of *Cosmopolitan* magazine. Again, what has been obscured are the more refined tastes and attributes to which he owns in his memoirs — his 'ele-gant clothes and educated vowels'. In one of her own few retrospective references to him, Greer confesses to the abiding *frisson* of his tweeds as well as of his heavy shoulders and commanding height.[21]

In their confident donning (or doffing) of costumes; in their physical and vocal swagger; in their capacity for a wide range of roles: here surely were the bases for as perfect a partnership as Greer might find in con-quering the stages of the world. She and Du Feu clearly saw each other — and the nature of their relationship — in the terms of quite particular per-formances, of actual dramatic scenes from plays or of specific sorts of actors in various parts. They didn't really agree, however, on which parts or on how these might be interpreted. In Greer's case, moreover, it is not so clear that she ever wanted a performing partner for long, however

perfectly matched. A penchant for going solo, amounting to a need, may
be detected in her academic work around this time. In the doctoral thesis
she submitted shortly before her meeting with Du Feu, she pays due
acknowledgment to various advisers on the work but also speaks of her
early resolve to proceed with the project largely on her own. It is another
of those comments, casual enough in their context, that take on a larger
pertinence when considered in the light of her whole sensibility and trajectory in life. 'Aloneness' in other senses (physical and emotional) she has
been increasingly inclined to represent as a great 'luxury', while also
acknowledging that she 'would quite like a husband intermittently'.[22]

The subject of her PhD thesis was the love and marriage 'ethic' in
Shakespeare's early comedies, considered in the light of some contemporary Continental drama on similar themes. She discoursed at length on
The Taming of the Shrew and Shakespeare's concern in that play with the
emotional equilibrium, the balance of loyalties and responsibilities, which
must be established between marital partners. The necessity of this process
in Shakespeare's time, where marriage was the norm and (once entered
into) a *fait accompli*, entailed and justified the taming to which the title
adverted: the bringing to an orderly maturity of the wild-child heroine,
Kate, by the shrewd and sensitive hero, Petruchio. In Kate's energies, properly harnessed, Petruchio sees a fruitful complement to his own energies
— fruitful for both partners, and for the equanimity of their relationship.
By marrying her, he offers her the chance to emancipate herself from her
self-destructive perversities. This was the burden of the play and the point
of the taming, Greer suggested. Hers was far from being one of those read-
ings which take the text at face value as a description — or prescription —
of wifely submission.[23]

When she recommended her own husband to read the play — as he
thought, 'to pick up hints on how to deal with her' — it might have been
helpful if she had given him her thesis as a guide to her own interpretation.
If she was inclined to cast herself and Du Feu in the roles of Kate and
Petruchio, it was with the ideal of their ultimate state of equilibrium in view,
and in their case, this involved at least a partial reversal of roles, whereby
she would come to do much of the taming. It is 'impossible for superiors
and inferiors to love', Greer was to remark in retrospect, defining love as

'unconditional tenderness'. By her account, Du Feu started laying down too many conditions almost as soon as their wedding had taken place, such as the amount of time she should be spending with him. She had her own conditions, too, he pointed out. These conditions may simply have been that she should have some freedoms as well as responsibilities within the marriage, but it is clear that there was a considerable clash (if not a *dis*equilibrium) of expectations, and that the marriage foundered on this. Even so, three weeks still seems an inordinately short time in which to have given this version of the Kate/Petruchio match any chance of reaching its ideal.[24]

Du Feu himself had envisaged Greer in more modern roles during the days of their courtship: her 'slight shifts of expression' were 'like a face in a movie close-up'; the 'flick of her head' could turn her 'into the wisecracking heroine of a 30's Hollywood comedy'. (Might he have had in mind, one wonders, Tracy Lord, the Kate-figure in Philip Barry's *The Philadelphia Story*, filmed in 1940?) She 'talked and clowned and enchanted me … Christ, it's great to meet someone who entertains you'. This attitude may have been part of that 'rejoic[ing] in each other's presence' which Greer later identified with true equality in a relationship; but without hearing anything about her response to him on this occasion, it might already have been nearer to that condescension which she found inimical. Whatever the case, by the time the marriage was coming to an end, Greer was still performing, according to Du Feu's recollection, but the performance had now reduced itself to what he called 'posturing': 'She told me how she would like to have two or three children by different fathers (but none by me) … I noted that her actions did not always tally with her flamboyant words'.[25] In the very brevity of its 'season', it might be tempting to see Greer's marriage as a kind of experimental performance in which some of the ideas for her first major book, *The Female Eunuch,* were conceived or tried out. There was nothing quite so calculated about either; although the impact of the marriage is palpably registered in the book, and there are some suggestive analogies with performance in the book's own genesis, arguments and presentation.

Her literary agent had first come up with the idea for the book as a suitable follow-up to Greer's television series, now that that show had finished its run. It was soon to be the fiftieth anniversary of the granting of female suffrage in England in 1918. By her own account, Greer lost her temper at the suggestion of memorialising (even by way of criticism) what had turned out in her view to be such a political non-event. It took an Indian publisher-friend she had known at Cambridge, Sonny Mehta, to encourage her to put this rage to use, and to embark on a study that would expressly concern itself with the relative powerlessness of women in their sexual and domestic arrangements for all the advances in their political status. It must not, he hinted, be an academic study, of the sort she was used to writing for university literature departments. As she herself soon realised, if it was to reach wider audiences of women who didn't have much spare time for reading, the book required of her an altogether snappier mode of presentation and tone of voice, closer to the style of her outrageous appearances in the underground press. It was a book *of* outrage: an exposé, a jeremiad, a manifesto.[26]

At the same time, it still contrived to be a dazzling show of Greer's erudition in fields far beyond her academic specialism. The sources she assembled, quoted, and assiduously documented drew extensively on her formal training in English literature, but they also reflected a confident command of the works of several other kinds of scholar from a range of disciplines — anatomists, psychologists, anthropologists, sociologists, criminologists, philosophers, historians and political theorists. *The Female Eunuch* was her first parade — there have been several more subsequently — of eclectic intellectual enthusiasms dating back over her whole life.

The book first appeared in England in October 1970. The period of its final drafting and editing coincided with the vigorous protests of radical students at Warwick and at various other campuses in Britain against the universities' administrative bodies. These battles were occasioned by local grievances, but they derived some of their fervour from the example of French intellectuals, who had joined with workers to battle against their government in the streets of Paris in May 1968, and of American students protesting against their country's involvement in the Vietnam War. Avowed radicals on the staff of English universities, such as Greer herself, generally identified themselves with the students' cause.[27]

The opening chapter of *The Female Eunuch* floated the idea that in time of 'Revolution' women 'ought not to enter into socially sanctioned relationships, like marriage, and that once unhappily in them they ought not to scruple to run away'. They may even be 'deliberately promiscuous' and certainly 'should be self-sufficient and consciously refrain from establishing exclusive dependencies and other kinds of neurotic symbioses'. 'Revolution' here is more likely a reference to a hoped-for global phenomenon of the future than to the dramatic but desultory displays of political ardour in the West over the past few years. Greer was to insist not long after that the 'communal vision' of sexual and family arrangements that she outlined in the book was 'a dream', as unconnected to any actual practices in the modern world as were the forms of communist anarchism she felt should provide the basis for all economic and political arrangements. But there can be no doubt that the substance of this vision was partly a reaction to the experience of her own personal battles in marriage in the recent past.[28]

In discoursing here on marriage and its trials, it was characteristic that the example she invoked should have been a married couple in a play — though a very different couple from Shakespeare's Kate and Petruchio, and in very different circumstances. It is Nora and Torvald Helmer at the end of Ibsen's *A Doll's House,* when Nora has decided to quit her marriage partly because of the very securities and comforts which it has offered and which she now sees as a crippling constraint on the development of her individuality. These 'approved buttresses', as Greer labels them — 'legality, security, permanence' — are what has threatened to turn Nora, representing all bourgeois wifehood, into the doll of Ibsen's title. Greer's own term for this condition, 'eunuch', is yet more dramatic.[29]

Calling her book *The Female Eunuch* confirms her talent for grabbing an audience's attention which had been evident in the titling of her articles for the underground press. Greer had been taken by the application of the metaphor, 'eunuch', to American blacks in Eldridge Cleaver's civil rights campaigns of the 1960s. Hers was certainly not the only book to catch what she had called in one of those articles 'the 1969 second wave of women's liberation movements'. Neither did it represent the most extreme tendencies of these movements. She openly eschewed the 'most radical and most elite' brands of feminism, with their highly theorised and absolutist views on men as the eternal enemy and their view of all heterosexual intercourse as a form of male rape. Her book, however, was to create the widest sensation, as far as coverage in the world press and other media was concerned; and the legends of its personal inspiration for the mass of ordinary women outside any specially committed feminist elite soon began to spread, continuing to this day.[30]

There had been some more moderate precursors in the 1960s which had attracted large international sales. The most notable of these works was Betty Friedan's *The Feminine Mystique,* first published in 1963. With its pitch directed mainly at professional middle-class women, its tacit equation of sexuality with wifehood and motherhood, and its goal of mere 'equality of opportunity within the status quo', Friedan's book was easily dismissed by Greer as 'not at all radical'.[31]

The end of the 1960s and the beginning of the 1970s produced an extraordinarily bountiful crop of feminist gospels, of varying degrees of radicalism: Juliet Mitchell's *Women's Estate,* Kate Millett's *Sexual Politics,* Shulamith Firestone's *The Dialectic of Sex,* Ann Oakley's *Sex, Gender and Society,* and Eva Figes' *Patriarchal Attitudes.* While all of them are now recognised classics of the genre, none quite achieved the *succès de scandale* of Greer's book at the time. Surveying their titles you can begin to understand why. You might enticingly call a university course in women's studies after any one of them, but it is hard to imagine how they could ever become a political slogan or a household name. Greer's 'Female Eunuch' had the power to become both. Its resonating force is registered (however palely) in the title chosen for a general onslaught on the feminist gospels — Greer's, and most of the others listed above — written by Arianna Stassinopoulos in 1973: *The Female Woman.* We have grown too accustomed to it now to appreciate how curious, how distinctive, how arresting Greer's own title must once have sounded, yet also how graphically precise it was in what it signalled. The book's jacket, sporting a rubberised female torso with straps at the top and side-handles around the upper thighs, was every bit as confronting.

These are the attention-getting qualities of some of the most successful advertisements in the press or on television, and it has been easy for chroniclers of the book's fortunes to document the canny complicity of these media in allowing *The Female Eunuch* and its author rather more publicity space than was accorded any of her fellow-propagandists in the feminist cause. Greer's striking physical attributes and her ready tongue, already deployed to such stylish effect in a range of public arenas, must have made it difficult *not* to single her out. The very sound of her name has a stylish theatrical ring: not quite as exotic as Firestone's or Figes' or Stassinopoulos', but less of a mouthful, and with a similar alliterative lilt to Greer Garson's — if not directly echoing the film-star's name. (Germaine de Staël's name and fame were too remote to have had a comparable echo effect for all but the most literate twentieth-century reader.) In an article in the *Bulletin* of 1982, in which he took Greer to task for her continual put-downs of Australia and paeans to England, Max Harris wittily played on the associations of her name with that of the Hollywood actress. He also predicted that Greer would take on something of the aura of the actress's most famous screen role: 'What we have seen … is the Garsoning of Greer. The youthful wildcat intellectual … will turn in her maturity into the Mrs Miniver of the Home Counties'. This shows some prescience. In Greer's present 'role' as the worldly-wise, charity-dispensing, Anglophiliac matriarch of Mill Farm, in Essex, there *are* odd touches of the Garson character in the 1942 film of *Mrs Miniver*. But how far has she relinquished the more feral qualities of her youth?[32]

Alert as she was to the opportunities as well as the dangers of media attention, the young Greer was not above exploiting the promotion machine put at her disposal as vigorously as it was exploiting her. Whether this was in the service of the feminist cause, or of her own book and personal reputation, we can't judge with any certainty. These things are not easily separable in Greer's case. Writing in the book itself, prior to any of the promotion for it, Greer had been emphatic about the disservice that many feminists did their cause in shrinking from the glare of media attention. The self-styled radicals were the worst in this respect, harping on the necessity of academic analysis and theory. What use was sitting alone in your university office or communing with your fellow-cognoscenti in cosy seminar rooms? True revolutionary life might be more than just a cabaret, but it necessarily partook of some of the qualities — disciplines as well as joys — of public entertainment. It was a 'festival of the oppressed', and any effective leaders of the women's revolution should be at the head of the promenade, putting as much work into flaunting as refining the movement's ideas, in whatever market-place was available. 'No publicity is still bad publicity'.[33]

While still on the staff at Warwick University, Greer visited America in the northern spring of 1971, to join in the celebrations and promotional activities organised for the book's release there in April. It was her first brush with the country which had invented the star system, and she was less reticent about submitting herself to its mechanisms than some of America's own stalwarts of the women's movement. She was invited not just as the guest but to take over as the host on a popular television chat-show, usually compered by Dick Cavett. One of the country's literary megastars, Norman Mailer, had issued an invitation to leading local feminists (including Kate Millett) as well as to Greer, to debate publicly with him the issues of women's roles and rights. The venue was to be the aptly-named 'Theatre of Ideas', housed in the New York Town Hall. Millett and various others turned down the invitation. Greer accepted, and couldn't be persuaded to renege when some of her political sisters tried to persuade her to do so.[34]

Other women had agreed to appear on the platform that evening — Jackie Cellabos, President of the New York chapter of the National Organization for Women; the comedian and writer, Jill Johnston; and one of the *grandes dames* of American literary criticism, Diana Trilling — but none attracted as much attention as Greer. It was she, Mailer acknowledged at the outset, who had 'done a great deal to fill the house'. Judging from a film that was made of the proceedings (entitled *Town Bloody Hall,* after a phrase Greer had used during question-time), she fully played up to the role of an up-and-coming international star. In starkest contrast to Johnston, all in denim, Greer was to be seen in an elegantly slinky long black dress, with a fox fur stole draped over one of her otherwise bared shoulders. The fur was nonchalantly tossed aside when she got up to speak. This ensemble was 'worn for fun and satire', she later claimed; but 'the humourless and unsophisticated New York press' lapped up the outward image of sexy luxury. When Norman Mailer announced her as the 'young, formidable lady writer, Germaine Greer, from England', she did not bother to correct this half-truth; and although the punctilious flutings of her voice, as recorded on the film soundtrack, don't quite represent 'the true accent of Cambridge (England)' which the American press ascribed to her, they were rather more English-sounding than the 'Australian/English/ American hybrid accent' that she ascribed to herself on this occasion.[35]

It was not till Johnston directly asked her 'Were you born in Australia?' that she acknowledged anything of her origins. Such details were hardly relevant to the case she was arguing on this occasion, but it was shrewd of Johnston to suggest the strong element of performance in Greer's self-presentation. Manhattan's *Village Voice* did so in more explicit and conventional terms when, in describing Greer's appearance at the Theatre of Ideas, it hailed the possessor of 'so silky an accent, so drawing room a gown, so smart a vocabulary, so exuberant an auburn hairdo, so stylish a stage persona'.[36]

Greer had taken the stage after Cellabos, announcing herself as 'also a feminist'. No surprises there. Having a dig at Mailer, perhaps, while also alluding to the research she was doing for her book on women painters, *The Obstacle Race,* Greer went on to say that 'for me the significance of the moment is that I am having to confront one of the most powerful figures in my own imagination, the being, I think, most privileged in male elitist societies, namely the masculine artist'. This figure, Greer argued, was possibly 'more a killer than a creator' — a type to whose ego 'lesser talents' were all too easily sacrificed. What is surprising here is the degree to which she foreshadows her arguments, not just in *The Obstacle Race,* but in the recent *Slip-Shod Sibyls,* which supposedly turns against the earlier book. There is not only the assumption or assertion that women have been 'lesser talents' in creative fields. There is not only the attack on men or a male-dominated culture for encouraging the eclipse of such talents, for compounding the misfortunes of the female artist. There is also the attack on her own sex for being complicit in their misfortune. 'No woman yet', Greer told her New York audience in 1971, 'has yet been loved for her poetry ... and we love men for their achievements all the time ... Sylvia Plath's greatest poems were sometimes conceived while she was baking bread. She was such a perfectionist and ultimately such a fool'.[37]

Greer's taste of international success on a public stage may have provided her with the confidence — as the sales of *The Female Eunuch* certainly provided her with the means — to quit her lecturing job at

Warwick University. She resigned from there in 1972. She now also had the freedom and the means to live where and as she chose. London remained an obvious base in England for the freelance journalistic and broadcasting work which increasingly came her way. She could now often be heard on various panel shows on BBC radio, she reviewed books for the *Spectator*, and she started writing a regular column for the *Sunday Times*, as well as continuing to contribute to the alternative press, notably the Amsterdam-based 'sex paper', *Suck*.[38]

As a retreat from the public eye the Italian countryside most readily suggested itself, as she had spent three happy and productive months in a Calabrian village just before the submission of her doctoral thesis. There was also a sense of ancestral affinity, as her mother had been of partial Italian extraction. It was to be to a valley in Tuscany — a popular haunt of other distinguished Australian expatriates, including David Malouf and the painter, Jeffrey Smart — that she eventually repaired, choosing a little farmhouse there with enough surrounding land to indulge her passion for gardening. Even on these domestic pursuits she was prone to invite the gaze of an audience.[39]

From her youthful days with the alternative press in London (and continuing until very recently, with the regular spot she was given in the *Oldie*), Greer developed the role of a sardonic garden-columnist, who became known familiarly as 'Rose Blight'. Under this witch-like persona, she took special relish in rehearsing the grimnesses and frustrations of trying to maintain a garden in a dreary climate like London's, while at the same time showing off her arcane knowledge of horticulture's more grotesque byways. The collection of some of these writings which she eventually published, entitled *The Revolting Garden*, constitutes a brilliant sort of 'anti-herbal' for modern times. It is also the most substantial monument we have to the brilliance of her talents as a comic, whether in rattling off one-liners on particular botanical specimens (the 'Shiitake': 'no relation presumably of the Piisstake') or more extended set pieces, such as her hymn to 'The Toad' ('like all nice people, toads make love just after they have woken up, which happens once a year … after a hug lasting several days') or her lecture on 'The Lawn' ('A good lawn is a sign of neurosis triumphant, and obeisance to the mind police').[40]

Gardening was never to become a central preoccupation, for all that she complained to David Plante, one of her visitors in Tuscany, of the time taken away from her writing by the cares of property. The main point in extricating herself from the routines of English teaching in a provincial university was not to retire to an even remoter backwater but to advance her career as a publicist for feminism. To an interviewer from *Playboy* magazine, who visited her in Tuscany in 1972, she stated that 'my life's work is to make the feminist position more and more comprehensible to more and more people'. Strutting her stuff in popular men's magazines like *Playboy* was itself a part of this venture: 'My role is to preach to the unconverted ... exposing myself to the worst kinds of prejudice and antagonism and doing my best to discredit them'. Up to the mid-1970s at least she also devoted considerable periods of her time to attending various international conferences relating to women's issues, and reporting on their proceedings for a range of prominent newspapers or periodicals in Britain as well as America. If she had not already taken a centre-stage position with *The Female Eunuch,* of course, it is unlikely that such reports would have been commissioned or accepted from her. At least as much as her subject matter or ideas, she was now unfailingly good copy. Germaine Greer the character, as well as leading performer, in the historic dramas of feminism was fully launched; though its development was probably less under her own control than the persona of 'Rose Blight'.[41]

In the second half of the 1970s, she had clearly preserved sufficient independence and time to make steady progress on *The Obstacle Race.* Her Tuscan habitat provided a particularly convenient and conducive base for completing this book. As well as documenting the various restrictions to the freedom and opportunities of women artists, Greer was also attempting a critical assessment of their work, their techniques, and their iconography. While she extended her hunt for source materials to museums and archives all over the world, the bulk of the research institutions she used for her studies were in Italy.[42] The works surveyed dated back to the early Renaissance, and the artists concerned were mainly European (many of them, again, Italian).

The Obstacle Race confronted its audience with a large cast of real-life historical characters in another show of dense erudition. Too large and too dense: even Greer herself confessed to 'a feeling of vertigo about this book' when she looked back on it the year after it was published.[43] The parade of case studies in frustrated creativity is in danger at times of lapsing into a rather desultory catalogue, unrelieved on the whole by the withering asides and swanking personal anecdotes that we find in *The Female Eunuch* or by any of the mordant patter of *The Revolting Garden.*

As with so much of her writing, however, *The Obstacle Race* provides some arresting if tangential insights into the course of Greer's own career as a historical character or performer. Commenting on Artemesia Gentileschi, for instance, she remarks of the seventeenth-century Roman painter:

> The retired life of women was an impossibility for her and so she lived aggressive, independent and exposed, forcing herself into the postures of self-promotion, facing down gossip, and working, working with a seriousness that few other women ever permitted themselves to feel.

Here is a somewhat more positive and sympathetic view of a fellow self-promoter than she was to take of any of the sexual radicals of the nineteenth and earlier twentieth centuries. There is a sense of the irresistible and ineluctable pressures which occasion such postures, both from within an individual and from without; though it is significant that Greer should still choose the word 'posture', with its negative connotations. There is an echo here of the charge of posturing which her own husband had brought against *her* when describing the last phase of their brief marriage. She echoes it again in her highly critical account of the poet, Marina Tsvetaeva, in *Slip-Shod Sibyls.*[44]

In speaking of herself, Greer can be at least as equivocal as when she is delivering judgments on others. 'I'm against the cult of personality', she had told the *Playboy* interviewer back in 1972, 'but I think we have to use whatever weapons we've got. And I have always been a personality'. Later in the same interview she claimed: 'That's my problem. I'm an individualist but I'm not proud of my individualism'.[45]

Greer's equivocation in such instances, her feelings of ambivalence, suggest a more illuminating way of understanding her career and thought than the talk of inconsistency, self-contradiction, betrayal, hypocrisy. While she doesn't expressly, even consciously, identify the posturings of her historical characters with her own inclinations, she is certainly alert elsewhere to the tendency of writers, critics and artists to make covert autobiography out of their subjects — talking about themselves while appearing to talk (often quite critically) of others.[46] When she went on, in *Sex and Destiny,* to berate the likes of Mrs Besant, Marie Stopes and Margaret Sanger for their promotional antics, her judgments might be said to show her up not so much in a hypocritical as a self-critical mood. From her own experience, she has known not only the pressure (psychological, social, economic) that can lead to such role-playing and posturing; she can also appreciate the constructive uses of these strategies, especially for a woman. But she is equally sensitive to their limitations and excesses.

At their most constructive, they are part of a process of escaping oppressive social conventions. In her doctoral thesis Greer expressly commends the heroine of *The Taming of the Shrew* for striving to escape other people's expectations and interpretations of her behaviour. Greer's own trajectory represents a series of escapes — or 'bolts', to use her expression — as much as a succession of performances. Because the processes involved in escaping and performing are so closely related in her case, it is not surprising that she has been every bit as equivocal about the effectiveness of the escape strategy — fully awake to its limitations as well as to its opportunities. In *The Female Eunuch* she specifically cautions young women who 'dream of acting as a way out' of some of the problems facing their sex.[47] As further study of Greer's own development confirms, one of the inherent hazards of the escapee's existence is that of being returned to captivity in some new or former shape. There can be little rest for the bolter.

As she recalls, Greer first dreamt of escaping her family home in the Melbourne suburbs from about the age of twelve. She would escape to Europe — not such a vague or fanciful notion in view of her already blossoming talents in French, German and Italian. 'I decided that Australia and I were both deprived. It was boring.' Her home offered what material comforts were affordable on a single middle-class income of the day. Her father had gone back to a steady desk job with a newspaper advertising agency following his war service, while her mother had given up the chance of a career as a photographic model to raise the family. But for such a precociously gifted teenager as Greer was shaping up to be, the outward bourgeois decencies, the 'even tenor' of suburban life, became an offence when unmatched, unrelieved, by any stimuli for the life of the mind. Hers was a home, she has repeatedly claimed, that was virtually devoid of books, paintings, musical instruments.[48]

Immediate escape to Europe was an impossibility, except in fantasies; but while waiting to find the means to realise those fantasies she lit on a number of interim escape hatches. While offering only temporary, half-adequate retreats, of the sort that would eventually require to be escaped from themselves, there are enough of them recorded in her scattered recollections to raise some questions about her more dismissive generalisations concerning Australia as a whole. Even the environment of her childhood home, it emerges, wasn't quite as colourless as she is usually inclined to suggest.

In the world of books, where she found her first escape, 'there was wine, conversation, nights at the opera, ecstasy, despair, Chopin and Liszt' — a heady romantic concoction that accentuated as it relieved the monotony of her everyday home environment. But there seems to have been no want of opportunity for this sort of escape, and its associated pleasures were not always so vicarious. Greer has recorded that her mother served to introduce her to the world of opera by taking her to a film of *Il Trovatore;* thereafter, she says, 'I decided that this was the scale of passion on which people should live their lives'. Judging from the observations of others, Greer's mother, however philistine, settled little more for conventional suburban respectability than her daughter did. In 1971 a schoolfriend from Star of the Sea days remembers going to visit Greer on one occasion and finding her mother 'prancing around the house in black leotards with this mane of flying red hair. THAT wasn't being middle class if you go back 20 odd years'.[49]

There was a near neighbour in Greer's suburb who happened to have a house full of pianos. He tuned them for a living, and when he met Greer, around the time she was thirteen, he offered to teach her to read music so that she could accompany herself while rehearsing her singing for choir at school. Twenty years later, she was to devote one of her columns in the *Sunday Times* to a fond memoir of this man.[50]

Greer's memoir of her schooldays at Star of the Sea is full of appreciative comment on what the nuns did to introduce her to the study of art and architecture as well as music. By this account, the nuns also managed to satisfy her cravings for 'spiritual values'. 'Just not *their* spiritual values', she stresses. Her mother had been brought up a Catholic and also educated at a convent school; her father, she thought at the time, might be at least partly Jewish, although she was to discover later, when she went about tracking down his origins, that he had been of Anglican stock. He had had to take instruction in the Catholic faith when courting her mother; but in their day-to-day lives, neither parent set an example of any religious commitment. The nuns, on the other hand, were over-committed, by virtue of their unquestioning belief in an absolute deity and their adherence to the rules and dogma of an institution. These were the sorts of constraint which a compulsive escapee could hardly abide for long. Before she had left school she had decided she was an atheist.[51]

She recalls how she had 'loved the way the nuns looked', though her images of them are typically equivocal: 'a gang of mad women in flapping black habits'; 'beautiful, really elegant'. She might be seen to have been divesting herself of any lingering attraction even to their costumes — literally divesting herself — in her striptease-nun act of later celebrity. According to the record, however, it was not a total strip in the manner of her breast-bearing on the covers of *Oz*. This was itself symbolic, perhaps, of her ambivalent feelings about her religious upbringing. *The Madwoman's Underclothes* was to be the title she chose for her collected journalistic pieces up to 1985; and while it contains only a couple of direct (and playful) references to her 'convent education', implicit vestiges of this are to be found throughout the volume, most notably in the passionate tone with which she takes her old faith to task for some of its attitudes and policies, especially in matters of sex. But Protestantism comes off even worse in this department, it should be noted. Moreover, for all her criticism of Catholic beliefs and attitudes, she retains throughout an admiration for the nuns' communal way of life, which she sees as a standing rebuke to the materialistic values of ordinary domestic life in the suburbs.[52]

School still had its boring or onerous moments — maths lessons, games — but she could satisfy her intellectual appetites undistracted by escaping from the suburbs to the great domed reading-room of the Public Library of Victoria, situated in central Melbourne: 'my Valhalla', as she has deemed it. The city itself appears to have offered few other pleasures for her, but here was a structure that offered some prevision of the longed-for Europe. Not only was its architectural design modelled on that of the British Museum's Reading Room; it also boasted one of the richest collections of nineteenth- and twentieth-century publications in the Empire. Here, too, was a home away from no-home, a public arena that provided privacy, an escape-hatch that didn't demand — indeed, would have discouraged — any performing antics.[53]

'Home is an illusion', she was to entitle one of her columns in the *Guardian* (her most regular performing space of recent years until she bolted from that too, when her fellow-columnist, Suzanne Moore, offended her by spreading Richard Neville's story about her alleged hysterectomy). 'If you believe there is a place where you belong you'll break your heart looking for it … I regard the happiest day of my life as the day I ran away from home. It was a long day, because I didn't stop running till I fetched up in Europe.' Yet it is the memories of her labours in her home-town library, rekindled on a return visit early in 1987 when carrying out the research for a book on her father, that produced the following reverie not far into that book:

> So the habit of a lifetime was formed … My dream was to live in this heavenly building … Libraries are reservoirs of strength, grace and wit, reminders of order, calm and continuity, lakes of mental energy … *In any library in the world, I am at home, unselfconscious, still and absorbed.*[54]

A brisk ten-minute walk north of the Public Library brings you to the University of Melbourne, founded around the same time, and still the city's only university when Greer first enrolled there in the mid-1950s. 'I knew it was going to be mine', she recalled in an interview with Clyde Packer nearly thirty years later; and yet a little later in the same interview she says, 'I knew it was second rate'. There are several apparent inconsistencies, even self-contradictions, in her account of the place, though it usually turns out that she is talking of different phases, different facets, of her time there, and some degree of equivocation is inevitable in view of the range of her experiences, both personal and intellectual.[55]

Commuting to the university on a daily basis offered further opportunities for at least a partial escape from the dreariness of her suburban home; the family had by this time moved from Sandringham to Mentone (just a couple of stations down the track from Highett, where Edna Everage, it should be remembered, was 'dying to try it' a few years later). The dreariness was only rubbed in, however, by the train journey in the 'deep, intractable seaside cold' of Melbourne's winter. She even remembers, with a shudder, the gaberdine raincoat she had to wear: nothing beautiful or elegant like the nuns' habits at school, but 'the current version of academic subfusc, dignified, drab and clerkly'. Greer was to make a couple of abortive attempts to leave home altogether during those years. Campus cultural life, as we have seen, offered unprecedented opportunities for the budding performer in her, a chance to escape from any kind of uniform into the more exciting dress-ups of the stage. The university milieu was also conducive (in a way her school could never have been) to making male friends, some of whom were to become the first in her succession of lovers.[56]

By her second year, at least, she was openly flouting any Catholic or bourgeois exhortations of the day to virginity. If, as Philip Larkin quips of England, 'sexual intercourse was invented in 1963', Greer was yet more radical for her young days than she likes to boast — clearly a leader of some extraordinary antipodean avant-garde seeking escape from the sexual inhibitions and prohibitions of the past. Writing in *Sex and Destiny* of 1967, the year she was first in Italy finishing off her doctorate, she noted she was already then 'a veteran of ten years' campaigning for sexual freedom'. She pushes this date back even further in her memoirs of her convent school where she notes, 'I began arguing against sexual guilt and hypocrisy while I was still a virgin. I mean that's a very nun-like thing to do'. What some of her recent critics have seen as an about-face on questions of sexual freedom in *Sex and Destiny* may be traced to much earlier equivocations during the years of her sexual apprenticeship. The one thing the nuns didn't do, she recalls of them at school, was to 'take sex for granted'. 'It's been an ongoing disappointment in my life', she continues, 'that other people don't give it that much importance'. And yet if she has always tended to emulate (or at least admire) the nuns in their regard for sex as 'something extremely powerful and holy', she differed from them early on in their more negative valuations of sex considered as a sin. They gave 'the distinct impression that sex is worse than stealing or lying or violence or cruelty', and she could never accept this.[57]

On any scale, one of the more unfortunate episodes of her sexual apprenticeship at university was the time she was raped by a fellow-student and fellow-member of her former faith. In her *Guardian* column, nearly forty years after the event, she rehearsed the scene and its aftermath in graphic detail, arguing that no rape victims ought to feel ashamed or reticent now about coming forth in this manner, and should not even baulk at publicising their attacker's identity, where they know it. Such a strategy, she claimed, may be a quicker and more effective form of redress than due processes of law. The international press, and stringent critics of her outburst from all sides, served to focus further recent attention on this incident and her attitudes to it. Some conservative male pundits suggested that it might be nothing more than a story to spice up her column, or a self-dramatising invention for dubious polemical purposes. Female lobby groups such as 'Women against Rape' lamented that the author of *The Female Eunuch* was now serving to undermine the legal advances made by the women's movement.[58]

There are no grounds for any suggestion that Greer has simply made up the whole incident on the spur of the moment. There is a self-dramatising element in Greer's reporting of it, but the only element of invention lies in the impression she gives that she is revealing the incident for the first time, and drawing fresh lessons from it. Her friends and acquaintances at Melbourne University seem to have been apprised of some such incident almost immediately afterwards. She publicly referred to it, if only in a throw-away line, some fourteen years later, in her *Playboy* interview of 1972. This was in the context of expounding her belief that rape in itself (compared to other crimes like murder) was not a 'terribly serious' crime, or that the most serious aspect of it was not its sexual but its violent nature, and that 'it is irritating that a woman can get redress only with great difficulty'. In the interview she had with Clyde Packer, published in 1984, there was a much longer account of the rape scene, as vivid as the one in the *Guardian* eleven years later, though the details were not completely identical. She also proclaimed here that when it came to sexual matters she believed in 'kicking ass and taking names, talking loud and drawing a crowd'. Editing the collection of her journalism a couple of years on, she recalled that as early as 1969, while working with the alternative press, she had tried to insist on 'naming names in sex news'.[59]

If the way in which she has recently rehearsed her own experience of rape has been at risk of undermining the work of women's law-reform groups, it is certainly not through any inconsistency with her previous positions, and it is quite consonant with the more anarchistic, anti-respectable strains in *The Female Eunuch*. Her avowed attitudes to rape and suggested solutions have also kept pretty true to those early equivocations about sex, going back to her schooldays, as something neither trivial enough to be a mere sport nor serious enough to be made a matter of institutional discipline and general dread. Greer's shock tactics in enunciating her position and her success in getting a rise out of her audience are as consistent in their way as the positions themselves, an integral part of them even. The compulsive urge to make a spectacle of herself has only gone on increasing perhaps because it has met with such encouragement (however unwitting) from vociferous critics as well as more forbearing sympathisers.

She might have made less of a spectacle of her rape at the time it happened not only because there was less of an audience but also because she had (as she saw it then) more serious things to worry about at Melbourne University. She was deeply equivocal about what she was learning and how it was being taught. Formal classes and curricula appear to have been as much a bind for her in their merits as in their deficiencies, and the need to escape or move beyond them was strong from the start. The French programme at Melbourne was plainly inadequate for her, but the English one (judged in the light of subsequent experience elsewhere) was 'as good as that offered at any university in the world'. It was too good: impressive to the extent of being oppressive. She singles out Sam Goldberg, already something of a legend as the chief purveyor of F. R. Leavis' literary and pedagogical gospels in Australia, among the several 'very good' teachers that she remembers from that period. Their influence was so strong that she found herself hosting an 'anti-seminar, maintaining ideas that ran counter to theirs'. It was known as the 'Alternative Seminar' at the time, and as recalled by another of its members, Chris Wallace-Crabbe, it was a social gathering over flagons of wine, cheese, bread and kabana, in which the members of the Honours class rediscussed the morning's topic without the presence of the staff. This was an occasion of both release and intellectual development, which generated great camaraderie.[60]

In the last year of her degree, Greer found herself a further escape-hatch or 'release' from the constraints of her home town when she took off to Sydney for a while. Some members of 'The Push', who were on a visit to Melbourne, persuaded her to return with them. Barry Humphries, Clive James, Robert Hughes were all drawn into the web of this legendary Sydney coterie for a while; but Greer was to become more absorbed in its activities than any of them. She was impressed both with the intellectual rigour of its discussions and its libertarian philosophy of life; she also fell under the spell of one of its leading lights, Roelof Smilde, with whom she was to have an affair. He could have been a brilliant student, but had jibbed at formal academic constraints, dropped out of university early, and chosen to be a wharf labourer. (Greer clearly had a *tendresse* for proletarians with intellectual pretensions — or vice versa — as her marriage to Paul Du Feu later confirmed. They offered at least the fantasy of an escape from her own class.) The philosophy of The Push 'was all against getting one's degree', she remembers, but she decided to return temporarily to Melbourne to sit her final exams. The scholar in Greer has remained as important a part of her self-identity as the libertarian in her.[61]

Partly owing to difficulties with the French component in her BA, she did not take first-class honours, but she gained a creditable enough degree to qualify for postgraduate study in English Literature. She took the opportunity to leave Melbourne, and enrolled for her Masters at the University of Sydney, where she could follow her scholarly interests while at the same time consolidating her relationships with The Push. She threw herself vigorously into the group's diverse social, intellectual and creative activities, as well as keeping up her active interests in the theatre. Within a couple of years she also managed to produce her MA thesis, which was on Byron, and for this she was to be awarded the 'First' that had eluded her in her BA degree.[62]

The Romantic poet has remained a hero of hers, as much for his sexual iconoclasm as for his literary achievement. In *The Change*, her recent book on women and the menopause, she has occasion to refer to Byron at a number of points. 'Truly irreverent' she dubs him there, and claims that he was 'genuinely interested in women as people and aware of the fundamental gravity of the woman question'. When it was only being whispered about, he had dared bring up the subject of menopause in one of his poems (just as the pubescent Greer had broken down taboos at school by bringing up the subject of menstruation). The question of Byron's treatment of the women in his own life has never been one to detain her. In her thesis of thirty years earlier, she concentrated mainly on his works, in which she saw enshrined a number of 'values' associated with irreverence: a protest against cant, and a promotion of pleasure, spontaneity and good humour.[63]

Choosing Byron as a subject for her MA thesis was something of an act of irreverence in itself, an escape from the values of her mentors, both at school and university. In her memoirs of a Catholic girlhood in inter-war America, Mary McCarthy gives us the measure of the Church's attitudes to him when she recounts how one of the nuns in her convent school had taken her to task for being 'just like Lord Byron, brilliant but unsound'. Byron was no great favourite of the Leavisites either. In his study of English poetry, *Revaluations,* Leavis had relegated Byron's work to a short 'note', declaring that 'the very essence of his manner is a contemptuous defiance of decorum and propriety' and that such 'irreverence moves towards a burlesque comedy that … is sometimes schoolboy'. Greer challenged Leavis' strictures, and those of many other critics, not just through a defence of Byron's values but by a closely-researched study of his poetic models (mainly Italian ones) and his poetic forms and methods. Her discussion of these subjects was dauntingly austere and technical at times.[64]

It is surprising, then, but consistent with herself, to find her signing off a television programme she made on Sydney nearly two decades later with the remark that she could never stay there long or her brain would turn to mush. After a hymn to the pleasures of the city's climate, topography, architecture and easy sociability, it was a dramatically arresting change of tune issuing from a master of the dramatic. The sense, too, that escape might be necessary from good things as much as bad conforms with a general pattern in her life. She expressed her equivocations about Sydney in a rather less stark fashion when interviewed by a local journalist during the making of the film: 'People here are amazingly rich in their life styles, and it is a land of lotus eaters; but, while a tremendous sense of wellbeing exists, the people become less and less curious about things'.[65]

The opportunity for escaping Sydney came in the shape of a Commonwealth Scholarship to Newnham College, Cambridge, awarded partly on the basis of her MA thesis. Here, too, were the means of realising her long-cherished fantasies of living in Europe. There was a method in her scholarly obsessiveness; it *paid* for her escapes. But there was a genuine passion and sense of intellectual commitment behind it too. Within a few months of arriving in Cambridge, Greer was bridling under the constraints of having to do another undergraduate degree (and one that she found quite inferior in the quality of its intellectual training to her Melbourne BA), and so she negotiated to switch to a doctorate, which enabled her to do pure research. Concentrating on Shakespeare and Renaissance literature was, she later mused, another way of escaping the Leavisite heritage that the Melbourne department had been expecting her to carry on — though this would have been news to Sam Goldberg who had studied Renaissance history and literature at Oxford and went on to write a major book on *King Lear*.[66]

'Six months at Cambridge is like a dream', she was to state in her interview with Clyde Packer. Speaking for those who love the study of literature, she meant a good dream, but there were other respects in which this was not necessarily the case, and especially not for the likes of her. The finite period she assigned this condition of reverie also gave her statement a characteristic double edge. The residency qualifications for a doctorate are rather longer than six months. In *The Female Eunuch* she was to allude to 'a women's college in which I had the misfortune to be immured for a whole year before I could escape'. The 'strikingly beautiful' buildings and gardens were not sufficient compensation for the lack of social liveliness, political activity and sexual freedom she felt at Cambridge. The Sydney she had left was both beautiful and sexy, but there could be no thought of going back if the very abundance of those things threatened to sap intellectual rigour.[67]

An escape deeper into Europe offered itself when Greer acquired an Italian lover. As it happened, he wanted to end the affair as soon as she arrived in Italy, and he arranged a trip for her that would take her to the remote Calabrian village where she completed her doctoral thesis. The complexities of Italian sexual culture were to elicit further equivocal responses in her. (At least the Italians had a sexual culture to speak of.) There was the personal agony of her ex-lover's 'cold-blooded thoughtfulness' to bear, on the one hand; on the other, she reports how, once installed in Calabria, she cherished 'the opportunity to live with people who have simplified and streamlined sexuality in order to knit this wild strand into their social fabric'.[68]

Once she had returned to England and submitted the thesis, ways of escape from the repressive atmosphere of academic life were provided in the form of the work offers she received from the wider worlds of journalism and television. Her marriage provided no effective escape at all. It was producing *The Female Eunuch* which afforded the greatest opportunities for her own liberation so far — not just through the money it brought her but in the very process and mode of its composition. In her two postgraduate theses you find the occasional witty aside or aphoristic cadenza that suggests an impatience with academic proprieties, but there is none of the uninhibited playfulness of her first book. What remains breathtaking about *The Female Eunuch* is its tone of wilful defiance, as she sprinkles around the names of a mass of scholars and pundits in fields far outside her speciality, blithely rejecting or rechannelling their ideas to facilitate the flow of her own: 'Perhaps my treatment of their highly sophisticated arguments has been brutal, but reverence before authority has never accomplished much in the way of changing things'.[69]

Reflecting retrospectively on her decision to quit academe in the wake of the book's success, she declared:

> I wanted to escape from the stereotypes imposed by our society, and look for new possibilities in different human contexts, above all, for a different notion of woman, for it seemed to me that consumer society could never regard human qualities as anything but commodities.

Even this sort of escape was not without its own catches. Liberation from the constraints of externally-imposed roles demands constant energy as new roles have a way of turning into traps themselves. In the very mode of

Greer's escape there were the risks of becoming captive to other forms of stereotyping as well as of becoming a commodity in herself. She had noted in *The Female Eunuch* how the 'gargantuan appetite of the newspapers for novelty has led to the anomaly of women's liberation stories appearing alongside ... all the rest of the marketing for and by the feminine stereotype', and by the time of her debate with Norman Mailer in America she was reflecting fatalistically on how both of them had now become 'creatures of the media'. The self-liberator must also face the constant possibility of being returned to the constraints of older selves or incarnations, if not of the particular societies, cultures, institutions, that served to nurture these things. 'In order to survive', Greer recalls in her most recent book, *The Change,*

> I had to fashion a self and project it. A woman, any woman, has to fashion a self that will attract ... She may be aware of the process that holds her captive, but she cannot escape it. Though I protested about it as a thirty-year-old feminist, I was still its victim and its beneficiary.[70]

In the book she wrote as a thirty-year-old feminist we find her protesting already (if in a different context): 'We cannot be liberated from ourselves'.[71] Much of her writing between *The Female Eunuch* and *The Change* can be read as a personal reflection or embodiment of these dilemmas and as an (at least tacit) attempt to confront them. Her life and career over the same period exhibit various sorts of 'return' as much as any further bids for escape.

In fashioning a role for herself as one of the pioneers of 'second-wave feminism' in the 1970s, Greer was bound to project some images of her personality and thought that would be seized upon in various quarters as quintessentially hers — and archetypally feminist. Some of her fellow-feminists seem to have needed an identifiable character of this sort — a mythological figurehead for the contemporary women's movement — as much as the mass media did. The need is suggested in this extract from a lecture given by Camille Paglia in 1991:

> Germaine Greer ... What a *loss*! If that woman had stayed on her original track, all of feminism would have been different. She was sophisticated, sexy,

> literate. What *happened* to her? ... [S]he turned into this drone, this whining, 'Woe is me, all the problems of this world!'[72]

Paglia's sense of betrayal here (though considerably modified in some of her more recent statements, where she has started defending Greer against other critics) is as strong in its way as Susan Faludi's critique of *Sex and Destiny*. Faludi takes Paglia herself to task as an 'anti-feminist' on the same page as she bemoans the apparent regressions in Greer's career, and stance. The issues here seem to reduce themselves to questions of propriety as much as of semantics: not just 'what is a feminist, or a feminist leader?' but 'how should she or he be expected to behave?' In the case of Greer in particular, this sort of reductiveness, based on some ideal model, seems to be not just beside but against the point of her whole work. The need to resist stereo-types of female behaviour *was* her 'original track' and has remained her general point. How can stereotypes of feminist behaviour or feminist belief — especially prescriptive ones that question the credentials of those who don't conform to type — be any more acceptable? Greer has certainly never spared the behaviour of other self-styled feminists the rough end of her tongue; and her tongue is becoming more violent, if the recent spat with her fellow-columnist on the *Guardian*, Suzanne Moore, is anything to judge by. Even in this vitriolic personal attack, however, where Moore is caustically described if not typed as 'a feminist of the younger school', Greer nowhere questions — she goes on affirming — Moore's feminist status. Greer's own feminist critics have tended to do the opposite in dealing with her.[73]

Faludi for one has roundly impugned Greer for deviating from the track of feminism *tout court* in her defence of certain marital or sexual cus-toms associated with traditional peasant societies and in her attack on 'the ideology of sexual freedom' associated with more modern Western prac-tices and policies. There is the clear suggestion (paralleling Paglia's) that Greer's *Sex and Destiny* also deviates from the author's own track in *The Female Eunuch*. Again, what bedevils discussion here is the assumption that there is some uniform or essential programme, some single line of thought, that is called feminism, and anything or anyone who doesn't conform to it at every point is not feminist. It is just this prescriptive sort of feminism that Greer may be said to have challenged in *Sex and Destiny*

— this stereotyped or formulaic notion of it from which she felt her instinctive need to escape, and to help her readers escape.

Greer was not attacking the particular sexual freedoms for Western women that she had so passionately advocated in *The Female Eunuch*. What she attacked was the ideology which she felt had been built up around these freedoms: a new 'sex religion' which preached that any form of repression or restraint was inherently bad, attempted to impose this dogma on the whole world, and was encouraged in the exercise by commercial forces in whose interest it was to make of sex a profit-making commodity. The general assumption behind this ideology was that any kinds of society which encouraged arranged marriages or enjoined chastity must be backward and oppressive; there was no understanding that they may just be subscribing to a 'different economy of sex'. In defending such societies against this assumption, Greer was nowhere proposing that their practices — or their own ideologies — should be re-imposed on 'Western folk, who have discarded chastity as a value'. The practices at least did strike her, however, as having a value in themselves, in their own context, and one that might provide the West, not with a model of wholesale emulation, but with some salutary alternatives, some correctives to its increasing propensity at once to revere and trivialise sex.[74]

The research for *Sex and Destiny* involved her in extensive first-hand observation of Third World countries — particularly India. The whole project may be seen as a form of escape from her own cultural paradigms ('occidental certainty'), of which a stereotype of feminism, and of sexual radicalism, was now a part. She was well aware, however, that the notion of Western culture in itself was susceptible to stereotyping. There were still peasant societies to be found in Europe, and she had had her first sustained exposure to one during her spell in southern Italy in 1967. She expressly invoked this experience in *Sex and Destiny*, alongside her more recent observations of India. The marital and domestic customs of such societies were no 'new role model', as Faludi has tried to make out. In the introduction to her collected journalism published a couple of years after *Sex and Destiny*, Greer remarked how her 'critique of the nuclear family' could be traced back to those earlier experiences in Calabria which had first opened her eyes to the operation of an alternative, 'multi-woven' family structure, and its distinctive opportunities for women 'as adults, … as workers, … as female rather than feminine'. She called this the 'stem family' in *Sex and Destiny,* and with typical equivocation did not deny its 'oppressive' aspects. But these did not compare in her view to the oppressions of the nuclear family — for children and men, as well as women — which we find her cataloguing and condemning as early as *The Female Eunuch.* There, too, we find Calabrian society already being invoked as the basis for her alternative ideas of a genuinely communal society or 'organic family'.[75]

The nuclear family is the institution about which Greer has been least equivocal. On this subject she seems to have remained obdurately negative. It is fairly evident that the depth of her reaction against it goes back to her own particular experiences of family life long before she ever witnessed the possibilities of an alternative in Calabria. Those experiences were to be recorded in their greatest and grimmest detail in her book, *Daddy, we hardly knew you,* published five years after *Sex and Destiny.* The negligent, dissimulating father of the title is exposed to relentless posthumous scrutiny here, although it is not as remorseless a picture as the one which Greer presents of her mother, still alive at the time the book was written, and as spiteful, domineering and prurient as she had ever been, according to this account. Only when Greer discovers that her father has been a philanderer as well as a phoney who has invented his past is there a fleeting moment of sympathy with her mother, and even then Greer describes herself as 'wrestling' with this 'unfamiliar experience'. There has since been a further softening in her attitude to her mother, and more of an attempt to understand her weaknesses and excesses in the past. Yet Greer does not contradict the earlier picture of their relationship. In 1992, recalling her early childhood, she wrote:

> There was a war on. My mother was barely 20 when I was born. She wasn't ready for marriage. She wasn't ready to be left with a baby … I actually feel sorry that Mother was reduced to such deep frustration. But what's the point of pretending mothers don't behave that way — with brutality and aggression — when their lives are torn apart?[76]

Though Susan Faludi sees the 'demonisation of mother' in *Daddy* as yet another sign of Greer's contribution to a backlash against feminism, it is in fact fully consistent with the glimpses she gave us in *The Female Eunuch* of this 'nagging', 'badgering' virago who took every opportunity to 'tyrannise the children and enlist their aid to disenfranchise my father completely'. In the earlier work, painful memories of the sort of family structure she herself had to cope with when growing up are clearly discernible in her representation of the alternatives: 'The point of an organic family', she proclaims in *The Female Eunuch,* is 'to release the children from the disadvantages of being the extensions of their parents so that they can belong primarily to themselves'.[77]

Has there been any such 'release' for Greer herself? She has made several attempts to communalise her own domestic arrangements, from accommodating a wide range of visitors in her Tuscan farmhouse for prolonged spells to offering the facilities of her more recent home base back in England to any homeless persons who could fit — or fit in with her. It would be easy to dismiss these as the gestures of a Lady Bountiful, of the sort she had stigmatised in Margaret Sanger. Even the 'fake homeless', as Greer calls the reporters who insinuated their way into her house as a way of testing out her most recent offer, are reminiscent of the imposters who gained admission to the house of the 'original' Lady Bountiful in George Farquhar's play, *The Beaux' Stratagem* (1707). Her own genuineness in this matter has been difficult to impugn, however — least of all by the journalists concerned. What is more disturbing in the reports of any of those who have been on the receiving end of her largess (and, indeed, in her own reports on the same occasions) is the ineluctable sense of a bossy matriarch presiding over her fellow-inmates with a punctilious monitorial eye. 'At dinner he drank a whole bottle of designer water', she recalls of one of the fake homeless.[78]

No one doubts her genuineness more than herself. 'I am a bounder's child. The blood of bounders runs in my veins', she ruefully reflects a little over half way through *Daddy, we hardly knew you.* In various ways that book dramatises the inescapable hold on her of parental inheritance — mainly from 'Daddy' (though more recently she has voiced concerns about what she may have inherited from her mother, including 'the unpredictability of my thought processes' and the 'use of language as a weapon, as a tool for manipulation'). There is a suggestion in her book on her father that the compulsive urge to escape may itself have a hereditary physiological or psychological base: 'Like Daddy I'm claustrophobic. Seriously claustrophobic', she remarks at one point. She fears the inheritance of hypocrisy and masquerade yet more. Her father turns out to have been a budding singer and stage performer in his youth, just like his daughter, as well as the manufacturer of aliases and 'cheap props' in the conduct or presentation of the rest of his life. Terms such as 'character' or 'charade' or 'act' or 'performance' crop up as often in her descriptions of his activities as the more direct 'phoney', 'fraud' and 'bounder' do. She catches herself playing around with possible aliases at one point: '"Germaine Greer" indeed. I call myself Frances Greeney, and realise glumly that I am simply carrying on the Reg Greer tradition of aliases. There is no bucking the genes'. The name passed on to her by her father, now an inextricable part of her starry lustre, can do nothing to make her feel more genuine or independent; it serves only to rub in her dodgy inheritance and identity: 'the ersatz phenomenon of Germaine Greer, celebrity'.[79]

None of these anxieties about genetic inheritance should be taken too literally — save in the case of her claustrophobia perhaps. There remain some grounds for believing, however, that if her father's genes are not implicated in how she acts and thinks, his behaviour has always been an influence on her, and a model or counter-model. It continues to extend its shadow to this day. His dissimulating ways, even when she only had some dim intuition of them, may serve to explain the roots of her instinctive suspicion of performers. Now, as shown in her more scholarly work in particular (including the editions of women poets brought out by her own publishing firm, Stump Cross Books), she has developed an almost obsessive 'concern for authenticity' in the matter of literary texts, and an uncanny nose for the 'shadier' kinds of author or editor.[80]

Her own compulsive performing tendencies from early days, and the continuing impulse to make a spectacle of herself, to keep on shocking and outraging a public audience, could also feasibly be traced to her father's behaviour towards her, or to her impressions of this as a child. Of her years as a schoolgirl, she claims in *Daddy, we hardly knew you*, 'I did my best to be good. And there was never a word of encouragement. He never noticed anything I did'. When sitting next to Norman Mailer at a dinner party following the New York Town Hall debate, she felt she was 'struggling like a neglected and ugly daughter for my father's esteem'. It has been one of the joys for her of becoming an older woman, as she records them in *The Change,* that she can now go out walking and 'neither expect nor hope to be noticed'. It is notable that she doesn't say 'need' here. Her advice to other post-menopausal women in this book is that they should now use their creativity, hitherto taken up with family responsibilities, to contribute to 'a wider stage, a different stage. This need not be a public stage …' But judging by her own recent activities — not just her newspaper columns but her brief return to a regular television series with her chat-show, *The Last Word* — her own need is still very much for a public stage. If there is an eventual need to escape these roles as well, the exit can be even more attention-getting than the rest of the performance. She is reported to have commented on the outburst leading up to her recent resignation from the *Guardian:* 'I have behaved badly … but I was sick of behaving well'.[81]

In some quite palpable ways the research for *Daddy, we hardly knew you* had involved a return to the nuclear family from which she had been escaping most of her life. Her father was no longer around to notice, or not notice, how she was behaving, but her other close relatives were, and in some of the same settings. Her mother, for one, still occupied the house in the Melbourne suburbs — the dreaded nucleus itself — that Greer had fled from as a twenty-year-old. What was in one respect an attempt to exorcise the demons of the past was in another a renewed involvement with them. But the very palpability of these physical presences and physical places allowed them to be escaped from again, ensured that the return need only be temporary. Her father, now a spectre, was bound to prove more haunting.

There might have been some lingering scenic charms for her in other parts of Australia, but, as she had decided years before, charms were also forms of delusion that made you forget 'the poor in this country', and especially its original black occupants. Her abiding conviction has been that 'Australia is, was, and ever shall be someone else's country'. It is this conviction which evidently lay behind her refusal to be drawn into the bicentennial celebrations of Australia's settlement by the British, in which two of her fellow-expatriates featured in this book, Clive James and Robert

Hughes, agreed to participate. And it is among the motivating impulses for her attack on a recent novel by David Malouf (her near neighbour in Tuscany for many years) whom she has accused of invoking 'the unending tragedy of the settlement of Australia by Europeans to use it only as a background for flights of invention so self-indulgent that the reader is almost ashamed to participate in them'.[82]

There could be no return of *this* native to the bleak heath of Melbourne suburbia, not because of its bleakness, necessarily, but because she didn't consider herself a native to start with. By her account she doesn't feel a native of anywhere. She has shifted her main base again from Tuscany back to England, clearly prepared to face another kind of bleakness in this 'country of the grey underpants', as she once described it; but even here her affinities are less with the title character of Thomas Hardy's *The Return of the Native,* swapping Paris for the austerities of his childhood haunts on Egdon Heath, than with those 'unaccommodated' folk on the storm-tossed heath in *King Lear* — the 'poor, bare, forked' creatures which Shakespeare's old patriarch sees about him.[83]

Poverty, admittedly, is not the first thing that comes to mind when you see the sort of rags she covers herself with on television today, but it is remarkable how often storm- or heath-like scenes have appeared in her writing, how many 'bare' and semi-bare figures she has observed around her on her travels (even in libraries), or how much of her own nakedness she has felt compelled to expose: the stripping nun, the *Oz* cover-girl, the madwoman in her underclothes who divests herself even of these in a leap to liberation and will always 'suffer greatly if obliged to sleep dressed'. In *Daddy, we hardly knew you,* there is an explicit image of herself as Cordelia to her father's Lear at one point; though she fears that the hardness involved in not pandering to his delusions — in so ruthlessly exposing them — may turn her into a Goneril or a Regan.[84]

Some comfort, however cold, is still to be taken in the rigours of the heath. They have their redeeming, if not redemptive, features. They can be tests of the will which prove your strength and resilience. (We see her surviving a storm in outback New South Wales that has another Shakespearean echo for her: 'just like the witches in Macbeth, I thought'.) They can even provide the model of an ideal world order. In her little book on Shakespeare which appeared before *Daddy, we hardly knew you,* she links the heath in *Lear* with the Forest of Arden in *As You Like It* as types of 'anarchist community run on the principle of co-operation between equals'. There are three overlapping and characteristic voices here. There is the voice of the Shakespearean scholar who revels in arresting interpretations. There is the voice of the faithful anti-state communist. (In her contribution, a few years later, to the final issue of *Marxism Today,* which focused on 'The Left after Communism', we find her hoping against hope that the baby can still 'be snatched from the bathwater', that 'the idea of socialism can rise from the ashes of state monopoly'.) And there is the voice that can always locate the good in the bad, as it can the bad in the good: the eternally equivocal voice.[85]

It is the weight of the good she sees amidst the bad in England that has made a return there relatively easy — or harder to resist. The good there has some palpable, physical forms, but it is connected in a yet more captivating manner with intellectual and spiritual qualities that she has always craved, and it can provide these in greater concentration than anywhere else she knows. The book on Shakespeare, written at the height of Margaret Thatcher's ascendancy in England, affirms that

> As long as Shakespeare remains central to English cultural life, it will retain the values that make it unique in the world, namely tolerance, pluralism, the talent for compromise, and a profound commitment to that most wasteful form of social organization, democracy.

It is a hymn to compare with John of Gaunt's 'This England' speech in *Richard II* or Jane Marryot's combined toast to the 'future of England with the past of England' at the end of Noël Coward's *Cavalcade.* There is still a sly, nicely undercutting note of equivocation in the last phrase; and both fellow-anarchists and fellow-feminists might find some of Greer's direct comments on Thatcher in other places too equivocal for comfort. One journalist observed flatly of Greer in the year her Shakespeare book came out: 'Her dislike for Margaret Thatcher is potent; she refers to her as Boadicea and "the nanny of Britain"'. Yet in *The Change,* a few years later, Greer was to write: 'We hear that she uses hormone replacement, but do not know whether to be encouraged or disheartened by the result, especially now that she has been tossed out by her male colleagues ...' It is difficult to gauge how far her tongue is in her cheek here. On a television programme about the painter, Paula Rego, Greer expressed clearer sympathies with Mrs Thatcher, and concern at the difficulties faced by the former Tory Prime Minister in having to play by the masculine rules of her party.[86]

In the middle of *Daddy, we hardly knew you*, there is an extraordinary and protracted hymn to the part of England where Greer had first settled — Cambridge University; or, more precisely, to a particular college of Cambridge, St John's, where she found herself dining at high table in 1987. Her idyllic picture here was punctured by none of the barbs she had directed at her own former college in earlier accounts. She had returned briefly to academe at the end of the 1970s when the University of Tulsa in Oklahoma appointed her to its graduate Faculty of Modern Letters, first as a guest professor and subsequently as the founding director of its Center for the Study of Women's Letters. The encouragement to combine her feminist interests with academic life was obviously an incentive to returning. According to David Plante, who was also a guest of Tulsa's at the time, 'she was devoted to her Center and the students in it', but there was nothing there (as there had been nothing at Warwick) to match the sort of intellectual conviviality of the high tables of the older English universities. 'What a fucking provincial place I've come to', Plante also remembers her saying of Tulsa. Greer left her position there at the end of 1983 after an altercation with the University over the funding of her Center.[87]

Sitting among the dons of St John's, what took her attention and her fancy was 'the playfulness of perpetual students' that characterised their talk: the mixture of wide-ranging erudition and entertainment that has characterised her own work. The vintage burgundy, good coffee, fine tobacco, oak panelling and stuccoed ceilings appear to have completed the seduction, breaking down some old reservations about the quality of the teaching at Cambridge which she had casually reiterated only three years earlier in *Sex and Destiny*. In as short a time, she was to be back teaching at Cambridge herself, back to her old college even. She has since made attempts to apply for the headships of two older colleges, Sidney Sussex at Cambridge and Wadham at Oxford. These proved unsuccessful, though even reaching the shortlists for positions at such traditionally all-male bastions suggests the strength of her own seductive powers, intellectually and vocally. 'Germaine's been a bitch all her life', a fellow-Australian feminist has recently remarked; whereas a male pillar of the English intellectual establishment, Paul Johnson, observed of Greer only a couple of weeks earlier: 'she is, despite all her efforts, a lady'. Judged by her own standards of invective, her retrospective dismissal of Sidney Sussex as 'the dullest college in Cambridge' seems the most ladylike of bitcheries.[88]

Bitchery or witchery? Newnham College, from being the place against which Greer had muttered curses as a graduate student, remains to provide a good base for muttering curses against the rest of the world, or so her fellow-feminist, the American novelist, Marilyn French, has intimated, following an invitation to high table there by Greer in 1994: 'The dons there are like my coven, full of fun and support', French observed. This image fits Greer's own Rose Blight persona and the admonitions to happy cronehood that are sprinkled throughout her recent guide for the post-menopausal woman, *The Change*. More recently she has placed herself in the company of 'the witches of Essex'.[89] But there is another image, evoked in the last paragraph of *The Change,* which suggests that returning to Newnham might represent something of a return for Greer to an earlier model of community in her life: the convent.

The Change closes with a sort of 'aria' (David Plante's term for Greer's lecturing style back in the early 1980s) in which she pictures the older woman of today 'climbing her own mountain, in search of her own horizon' and knowing that 'when she has scrambled up this last sheer obstacle, she will see how to handle the rest of her long life'. We might be pardoned here for detecting a faint echo of the Mother Superior's 'aria' in *The Sound of Music,* exhorting the young problem novice, Maria, to 'Climb Every Mountain'. We could also be pardoned for imagining the nuns at her old school chanting, in the fashion of another song from the show, 'How do you solve a problem like Miss Greer?' Plante himself after all has evoked the strange potency for Greer of the film version of *The Sound of Music* which he and she found themselves watching on television one evening in Tulsa. 'This is shit', she declaimed — with tears streaming down her cheeks. Equivocal views on convents — not just the ones she remembers from her schooldays — are scattered throughout her writings. In a secularised form

— and a sexualised one, to the extent of allowing the inmates some choice in the matter of chastity — this sort of institution has come to provide her with the nearest to an ideal of collective life for the single woman: for the individual who (like herself) goes 'more or less alone' in the world. Here she might be 'bound together in mutual support' with other such women, forming (as a friend of Greer's puts it) 'a vast and cheerful sisterhood … a kind of refuge'. If her dream of wanting her own house to be like a 'secular nunnery' out of Rabelais has never quite materialised, Newnham in the 1990s has served as a reasonable surrogate for Greer, with fewer of the old inhibitions but most of the old accoutrements ('good conversation, good books, … and lots of time for contemplation') that non-secular convents provided.[90]

'Secular' doesn't mean unspiritual in Greer's lexicon. She still believes in a concept of grace, as she told Phillip Adams in an interview she gave in 1992; though she doesn't define it in any of the usual Catholic senses (divine grace or 'sanctifying grace') but rather as 'a feeling of connectedness to things'. On returning to live near Cambridge she has also returned to churchgoing and choirsinging — though, interestingly, in an Anglican church, which represents another sort of return: to the observances of her ancestors on her father's side. Whether this signifies or portends a return to any sort of Christian *belief* is rather more doubtful. She has declared recently, in almost a single breath:

> 'I am still a Catholic. I just don't believe in God. I am an atheist Catholic … I don't want to escape from it, I'm very glad to be a Catholic … I think there's something to be said for nunneries. I'm *not sure* that there's anything to be said for Catholicism.[91]

There is nothing that Greer is less sure, more equivocal, about than religion. It doesn't mean she is inconsistent. Despite the dogmatic assertiveness of her customary tone of voice, being equivocal may even be said to provide the consistent principle *in* her life, the ideal condition towards which she aspires and to which she attempts to nudge her audiences. Richard Neville writes of the young Greer in Sydney, completing her thesis on Byron while dominating the local student-theatre scene: 'Self-assured, with … an appalling certainty, she would rather be wrong than ambivalent'.[92] But if this is true of her earlier years before she left

Australia it doesn't wholly fit the person she has become, or tried to become. The journey away from certainty may have already begun before she stepped on the boat to England.

Among the qualities which even a stern critic of Byron like Leavis found himself admiring was the poet's unity in variety. (As he spelt it out: 'Byron's variety and flexibility … relate to no stylisation or impersonal code — the unity is our sense of Byron's individuality'.) If there is no direct evidence that Greer was instinctively attracted to such qualities when she embarked on her MA thesis, it becomes clearer in the case of her second thesis subject. In the acknowledgments included there, she thanked her supervisors at Cambridge for helping to rein in her certainty. But Shakespeare himself provided the best lessons for her in this respect. While she did not fully imbibe or register these lessons at the time, her book on Shakespeare produced nearly twenty years later is rich testimony to their sustained (and sustaining) impact over the years. 'Intellectual life in the Shakespearian mode', she writes there, 'is a never-ending learning process; each of the plays enacts the mental adventure of scepticism'. From his various sources, according to Greer, Shakespeare took a 'mass of conflicting notions', shaping these into a compendium of wisdom that allowed them all 'full imaginative development'. The result was not prescriptive propaganda, but a 'theatre of dialectical conflict': something 'exciting and alive, repaying all kinds of analysis and suggestive of all kinds of alternatives'. It was this 'myriad-mindedness' in Shakespeare, or what Keats dubbed 'negative capability', which had helped make possible the 'pluralism and tolerance' that Greer had so come to cherish in English life and thought: 'the freedom from aggressive certainty'.[93]

In the methods as well as the themes of Greer's other books we can witness her attempts to abide by these lessons, meet these ideals. No one is more aware than she of the traps and difficulties involved, and of her own deficiencies in the process. Yet she seems powerless to do anything about these. Shakespeare's is a hard act to follow, she suggests — and particularly hard for one of her own disposition and compulsions — because in a sense it is the very opposite of an act. Referring to his biographical elusiveness, she says: 'Nothing but a complete lack of interest in self-promotion … can explain Shakespeare's invisibility'. It is an elusiveness she yearns for herself, if her rebuffs to any prospective biographers of her are a sign; yet ironically those rebuffs can be as noisily self-dramatising as so much else in her career, drawing rather than deflecting further public attention. There is a related irony at the heart of her consistent efforts to remain equivocal. In resolving to free herself and her readers from the perils of certainty, she cannot escape from aggression. Shock tactics have become almost essential to the enterprise, certainly difficult to avoid.[94]

The opening pages of *Sex and Destiny* candidly explain her practice of aggressive *un*certainty. Good books, she says there, are to be judged by their ability to stimulate creative thought, and this means 'producing confusion in place of certainty, melting concepts so that they may reform and coagulate in new relationships'. Such a process will possibly be 'quite violent, for settled certainties resist corrosion and demand vitriol'. For this she makes no apparent apology, and later in the same book, if in a different context, she had occasion to pronounce: 'human kind cannot bear very much harmony'. The line is most obviously derived from T. S. Eliot's 'human kind/Cannot bear very much reality' in the first of his *Four Quartets;* though the sentiment contains stronger echoes of a speech at the end of *This Happy Breed,* given to Frank Gibbons, whose sister, Sylvia, Greer had played in Melbourne many years before:

> Human beings don't like peace and good will and everybody loving everybody else. Human beings like eating and drinking and loving and hating. They also like showing off, grabbing all they can, fighting for their rights and bossing anybody who'll give 'em half a chance.[95]

Some fifteen years before *Sex and Destiny,* Greer had made a more cautiously judicious pronouncement on the combination of aggression with creative uncertainty. It was in an article she published in *Oz* magazine before she had written any of her books. Discussing the general strategy of the current political and cultural 'Underground', she explained:

> it is principally a clamour for freedom to move, to test alternative forms of existence to find if they are more practical, and if they are more gratifying, more creative, more positive than endurance under the system. This partly explains the lack of ideology which combines so oddly with the

growing peevishness ... , peevishness now developing into belligerence, with the threat of violence.[96]

She is not consciously talking of herself here, but perhaps nothing else in her writings so succinctly summarises the nature of her life's journey, with all its costs and hazards as well as its enabling strengths.

Chapter Five

The Nostalgia of the Critic

The Unbalancing of Robert Hughes

Just after Christmas 1970 the unsigned 'Art' column in *Time* magazine could be found contemplating the fate of the angel. 'Whether God is dead or not', it began, 'his angels seem to be'. Yet it ended on an appropriate note of seasonal uplift, reflecting that: 'As the rigid boxes of nineteenth-century positivism disappear from our culture and new epiphanies of consciousness unfold themselves, it is possible that we may return to that receptiveness in which earlier civilizations saw their angels. Except that we will inevitably call ours something else'.

Following stints as an art columnist for various Australian and English newspapers, and the publication of two major books, *The Art of Australia* (1966) and *Heaven and Hell in Western Art* (1968), Robert Hughes was invited to New York to write for *Time* in 1970. His first signed column — a review of a retrospective of modern American sculpture, held at the Whitney Museum in Manhattan — appeared in the first number of 1971, one week after the piece on angels. It does not seem too fanciful to speculate that both articles were by the same hand.

Their particular subject matter may be widely divergent, but that in itself is not uncharacteristic of Hughes. The obsessive urge of this antipodean prodigy to gobble up a world of knowledge and sensation from which he had felt so removed when growing up is a familiar enough trait of many of Australia's cultural and intellectual expatriates, including the others featured in this book. A more distinctive signature can be discerned in the peculiar, almost compulsive, poise of the articles. This is reflected not just in their stylistic mannerisms (usages at once bold and exact; the combination of punchy rhetoric with fluent cadences), but more generally in the sense of balance about the judgments each delivers.

'And yet, and yet … The thought that angels are dead is a nagging one. It is unsatisfactory.' This note of uneasy reservation following apparently confident assertion has an echo in the discriminations voiced in Hughes' first signed piece for *Time*. He doesn't hesitate to apply the word 'dazzling' in describing the effects of the two sculptors under review — Nancy Graves and Duane Hanson. But in the second instance, he worries over the implications of this routine journalistic superlative, suspecting that 'there may seem to be something too easy, almost flip' about Hanson's work. Trying to resist the same hazards in his own dazzling prose, he puts occasional breaks on its headlong pace and flow, reins it in to reconsider its general direction and effect. In its syntax as much as its import, the opening paragraph of his first signed review is characterised by just such a balancing act: 'In general U.S. museums do not just reflect art history. They program and write it through their selections, their theme shows, and their imprimatur. But Manhattan's Whitney Museum, with dedication, if not full impartiality, has clung to the principle of the survey'.[1]

Balances, or attempts to achieve and maintain balance, form a recurrent motif of Hughes' career and ideas, as well as of his prose and mode of argument. The balances respond to various tensions in his life and sensibility, and they have provided ways of containing those tensions — till recently, at any rate. From within the cultural milieu he inhabits there have emerged some new forces over the past decade and a half which have served to upset his balancing act in various ways. There have been no substantial or sustained signs of recovery from this upset; and it looks increasingly as if he has lost even any desire for recovery.

One can chart the process through his continuing work for *Time* over this period, particularly in the reviews from that magazine which he selected for re-publication in his book, *Nothing If Not Critical*, published in

1990. Significantly, this selection does not reprint any of his earlier offerings in the magazine, such as that tactful and even-handed piece on the American sculpture show. A more unsettling symptom is the title of the book, plucked as it is from the mouth of Iago, one of literature's subtlest villains, and the most obscurely motivated. Many of the individual items are not anywhere near as negative or dark as this may suggest; but that is their overall impression as Hughes traces the decade of the 1980s, through its art, contrasting it implicitly (at times explicitly) with previous generations and centuries. Cumulatively, these pieces fall little short of an all-encompassing jeremiad against the 'post-modern' world, which (for all that he denounces the very epithet for its vacuity) he has to concede is ineluctably ours as we approach the new millennium.[2] His subsequent writings in *Time*, and elsewhere, have done little to mitigate and much to deepen the malcontent tone.

Although he has not yet ventured on any full-scale autobiography, Hughes has always seemed willing to flaunt the tensions in his life, his personality, his beliefs, and in the series of influences (geographical, familial, religious, educational, political, moral and aesthetic) that have helped shape his brilliant career. As a worldly and sophisticated critic of European and American art, he has made no secret of — will often invoke — his upbringing as an Australian of Irish-Catholic origins. His public persona has tended, if anything, to play up the boozy, pugnacious, larrikin stereotype.

Not for him the 'imperturbable tweeds' (Hughes' description) or clipped vocal intonations of Kenneth Clark on *Civilization* — that seminal exercise in television arts programmes of the sort in which Hughes himself has come to specialise. In more youthful days, at least, Hughes thought nothing of sporting a stetson hat above a suede jacket and plush trousers, or kitting himself out as a bikey in full black leather garnished with metal studs and snaps. But his imposing face — part-cherubic, part gladiatorial — was as likely to stare out at you from beneath the dome of a homburg, topping a Savile Row suit, or under a panama, crowning a cream blazer and striped poplin shirt. A fine succession of floppy bow ties adorned his neck in his first incarnation as host of a television series — the programmes he made on Australian painting in 1975, *Landscape with Figures*.

In subsequent series he has preferred open necks and smart, 'preppy' casuals — his now customary mode of dress off-screen as well.[3]

All this may display a playful chameleonism rather than any true balance. There has been more of a sense of balance, and of a consistent one, in the qualities of his voice. Notoriously resounding throughout New York bars in the 1970s and 1980s (until he made a decision, on medical advice, to give up regular drinking), its gruff boom and thrust were made familiar to much wider audiences around the world with his BBC TV series of 1980, *The Shock of the New*.[4] But there were always associated subtleties for those attuned to them. His accent is what used to be called 'educated Australian', although some of his non-Australian audience, brought up on the likes of Kenneth Clark, don't appear to have caught this refinement at first. When *The Shock of the New* was premiered, one newspaper critic in England deeply annoyed Hughes by bemoaning his 'antipodean honkings'. The accent has changed very little with the years, in spite of his spell in America since 1970, and before that (for six years or so) in England and Europe. With slightly more discrimination, a recent English commentator has remarked on the 'rich, brown Australian' of Hughes' voice, and another has observed how 'Hughes's Aussie diphthongs still amaze and entertain'.[5]

As suggested by the subtler tones of his accent, his Australian-Irish-Catholic upbringing was not of the rural or working-class varieties but urban-professional. He was born in Sydney in 1938 into a long-established dynasty of lawyers and businessmen. Observers in Australia have often remarked on the Hugheses' 'patrician' demeanour (a mixture of confidence and reserve), some dubbing them 'an Australian aristocracy' or even 'Australia's Kennedys'. They have never been as exalted or prominent as this; though their lineage has been respectable enough.[6]

Most of the Irish who came to Australia in the nineteenth century did so either as convicts, sent out under the transportation system of the British government's penal policy from the 1780s to the 1840s, or as refugees from rural poverty. Robert Hughes' most famous book, *The Fatal Shore*, published between *The Shock of the New* and *Nothing If Not Critical*, graphically focused on some of the more horrific experiences of the convicts, Irish and otherwise; but whatever his motives in producing this exercise in Grand Guignol, they cannot directly be attributed to convict origins. His Irish roots may have had something more to do with it — though they are Irish only on his father's side. The first Hughes to come out to Australia, Tom Hughes of County Roscommon, did so as a free settler, though he found employment in the penal system as a clerk at Darlinghurst Gaol in Sydney. This was in the late 1830s, a few years before the Irish famine.

Tom Hughes' son, John, made good in the grocery business, and started to buy up large tracts of valuable land in and around Sydney. In a fit of piety in his later years he was to give much of it away (including the large family home bordering the Harbour) to the Catholic Church. Without making them aristocrats, however, his initial acquisition of prime property had served to raise the family's social standing considerably. One of his sons, also called John, went on to become a Minister for Justice in New South Wales. Another son, Tom — Robert's grandfather — ended up as Lord Mayor of Sydney, the chairman of the brewing company, Tooheys, and a director of the Commercial Bank of Australia. Their family's status was confirmed when Tom was knighted.

Sir Thomas' son, Geoffrey — Robert's father — followed pretty much in his own father's footsteps; though there were limitations to his career which reflected something of the sectarian rivalries in Australia at the time, and the difficulties that Catholics experienced in making it to the top in a country that was still dominated by Protestants. He won considerable repute as a solicitor and businessman, becoming deputy chairman of Tooheys, and a director of the Commercial Bank as well as of a Sydney insurance company. He achieved sufficient distinction in these capacities to be made a papal knight. He could also boast a dazzling military record from his days as a fighter pilot in Europe during the First World War. Lord Bruce, the Prime Minister of Australia between 1923 and 1929, was supposed to have considered him seriously for the position of Minister for Air, but Hughes lost out on pre-selection for a parliamentary seat to a freemason. This setback was not forgotten in the family.

It was while in England during the war years that he met his wife, Margaret Sealey Vidal. There is relatively little mention of her in any of the Hugheses' published records, though from what fragments exist, it seems that she hailed from a West Country family, and had been courted by Geoffrey Hughes' playing loop-the-loop with his aircraft over her home in a village rectory. He persuaded her to convert to Catholicism, and to return to Australia as his wife. They settled in Rose Bay, one of the prosperous eastern suburbs of Sydney. Robert was their youngest child, being preceded by two other sons and a daughter. One of the few characteristics of his mother's which he records is her English accent — something which helped modulate his own, as he acknowledges. In a short memoir of his schooldays, he provides a vignette of her running the tuckshop committee. She was clearly a good businesswoman in her own right, having managed one of the first ski-equipment stores in Australia, and (during the Second World War) a shop selling goods to raise funds for servicemen's wives and widows. She herself was to be widowed a few years after the end of the war.[7]

Robert was twelve when his father died, and was just entering upon his secondary education at St Ignatius' College: 'a repository for the sons of well-to-do Catholics, run by Jesuits', as he describes it in his memoir of the place. Both his elder brothers were sent to the same school. Tom, older than Robert by fifteen years, had long since left, and with an air force career in the Second World War behind him, had just been admitted to the Bar. The first peak of his career was to come in the late 1960s, when he was appointed Federal Attorney-General by the Australian Prime Minister of the day, John Gorton. This might have made some amends for his father's failure to gain a cabinet post, though Tom Hughes was to be stood down by Gorton's successor, Billy McMahon, in 1971. The middle brother, Geoffrey, who broke the news of their father's death to Robert in the school cloisters, also went on to follow a legal career, as a solicitor. Robert, by his own and his elder brother's accounts, would probably have gone on to do much the same if his father hadn't died; he had been especially close to him, but the premature end to their intimacies served to cast the young boy adrift from his family in all kinds of ways, and he has remained 'a bit adrift since', Tom Hughes remarked in 1995. The most tangible symptom of this was to be his expatriatism; and, in attempting to understand his decision to live away from his homeland, it is important to keep in mind that the other expatriates dealt with in this book also suffered various kinds of curtailment or frustration in their relationship with their fathers.[8]

His family and schooling presented other sorts of frustration for him but also more positive stimuli. In these experiences we will find some of the earliest sources and models of his search for balance, and at the same time the seeds of the imbalance observable in his later career.

Geoffrey Dutton, the South Australian-born critic, and an early mentor of Hughes, observed of him and his family: 'He wasn't conservative, and they all were'.[9] Politically speaking, the young Robert wasn't particularly radical either — until the years of the Vietnam War at least. The distance which he started to feel from his surviving family in his teenage years, and which served to deflect him from any commitment to a legal career, had more to do with his nascent artistic promptings. There was no one to share these with at home, or so he seems to have convinced himself.

'My family had no interest whatever in the visual arts', he recalls in a profile recently published in *Vanity Fair*. This may be a little unfair on his sister, Constance, who dabbled modestly in painting of a sort ('ballerinas on cold cream jars') and who later trained as an architect, providing a model for an alternative career to law in the family. If only an incidental manifestation of their socially superior status, there was a cultivated feel to the Hughes household that far exceeded the offerings of the Humphries or James or Greer households. This was evident in the level of everyday discourse among family members and also in their possessions and adornments. Hughes fondly remembers the Arthur Streeton landscape purchased by his grandfather, and more wryly a Norman Lindsay etching which he discovered as a teenager stuffed behind a stack of trays in the pantry at home. He reflected on this find nearly a quarter of a century later: 'A great many of our primal art experiences do come from bad art. No one is born in the Uffizi'. But not so many are born into families that own any kinds of original art. An eccentric aunt, Hughes recalls, had bought up 'great quantities of Donald Friends and Justin O'Briens'. There was no comparable collection of paintings in his own home, but there was some 'good furniture, glass, china', and a 'great many' books in his father's library. He was addicted to reading by the age of nine, he claims; and in those pre-television days the family 'even read aloud to each other'. The range of books was very wide, if not particularly adventurous: 'from *Paradise Lost* to Andrew Lang's *Purple Book of Fairy Stories,* from Shakespeare to our national doggerelist Banjo Patterson [*sic*], from Xenophon's *Anabasis* to *Kim, The Jungle Book* ... and *The Hunting of the Snark*'. More significant for the development of Hughes' career, there was almost a complete set of the periodical, *Art in Australia,* and 'a lot of Ruskin'. Hughes notes that Ruskin was 'the first art critic that I read as a child. The power of the prose in the great descriptive passages and the minute character of the observation certainly teach you something about writing when you're young'.[10]

Influences of any kind are notoriously difficult to trace in a precise way; but there are good grounds for arguing that Hughes' early immersion in Ruskin also helped to teach him some of his most fundamental values about art, or at least to initiate him in the contending issues and criteria involved in judging it. Various other sources of influence are detectable in Hughes' tastes. It is in the range of critical precepts, and the sorts of relationship between them, that his correspondences with the Victorian critic are particularly evident.

Hughes has always been clear that the judgment of true masterpieces has nothing fundamentally to do with the money value by which a dealer or gallery owner may try to define them in order to impress prospective clientele. Nor, on the other hand, should this judgment depend exclusively on the ideological commitments (whether political or religious) evident in their subject matter, or on the pleasure-giving capacity (whether to *cognoscenti* or much wider audiences) of their style or form: these are competing, but also closely interlocking, considerations; and there has been a continual search in Hughes for some kind of balance between them.

Over the years he has looked for each of the following attributes in painting, singly or in various combinations: the freshness of the stylistic conventions, at successive historical stages, by which an artist's experience of space and form is expressed; the degree to which the work opens up a passage from its creator's personal experience or feeling to more general social or moral or religious meaning; the potency with which symbols, philosophic implications, myths, are manifested and transmitted. 'Significant content', deep emotion, spiritual values, stylistic and technical virtuosity, aesthetic enjoyment and delight: all need to be assessed and weighed, though there is no precise formula laid down for judging the appropriate proportions of each.[11]

There are certainly some broad parallels and points of sympathy with Ruskin here, even if they don't prove direct influence. Here is the Victorian sage on the relation of money to artistic judgment: 'the greater number of persons or societies throughout Europe, whom wealth, or chance, or inheritance has put in possession of valuable pictures, do not know a good picture from a bad one'. Add Australia or America here, and you have Hughes' views in a nutshell. There is another pronouncement of Ruskin's which enshrines within it the very principle of balance by which the older and the younger critic have attempted to make their own discriminations between good and bad:

> I never met with a question yet, of any importance, which did not need, for the right solution of it, at least one positive and one negative answer … No chance of our getting good art unless we delight in it: … no chance of our getting good art unless we resist our delight in it.[12]

On some other questions, relating to politics in particular, we shall find that Hughes diverged from Ruskinian paths, as he grew more politically conscious in early adulthood. Before this time, however, he had found a still living and still active model in the English critic Cyril Connolly. When Hughes was sixteen, he came across Connolly's book, *The Unquiet Grave*, on his sister-in-law's shelves. Produced about a decade earlier, this pot-pourri of aphorisms on love and art had acquired instant cult status. Patrick White later recalled that it was 'my Bible almost during the War'. Hughes has been as emphatic as White about its impact on him — though this proves to be no simple matter.[13]

'If it hadn't been for reading *The Unquiet Grave*', he recalls telling its author when he bumped into him in London, 'I never would have come up with the courage to leave Australia'. That he didn't leave permanently till 1964, some ten years on, leads you to wonder a bit about this, though he had made a temporary overseas trip of a few months during 1959, and he remarks of the book elsewhere that he used to 'reread it like a sacred text' year after year. He still doesn't make clear why this work should have provided such encouragement for him to leave his homeland, compared to other possible incentives and pressures. Connolly himself was clearly bemused or unimpressed by this information. As Hughes relates the meeting with him, he retorted that he couldn't be held responsible for the 'accidental effects of my juvenilia in distant countries', and turned on his heel and left.[14]

Examining the book itself suggests the more immediate kinds of influence that it might have exercised on Hughes while he remained at home. Produced originally towards the end of the Second World War, before the final victory of the Allies had been secured, Connolly's work exuded a certain bleak weariness about the human condition that chimed with the angst-ridden mood of the currently fashionable existential philosophy across the Channel. (Hughes has also recalled his youthful dabbling in the works of those two great gurus of existentialism, Albert Camus and Jean-Paul Sartre.) According to the narrator of *The Unquiet Grave*, 'the old platitudes of Liberalism' might be revived 'in all their glory' as a buffer of consolation against the spectacle of 'absolute States and ideological wars', but they could offer nothing more substantial; and the arts were now advancing 'further and further into an obscure and sterile cul-de-sac' — a symptom of a 'triple decadence', in language, religious belief, and society. Finding himself in a part of the world that had remained relatively insulated from the worst atrocities of the war, Hughes was still trying, according to his recollections, 'to introject angst into the Sydney environment' of the 1950s. In part, this came to involve an exaggeration of the 'dark side' of contemporary Australian painters as he started to acquaint himself with their work and to pick up his pen in a critical engagement with it. Connolly proved as apt a muse in this venture as Camus or Sartre.

Connolly might also have served as a muse in a more positive sense. *The Unquiet Grave*, with all its cosmic angst, was not entirely a textbook of despair. It proclaimed an underlying 'faith in the unity and continuity of Western culture in its moment of crisis', and in picturing the decadence of twentieth-century Europe, it reflected that 'the goal of every culture is to decay through over-civilization' and that 'the civilization of one epoch becomes the manure of the next'. Persisting with artistic endeavours was not a futile activity, however inclement the current cultural climate appeared to be. On the contrary. 'The more books we read', the narrator counsels,

> the clearer it becomes that the function of a writer is to produce a masterpiece, and that no other task is of consequence ... Every excursion into journalism, broadcasting, propaganda and writing for films, however grandiose, will be doomed to disappointment. To put our best into these is

> another folly, since we thereby condemn good ideas as well as bad to oblivion. It is in the nature of such work not to last, and it should never be undertaken … How many books did Renoir write on how to paint?[15]

This ringing exhortation was made at the very start of the book, so readers could scarcely miss it, however selectively they may have scanned the rest. Hughes' eventual 'excursions' into the very fields marked here as dead ends may suggest that in the long term the book's effect — or the effect of that stinging put-down from its author — was to provoke him into a defiance of its preachings. But in the short term its role may have been to help him defy the more conventional preachings to which his family and school were subjecting him. It was just around the time he first came across this book that he started to lose his faith in Catholicism. There were quite independent reasons for this, to do partly with his burgeoning sexuality, and the difficulties which he had in reconciling this with his Jesuit teachers' condemnations of sexual pleasure outside marriage. Broader doubts about their version of God and about His much-vaunted wisdom and benevolence began to assail the young boy. In this dilemma it is not surprising that he should have sought and found an alternative 'sacred text' in a book like Connolly's. Art as 'a substitute for religious experience' was to be one of the themes of his explorations of Modernism in *The Shock of the New*. And to become an artist of some sort, if not to 'produce a masterpiece', was for several years to be an abiding goal for him.[16]

His Jesuit school, however inadvertently, provided some positive encouragements and examples for him in this endeavour. From its admittedly kitschy spiritual hub — a chapel 'full of ugly plaster saints' — he recalls how he 'learned a common ground of iconography'. Forbiddingly austere and gloomy, the architecture and physical fabric of the buildings were packed with visual interest for an imaginative child, even if he couldn't fully register all the historical and cultural associations at the time. As Hughes put it, in a memoir of the school which he wrote nearly a decade and a half after leaving: 'St Ignatius' … was a minatory place, a blockish palazzo of Hawkesbury sandstone, dark and frowning, with a Berninesque facade, [and] resonant cloisters …' Everything about the building (even that local stone, as it turns out) pointed to Europe, and not

only Renaissance or Baroque Europe. For Hughes the cloisters have res-
onated with more than the sound of his fellow-inmates' everyday
perambulations; it was down this long arcade that his brother Geoffrey
had approached him with the news of their father's death, and the memory of those ominous, resounding steps, he told one interviewer, still
cropped up in his mind when he looked at a de Chirico: 'you know, that
long, vanishing perspective of the sandstone'.[17]

He didn't have to wait to go to Europe to be initiated in de Chirico or
in various other Modernist painters. There had long been a practice at the
school of pinning up a selection of postcards of famous paintings on one
of the main notice-boards. These had mainly consisted of Renaissance
madonnas and the like; they were probably there more for the boys' spiritual edification than for aesthetic purposes. But one of the priests in
Hughes' time at the school decided to confront the boys with the subversive horrors — or, did he furtively think, delights? — of twentieth-century
secular art, and pinned up reproductions of 'paintings which he considered to be surrealist' (by the likes of Rousseau, de Chirico, Tanguy and
Miro). Hughes recalls being duly horrified — and fascinated. There was a
similar mix of feelings when he first spied a Miro original at an exhibition
held in the New South Wales Art Gallery in 1953, but he was soon won
over entirely. This 'magical and free' image, as he was to evoke it over
thirty years later, 'didn't have any of the overpowering, overwhelmingly
structured character of Jesuit education. Also it seemed to have something
to do with sex'. He has reflected yet more recently: 'Surrealism … for many
Catholic kids with artistic ambitions was the door out of orthodoxy'.[18]

Within the official routines of Jesuit pedagogy in the 1950s there was
not much opportunity to *practise* art as such. (Many schools of that period, whatever their religious bias, did not give a high priority to painting or
drawing as formal subjects at senior level.) As for sex practices, they were
ruthlessly proscribed. Finding sexual outlets when the authorities weren't
on guard was made even more difficult if you were as timid or ignorant
about homosexuality as Hughes says he was. He remained a virgin, he tells
us, till his final year, when he 'succumbed' to a local shopgirl. The official
line on sex drew no moral distinction between fornication and masturbation. The evils of both formed the subject of a lurid hellfire sermon

delivered to the boys by 'a Jesuit with special oratorical powers ... brought from outside the school'. Yet this could have the effect of glamorising sex, heightening its power as a transgressive weapon. In another context Hughes has associated masturbation with the kind of art in which he was becoming interested as 'a symbol of revolt against the family and authority'. Modernism — and especially Surrealism — represented a form of sexual liberation for him as much as it did a displacement of religious faith. 'All kids get off on Surrealism', he claimed to one interviewer, 'because it's about revolt, the overthrow of authority, the realm of the subconscious. Above all, it's about sexual freedom which is what you want when you're that age — certainly what I most wanted.'[19] As a result, you had to be almost as furtive about these artistic tastes and inclinations as about actual sexual activity. Modernist literature was no less suspect. Hughes has described how he used to conceal a copy of the works of Apollinaire (the Symbolist poet who had greatly influenced modernist painters, and had coined the term 'surrealism') within the covers of a Latin textbook. A more liberal-minded Jesuit on the staff, Hughes' senior English master, lent the boy a James Joyce anthology on one occasion, though both of them got into trouble over this.[20]

Hughes was not prevented from writing poetry himself; there was even some positive encouragement given for this activity to the boys in general, though it was carefully monitored. There was a prize offered for poetry which Hughes managed to win one year, with a shrewdly-tailored piece on the conquest of Mount Everest that managed to turn this achievement into a triumph of the faith. The judge was the noted Catholic convert, and leading anti-modernist poet, James McAuley. McAuley had nursed something of a passion for Apollinaire in his own youth, though it was the classical discipline and restraint of the English Augustans that he took as a model in his maturity. A few years later, in a cartoon of McAuley which Hughes dashed off for the periodical, *Australian Letters,* he neatly if not too subtly crystallised the poet's religious and literary allegiances by depicting him as an angel with a cruciform pen poised over a scroll, on which was inscribed the words: 'I love Pope'.[21]

Determinedly out of love with the Catholic Church, yearning to consolidate his discovery in art (and in sex) of an 'alternative to my Jesuit

upbringing', Hughes was none the less adept at fitting in with the structures and disciplines of his school while he had to, and they have
ineluctably marked him in various ways. Germaine Greer is supposed to
have said on one occasion that he is 'still a Catholic'. When an interviewer
quoted her to him on this issue, Hughes responded:

> I know what she means because there's a sort of Jesuitical cast of mind that
> never leaves you. You're capable of entertaining two sides of the question. It's
> a method of argument which is not ultimately based on Loyola but upon clas-
> sical structures transmitted through seventeenth-century education. But I'm
> extremely glad I had that education.

Being able to entertain two sides of a question is not the same as arriving
at a balanced or even-handed view — it might leave you aggressively
equivocal, as in Greer's case — but it's surely a prerequisite of balance.
Neither knack, of course, could be considered an exclusive preserve of
Jesuit (or more broadly Catholic) intellectual traditions, and there are
alternative, though not unrelated, explanations for the balancing acts in
Hughes' style and thought.[22]

He had extensive experience as a debater during his years at St Ignatius',
and it is one of the ground rules of school debating that you have to be prepared to take any side of an issue. Hughes ended up winning the
championship in the debating competitions with other elite Sydney
schools. This wasn't just a Catholic elite, and the nickname he earned after
this triumph, 'Fucking Churchill', suggests a rather different model from the
Loyolan or Jesuit one. Being prepared to take any side of an issue is a technique lawyers have to learn as well, and Hughes may have first imbibed the
rhetorical skills involved in this technique from his father and brothers,
particularly his brother Tom, who had been called to the Bar as early as
1949, two years before Robert entered St Ignatius'. Tom had been sent to the
same school, of course; though if we are to believe some accounts of his
career, his training by the Jesuits was the last thing to have lent any balance
to his frame of thought. It is a quality he has expressly prized in his later
years as a principle of good lawmaking, speaking for instance of how governments need to preserve a 'balance … between the need to deal with
crime and the fundamental legal rights of people'. But it is not something

for which he's been noted in his own style of advocacy or 'attitude to life'. A legal colleague once said of him: 'I've never known him to vacillate. If he's wrong he'll be very wrong because he won't retreat from any position he takes up'. And in a profile of Tom Hughes written in 1978, his future son-in-law, Malcolm Turnbull, observed: 'there are dangers in being trained by the Jesuits. They teach discipline at the expense of flexibility and their disciples tend to see straight lines and clear distinctions where none exist'.[23]

On the death of their father, Tom Hughes clearly became something of a father-figure for Robert — the first of a succession he has found in various guises down the years. Cyril Connolly was to be another, in an indirect and more strictly intellectual fashion. Robert's relations with these figures have often mixed defiance with awe. There were occasional moments of closeness with his brother, such as when they went on fishing trips together in rural New South Wales, which Robert clearly enjoyed, and continued to treasure in his memories, but for many years he identified Tom with those austerities and disciplines of their old school from which he had sought an escape. In his 1969 recollections of St Ignatius', he claimed that the memory of the corporal punishments meted out to him and his fellows by the Jesuits meant that 'To this day, I can't open a letter from Authority — bank manager, elder brother, tax department — without hesitation and a flicker of that desire to hide'. But he had already engaged in more assertive forms of resistance against such authorities.[24]

In their less brutal forms, the very disciplines of his school helped provide him with his first passport to greater freedom and independence from his upbringing. The academic training was very rigorous, and combined with Hughes' native intellectual talents, it brought him notable success in examinations. In his final year at school, 1955, he was the top candidate in English in New South Wales, and won fifth place overall in the state aggregate. These results brought him two scholarships to Sydney University. A biographical note on him in the revised edition of his *The Art of Australia* (1970), sums up his subsequent academic career thus: 'Hughes ... interrupted his degree course in 1956, and finally completed his studies in the faculty of architecture in 1962'. There was more than a bit of evasiveness here, though Hughes was probably not responsible for it. As he told the story in his school recollections of the year before: 'overcome with the sudden delicious absence of discipline, no strap, no lines, nobody to tell you when to work or punish you for not working, I did not work at all, failed Arts 1, and lost both scholarships at once'. His most recent account of this period adds that he had originally intended to combine his arts course with law and

> then become a barrister, like my elder brother. My conscious mind had per-
> suaded me that I could follow in his footsteps to the bar and maybe give him
> some competition. But alas, my unconscious led me to the wrong bar.
>
> Released after five years in a Jesuit boarding school, I discovered beer, girls
> and university journalism.[25]

He was never to complete his studies in anything, in the sense of qualifying for a degree. While he eventually enrolled in the Architecture faculty, and managed to sustain a better academic record there for a while, he was never wholeheartedly committed to it. Traces of his formal training in the subject are still to be glimpsed in the sure-footed technical precision which informs, say, his critique of the grand purist follies of Mies van der Rohe in *The Shock of the New*, his evocations of the medieval churches or the nineteenth-century covered markets of Barcelona in his book on that city, or his celebration of New York's Chrysler Building in his television series, *American Visions*. But there is no sense that he was ever serious about practising as an architect.[26]

Much of the year he was supposed to be completing his architectural studies he in fact spent following up research in preparation for *The Art of Australia*. The founder of Penguin Books, Allen Lane, had been introduced to Hughes the year before, when on a visit to Australia to investigate the possibilities of setting up a local branch of his firm. This enterprise got off the ground by the end of that year, and Hughes' book was among the first to be commissioned by one of the editors Lane had appointed, Geoffrey Dutton. By March 1962, just about the time the university term would have been beginning, Hughes had already started in earnest on the project, and was busy interviewing artists from various parts of the country. An advance of three hundred pounds which Lane secured for him finally encouraged Hughes to ditch his studies altogether, and by the middle of 1963 he had managed to complete a first draft of the whole work. There was to be a long delay, however, before it was released; various bungles and wrangles in the production stage, and last-minute reservations on Hughes' own part, had led to the pulping of the original printing stock.[27]

Hughes' facility as a critic had been spotted not long after he left school, and he had allowed it to be tapped over the next few years by a range of newspapers far beyond the world of 'university journalism'. Donald Horne, editor of the Sydney *Observer,* had employed Hughes as a cartoonist on that paper (as well as an economics reporter) in its first year of publication, 1958, but when the art critic had to be sacked for not attending the shows he reviewed, this job was handed over to Hughes. The earnings he received, combined perhaps with some support from his family, were enough to subsidise his first foray out of Australia the following year. He was in hot pursuit of a young Sydney dancer, Brenda Bolton, who had gained admission to the Royal Ballet in London. It was an unsuccessful pursuit, but during that jaunt in England he managed to have some of his writings accepted by the London *Observer* and the *Spectator:* quite a coup for a colonial tiro. (It may have been in these publications that Lane first came across his name.) He went through his money after a few months, and returned to Sydney, whereupon he was snapped up by the *Mirror* to be their art critic and political cartoonist. He also became a regular contributor to *Nation,* edited by the redoubtable Tom Fitzgerald, who was nurturing young Clive James' career around the same time.[28]

James had first come across Hughes (the 'Huggins' character in his autobiography) at Sydney University. He remembers him as 'the artiest young man on the scene', with a 'lanky form Englishly decked out in lamb's wool, suede and corduroy', an impossibly long cigarette protruding from his lips, and a folio under his arm, full of his sketches and drawings. He drew as compulsively as he smoked — as if making up for all that lost artistic time at school. He started taking classes with that 'superb draughtsman' and landscape painter, Lloyd Rees, and soon began to paint also. Rees' anecdotes of his days as an artist in Tuscany filled Hughes with a yearning to get to Italy himself.[29]

For a while he continued to pour out poetry — 'excited plagiaries and pastiches from Thomas and Seferis', as he described them nearly twenty years later. These derivative elements in Hughes' verse were to be remorselessly anatomised in an article published in the undergraduate newspaper, *honi soit,* in 1961 by Geoffrey Lehmann. He was an aspiring poet himself, and when a pupil at Sydney's top Anglican boys' school, Shore, he had clashed with Hughes in the debating competitions. Hughes might have comforted himself that this exposé was partly a score-settling affair, with its roots in rivalries that had little to do with the artistic qualities of his work. But he appears to have harboured serious doubts himself about the originality of his verse for quite some time before, and claimed in later years to have 'stopped writing "poetry" when I was 20'. If this is correct, it was a good three years before Lehmann chose to strike.[30]

In retrospect, Hughes has also been inclined to pooh-pooh his ventures in painting as too-slavish versions of the work of his cultural heroes in Europe and America ('purple De Koonings'). He told Clyde Packer, who interviewed him in the early 1980s, that he used to sell these paintings 'in order to subsidise myself as a writer … I couldn't possibly have made a living off art criticism in Australia'. In the memory, however, of a fellow-undergraduate at Sydney, Andrew Riemer, Hughes' widely-announced ambitions twenty years earlier were 'to find some place — England? America? — where his talents might be better appreciated' *and* to become a painter. Certainly, apart from the year and a half or so he took to complete the first draft of *The Art of Australia*, painting was the chief focus of his energies during his remaining years at home.[31]

Even before his first brief foray abroad in 1959, he had exhibited in a show of the Sydney Contemporary Art Society. He started to mix with other aspiring painters, such as Colin Lanceley, who have since gone on to prominent artistic careers, and who at the time were crystallising into a self-consciously iconoclastic group that became known as the Annandale Imitation Realists. They had their first group show in 1962 (riotous Dadaesque collages of discarded objects from funfairs and the like). By 1961 Hughes had already produced enough to have an exhibition of his own in Sydney; and he was to hold another of these one-man shows in Melbourne in 1963. (His chosen modes and media here were rather more conventional than the Annandale group's: semi-abstract landscapes in oils, and some gouaches). He wowed at least one prominent private collector — the madcap millionaire major, Harold Rubin, who wanted to buy up the entire contents of Hughes' studio. Only a monumental eccentric could be so attracted to his work, Hughes later made out; though a reviewer of his Melbourne show shrewdly noted its 'plainly comprehensible', 'finely weighed and balanced' nature — 'close to his qualities as a writer'.[32]

Hughes couldn't take much pleasure in the good reception accorded him by local critics because this would have been to comply with a 'depressingly complacent culture', as he dubbed his homeland in the original version of *The Art of Australia.* The place was too small, too cut off from the world's great artistic and intellectual centres in the northern hemisphere, too lacking in major historical and political dramas, to be other than complacent — and culturally 'immature'. There had been outbursts of artistic competence, even inspiration, in the past, which it was part of his business to trace in the book, and there had been a positive 'efflorescence of talent' since the late 1930s; but this, he averred,

> has solved no problems. It has posed new ones, because it has confronted Australian sensibility with the painful duty of growing up. If this isn't met, we will be cosily sitting on the other side of the hairline which separates the provincial bore from the regional artist.

In Hughes' eyes, as in Clive James', Germaine Greer's and Barry Humphries', growing up appeared to be inseparable from getting away. In the revised edition of *The Art of Australia* Hughes quoted an Australian painter who had said to him in 1966: 'you can't begin to grow up until you've left the place'. This was not just if you were a painter.[33]

Hughes had left Australia for Europe two years earlier, yet within a few months of arriving in the northern hemisphere he had relinquished his ambition of becoming a painter and decided to commit himself to writing about art. There was no question of his returning home, and he didn't do so in any professional capacity until invited to come back for a three-week lecture tour organised by the New South Wales Art Gallery Society in 1972. A dawning realisation (literally at dawn, as he relates it in one account) that he would only be 'a "middling good" or at the best a "promising good", painter' had prompted the reversal of one of his ambitions on leaving Sydney. What was the good of doing anything if it wouldn't one day result in a masterpiece?[34]

Cyril Connolly's harpings on the masterpiece in *The Unquiet Grave* were still ringing in Hughes' ears, perhaps; though the flea in the ear he had received directly from the same author may now have stung him into proving him wrong in his assumption of a rigid distinction between creative work and commentary on creative work. Why couldn't commentary or criticism aspire to the condition of a masterpiece in itself? (Connolly himself, as the former editor of the distinguished literary periodical, *Horizon,* and even as regular reviewer in posh weeklies like the *Sunday Times,* had proved himself more of a master in these journalistic excursions than in his pallid attempts at novel-writing. There were also those great exemplars of 'journalistic' criticism, Edmund Wilson and Kenneth Tynan, whose reviews of literature and theatre, respectively, had dazzled Hughes from his undergraduate days.) Hughes reports another traumatic incident involving an old idol of his which may have had a more decisive influence on his commitment to full-time criticism. Towards the end of 1964 he was staying at Porto Ercole in Italy, at the invitation of the famous Australian war correspondent and author, Alan Moorehead, who had a house there. His friend from the Annandale Imitation Realists group, Colin Lanceley, was also passing through, having won a valuable travelling scholarship for Australian artists. Persuaded that Hughes was not of the same mettle as himself, Lanceley apprised him of this by chucking his palette into the sea. Lanceley's robust candour was as much a relief, perhaps, as it was a jolt. It is possible that (as in the case of his poetry a few years earlier) Hughes had already begun to lose confidence in his potential as a painter of original masterpieces. Being suddenly exposed to so many of them in Europe might have been the opposite of inspiring to him in his own efforts; but this was in itself a part of his growing up.[35]

Whatever the reasons for his abandonment of painting, they did nothing to weaken his obsession with escaping the provincial cossetings of his homeland. To his way of thinking at the time, Australia was no more conducive to writing about art in a mature way than to practising it. 'Criticism here has hardly got beyond snapshots of surface reactions', he claimed in an article he published in *Nation* about a year and a half before departing. There were, as he conceded here, a few outstanding exceptions to this lack of rigour — such as the work of Bernard Smith, whose book, *Australian*

Painting, 1788–1960, had just appeared. But a 'few art historians', he wrote
in the conclusion to the original version of *The Art of Australia,* could 'not
provide a constant centre of critical thought'.[36]

His subsequent reminiscences of his days as a reviewer and critic in
Australia are often cast in terms of infancy or stunted growth, whether
referring to himself or to the critical culture at large. Someone else first
stuck the label *'enfant terrible'* on him, as early as his first year at university; and it remained his routine tag-name with journalists for years. While
he has expressed some reservations about how *terrible* he was, he has readily accepted and accentuated the image of the child. 'All I really was', he told
an interviewer from *Vogue* in 1975, 'was an energetic kid who was trying
everything I could in order to find out about it — how to do it'. About ten
years later he told Geoffrey Dutton:

> Australia in 1958–63 was the only place in the world where someone as igno-
> rant as I could have conducted his basic art training in public without being
> laughed offstage. If I saw my then self now, I would sternly tell the little guy to
> go to school. But there were no schools — at least not for art critics.

From the late 1940s Melbourne University had boasted a Fine Arts
Department, which trained art *scholars,* at least; though it's true that
Sydney University did not have an equivalent for another two decades. In
the absence of such training grounds (which he might have felt con-
strained by, anyway, judging from his more recent expressions of disdain
for the insulations of academe), the 'little guy' had found lots of chances
through the world of journalism to learn the ropes of what would become
his profession, but, he has insisted subsequently, they were all 'little
chances'. Local newspapers provided little remuneration for art criticism,
and little space for it, partly because there was only a little market to support it . Though *Nation* offered him slightly more space than usual, there
was precious little to write about, unless it was about the shortcomings
themselves. Consistent with the image of the *enfant terrible,* Hughes has
described how he left Australia 'muffled in Oedipal rage, dying to get out'.[37]

In his interview with Clyde Packer, we find him turning these personal feelings into a general condition, into a collective myth about all those
(in his generation at least) who did get out. 'Expatriation', he contends, 'is

very largely about Oedipal revolt, it is about the feeling that if you're not going to kill your father, at least you're going to kill him symbolically by getting away from him. You find a new father'. An echo of this is certainly to be found in Barry Humphries' talk, when interviewed by John Lahr, of murdering his parents 'symbolically'; although Humphries was referring to the function of his theatrical impersonations rather than of his expatriation. In Hughes' case, as his own father was already dead by the time of his early adolescence, it was not just the act of murder that had to be symbolic but its avowed victim as well. It was easiest to make a symbolic father out of his elder and rather stuffy brother, or out of predecessors and mentors in his own field of art criticism, such as Bernard Smith — 'the grandfather of Australian art history', as he has been dubbed in a recent profile of Hughes' career. (*The Art of Australia,* Hughes indicated, while 'indebted' to Smith's *Australian Painting,* was at the same time 'radically opposed … , both in technique and in emphasis'.) But Hughes also found ways of identifying his paternal line with broader aspects of Australia's social, political and cultural milieux.[38]

'Grandad's Gallery', he entitled his first article for *Nation,* a slashing attack on the Art Gallery of New South Wales. This institution sported Streetons in abundance (compared to the solitary one his own grandad had purchased); there were some Lindsays, too, which might have sealed the associations with his home. A sprinkling of other nineteenth- and early twentieth-century Australian or English artists were represented well enough — all of impeccable respectability. But where were the works of those artists whose names were emblazoned in brass on the façade of the building: 'Ghiberti, Giotto, del Sarto, da Vinci, Bernini, Inigo Jones, Wren and so on'? Not one was to be found within the Gallery's walls. This could be construed as false advertising, Hughes intimated. There's a sardonic note here that corrects any tendency to over-earnestness. The imputation is consistent, however, with the charges of cant and dodgy ethics that he was to bring against the nineteenth-century merchant class of Australia in his 1975 television series, *Landscape with Figures.* This was, of course, the class of his forefathers.[39]

It was in the Art Gallery of New South Wales that he had first set eyes on magical, sexy Miro, but it was the only Miro on view and part of a visiting exhibition. This made it as frustrating and tantalising as a peep show. The situation was typical of Australia. If able to be seen at all, original works by the great masters of European art were represented only by a few specimens, even in the major galleries of Sydney and Melbourne. Substantial touring exhibitions from abroad were rare events. The only hope of seeing anything approaching a representative sample of these artists' works on the spot was in the form of reproductions, such as on the postcards displayed at his school, or in prints, art books and magazines. The only hope of seeing the originals was to leave Australia. In *Landscape with Figures,* Hughes clearly identified with the escape strategies of a generation of Australian artists — slightly older than his own generation — who after the Second World War had to cope with a deeply conservative political regime as well as a complacently provincial cultural scene. Referring to the work of Albert Tucker, Sidney Nolan and Arthur Boyd, in particular, he said:

> Neither social realism nor militant expressionism had very much of a role in the brave new Australia presided over by *our great white father, Robert Gordon Menzies.* It was time to get out, therefore — time to get to Europe and to learn what they had really been looking at in reproduction for so long.[40] [My emphasis]

Menzies was to remain Prime Minister of the country for a further two years after Hughes himself got out.

Hughes has recently re-emphasised the sense of deprivation involved in being forced to make do with reproductions. In the introductory essay to *Nothing If Not Critical,* he wrote: 'There is no tyranny like the tyranny of the unseen masterpiece. In Australia we had art schools teaching people how to make Cézannes, but our museums had no real Cézannes to show us'. And in a lecture he gave back in Australia in 1992, on the subject 'What's a Museum For?', he declared: 'All art education begins at that moment of contact — not with a reproduction or a replica, but with the real thing'. One of the purposes of a museum, he wrote the following year, 'is to defend the audience's experience of the original work against its possible clones; to stand for the first-hand, as against the simulation and the copy'.[41]

Hughes risks overstressing the limiting effects of such deprivation. Elsewhere he has suggested that it need not be such an oppressive force.

Two of his favourite artists of the twentieth century (the *émigré* German Londoner, Frank Auerbach, and the New Yorker, Joseph Cornell) have, on his own showing, resolutely shied away from any extensive touring of the great collections, even though these have been far more accessible to them than to Australian-based artists. According to Hughes' account of the buildings of Antoni Gaudi, photographs of 'caliphs' palaces in North Africa, Persian towers, Indian stupas, arcaded pavilions and mosques in Cairo' provided the Catalan architect with an indispensable source of information and inspiration. Gaudi never personally visited any of these places, but this never made him less than a genius. Conversely, if we credit Hughes' accounts of the various Australian painters (from Streeton to Whiteley) who eventually did expatriate themselves, their careers took a nose-dive into mediocrity or glibness thereafter. Back in the early 1960s Hughes was even to be found stressing the 'stimulating', 'productive', 'exhilarating' effects of isolation from European masterpieces.[42]

Lack of ready access to major collections may be more frustrating for ambitious art critics, eager to secure (and demonstrate) a knowledge of their field beyond the familiar horizons of their immediate locality. Hughes was reported as claiming in 1971: 'I could never have functioned as a critic if I had not left Australia — you must seek something new and greater'. To have ended up, say, 'the world authority on Tom Gleghorn' — much as he had respected some of this artist's work — was never a fate Hughes could have willingly entertained. Even to achieve authority in writing about local artists demanded a wider frame of reference, a serious and sustained engagement with the international context, both past and current. Hughes said in 1974: 'The effort is to see for good or ill Australian art as part of world art'. This required more than airy assertions of influence and vague invocations of tradition. From his days in Australia a decade or so earlier, he could remember 'the reviews that used to talk about the great tradition of European portraiture as exemplified by Rembrandt, Goya and Dobell, just total fantasy, a fantasy generated by being locked out of access to the Rembrandts and the Goyas and wanting to get a local boy [Dobell] who would serve both purposes'. For Hughes himself, at least, occasional trips abroad would not suffice to make up for this deprivation. He wanted to be able to 'cross the street and look at Rembrandts', as he put it in 1975.[13]

Hughes had had an opportunity to become regular art critic of Australia's first national newspaper, the *Australian,* when it was launched in July 1964; but there were greater incentives for him to leave the country for good around this time. From the sales of his paintings, as he recalls, he had made or saved about $2000 — enough for a passage to England, for some travel *en route* (he chose to go via America), and for establishment expenses in London while he started to look for work. According to Clive James, Hughes had never had to worry about accommodation in London, as there were family quarters already set up in one of the swishest areas of the metropolis. Hughes doesn't mention any such cushioning from his family — and it wouldn't easily fit his self-image as oedipal tearaway — but he has richly acknowledged the patronage (in various ways) of another of his father-figures, Alan Moorehead.[44]

Born in Melbourne in 1910 — just over half way between the birth-dates of Hughes' father and older brother — Moorehead had travelled to Europe, and decided to settle there, in his mid-twenties, just about the same age that Hughes would resolve on a similar course decades later. After the Second World War Moorehead and his wife based themselves in Italy, and, on the proceeds of his journalism and best-selling books, bought their villa at Porto Ercole, a fishing village on the Tuscan coast, in 1960. He returned to Australia for a visit early in 1964, and having already become acquainted with some of Hughes' journalistic writings, he made contact with the young man, 'out of the blue', to tell him how impressed he was with his work, but to offer him a word of warning, too. 'If you stay in Australia the way you are', he is reported as having told Hughes on the telephone, 'Australia will remain very interesting but you are going to become a bore'. As Hughes recalls their conversation on meeting, Moorehead went on to say to him: 'What you should do is leave Australia and go to Europe because you're not going to be able to find a publishing situation here which you can really develop. There aren't the papers; there aren't the magazines'. Nothing could have chimed more with Hughes' own intuitions; and the advice came at an opportune moment. Hughes has recalled how 'at that time my mother had died, thus freeing me to go to Europe again'. Moorehead promised to arrange introductions for Hughes to publishers and agents in London, and assured him of a bolthole at Porto Ercole any time he needed a retreat.[45]

Hughes was soon on his way. He did write an article for the *Australian*, in its fledgeling months, but this was dispatched from Hawaii, where he could hardly believe his luck in happening upon the 1964 Guggenheim International Award Exhibition held at the Honolulu Academy of Arts. He made it the occasion for some general reflections on the contemporary art scene. It was full of the *enfant*'s wide-eyed wonder at a new and larger and lusher playground, with some vestigial scorn for the constrictions of the one he had now outgrown and put behind him. Underlying both the enthusiasm and the scorn was a search for balance and a faith in the capacity of modern art to embody and enhance this quality within its own forms:

> Once every five years, less in Australia, some critic raises [*sic*] to hail the Death of Abstract Art … To speak of conflicts between abstract and figurative is to vulgarise and distort the whole history of modern painting. They coexist and modify one another … Not the least achievement of modern painting is that it has expanded, enriched and strengthened our ideas of what imagery can be … There has been … an 'iconographical explosion.' It seems big enough to blow the Jeremiahs off the face of the map, for art itself never loses its human value, no matter what form it takes.[46]

Hughes didn't publish much else at this stage. He had brought down his valedictory verdicts on Australian painting. As well as *The Art of Australia*, he had produced an affectionate — though far from uncritical — monograph on the paintings of Donald Friend, which was published in Sydney in 1965, making it in effect his first book. Its criticisms were focused mainly on the cultural milieu in which Friend was raised and which he, too, had to escape: the Sydney art scene of the inter-war years, that 'rabbit warren of ignorance and prejudice', as Hughes took relish in calling it.[47]

Ideas for new books on wider artistic themes were already at the back of his mind but he had a lot of catching up to do in the galleries and museums of the world before he could begin to commit them to paper. There were also plenty of diversions for an unwary 'innocent' abroad that had nothing — seemingly — to do with art or art criticism. Hughes recalls picking up a 'floozie' in Los Angeles who persuaded him to take her to Las Vegas, where he lost much of his savings on the slot machines. One of the very first 'visions' to which he treats his audience in the recent series,

American Visions, is of the 'weirdly mutilated', high-kitsch architecture of Las Vegas casinos, so his own youthful exposure to them may have yielded something in the end. He was to press on to New York where he arrived in time to catch the World Fair and a glimpse of the *Pietà* of Michelangelo, 'visiting' from the Vatican, and flanked by armed guards. His eyes were still set on viewing the great masterpieces in their proper (European) context, but something of the ambiguous allure of America, that would take him back there on a permanent basis six years later, had perhaps already begun to work on his unconscious.[48]

He finally arrived in London, but in his reduced circumstances it was only a matter of months before he felt impelled to take advantage of Moorehead's invitation to Porto Ercole. Save for the fact that it happened to be where Caravaggio had spent his dying days over three and a half centuries earlier, this place had no artistic associations or appeal itself, but it proved a convenient centre for his sustained visual raids on the museums and galleries of neighbouring towns and provinces, and he ended up basing himself there for a couple of years, mastering the language as well. Learning Italian was no mere functional acquisition. Its special boon for him, as he related it to Clyde Packer, was that he was 'able to read Dante in the original [and] ... connect myself with all this material' from which he had been cut off as a child growing up in a faraway place. That art in such abundance helped provide him with a salve for other painful 'disconnections' in his childhood is suggested by his curious remark, in the same breath, that this whole Italian jaunt constituted a period 'with the unfound father'.[49]

Elsewhere in the Packer interview, Hughes suggests that his close proximity to Moorehead during this period provided him with further help, of a more clearly paternal nature, in transcending the rawnesses of his youth. Moorehead was completing his book on the baleful influences of European exploration on the South Pacific, *The Fatal Impact;* and every morning he would disappear into his studio at the bottom of the garden for five hours or more and make himself complete a thousand words. Here was an 'invaluable, indispensable ... model of professional conduct'. Hughes was still too youthful at the time not to be daunted by and slightly scornful of this unvarying routine ('all that *enfant terrible* stuff in Australia had conditioned me to think that I could rely upon inspiration'), but it was an example that eventually came to form the basis of his own practices, and which he continues to follow today.[50]

Other seeds of Hughes' later work were planted at this stage, however unknowingly. He admired and envied the epic scope of Moorehead's theme in *The Fatal Impact,* but having just quitted the area of the South Pacific, it was the last thing he felt that he himself could ever return to in a book, and he derisively dismissed Moorehead's prediction that he eventually would do so. It was a way of paying tribute to Moorehead's foresight when he echoed the older author's title (as well as something of his broader subject matter) in his own book of two decades later, *The Fatal Shore.* (The title was derived more directly from a phrase in a convict ballad of the 1820s.) One of the non-Australian subjects that Hughes did have in mind to write up as a book while staying at Porto Ercole was the Dada and Surrealist movements, the passion of his schooldays. Nothing came of this project (not directly or immediately, that is, although there were to be substantial sections on these movements in *The Shock of the New).* Even when he attempted to settle down to some writing in the mornings, Hughes has recalled, 'I'd fail', owing to endless hangovers. He was not entirely unproductive, however. He still managed to dash off some spritely journalistic pieces based on his dartings about provincial Italy and its cultural treasure troves; and a selection of these (one on Caravaggio, one on Duccio's altarpiece in Siena cathedral, the *Maestà,* depicting the Virgin enthroned in heaven, and one on the frescos of heaven and hell which Andrea Orcagna painted at the monumental cemetery in Pisa) found their way back to Australia and were published in major newspapers there early in 1966. If he was not already planning it consciously, Hughes was clearly gaining the expertise and the confidence which enabled him, only a couple of years later, to produce his next book, *Heaven and Hell in Western Art.*[51]

The immediate function of his journalism would have been to provide him with some cash for daily living expenses and more extensive travel in Europe. He has recorded some brief recollections of serene days spent in the 'museums of Europe' in the mid-1960s just before the days of regular jet travel and mass tourism. He mentions not just the Uffizi, so near at hand to his Tuscan base, but also the Albertina, the Louvre and the Prado. It was in the (northern) spring of 1966 that he first went to Barcelona, which had been the home of his beloved Miro and a way-station for Picasso in his youth. 'It reminded me of Sydney, only with art', he quipped many years later in explaining its special appeal for him. Here was an incentive to add to his languages; he had little Spanish and no Catalan when he first arrived. Here, in the long run, were the seeds of another of his books, though he has indicated that he didn't start thinking about such a project consciously for another seventeen years or so.[52]

With his head stacked full of the thousands of images to which he had exposed himself over two years he finally felt sufficiently fortified to make a renewed break for independence, quit Porto Ercole, and try his luck in London again. As he explained it to Packer, his pilgrimage to the shrines of European art

> enabled me to overcome my inferiority complex about not being an heir to Europe. It enabled me, when I ran into an Englishman who was talking about Piero della Francesca, to think, 'Yes I know that ... too. I have seen it ...' It was the belated equivalent of a proper university art-history course, except it was conducted in rather a gutsy manner, with a great deal more passion; and wasn't done from slides. So one's inferiority complex was more or less conquered.[53]

'More or less'. As that slight (and characteristic) note of reservation suggests, there were still lingering tensions or uneasinesses. Hughes was very apt to run into cultivated Englishmen, and not all were as offputting as Cyril Connolly. He now got to know both Kenneth Clark and Anthony Blunt, and each assumed a benevolent fatherly role for him, though one which still had to be resisted in various ways, it appears.

Clark's 'imperturbable tweeds' may have triggered off instant memories of his own father in a very different setting. In the recollections of his schooldays, written shortly after his meeting with Clark, one of the first impressions Hughes records is of himself as a five-year-old breathing in the 'smells of wet tweed and tea from the parents' enclosure' at a football match. In 1980, when *The Shock of the New* was first screened, and comparisons were being bandied around with Clark's *Civilization* of more than a decade earlier, Hughes was eager to dismiss any direct legacy from the older performer, but he acknowledged to one interviewer that 'when I was a baby critic, he [Clark] had a tremendous effect; he seemed to be a model of detached and eloquent diction'. Clark had been yet more impressed by this foundling from the antipodes. On returning to London from Porto Ercole in 1966, Hughes had started making himself known again by publishing articles in the posher newspapers and periodicals, as he had back in 1959, and he also began to pop up on various arts programmes screened on BBC television. Clark is said to have commended him to George Weidenfeld (who later published *Heaven and Hell in Western Art*) as the 'most brilliant young art critic' he knew. There are stories that the BBC even tried to co-opt Hughes as a collaborator on *Civilization,* but that Hughes soon found he 'couldn't collaborate with Kenneth Clarke [*sic*] on anything' and ended up deeming the finished product a disaster. Certainly, Clark and his programme soon became a model from which to depart. Three years before *The Shock of the New* was screened, Hughes was quoted as saying that *Civilization,* while it had pioneered 'the landscape of cultural television' was 'essentially a set of beautifully and very sumptuously filmed lectures in which at great expense slides were projected upon a screen. TV is not slide lectures ... '[54]

Hughes has recalled how he still had 'a nostalgia for the idea of scholarly respectability' when he went back to England in 1966, and that this drew him into the ambit of Anthony Blunt, who was then Professor of the History of Art at the University of London and Director of the Courtauld Institute. Hughes found Blunt 'very approachable — partly, I suppose, because he was gay', and he would drop by to take tea with the Professor and absorb the lessons he offered in looking at pictures and sculpture. Here was another model Hughes might have followed but which he ultimately rejected. He was to reflect:

> If ... I'd gone the academic route and become a student at the Courtauld ... and committed myself to a life of art scholarship, I would never have been able to do 'The Shock of the New' because I would not have been able to handle the material journalistically. I'm very interested in the kind of information you can get across to mass audiences without damaging the subject.

It was a matter of balancing knowledge with easy communicability. Blunt's personal style and pedagogical manner were too mandarin, perhaps; and his customary intellectual milieu too wedded — even more than in Clark's case — to instruction by lecture and slide. There was no question that his 'extracurricular activities', as Hughes neatly calls Blunt's political dealings with the Soviet Union, had anything to do with Hughes' eventual retreat from him: 'He wasn't going to let on to some sprog from Australia that he was a spy'.

If Blunt's anti-establishment leanings had been clearer from his writings and teachings in art history, it is possible that Hughes may have found him not less but more appealing. But for his mask to stick as long as it did, Blunt had to play up his English-establishment demeanour, and this couldn't help form something of a barrier in their relations given Hughes' own self-consciousness as a colonial. (The phrase 'some sprog from Australia' suggests how acute that self-consciousness was, and perhaps remains.) Furthermore, there was a part of Hughes at this stage that regarded himself as 'bohemian', 'anti-establishment', even a bit of a revolutionary, or at least these were the qualities which *he* felt impelled to play up in front of his peers, the masks *he* had to wear in order to persuade them (and himself) of his independence from his family. As a consequence, he recalls, he led 'this funny kind of split-level life', sipping tea with Blunt at the Courtauld, but also 'on the fringes of the *Oz* set'.[55]

Back in Sydney, in 1963, Hughes had designed a cover for *Oz* magazine before that publication — like himself — migrated to London. Several years later he was still contributing occasional articles to it. In an issue of 1969 he inveighed against the extravagances of the American space programme which had just managed to land a man on the moon. The following year, in the notorious 'Schoolkids Oz' issue, for which the editors were to be put on trial and convicted on obscenity charges, Hughes published a review of *The Making of a Counter Culture*, by Theodore Roszak, one of the great gurus of 1960s and 1970s 'alternativism'. He had originally been commissioned to write the review by that altogether more respectable organ of British opinion, the *Spectator*, but the *Spectator*'s editor of the day, the young Nigel Lawson, had rejected Hughes' piece as 'mindless ranting'. Unlike Clive James, who had reviewed the same book around the same time and dismissed it as 'shallow' rhetoric and a 'hopeless analysis', Hughes had thrilled to its invocations of 'revolutionary will'.[56]

Of his early circle of friends at Sydney University in the 1950s and 1960s, Hughes was to recall: 'We were a politically unconcerned bunch of aesthetes and artists'. As with many middle-class Australians of that generation, he was shaken out of this apathy by the Vietnam War, to which Australia's so-called Liberal government, under Robert Menzies, had started committing troops, on the anti-Communist side, within a year of Hughes' departure for Europe. Some signs of Hughes' outrage at these events in South-East Asia, and at his own country's interference in them, can be found in the art criticism he was producing at the time. Into his book on images of heaven and hell in Western art, he found an occasion to invoke his own graphic image of an 'oafish, grenade-festooned corporal, kicking in the teeth of a Vietnamese adolescent', and in the preface he wrote to the revised edition of *The Art of Australia,* he suggested that a visiting exhibition of American art to Australia in 1966 had been motivated by the United States government's 'gratitude to its enthusiastic accomplices in Vietnam'.[57]

According to the recollections of *Oz* publisher, Richard Neville, Hughes had much grander forms of protest in mind. He elaborated on these to Neville over a lunch they had together in London in April 1970. Round up a few of the most notorious international revolutionaries of the day (several of them were personally known to the *Oz* set, if not a part of it); charter an aeroplane; fly them out to Australia and shake up the place with a spectacular exercise in street theatre; subsidise the project and give it maximum publicity at the same time by making it the subject of a film, the 'treatment' for which (to be written by Hughes and Neville) could be published in *Oz* in order to attract a backer: 'We must make it clear', Neville recalls Hughes as saying, 'that the evils which our country epitomises exist all over the world ... Make it a world news event — in fact, if we can't make it a world news event, then it's not worth doing'.

The imperative to resist provincialism even in working on a provincial stage does sound like Hughes, however inexact the recollection of this conversation may be. Neville's subsequent explanation of Hughes' motives also has a ring of truth to it, even if the truth is not quite as simple: 'Bob', he claims, 'was pitting the strength of his radical credentials against the opposite inclinations of his older brother, Tom, who had just landed a position at the core of the establishment — Attorney-General of Australia'.

During the years of the Vietnam War it was part of the Attorney-General's responsibilities to enforce the contentious Conscription Act of the ruling Liberal–National Party coalition, and Tom Hughes was to gain considerable notoriety for his 'single-minded vigour' in pursuing this role. Just four months or so after the Neville/Robert Hughes lunch in London, Tom hit the headlines back in Sydney for brandishing a cricket bat at some student demonstrators who had assembled outside his house to protest against conscription — although he also went on staunchly maintaining the right to dissent 'within the limits of the law'. If it had ever gone beyond being a lunchtime fantasy, young Robert's planned spectacular with a cast of subversive superstars would have been a revealing test of the limits of his brother's tolerance.[58]

Even as mere fantasy, it suggested the persistence of his 'oedipal' rage — and not just against the father-figure of his brother. There was also the 'great white father' (as he was to call him) of the party that his brother served, Robert Menzies — undoubted father, too, of Australia's Vietnam policy. And now that he had retired, there were Menzies' successors as party-leader, among them John Gorton, who had appointed Hughes' brother to his position of power. Early in 1971 Hughes was quoted as saying how he 'rather likes his elder brother' but that

> the politics of the whole Gorton government in fact are a disaster ... The attitude of Gorton and his whole cabinet on the Vietnam War is built on the premise that should the North Vietnamese take Saigon, it would be used by China as a springboard to invade Australia.
>
> I've seen absolutely no evidence to remotely suggest that the Chinese, or anyone else in Asia for that matter, wants to invade Australia.

Through such pronouncements, Hughes may also have been taking a side swipe at the spectre of his real father, who, 'when he spoke of Asia ... saw it as a threat'. Remembering these views of his father some fifty years on, Hughes can see some historical justification for them ('Australia had been at war with Japan from 1941 to 1945'), but that was not something which his more youthful self could, or wanted to, acknowledge.[59]

In the late 1960s there were family pressures of a new and very different variety impelling Hughes to maintain a show of radical rage. Through his *Oz* connections he came to meet and marry Danne Emerson in 1967 and they produced a son, Danton, the same year. While they had drifted permanently apart by the mid-1970s, the marriage was not officially dissolved till 1981. Not long after, Hughes described his former wife to Clyde Packer as 'a woman of many extraordinary qualities but also a flying test-bed for every fad that existed in the 60s'. The naming of their son after one of the leaders of the French Revolution — not the most militant of them but the most brazenly charismatic — might be seen as a small symptom of this faddism. Not only hers, of course. Hard drugs; 'fluid', non-monogamous relationships, even within marriage; an attraction to the causes and the circles of the most radical-seeming political or cultural groups of the day (Women's Lib., Black Power, the 'Living Theatre', along with *Oz* and the rest of the underground press): as a rebel against his conventional family, Hughes himself was clearly susceptible to all such things to start with. But one does get the sense that their drawing power would not have been quite as strong for him if it had not been for the influence of his wife.[60]

She was the product of 'a conventional upbringing' in a Sydney suburb — Maroubra (on the same side of the city as Hughes' childhood home, but distinctly downmarket). At Sydney University, where she graduated in Arts and then went on to train as a teacher, she had started to mix in the heterodox world of 'The Push'. She had once fought for the favours of one of its male members against none other than Germaine Greer, building up antagonisms between the two women which later exploded in a legendary slanging match between them at a party in London in the mid-1960s. The competition between them was as much political as sexual. They were to find themselves at loggerheads again in November 1970, at the 'Wet Dream Film Festival' in Amsterdam, where Danne Hughes reproached Greer with betraying the integrity of one of the guest artists by objecting to the threatened violence of his act. He was about to torture a live goose.

Robert Hughes, meanwhile, was poised to settle into his job with *Time* magazine in New York. This was not yet to be quite the end of his marriage to Danne — the couple even returned to Australia together for his lecture tour of 1972, with Danton in tow. But it was the beginning of the end, as she now began (according to Richard Neville) to throw herself 'into the affairs of the Underground press, as well as affairs with its writers'.[61]

As Hughes put it many years later, quoting from the old ballad, she ran away with 'the raggle-taggle gypsies-o'. His almost visceral recoil from the romanticised messiness of 1960s alternativism is suggested here. ('You'd get up in the morning', he elaborated, 'and there would be some character boiling up his morning fix on the stove'.) If the worlds of *Civilization* and the Courtauld were too stuffy, the world of the 'Underground' was too scruffy — and still too dreamily juvenile for one who had left his home-land in order to grow up. It was a matter again of attempting to find some balance between these extremes. Hughes declared to Packer:

> the 60s were a pretty fraught time for everybody in London. I am by nature somewhat conservative, but I was trying not to be when I was in London … There was something babyish about the quality of hope in London then, par-ticularly in those around *Oz*. It was a difficult time for anybody to develop as a writer because of the prestige that formlessness and spontaneity enjoyed. I was low in London because I felt culturally out of sync. Also, I did recognise that there was actually some point to some of the so-called underground. So, I didn't feel in sync with the people who took rigidly conservative stances against it either.[62]

In political terms, at least, here was a marked divergence in Hughes' atti-tudes and sensibilities from his childhood hero, Ruskin. Summing up the politics of his own day, in Victorian England, Ruskin had noted the 'oppo-sition between liberals and illiberals, … between those who desire liberty, and who dislike it', and firmly declared himself a 'violent Illiberal'. He was equally attracted to, could not resist or mediate between, the extremes both of Toryism and Communism. (There's a vague foreshadowing here of Blunt, perhaps: 'Master of the Queen's Pictures', as he became, and Soviet agent.) Hughes' instinct, as he has matured, has been to seek a path between the extremes of right and left. He has generally found this path in the ideals of liberal democracy, spawned by Enlightenment philosophy, and further shaped and refined by Ruskin's contemporary, John Stuart Mill. Hughes has not been uncritical of what he sees as liberalism's own limitations, excesses and distortions, as reflected in the policies of various governments or political leaders that have called themselves liberal. He could have been afforded no better insight into the distortions than the

Vietnam policy of Australia's Liberal–National Party coalition government, with its violation of the very old liberal principle of national
self-determination. There's a sense in which the social and domestic policies that Mill himself came to advocate, in his later years, went too far in
the direction of state intervention to be accounted truly liberal. Hughes
nowhere specifically comments on this; though he has recently hinted at
some misgivings on his part about 'areas of bloat' in public funding of
social security. For him, the great hero in the liberal pantheon remains
Thomas Jefferson, draftsman of the Declaration of Independence in 1776,
and America's President from 1801 to 1809.[63]

The extraordinary intensity of the President's energies and passions in
all kinds of directions — architecture, education, technology, as well as
politics — makes him no obvious model of balance. 'Under the surface of
the eighteenth-century Whig reasonableness', Hughes states in the first
episode of his *American Visions,* 'there was something immoderate and
crazy about Jefferson'. But this doesn't detract from the 'overwhelmingly
attractive cast of his mind ... building up everything from first principles
... without a trace of fanaticism or self-pity or cant'. Hughes' decision to go
and live in America himself had nothing directly to do with any such hero-
worship of the country's liberal traditions and exponents; it was more
fortuitous, more pragmatic and more sceptical than that, as he has related
it. Subconsciously, however, it was his own declaration of independence
from both England and Australia, a further bid for freedom from 'babyish'
constraints and entrapments.[64]

How did it all start? There was just a phone call 'out of the blue',
Hughes has been apt to say — the same way he has described his equally
momentous first contact with Alan Moorehead. On this occasion the call
was long-distance from New York, and the caller did not immediately
identify himself. Hughes suspected it might be the CIA at first, checking up
on the renegade brother of Australia's new Attorney-General, but he finally ascertained it was *Time* magazine, offering to fly him over to New York
and try him out as their new art critic. The magazine's Managing Editor,
Henry Grunwald, had seen a copy of Hughes' *Heaven and Hell in Western
Art,* and been impressed with the quality of his writing — not a pre-emi-
nent quality of your regular art school graduate in America, Hughes

himself reflects. There were a couple of other contenders for the post — an Englishman and a Frenchman — but Hughes won.[65]

This story of his appointment is too good to be the whole truth. In a later version, Hughes suggests that there was a slightly more elaborate procedure of courting (and vetting?) by *Time*. Early on in the negotiations, one of the magazine's reporters from its London bureau was deputed to take Hughes out to lunch at a fashionable restaurant where various issues relating to the job were thrashed out. Doubtless, one of these was money. The financial incentives that were offered him turned out to be very considerable. Records are patchy, but from what he lets on, his salary had climbed to about $50 000 (US?) a year by the end of his first decade with *Time*, in 1980, and only a few years after that to $80 000 ('plus expenses and stock options').[66]

'America made me free', Hughes told an Australian interviewer in 1981. Free in the material sense, he meant here. He was released from the financial uncertainties of casual journalism and television work which had been his lot in England. But his job with *Time* was to involve other kinds of freedom, too. Because the magazine formed a part of one of America's largest media corporations, friends had cautioned Hughes that if he took the job he would be under constant scrutiny for his opinions and forced to conform to the rigid house style for which the magazine had become legendary among journalists. But this never turned out to be the case, according to Hughes. He had been reassured at that preliminary lunch that he certainly wouldn't have to conform to any dress codes. He had been worried at that stage that the magazine's bosses might have expected him to cut his hair or give up his motor cycle. But, no, he was told, such individuality would be cherished. When fine-tuning his contract, he even found the board of management amenable to dropping its traditional policy of contributor-anonymity and giving him a by-line. To a degree, of course, that let them off the hook as much as it did him. If he proceeded to smuggle any controversial political references into his art criticism (as he had done in the book which first brought him to the Managing Editor's attention), that could be explained away as his personal opinion, and not necessarily the magazine's. But did this matter as long as his own independence was assured?[67]

After more than a decade working for *Time,* Hughes could tell Clyde Packer: 'I've never had so little editorial interference from a magazine in my whole life. They don't rewrite me, they don't do any of that sort of thing'. In 1990, looking back over two decades, he commented to another Australian interviewer on 'the kind of liberty' the magazine had allowed him in practising his profession. He insisted that art critics were 'not given it in Australia. No paper here is really committed to serious, independent criticism on a regular basis. Most of the time you tend to get "lifestyle" stuff — auctions, prices, art as an investment ...' He returned to this theme yet again in 1995, when he said of his employers at *Time* that, as well as continuing to pay him a good salary, 'they give me complete freedom'.[68]

The sheer size and range of America's population, and the sweeping scope of her cultural influence beyond her borders, have been key elements of the sorts of liberty he associates both with the country at large and, on a more personal level, with his job there. It's the land of the 'huge big chance', he told Clyde Packer in 1980 — maybe only one chance, but sufficient to 'change your life', and a striking contrast to all those frustrating 'little chances' which his homeland had offered him. He has recently elaborated on the contrast:

> This polyphony of voices, this constant eddying of claims to identity, is one of the things that makes America. It is, I repeat, why the foreigner is grateful to be here ... Nothing could be less like the tiny, homogeneous Australia of my childhood than this gigantic, riven, hybridizing, multi-racial republic, which each year received between a half and two thirds of the world's emigration.[69]

The Statue of Liberty in New York harbour, he explained recently in his *American Visions,* 'meant freedom, meant America' to the millions of foreigners who had entered the country since the late nineteenth century, but its real subject 'was not America welcoming the exile but liberty enlightening the world'. The way he has spoken about *Time* magazine suggests that he sees it as fulfilling a comparable function. One of the best things about it from his point of view is that it addresses not just 'a large, reasonably visually literate audience, in America' but also 'a large, intelligent, international readership'. (Estimates of the early 1980s placed its audience at anything between nineteen and thirty million, worldwide.)

Time is 'the kind of forum that can reflect the pluralism that occurs in culture'.[70]

Independence, liberty, freedom: these things were what people had settled the New World for, and they were related to that sense of newness about the place as much as they were to the growing heterogeneity of its population. The pursuit of the new, in fact, was one of the oldest concomitants of the quest for freedom. Hughes' pilgrimage to America as an art critic was just a variant on these earlier patterns, or at least it started out that way. In *American Visions,* he demonstrates some of the palpable ways in which the founding fathers of the American republic — notably Jefferson, through the buildings he designed — were to be seen 'rejecting the Englishness that was all around them': seeking 'cultural independence' as well as political independence. This was to be a very gradual process, however, and especially in the field of painting. 'In art', Hughes observes, 'America really disliked the new — at first'.[71]

Over a century and a half earlier than Jefferson's Declaration of Independence, the pilgrim fathers had settled in what they called *New* England. Apart from the territory concerned, what was new about this was the freedom of worship they had gone there to establish and enjoy. Artistic enjoyment, or the 'sensuous ordering of sight', was not a high priority for them, and especially not where worship was concerned. 'You don't have pictures of a kind a Catholic might have', says the ex-Catholic, Hughes, in a staged 'interview' with dressed-up replicas of the pilgrim fathers on *American Visions.* But in its own way, he affirms, their puritan asceticism did 'have its aesthetic' (the aesthetic of 'radical bareness' exemplified in their architecture); and it certainly didn't mean they were 'conservative'. 'The truth', says Hughes, 'is very nearly the opposite. They invented the idea of American newness'. It was inherent in their theology of 'a new heaven and a new earth'. All the same, he has recently remarked elsewhere, 'almost all Americans before 1820 breathed a very thin aesthetic air'.[72]

The great boost to newness in art came with another, much later, much larger, and very different group of immigrants: the vast mass of Europeans who transplanted themselves in America at the end of the nineteenth century and the beginning of the twentieth. These, as Hughes puts it in *American Visions,* embodied a 'culture of mobility and displacement that would give America new vernaculars and help turn New York into the ground zero of a modernist explosion'. Between 1900 and 1930, he notes, New York 'turned itself into the exemplary modernist city, infused with a giddy sense of possibility and freedom'.[73]

When Hughes transplanted himself to New York in 1970 — his second great 'displacement' in a sense — it was a part of his ambition, as he expressed it in an interview with Don Riseborough a year after arriving, 'to discover and interest ourselves in new art forms'. As well as looking at the more prominent practitioners of these (and older) forms, he felt some responsibility to 'consider some of the unknown painters as they may be involved in some movement that the public wants to know about'. Looking back on this period a quarter of a century later, in the penultimate episode of *American Visions,* he claims that around 1970 it was 'simply taken for granted that New York was the centre of world art. Today we are not so sure about that but we were then'. And in the last episode, he declares: 'Today New York is still a world cultural capital but it's not the imperial centre. No place is. But in 1970 it was'.[74] It appears from his comments at the time, however, that he was 'not so sure' about this almost from the start of his New York venture, and that he harboured some uneasy reservations about the newest of the 'new art forms' to which he began to expose himself.

Quizzed by Riseborough in 1971 on the notion of New York as the 'art centre of the world', he is reported as replying: 'I really don't know if New York is the centre at the moment or not. The big boom in the sixties is dead, finished, gone. I don't mourn it. It's very much tougher, eclectic'. Among the new art forms being developed, he went on to explain, was Conceptualism — 'that is, art as an idea rather than as a substance. It is art as a proposition. I don't enjoy it very much. But I hope to get to like it'. Interviewed by the rising journalist Derryn Hinch a year later, Hughes was clear that 'New York is no longer the beginning and the end of the art world. The rule used to be that if anybody was any good he'd eventually be seen in New York, but a lot of good painters now reject New York'.[75]

With 'more exposure than any other critic in the world', Hughes could still comfort himself from his new perch at *Time* that he was at the great centre of journalism and also at a great centre of serious and sophisticated critical debate about art and literature. 'New York is still the most interesting place to work in — there is nothing comparable in London', he told Riseborough. The city had been the seat of one of the god-critics of his youth, Edmund Wilson (still alive when Hughes first settled there). It was also the base of the high priest of modernist art theory and criticism, Clement Greenberg, whose writings Hughes had invoked back in his Sydney days to show up the relative primitivism and superficiality of Australian writings on art. The American metropolis gave its name to three other world-famous publications: the *New York Times,* the *New Yorker* and the *New York Review of Books.* (The last of these would winkle several articles out of Hughes over the years, and allow him a yet more generous spread than his regular page or two in *Time.*) 'The big cultural scenes', he maintained, 'are still here — the big glossy art magazines are still here'.[76]

At first Hughes was clearly euphoric about just being there, and soon showed his commitment to staying by buying himself a loft in the lower Manhattan area known familiarly as SoHo. (This was before it became a mecca of radical-chic, he has been eager to point out subsequently. 'It wasn't even called SoHo then.') But his passion for his new-found home did not entirely blind him to its traps and limitations. Derryn Hinch reports him as saying in 1972: 'I love New York. I think it's the greatest place in the world, but people here are so insular … they forget that New York is not America'.[77] As if, perhaps, to remind himself that New York was not the world, he accepted the invitation of the New South Wales Art Gallery Society in the same year to return to his old home and deliver three lectures.

The lectures showed a characteristic balance of tone, approach and interests. They were 'not scholarly', noted the portrait-painter, Judy Cassab, in her diary, 'although that was there; showbiz, personal charisma, bad taste, and a delightful shower of words'. The topics were 'Heaven and Hell in Western Art'; 'Postwar American Art' and 'Leonardo da Vinci'. The last probably drew on materials that he had been collecting for a biography of Leonardo, originally commissioned by George Weidenfeld as a successor to *Heaven and Hell.* (It was never to be completed.) The middle lecture would have served as a testing ground for some of the ideas on American modernism which surfaced a few years later in *The Shock of the New.* There was nothing in the series that related specifically to Australian art; though he did address himself to this subject in a talk he did for ABC radio. The talk

was mainly an attack on the rise of the art dealer in Australia, and the iniquities of the art market, though he did rehearse (and with yet greater
ferocity) some of his old complaints about the provincialism and isolation
of the art scene as a whole. Most of the painting he had seen was 'sweet and
hedonistic and decorative and unchallenging'. The 'existential toughness
and the hardness' which had once been touted as a feature of Australian art
was 'mostly a fiction', he now concluded.[78]

These views did not prevent his returning again two-and-a-half years
later to make his ten-part series on Australian art for ABC TV, *Landscape
with Figures*. Without pulling any of his customary punches, whether at
painters, museums or the market, the conclusions he drew at the end of
this series were altogether more hopeful. This was partly because of the
impending opening of the Australian National Gallery in Canberra, the
collections of which (both in local and overseas painting) impressed him
far more than those of the older galleries ever had. It had even purchased,
amidst cries of outrage from more conservative quarters in the country
and much of the press, a major work by one of his favourite American
modernists, Jackson Pollock. But one can also detect behind his new optimism about Australian art a growing lack of confidence in the cultural
strengths of his adopted home as it entered a so-called '*post*-modernist'
phase. *Landscape with Figures* ends with the words:

> In the not far distant days when new art had a strong compact centre and a
> wide weak periphery, Australian painters had very little option but to behave
> and think of themselves as the colonials of modernism ... But it has ceased to
> matter very much anyhow because now, the centre as once constituted is slow-
> ly coming apart. There is no glue left except that afforded by the art market.
> And in the meantime the periphery, that once despised area, seems to be firm-
> ing. In time, therefore, I think it is possible that Australian art will learn to
> relax and that it will stop getting paranoid about a world role which it has
> never in fact had and probably never will possess. At that moment its climb
> upwards from being a provincial culture will have well and truly begun, and I
> think we will all be vastly the better for it.[79]

A decade's distance from his homeland served to rekindle his interest
in it. Some segments of *Landscape with Figures* were filmed at Port Arthur,

the site of a ruined penitentiary, and one of the more gruesome remnants from Australia's convict past. It struck Hughes how little he knew, or had ever known, about this past. There were a few good academic histories of the subject to make up for the 'potted version' in tired textbooks to which he'd been exposed in his schooldays, but none of these, as he saw it, sufficiently fleshed out the human story of the convicts' own experiences. Here, at last, was the sort of big historical theme, relating to his homeland, which he had felt a vague hankering for when watching Alan Moorehead at work back in the Porto Ercole days but then dismissed as a fruitless fantasy. Now, it appears, the sorts of subject he had felt more excited about at first in Italy had themselves begun to pall. His Leonardo had languished when he had elected to spend his spare time from *Time* doing up his Manhattan loft. 'Art books don't sell', he told an interviewer in 1977. 'Also, I don't want to spend my time writing long books about other people's fictions. At this time, I want to write about the real world'.[80]

The result was *The Fatal Shore,* though it took him another ten years to produce. The book's working title was *Chains.* As the descendant of a free settler in Australia, Hughes had no clanking ghosts of convicts in his own family's history to appease; but related spectres from his personal past were clearly pressing to be exercised — if not exorcised — when he embarked on the book. He has been happy to acknowledge the presence of some of these. One of the effects of his *Heaven and Hell* book, he claimed many years after its publication, was 'getting the Jesuits out of my system'. Not long after he had started his basic research for *The Fatal Shore* he was already declaring that 'the whole thing has everything to do with my Catholic background. Absolutely'. His interest in the subject and the approach he was taking to it reflected a fascination with various dichotomies that were at the root of the Church's teachings: 'punishment and reward', 'extreme pain and extreme pleasure', and, once again, heaven and hell. As it happened, the two predominating images of his homeland's early culture were 'Australia as a paradisical continent and Australia as hell-hole'.[81]

When *The Fatal Shore* finally appeared, several authorities in the field of early colonial history were to take it to task for over-emphasising the darker, more oppressive aspects of the convict system, and it is certainly true that the main impression he conveys of places like Port Arthur or

Norfolk Island — sometimes quite explicitly — is of a peculiarly terrifying hell on earth. He did make plain at the outset, however, that it was precisely his intention to highlight the grisly extremities of convict history and not its more normal, less dramatic course. 'Normalizing' the *whole* experience would be just as distorting, he suggested. It was hardly a way to grip a wide audience, either, and persuade them to buy the book. The darker aspects, as it turns out, are far from being the only impressions of early colonial Australia that he registers here, whether from his own imaginings or from the reports of his contemporary witnesses. Dwelling on the hellish, he is no more blind to the heavenly representations (Australia as paradise, Eden, Arcadia) than he was in his earlier study of those 'two master images' of the Western mind. His very sense of a dichotomy between those images involves him in invoking specimens of both and thereby, to some degree, correcting the imbalances of his chosen emphasis.[82]

Hughes has been less happy to accept the notion that *The Fatal Shore* represents some sort of atavistic, or personal, 'revenge upon the English'; and commentators on the book surely do go too far when they suggest that its author is using it as part of some 'defiant score settling for his Irish-immigrant forebears' or exploiting an opportunity 'to deliver a colonial left-hook to the stiff British upper lip'. It needs re-emphasising that his own Irish forebears never suffered under the convict system, even in its more 'normal' incarnations, and that his forebears on his mother's side were themselves English, not Irish. At the same time, the book draws explicit attention on occasion to English snootiness about Australians, an attitude (so Hughes made out) which stems precisely from Australia's origins as a dumping ground for the detritus of British society. The time was long past, he recognised, when 'Australian' was automatically 'a term of abuse', but right up to 1960 or thereabouts, even an upper middle-class Australian with no known felonious skeletons hanging in his family closet 'risked hearing languid sneers directed at his convict ancestry'. Hughes adduced no direct documentary evidence for this (and was to be challenged on the point by one English reviewer). What he did have, however, was direct personal experience of that *kind* of put-down — whether from the likes of Cyril Connolly or from the more barbed species of English television reviewer. Their sneering had been free of any taunts (any conscious thought, even) about convicts, but its victim, in brooding on the matter, might well have been led to start pondering its more remote historic roots. What would have made these put-downs particularly rankling in Hughes' case was the very fact that he was half-English himself.[83]

The most provocative and publicised aspect of *The Fatal Shore* was its hypothesis that the transportation system devised by the British contained within it the effective blueprint for the 'Gulag', or forced labour camps of the Soviet Union. Hughes flirted with this hypothesis in his Introduction, but he didn't press the analogy too closely thereafter, let alone subject it to any thoroughgoing historical analysis and comparison. It should be regarded mainly as a literary device, a trope, designed to provoke curiosity and sales rather than provoke the British. (In an interview about his work-in-progress on the book, published by an Australian newspaper in 1977, Hughes can be found acknowledging that 'however brutish Georgian England appears to us now, it was nevertheless very liberal by the existing standards of European absolute monarchies before the French Revolution'.) If his Gulag theory can be related to anything in his cultural or personal background, it is to what he himself once diagnosed in another context as an 'Australian tendency to feel nostalgic for the Tragedies one has not experienced'. Elsewhere, seeking to explain the tepid prettiness of so much recent Australian painting, he was prompted to remark: 'When I was growing up in Sydney in the late 40s and early 50s, the harbour was our watery paradise. Our experience had absolutely no dark side'.[84]

To escape from paradise precisely *because* of its sequestered serenities was a driving force of all the birds of passage dealt with in this book. Heading for New York, making a nest in what was then one of the city's seediest quarters, was Hughes' way of correcting the stultifying imbalance in his youthful environment — but such a radical way that it has required correction in turn. He came to find this balancing device partly through remarriage. In 1977 he met a Californian woman, Victoria Whistler, while he was in San Francisco to give a lecture on Robert Rauschenberg — 'one of the most wildly uneven artists in American history', as Hughes later called him. He was on his way back to Australia at the time to pursue his research for *The Fatal Shore*. She had attended his lecture, invited him to dinner afterwards, and was then to pursue him in New York once he returned there. They married four years later after his divorce from Danne Hughes became final. While bearing the surname of one of America's most distinguished expatriate artists of the nineteenth century, she was not an artist herself, nor a critic. This was possibly a part of her attraction. Her one connection with the art world was that she was 'in the framing business' — a job she gave up after starting her relationship with Hughes. The *Vanity Fair* profile of Hughes in 1990 tells us that 'he is extravagant in his praise' of the 'sense of order and stability ... she has brought to his life'.[85]

He continued to conduct much of his professional life from his loft in SoHo and his office at *Time* magazine, but his domestic and recreational life came to be centred at a farmhouse he bought on Shelter Island, part of Long Island on its eastern side, about a hundred miles out of Manhattan, and accessible only by ferry. There are some interesting convergences here with his older brother's life back in Australia. Tom Hughes was also married for the second time in 1981 (having divorced his first wife in the 1970s); he, too, divided his time each week between his city office and a country property (a rather larger one than his brother's, with sheep and cattle and horses on it). 'He says the farm provides a nice balance to his life', a journalist reported in 1994. The same journalist, and various other chroniclers of Tom Hughes' recent career, have reported something of a mellowing in his temperament and opinions since the early 1970s. While remaining 'at heart ... a Liberal' — a supporter of Australia's Liberal Party — he was to become increasingly critical of it from 'a small "l" Liberal' perspective, and persuaded that its commitment to the Vietnam War 'was a mistake'.[86]

Not too much should be made of the convergences between the two brothers in their later years. Robert Hughes has not budged from his avowed liberal opinions and perspectives, but his tone of voice in supporting these opinions has, if anything, become more belligerent and dogmatic. Finding a new order and stability in his personal life appeared to provide him with the conditions under which he could contemplate a return to writing art books, but the books concerned have all been testaments of various kinds to a fast-diminishing faith in the art of the present day — and in the art of the past to fulfil the hopes and expectations of its makers. For all his earlier talk of getting the Jesuits out of his system, one begins to wonder whether vestiges of his old religious faith and training have not begun to resurface as the challenges to his faith in art have grown apace.

His first art book to appear since the revised edition of *The Art of Australia* in 1970 was *The Shock of the New*, published in 1980. It didn't start out as a book but as a television series made for the BBC over a three-year period and first screened in 1979.[87] Subtitled 'Art and the Century of Change', its conception of the 'New' was a broad historical one, embracing the whole history of modernism, as distinct from a notion of new as 'most recent' or 'the latest'. Hughes didn't entirely ignore the latter categories, but they were not the main focus of his explorations as he had said he would make them when he had first arrived in America. And they were far from being the focus of any enthusiasm on his part.

His hopes that he might come to like conceptual art had proved vain. In *The Shock of the New* he dismissed this movement in all but a sentence. Minimalism (with the exception of one or two of its practitioners) hardly came off any better. He talked of its 'polemical numbness', and even associated it with a species of fascist art at one point. High Modernism itself, of course, had its own darker moments, as he readily acknowledged. 'We like to think that modernism is left-wing, or at least virtuously liberal, by nature. But to think so is to reckon without Futurism, which became the house style of Italian fascism.' Modernism, as Hughes demonstrated, was also enshrined in certain styles of urban architecture around the world that represented the bleakest authoritarian and bureaucratic tendencies in social planning, whether on the right or the left. For all these excesses, it was still something worth celebrating overall, as a radical breakthrough in the history of painting and sculpture which had managed at the same time to be 'grounded in tradition'. In *The Shock of the New* Hughes set out to recapture both its novel excitements and its venerable provenance for a much wider audience than it had ever enjoyed before.[88]

The celebratory hymn took on a note of threnody in its closing stages, as Hughes contemplated the 'end of modernism': a prospect 'no longer possible to avoid', he sadly reported, 'for the idea that we are in a "post-modernist" culture has been a commonplace since the 1970s'. Elwyn Lynn, an Australian critic who had locked horns with Hughes on more than one occasion, waggishly summed up *The Shock of the New* as 'an Irish wake, over the death of modernism', while noting as well the hectoring tone and 'dogmatic finalities' that characterised the obsequies. It is true that Hughes' lament for modernism is never sentimental or dewy-eyed, but it can't escape that higher nostalgia, characteristic of the pastoral strain in literature and art, for a vanished golden age in the world's history or in the artist's own youth. Referring derisively to the 'good taste' of some Sydney painters of the 1940s in his book on Australian art, Hughes had claimed that 'being nostalgic, it is a useless instrument for measuring the new'. It is not a warning he appears to have heeded himself in addressing the art that has followed after modernism.[89]

'The Nostalgia of the Poet' is the title of a painting by de Chirico, one of the modernist masters to whom Hughes was first exposed at school. In the collection of his 1980s criticism from *Time*, he reprints a particularly acute and discriminating essay on the development of the Greco-Italian's work over eight decades or so. This documents a 'long slide into mediocrity', as the painter's early state of mind, signifying 'alienation, dreaming and a loss', and reflecting on the processes of nostalgia, becomes in itself 'nostalgic, and flatly so', regressing to an ersatz classicism. The trajectory of Hughes' own career as a critic could not fairly be described in these exact terms; the de Chirico essay — though a relatively early one (1982) — is testimony alone to how far from mediocrity he has remained in the post-modern decades. Yet his very arguments about de Chirico's decline, and more generally his arguments against subsequent developments in the world of painting, makes of modernism itself a focus of retrospective (if not regressive) yearning. His is a case, clearly and increasingly, of the 'nostalgia of the critic'.[90]

In the recently updated edition of *The Shock of the New*, published in the wake of *Nothing If Not Critical*, Hughes can be found retreating from this position slightly. He acknowledges that modernism's influence at least may not be entirely dead as yet, and he challenges the pretensions of self-styled post-modernists by stigmatising their 'ill-defined' historical and theoretical perspectives. As in his post mortem on angels in 1970, he is still clearly capable of reserving final judgment, of saying and thinking 'And yet'. And yet, the note of reservation here sounds more confused than balanced. For much of the burden of the revised section of this book is to arraign the same vague movement for facilitating the end of much more than modernism — something close to the end of art as the Western world has known it:

> The contrast between our *fin-de-siècle* and the last seems binding: from Cézanne and Seurat to Gilbert and George, in just a hundred years. The year 1900 seemed to promise a renewed world, but there can be few who watch the approach of the year 2000 with anything but scepticism and dread.[91]

Some such indictment runs right through *Nothing If Not Critical*. It provides the sub-text of all the reviews collected there, whether favourable or unfavourable, and of whatever period in art history (pre-modernist, modernist, or post-modernist). Hughes won't deny that 'there are a few living American artists whose latest shows one would always feel eager to see' (and he adds a few European ones to the list in his more recent book, *Culture of Complaint*); but that phrase 'a few' damns all the rest: those participants in 'the cultural gorge and puke of the early eighties', or their promoters. The death of the American painter, Mark Rothko, becomes a symbol for the death, or rapid erosion, of those 'old purposes of art, the manifestation of myth and the articulation of social meaning'.[92]

Hughes has continued elsewhere to champion some surviving artists of the modernist era like Frank Auerbach, Lucian Freud, or Colin Lanceley; though in the monographs that he has devoted to each of these he can't resist taking broad pot-shots at their post-modern successors. He is aware of the 'conservatism', by post-modernist canons, of his remaining favourites; it is a quality he can even prize in them now. Yet there is a crucial loss entailed in this too, for which those same canons are held to blame. By his accounts, post-modernism did not provide a new avant-garde to replace the old modernist one; it effectively killed off the very notion of such a thing, embracing in the 1980s a mindless and pseudo-populist eclecticism. It grew into a kind of guard or army itself; but its chiefs (such as Andy Warhol or Julian Schnabel) proved to be a vacuous as well as vicious lot, whose corruption and decadence were reflected in the activities of their lieutenants (critics turned hype-merchants; connoisseurs turned dealers) as well as the institutions which accommodate them or recruit their successors (museums, such as the once-responsible Whitney, now suffering a discernible 'loss of intellectual fiber'; and art schools that have given up any discipline but deconstruction, out of a 'woozy sense of aesthetic democracy').[93]

There is no genuine discipline, or genuine democracy, here. Nothing exposes more clearly for Hughes the hollowness and pretensions of post-modernism than the jargon favoured by its theorists, most notably Jean Baudrillard, Jacques Derrida, Michel Foucault, and Jean-François Lyotard. Baudrillard's attempt, in his book *America,* to deconstruct the cultural codes of contemporary capitalism, is at once impenetrably arcane and transcendently vague, according to Hughes' review. Originating avowedly from a position on the left, this book's oracular pronouncements can make an equal appeal to those from the opposite extreme of the political spectrum. It is a species of cult literature that wilfully excludes the bulk of readers by a form of verbal intimidation. The very style of the book is an affront to Hughes' liberal conscience.[94]

'Life goes on despite theory, and so does art', he declares at one point, in exasperation at Baudrillard's apocalyptic rhetoric, and yet at various other points, Hughes' own plain speaking can evoke as portentous a vision of the current risks to humanity and all its endeavours, artistic and otherwise. If the end of the world is not yet nigh, it may be nearer than ever before, and artists, let alone critics, have no capacity to stop the process (if they ever did). A review from 1986, reprinted in *Nothing If Not Critical,* exclaims at one point: 'How touching our grandfathers' faith in the future seems, in our day of acid rain, exploding shuttles, decaying inner cities and general creeping dystopia'. He told one interviewer in the year *Nothing If Not Critical* was published: 'Turns of the century are always accompanied by catastrophist thinking. But we're not just at the end of a century, mate, we're at the end of a millennium'. Even those last vestiges of faith, such as Cyril Connolly had been able to cling to, seem to have exhausted their viability now, and the consolations of the liberal ideal to have grown still more tenuous. In a review of a Goya exhibition, held in New York in 1989, Hughes has occasion to wonder how the speech-writers and television preachers of the Reagan era 'could so easily turn America's noblest tradition of political thought into the "L" word'. He pronounces the process 'obscene'.[95]

It is still possible, as in these examples, to use art criticism as a vehicle for political and social critique — but with little hope of effecting any change. It would be even more vain, by Hughes' account, to expect any assistance in these tasks from artists themselves. As early as 1971 he was declaring: 'Let's face it … art doesn't have any effect on politics'. But 'I don't mean that it's dying', he had emphasised then. In 1980, while acknowledging that there was still some good painting or sculpture around, he said that he didn't 'think it's capable of performing the social roles which modernism hoped it would'. In the 1991 edition of *The Shock of the New,* he denies any positive role to art in helping to 'stave off the horrors of the eighties from AIDS to crack to the impending greenhouse effect'.[96]

In *Nothing If Not Critical,* he goes further than this, implicating art's most recent forms and manifestations in what has helped to bring the horror about. They are still too lacking in potency to be directly responsible, but they are part of the same irresponsible milieu. 'Cultural Reaganism' is how he dubs the exhibiting strategy of New York's Metropolitan Museum of Modern Art in 1984; a mini-version of the 'private opulence, public squalor' in the world outside. Warhol (whose earlier work in the 1960s he was inclined to take more seriously) is already shaping up to be court artist and chief flatterer at the White House. In his 1987 attack on Schnabel, Hughes reinvokes the image of the exploding shuttle from his 1986 essay, applying it now to the art careers of that decade which, he claims, have risen 'amid roars of acclamation and pillars of smoke — and then, like Challenger, detonated'.[97]

The spectacle here of the Manhattan art world is not far removed from those kitschier representations of hell which Hughes discussed in the opening pages of his *Heaven and Hell in Western Art.* Associations with the underworld are clinched in the sentences immediately following: 'Who now remembers graffiti, the hot ticket of '83? Or the East Village scene in general? Out to limbo, … permanently remaindered'. There are signs that the sermon on hell to which he was treated as a schoolboy by a Jesuit teacher may have had as lasting an impact on him as his baptism by postcards in the modernist faith, administered by another Jesuit at his school. These signs are at their most overt in the depictions of convict Australia in *The Fatal Shore;* but the counterbalancing images of paradise to be found there are nowhere in evidence in his visions of contemporary New York. He declares flatly in the introductory essay to *Nothing If Not*

Critical: 'New York had never been a paradise'. Certainly, there are no angels of the kind that the *Time* reviewer, twenty years earlier, could still hope existed: the 'new epiphanies of conscience' in the Manhattan art world are nearer to signalling the work of devils, or at least would-be devils. Hughes invokes here the image of 'the overrated photographer', Robert Mapplethorpe, 'sticking a bullwhip up his ass and pretending to be the devil in front of his own Hasselblad'; and three years later, in his more sweeping critique of American art and society, *Culture of Complaint* — where the puritan heritage of Mapplethorpe's censors is even more a target of Hughes' scorn than the photographer himself — the same image is re-invoked, with an added satanic touch of Hughes' own devising: 'One can almost hear the shade of the late Robert Mapplethorpe rustling its leather wings in mirth'.[98]

For all their grimness, there is nothing glum about Hughes' jeremiads and prophecies in *Nothing If Not Critical*. At times the tone can verge on fiendish glee, as if Hughes has become a bit of a devil himself, determined to take some kind of revenge on a world that has disappointed his earlier hopes for art. There is an associated guile as well. Some of his previous books have had rather more portentous or apocalyptic-sounding titles. By comparison with *The Fatal Shore* or *The Shock of the New, Nothing If Not Critical* sounds nothing if not tame — unless you pick up the allusion to Iago. Apart from the author's photograph on the back cover (no cherub here; more a scowling gargoyle) there is nothing to prepare you for the ferocity inside the covers. It creeps up on you stealthily, as in the case of Shakespeare's villain.

The difference from any regular human devilry is that Hughes means well, not ill, by his guile. Behind it is a clearly moral imperative: to expose the devilish ills of others in the world around him. It is hard to resist seeing in this a throwback to the faith of his upbringing. He himself has compared a fellow art critic, 'who spent fifteen years in New York never doing a negative review of anything' to 'a sort of priest going around issuing benedictions'. Hughes is more like an inquisitor. The stratagems he devises for outsmarting his particular *bête noir*, Julian Schnabel, have an elaborate deviousness about them that might even be termed jesuitical, in the colloquial sense.[99]

In both a colloquial sense, and in more precise historical and theolog-
ical senses, Hughes often deploys the terms 'puritan' and 'evangelical' to
describe or explain the ills of American culture, as he sees them: the battles of the right and the left in cultural as well as political arenas (which he
compares to warring puritan sects); the overt or covert censorship of the
arts (such as directed against Mapplethorpe — an ex-Catholic himself);
the prescriptions of 'political correctness' in speech and behaviour; the
valuing of art as a form of therapy or instrument of ideology rather than
as a focus of pleasure or object of beauty. For all its own oppressive rituals,
Hughes continually suggests, there is nothing quite as 'fundamentalist',
'irrational', 'vulgar' — or plain destructive — about Catholic culture. Don't
we catch just an echo here of the kind of name-calling which characterised
the cultural and religious 'wars' between Catholics and Protestants in the
Australia of Hughes' childhood? One has to wonder whether he is not subconsciously reflecting on a version of himself in this recent review
(post-*Nothing If Not Critical,* post-*Culture of Complaint*) of the Detroit
artist, Mike Kelley:

> He is an ex-Catholic but in some crucial respects a Catholic still, and his work
> is charged with religious references and rhapsodical diatribes of moral insult
> that verge on panic ... He is as deeply immersed in the religious aura of his
> infancy, pre-Vatican II, as any Chicano postmodernist doing lurid madonnas.[100]

Unless you happen to be an object of them yourself, there is as much
relish to be had in observing Hughes' remorseless attacks on this or that
new cult of the current American art world as he has in making them.
There is probably no other art critic in his generation, of whatever sympathies or antipathies, who combines such resources of erudition, wit,
fluency and panache. And the depth of his present antipathies is easy
enough to understand in the light of what we know of his past sympathies.
As he has witnessed it, over the past two decades, post-modernism
has come to challenge all the fundamentals of his own, or his mentors',
artistic faith: firm critical standards for art, based on the premise of a
demonstrable tradition of great works or masterpieces; the possibilities of
moral or spiritual or social or political meaning in art — without a didac-
tic tone or a tendentious programme; a belief and a pride in the unity and

continuity of Western culture. Modernism's challenges to the classical and romantic traditions of artistic representation were never so nihilistic or so empty-seeming. From where he has witnessed their activities most closely, at his base in New York, the practitioners and promoters of post-modernism have appeared to lack any of the visionary intensity or the brio of the modernist avant-garde in its heyday.

Hughes told the Australian journalist, Luke Slattery, in 1995: 'My belief in the capacity of the avant-garde to renew itself fell to pieces as a result of living in America, a country whose primary institutional culture is based on the idea of newness. This disenchantment ... affected me greatly'. What he went to America *for,* in other words — to pursue the new — turned out to be a fatal chimera. Yet its fatality for him has lain as much in its continuing intoxications in the midst of those disenchantments. 'Crossing the East River', he recalls of his own trajectory, in the final episode of *American Visions,* 'was like crossing the Rubicon. No way back'.[101]

For all the sport provided by Hughes' assault on the post-modernists around him, and for all that we may recognise the offence they represent to his (if not our own) most cherished aesthetic and political values, it is hard not to wonder whether the obsessive energies he has put into combating them are fully justified. The various inquisitions of the Catholic Church are probably more famous now for their excesses than for anything else; and so it may prove with Hughes' campaign. His chosen weapons and punishments may be even more disproportionate to the degree of threat involved. He himself has indicated just how shallow the current devils are, doomed to extinction by their own celebration of the transient and the fashionable if not by the decadence of their way of life. Were the offenders against his own religious faith — whether medieval heretics, or Reformation Protestants, or the Muslims and Jews in fifteenth-century Spain which he mentions in his book on Barcelona — ever so obligingly self-destructive?[102]

Hughes' intimations that post-modernism may be symptomatic of a more general self-destructiveness in the world of art, even the world in general, betokens another kind of disproportion in his vision. Can any kind of world-view reliably be based on such a narrow focus as New York — or even the larger one of the United States? He is aware of the inverse parochialism of the metropolis — its assumptions about its specialness or uniqueness, on the one hand, and about its cosmic centrality, on the other — and he is alert to some of the hazards, complacencies and delusions entailed in those assumptions.[103] But his own efforts to avoid them or transcend them have been fairly limited in practice.

His recent *American Visions* took him and its audiences out of New York for a lot of the time; but it was confined almost exclusively to *north* American visions. He has eloquently protested, in the *New York Review of Books,* at the way mainstream television in the United States contrives to ignore 'most of Latin America, except Mexico' for most of the time, and in *Culture of Complaint* he endorses the view of those 'multiculturalists' who argue that people 'can and should look across the frontiers of race, language, gender and age without prejudice or illusion, and learn to think of a hybridized society'. These cannot be dismissed as just pious liberal mouthings. There is evidence dating back to his mid-twenties of his interest in a number of contemporary Latin American painters: Ernesto Deira, Jorge de la Vega, Roberto Matta, Wilfredo Lam. In 1986 he wrote an extensive appreciation in *Time* — reprinted in *Nothing If Not Critical* — on the great Mexican muralist, Diego Rivera, and another one, more recently, on the Cuban, Lam. All the same, he seems to have lost all interest in their successors today, and doesn't encourage any in his readers. None of the work of Rivera's followers 'could compare to his own immense energies', Hughes confidently asserts in *The Shock of the New* — feeling no need to provide particulars, not even the painters' names. Years later he dismisses them as 'regressive Chicano realists': a more conservative version (are we to suppose?) of the type of 'Chicano postmodernist' to whom he compares Mike Kelley. There is surely something in these airy epithets of that 'proneness to stereotype' which he has observed himself in the people he has lived among for a quarter of a century.[104]

There is nothing in his writings to persuade us that he has examined in any depth the activities of individual painters, sculptors and installation-artists working currently within 'alternative' cultures over the borders of the United States. If he did take a considered look at these, he might be surprised to discover how far some of these artists question the usefulness of the label 'postmodern' themselves, as applied to their own work or to their economic and political circumstances (so different from those prevailing in the United States). He might also discover that there was still some life to be found in the notion of an avant-garde, with programmes and practices to match.[105]

In *Culture of Complaint* Hughes protests that there is at least a part of him which is 'more interested in difference than supposed mainstreams today', citing in support his 'longish book about Barcelona and Catalan nationalism'. The cultural and political history of the city are impressively meshed in this work, there are many bravura cadenzas in its prose which can match anything in *The Fatal Shore*, and the sweep of subjects and periods dealt with is prodigious. But there is a curiously truncated feel to the book, deriving from its very wide-rangingness. Taking on nearly two millennia of the city's history, the narrative suddenly cuts out with the death of Gaudi in the mid-1920s. There are incidental passages sprinkled throughout on subsequent phases in the city's development, but they are increasingly curt and dismissive the closer they come to dealing with the present day. Only one specimen of what he calls 'the smirking reflexiveness of Catalan PoMo' is anatomised in any detail: a discotheque called the Torre d'Avila, 'a medieval simulacrum'. Whether such architectural caprices 'will last', he says, 'is hard to predict. Its sheer awfulness may entitle it to preservation'.[106]

Hughes is not so pessimistic as to discount entirely the prospect of great art's re-emergence from places outside the so-called 'mainstream' — his native Australia, for instance. But it is a vague and purely speculative prospect as he presents it, and any possible grounds for it are nowhere explored, so that he hardly inspires his readers to take it very seriously as a hope for the future. An updated version of *The Art of Australia* or *Landscape with Figures* may be one way in which he could explore this prospect. There have been rumours every now and then of some such project getting off the ground, but no palpable signs of it as yet.[107]

It could hardly be argued that the completion of *The Fatal Shore* had exhausted Hughes' interest in his former homeland. Over the past few years he has made return trips almost annually. These have been mainly to visit his family here (and to pursue his favourite sport of fishing); but he has also become an active spokesman for the Australian Republican Movement. There is a family link here, in that the Chairman of that lobby group is Malcolm Turnbull, his niece's husband. But there can be no doubt of Hughes' personal commitment to the cause. As he sees it, Australia cannot assume a true independence and maturity until all formal links with its so-called mother-country are severed. 'The Republican issue … is one of self-governance and adulthood'. His stance on this, he protests, 'is not a matter of some sort of Oedipal resentment against England'. In recollecting his career elsewhere, he had been happy enough to admit to some such resentment — but one that was clearly directed against *Australia,* and that impelled him *towards* England. The hoped-for solace of England may still be interpreted in terms of his Oedipal analogy, however: running to the mother's arms after disposing of the father. Any rejection by the mother, any disavowals of her maternity through a 'languid sneer', was bound to be a cruel disappointment; and one may still catch a tinge of that disappointment — if outright resentment is kept at bay — behind Hughes' memories of the years of Australia's political and cultural dependence:

> Our education would prepare us to be little Englishmen and Englishwomen, though with nasal accents. We would not be accepted as such by the English themselves: we were not up to that … It seemed natural to us that our head of state, with constitutional power to depose any democratically elected Australian prime minister, should be a young Englishwoman who lived 14,000 miles away. What native-born Australian could possibly be as worth looking up to as this Queen?[108]

It remains the case that Hughes has not exercised himself in any prominent way over recent Australian developments in *art,* except for the odd directive to his compatriots to content themselves now with being 'local' — to embrace, indeed, what 'used once to be derided as provincial'. Coming from an old and brilliant derider himself, this seems quite a turnaround; though we saw the beginnings of the turn at the end of *Landscape with Figures.* There is no particular condescension here to his native land. 'The future belongs' to localists worldwide now, he makes clear in the same breath. But there is no particular interest either. He has made it pretty clear elsewhere that, with all its attendant horrors, New York is his locality now and he's sticking to it. 'On the whole I'd rather be privy to things in New York than Australia, at present', he told Geoffrey De Groen in an interview published in

1984. He was happy to be a consultant recently for the 'Antipodean Currents' exhibition in Manhattan, a group show of recent work by some of Australia's leading contemporary painters; but it's hard to imagine his becoming involved if the 'currents' concerned had not been flowing towards him.[109]

Those early days of his job with *Time*, when he imagined himself resolutely seeking out the new and the unknown, seem long past. As early as 1980 he was quoted by one Australian journalist as saying, quite bluntly:

> It's pointless to beat the stuffing out of Arthur Anybody's pastels in front of 19 million readers who've never heard of him. It's assumed if you're writing about someone in Time that that person is a significant figure.
>
> You meet winners, not losers, and this undoubtedly has some effect upon you, but I don't think it's my job to find unknown talent and promote it.

Another journalist in the same year, who quizzed him specifically on his attitude to Australian art, reported him as telling her that he 'would love to reacquaint himself' with the subject but that it would not be published by *Time*. This publication was

> a chauvinistic American magazine with its own particular cultural biases. Whether or not something is published in 'Time' has absolutely nothing to do with the actual quality of work going on in Australia. That's not the criterion, and it's not important. I used to think it was important before I'd spent ten years with 'Time'.
>
> I realise now the job does not involve discovering new talent and has a great deal less power than I once thought.[110]

These comments don't sit too easily with his testimonies elsewhere to the 'complete freedom' given him by his American employers, the total independence, the unparalleled liberty. More disturbing and more poignant here is the registration of his hopes for power and their clear disappointment as the years have passed. For all that the power concerned may be intended for good, not ill, it is this posture of thwartedness (akin to the bleak, hard gaze of the gargoyle that confronts you in recent photos) which makes sense of his own identification with Iago in the title and epigraph of *Nothing If Not Critical*. The association with Iago is partly prefigured in the Clyde Packer interview, when Hughes says of his job with

Time: 'I don't help run the magazine. As the subaltern said when asked about his role in the cavalry: "My job is to lend tone to the brawl" '. It's hardly an exact parallel, but Iago's public position as an 'ancient' or 'ensign' in the Venetian army — the lowest rank of commissioned officer — is a plainly subordinate one. Hughes' accounts of his position not just with *Time*, but in the New York art world generally, continually emphasise his peripheral status as a critic and his feelings of impotence. In 1987 he declared: 'Critics have become sort of adjuncts to the commercial process here. The art world is absolutely rotten with all sorts of unexpected corruption'. (Iago takes a comparably black view of his world in Venice; for him, what appears to be a mere social 'courtesy' in the eyes of his gullible side-kick, Roderigo, is in fact 'an index and obscure prologue to the history of lust and foul thoughts' — or so it gives him a grim pleasure to speculate.) 'Criticism', Hughes told one interviewer in 1990, is no longer 'needed by the art world. Its only use will be as an art form'. Making a similar point as a guest speaker at the Adelaide Arts Festival in the same year, he observed that power in the art world was now divided between dealers and collectors — 'with museum curators coming in third and critics a long way last'. He told another interviewer: 'It's not within the power of the critic anymore to create reputations overnight, or still less, to destroy them'. None the less, his belabourings of Schnabel, Mapplethorpe, the later Warhol and various other pin-up boys of the post-modern era suggest how powerful the destructive urge in him remains.[111]

Hughes has entertained some fine fantasies of destruction involving fellow-critics as well. One rainy night in Manhattan, a recent report informs us, he found himself driving a carload of some of the world's most distinguished writers on art — including rather more modish ones than himself, like Rosalind Krauss, co-editor of *October,* the house magazine for 'cutting-edge' post-modernists in America. According to the report, he joked in retrospect that 'he might have made a real contribution to the art world if he'd gone off the road'.[112]

His growing reservations about art criticism are not quite as clear-cut as Cyril Connolly's conviction of the pointlessness of such ancillary activities, but they tend to echo it across the distance of more than a generation. The contents of *The Unquiet Grave* have perhaps never entirely lost their discomfiting resonance for Hughes. However sporadically or dimly, memories of Connolly have continued to impress on him the marginality in being not only a colonial but also a critic. More generally, the kinds of disappointment in art and politics to which Connolly's generation were prey by the end of the Second World War have gradually caught up with Hughes as he has become part of an older generation himself. The particular objects of this disappointment may be different, but its broad focuses are similar. The main difference is in the tone of response. Confronting the prospects of doom and destruction, forty years on, Hughes' tone is far less measured, far less muted, than Connolly's. Rather than world-weariness, it exhibits an almost manic energy, and an irrepressible relish for aggression. Such traits comport disturbingly well with the figure of Iago; but, at the risk of stereotyping, they appear to represent as well some common lineaments of the tearaway Australian.

Chapter Six

After-word

'Like all Australian ex-pats', announced the Countess of Harewood in 1994, 'we share an extraordinary feeling of deep and inalienable attachment to the land of our birth mixed with an uneasy fear that one day we will wake up and find ourselves trapped there forever — *in the 1950s!*' These words were addressed to Barry Humphries on his sixtieth birthday. 'Dear Barry', the Countess continued, 'you *can't* be sixty! You're twenty and still struggling to get out from Down Under. Join the Club!'

Edna Everage might have a problem (as her compatriots would say) with the Countess's continuing subscription to this little Aussie battlers club. Only a Dame up to now, it would take all her self-possession just to bite her lip as she reflected on Lady Harewood's previous incarnations as Patricia Tuckwell, violinist, and 'Bambi' Shmith, Melbourne model in the dreaded 1950s. Trying to conceal her envy at this fairytale rise from the deerpark at the ends of the earth to the inner sanctum of one of England's 'nicer type of homes', Dame Edna could easily be tempted to fall back on one of her oldest *mauvais mots*. 'Hasn't she done *well?*', you can imagine her importuning us through gritted teeth.

.That it's a barb which might well be hurled back at herself (or at her creator, if we changed the pronoun) is something that her habitual envy and bitterness would not allow her to see. She would be as unlikely to notice the Countess's caveat. 'This irrational state of mind', Patricia Harewood acknowledges of her recurrent nightmare, 'has *nothing whatever to do with the Australia of today*'. Even some of her fellow-Australians who did register this acknowledgment may not be wholly appeased or impressed by it. (The more xenophobic Englishman's legendary cry to expats, 'why don't you go back to your own country?', has an echo in the aggressive stay-at-home's cynical refrain: 'why don't you come back, then?') Over the last couple of decades, however, there has grown up a common perception that things *have* dramatically changed in Australia since the 1950s, as well as in its relations to the outside world — and changed in such a way to make the expatriate a dying, if not extinct, species.[1]

It is easy to oversimplify the substance of such changes, and to exaggerate their pace and pervasiveness; but it would be impossible to deny their force (their symbolic force, at least) or their multifarious range. I can only give the merest sketch of them here. There has been crucial political change, to start with, or a change in political temper. The stable, if not-so-serene, stretch of 'the Menzies era' finally came to a close in 1972 (six years after Menzies himself had retired), when the coalition party he had once led was finally defeated at the polls by the Labor Party under Gough Whitlam. While Menzies' reign assumed an almost mythic length, appearing both to its friends and its foes like a story that would never finish, Whitlam's was notoriously brief, and as momentous-seeming in its bitter end as in its vauntedly radical beginnings. Three years was hardly sufficient to build up even a veneer of stability or serenity. Wherever one's political allegiances lay, it was never possible to say of Whitlam's Australia that it was 'the land where nothing happens'.

There have been associated cultural changes in Australia, or changes in the cultural temper, both in broader and narrower senses of the word 'culture'. In 1989, speaking at a conference in Italy, the Sydney historian Richard White spoke of 'the cultural confidence of the last twenty years: many Australians are no longer so convinced that Australia is boring, that real history happens elsewhere'.[2] This has been partly a result of a growing sense of cultural independence from Britain, even while formal constitutional ties (manifested most prominently in a governor general appointed by the British monarch in her ambiguous role as the Queen of Australia) remain in place.

There was no more dramatic historical 'happening' in this period — though it seemed more surreal than real to many observers at the time — than the sacking of Whitlam at the official behest of the governor-general of the day. For many of Whitlam's supporters this showed up the present constitutional arrangements between Australia and Britain to be a much greater hazard than they had imagined; but in the event the support for Whitlam was not sufficient either to save his political skin or to bring about any changes in those arrangements. Pressure for change has built up again more recently in a resurgent republican movement. Such pressure has never been as strong, however, as those forces which have served to erode Australia's cultural dependence on Britain.[3]

From long before the Whitlam years, before even the Menzies era, the composition of Australia's non-indigenous population began to change, to diversify, as government programmes, eager to build up the country's numbers, labour supply and internal markets in the aftermath of the Second World War, actively encouraged mass immigration among people from non-British, as well as British, backgrounds. 'Non-British' meant 'European', exclusively, for many years; it wasn't until the mid-1960s that residency restrictions on Asians began to be relaxed. It was one of the feats of the Whitlam government in the following decade to remove all remaining official restrictions. There has been an increasingly large section of the Australian population, therefore, that has no ancestral links or current family ties with Britain; and while English remains the lingua franca, this diversification in the ethnic basis of the population has started to tell — well, more than started; it is by now deeply ingrained — in many aspects and specimens of everyday life from school curricula to restaurant and household menus. 'By the 1970s', Robert Hughes noted recently, 'Australia had ceased to be a "basically British" country ...' If the 'cake and steak' derided by Patrick White in the late 1950s are still culinary staples, if there are still vestiges of the 'literary diet of steak and eggs' which so repelled the young Barry Humphries, these are now prepared and served in a myriad different ways reflecting a wide spectrum of separate and mixed cultural traditions.[4]

Humphries' own rise to prominence in Australia in the 1950s was itself a symptom that something was at least beginning to 'happen' in the spheres of culture relating specifically to the arts. White's decision — despite or because of his more negative feelings about his homeland — to commit himself to Australian subject matter in his novels was another such symptom. Each still had to face various forms of indifference, neglect, derision, and tacit or not-so-tacit censorship; but during the 1960s both the critical and popular reception of their work markedly improved, and Humphries, certainly, enjoyed a far bigger following in his native land than in England. His breakthrough in England in 1972, with the first film version of his Barry McKenzie cartoons, was also a breakthrough for the Australian film industry, according to one of the producers, Phillip Adams. As 'the first and one of the few Australian films to strike an overwhelming response in a wide audience', he recalls, 'Barry McKenzie kicked open the doors of Australia's cinemas and Britain's for Australian films'. Back in the 1920s a local film industry had briefly flourished, but by the following decade it had fallen victim to competition from Hollywood. The 1970s revival, boosted by government funding, has managed to sustain itself on an international as well as local level. The last two decades or so have also seen a blossoming of local specimens of art-forms like opera and ballet, which previously had relied almost entirely on the traditional European repertoire.[5]

'Suddenly', Clive James observed of the Whitlam era in his first volume of autobiography, 'Australia began offering its artists all the recognition they had been previously denied'. It was not quite as sudden as this. The previous government under John Gorton had already begun taking some important initiatives in this direction; and a growing audience base, reflecting a larger and more diversified population, was as crucial to the developments concerned as any increases in the state's interest and patronage. The same factors have helped boost the production of Australian literature. In the 1970s and 1980s there was a greater range of local commercial publishers in Australia than ever before, and although some of them have suffered from a recent downturn in trade and failed to survive, you would not suspect there was any 'crisis' in literature from the buzz of activity and popular excitement that is generated by that latest fixture on the Australian arts calendar, the writers festival.[6]

This type of event has a strong international as well as local component, of course (Melbourne's was initially called the Melbourne International Writers Festival), and part of the buzz derives from the sudden concentration in one place of so many literary queen bees from other hives around the world. There is nothing new about famous visitors from abroad, in various artistic fields, turning up in Australia for a brief season; and in the way they are still fêted by the locals, it might be tempting to see a vestige of Australia's so-called 'cultural cringe' — of that penchant for 'sidling up to the cultivated Englishman' which A.A. Phillips, leading diagnostician of the cringe, specified as one of its symptoms. But circumstances and conditions have undergone certain changes since the 1950s when Phillips first made his pronouncement. To begin with, the most fêted literary visitor is now as likely to be from Latin America or Asia as from England or a predominantly English-speaking country. If English writers still tend to predominate, and (as happens at special festivals) in denser clusters than ever before, this may reflect what another critic, Geoffrey Thurley, sees as the most sophisticated stage of cultural provincialism: the stage when a provincial society has come to 'acquire its own centre of gravity — a gravitational mass which may well indeed begin to attract the old parent society'. Part of this attraction may lie in the opportunity afforded the visitors to meet the 'province's' own leading writers. These local queen bees figure as regularly on festival programmes as the more exotic species, and they are as capable of attracting the local audiences at the festivals too. Australian-based writers have become more interesting to everybody.[7]

As early as 1975, narrating his television series on Australian art, *Landscape with Figures*, Robert Hughes could say: 'The speed with which art information now gets around the world has begun to erode the centre, and this may give a fresh interest to uncentral art, to provincial art'. By 1990 he was declaring: 'Today there is neither a centre nor a periphery'. The following year John Lahr quoted Barry Humphries as telling him: 'I've suddenly discovered that England is really a province of Australia'.[8] (He may have been partly reflecting here on his, and his fellow-expatriates', successful invasions of the English scene.) We don't need to go quite as far as these statements to see that, in a post-colonial world, words like 'local', 'periphery' and 'provincial', on the one hand, and 'international' or 'centre', on the other, have taken on new relationships or configurations — complementary and overlapping rather than antithetical — and have shed some of their older, more schematic connotations. Certainly, the all-but-pervasive assumption in the 1950s of the centrality of London (or New York), and the provincial marginality of Australia, has undergone some considerable refinement, if not radical reappraisal. Even where Australia is still regarded — or regards itself — as provincial, that tag is no longer an automatic by-word for 'inferior' or 'derivative'.[9]

Clive James, revisiting Australia in 1996 (as Robert Hughes had done the year before) to give the inaugural address at the Melbourne Writers Festival, acknowledged post-war immigration as the most important factor in his homeland's growing cultural confidence. Focusing on literature in particular, he suggested that true confidence had nothing to do with the sort of chauvinistic bluster about Australian achievement in this field which had dominated discussions of a national culture or national identity while he was growing up in Sydney in the 1940s and 1950s. (A.A. Phillips had typed this kind of bluster as 'the Cringe Inverted'.) Culture must grow through accumulated quality, based on individual initiative and effort, rather than through any orchestrated national ambition or consciousness-raising. The immigrants, as well as contributing to this accumulation through their own individual efforts, had helped save Australia from a 'self-imposed incubus of aggressive provincialism'. They were fleeing from just this form of oppression in their homelands, he said — around the same time, he might have added, that he was fleeing the version of it in his own homeland and travelling the other way.[10]

There have been rapid technological changes or developments since the 1950s, most notably in modes of travel, but also in communications, with the advent of the fax and e-mail, and considerable advances in international telephone services. Calls to or from overseas are cheaper and much easier to make now, with satellites doing the work of a team of manual operators; and the audibility levels of these calls have so improved that — save when they happen to ring you in the middle of the night — you can imagine that your best friend in London or your agent in New York is all but next door. While these are mixed blessings (invasion of privacy has never been easier, and how does a redundant operator earn a living now?), there is no doubt that they have helped shrink the 'psychological' distances between Australia and the rest of the world.

As early as 1962, prior to any of these electronic advances in communications (and four years before Geoffrey Blainey published his classic study in Australian history, *The Tyranny of Distance*), the expatriate writer and editor, Charles Osborne, could be found proclaiming in the introduction to a special Australian number of the *London Magazine:* 'In the past, many of us Australians have blamed the vagaries of our national character on our geographical isolation. But now there is no isolation, outside our own skins, anywhere on earth'.[11] He provided no details or explanations of this new development, but one of the factors he might have had in mind was the increasing recourse to air travel by his fellow-Australians, especially since the introduction of the jet a few years earlier, which cut the journey time between Sydney and London to just over a day. Ships were still taking five weeks or more to do the same trip.

Official statistics for the years 1962–64 reveal that for 'short-term' hops overseas (all destinations) aeroplanes were already the preferred mode of transport for Australians, whereas in the case of so-called 'long-term' movement (defined as an intention to stay in a country abroad for twelve months or more) the numbers going by air were still a minority but a rapidly shrinking one. Until the introduction of the wide-bodied jet a few years later, ships remained the standard form of long-distance, long-term mass travel, and were considerably cheaper. Most of the European migrants who had arrived in Australia between the mid-1940s and the mid-1960s had come by ship, and anecdotal evidence suggests that the great majority of Australian expatriates in 'the artist and intellectual class' (if we can invent a category that does not show up in the official statistics) also made their journeys by sea. Momentarily forgetting Robert Hughes' pioneering excursions by air, Clive James observed of the 1950s and early 1960s: 'In those days everybody you knew was too poor to fly', and Christopher Koch confirms that 'there was no question of going by air'. By 1972, however, a Melbourne newspaper, commenting on the fact that 70 per cent of migrants from Britain were now opting for air travel to their new home, concluded that 'the future of the ocean liner looks bleaker than ever'.[12]

Just around the time when aeroplanes were taking over from ships as the normal mode of international transport, and enabling more people to travel long distances than ever before, there was a noticeable growth or tightening of government controls over the entry of non-native citizens. For Australian citizens this was particularly noticeable in England, where they had been used, as a result of Australia's membership of the British Commonwealth and formerly of the British Empire, to fairly relaxed treatment from the immigration authorities. Koch recalls that when he first arrived in England in the mid-1950s, together with another Australian,

> the only formality we observed on entering ... was to flip open our passports, which stated that we were Australian citizens and British subjects. We didn't have to have any money, ... that didn't matter, as work was easy to get. Nor was there any problem about length of stay, as our dual nationality was real.[13]

Such freedoms gradually began to dry up over the following two decades, as the numbers of full-scale immigrants to Britain from her former colonies multiplied rapidly and governments began to yield to local demands to stem the flow. Australian travellers to England in recent years have had to line up under the 'Aliens' sign when arriving at British airports, and are often subjected to an intense grilling over their financial circumstances and job situation. Even long-term Australian residents in England, who are allowed to go on living and working there, must join the same queue if they do not have a British passport. Alluding to this situation on a television show which he conducted on the subject of 'Britishness' in 1990, Clive James said that he now spoke 'as a member of an excluded group', and was worried about what might happen to subsequent generations of Australians who 'won't be able to come and work here'. In 1995 Germaine Greer fretted that 'after 31 years of paying taxes in Britain' her 'permission to re-enter the country could be revoked at any time. If it could happen to the Ugandan Asians it could happen to me'. She was even more concerned about the increasing bureaucratic difficulties faced by Australian citizens seeking entry into some continental European countries.[14]

In view of such deterrents, will many Australian artists and intellectuals of the future even try to base themselves abroad for any prolonged period of time? In view of the changes in Australia's political and cultural climate over the last few decades, will many of them wish to do so? In view of the technological developments in transport and communications over the same period, will many of them need to do so? The general impression among those who have given some thought to such matters is that expatriatism is in a state of terminal decline — and especially the kinds of compulsive (or, as it seemed, almost compulsory) expatriatism represented by Humphries and James, Greer and Hughes, when they left Australia between 1959 and 1964.

As early as 1971, just before Gough Whitlam's brief ascendancy, the Melbourne historian Jim Davidson was predicting that the younger generation of Australians may soon come to take Australian culture as their 'primary point of reference'. They now regarded their native land as 'a fully autonomous society', he argued, and as 'their metropolis'. He cautioned at the same time, however, that 'the intellectual in Australia is still the odd man out ... Too often they have not been made to feel at home ... The ordinary people, in fact, feel that England is where the intellectuals really belong'. Only slowly was this changing, Davidson observed. He himself was based in England in the early 1970s. In some 'home thoughts from abroad' which he published in 1973, he noted that 'the greater number of our creative artists now live and work at home'; and by 1979, back home himself and ensconced as editor of one of Australia's leading literary magazines, *Meanjin*, he could speak of 'the demise of the classic phase of Australian expatriatism'.[15]

Another Melbourne historian, Geoffrey Serle, in the first edition of his voluminous survey of the 'creative spirit' in Australia, published in 1973, paused to observe:

> Expatriation has continued, but probably at a much reduced rate. There are still refugees who have fled permanently from a native-land they have found oppressively constricting ... They are usually unaware that the battle has been joined in recent years and that the tide has perhaps turned ... There are also still many unwilling expatriates, whose talents are recognized overseas but not at home, who are angrily impatient with the hidebound conservatism still prevalent in many areas of Australian industrial and professional life.[16]

In 1978 the Sydney novelist, Frank Moorhouse, was inclined to be far less cautious. While admitting that there was still no end to that anxiety which had always assailed Australian artists — the question of 'whether one could achieve excellence by staying in Australia' — he felt that 'we are at a ridge in Australian history now. Writers my age [he was forty at the time] and younger did not become expatriates … [T]he historical fact is that we are not going away to live'. Two years further on, in 1980, he talked of the ridge again, identifying it with the whole of the previous decade, which he said was the time when 'writers, at least, stopped going away to live in other countries — the end of the expatriate tradition'. Perhaps reflecting on the fact that Moorhouse himself subsequently contradicted this trend by going away to live in Europe for several years, the editors of a recent anthology of modern Australian travel-writing deem his earlier announcements 'too dramatically definite'. They none the less conclude that expatriatism since the 1960s had proved 'a less common option or necessity as Australians became more satisfied with their own culture and more confident about it'.[17]

In the view of two recent historians, expatriatism has also become a less common, less urgent, subject of concern, whether for those who still do move away from their native land or for those who stay. In his *Australia. A Cultural History,* John Rickard argues that 'the rise of the global village has done much to blunt the impact of expatriatism, and the decision to travel no longer carries the same connotation of escape or desertion'. In her study of Australian women abroad, *Duty Free,* Ros Pesman concludes with a reflection on her own daughter, who now lives and works in Paris but — as part of 'the global village' — proceeds to commute 'between Europe and Australia at will'. For her, 'identity is not a problem', and 'the problem of whether she is or will become an expatriate is … not an issue'. That sort of debate, Pesman continues, 'is now confined to an aging, if still voluble cohort, the leftovers of the 1950s and early 1960s'.[18]

For better or worse, it is true that we probably won't see their like again: these 'leftovers' of a peculiar phase of Australian (and global) history — this 'cohort', of which the four figures examined in this book are among the most voluble representatives. But if expatriatism is not now an issue of concern, except perhaps to them, it is important for Australia's future cultural and intellectual development that it should not become a matter of general complacency. It is impossible that 'the tide' (to use Geoffrey Serle's metaphor) should ever turn back to the 1950s and 1960s — Sir Robert Menzies was as distinctive a creature of those decades as Humphries or James, Greer or Hughes, and we shan't see Menzies' like again either. But there can be no guarantee that the tide won't take another, different turn, which is even more inhospitable-seeming to 'word children' of the future, or to creative and inventive minds in general.

In 1992, when Paul Keating's Labor Party was still in power, a senior academic at the Australian National University in Canberra warned that 'increased government and bureaucratic intrusion into the tertiary education system could lead to the death of intellectual life in Australia'.[19] He was referring to what he saw as a growing tendency of government officials and committees to take a hand in deciding academic policy rather than sticking to their administrative role. This sort of intrusiveness was accompanied by a substantial contraction in government funding for universities. There is no sign yet that such tendencies are abating, or are likely to do so, under the government which has replaced Keating's.

It is alarmist to speak of intellectual death, but recent official figures of 'permanent departures' from Australia by former residents, especially among native-born Australians, would give no comfort to anyone who fears that a drain of creative and inventive talent from this country may be opening up again. There was a fairly steady fall in the number of such departures from the mid-1970s to the mid-1980s, but from the late 1980s there have been considerable fluctuations in these figures (probably reflecting new uncertainties over the availability of employment), and from a low of just under 9000 in 1986 they climbed to an all-time high of over 16 000 in 1990, with no indication of any significant drop thereafter.[20]

It is difficult as ever to specify the number and proportion of 'artists' or 'intellectuals' included in these figures; they are perhaps an inherently elusive category for the statistician. How far the official category of 'permanent departures' can be equated with the more subjective one of 'expatriates' also remains a problem. Furthermore, there may still be some unintentional expatriates, and even some dissimulating or uncertain ones, hidden in the much larger figures for so-called 'temporary departures' of under a year. More fluid now, with the rise of the so-called global village and the provisions for global commuting, the category of expatriate may have become more subjective than ever — a question of state of mind at least as much as of choice of domicile. It is also more contestable as a concept. There remains a wealth of testimony, however, of an unofficial kind, to the persistence of the term, and (in however diffuse and attenuated a form) to the persistence of the phenomenon among highly creative Australians.

One cannot begin to catalogue here, or even just enumerate, the continuing succession of interviews with, profiles of, and articles about Australian novelists, Australian poets, Australian painters, Australian photographers, Australian film-makers, Australian actors, Australian dancers, Australian musicians, Australian singers, Australian designers, Australian academics in myriad fields, not to mention Australian businessmen, Australian sportsmen, Australian models, who in the last twenty years or so have shifted and generally retained their main working base abroad. Open the most mandarin of literary or art magazines, glance at the most populist of newspapers, tune into any arts programme or celebrity guest show on the radio or the television, cruise every festival, and it would be unusual not to find at least one of these displaced persons staring out at you or begging to borrow your ear. If they are not back home on a visit, they are being beamed, snapped or taped from their new home far away; and it is surprising how often that new home will turn out to be in one or other of the oldest destinations known to peripatetic antipodeans, and how you can still catch them saying that while they may not regard it (or anywhere else) as their real, emotional home, it constitutes the 'centre' of their creative being, or a larger chunk of that centre than their real home could offer them. If they don't want to be there, they have to be there. Or so it seems to them.

London at Christmas-time, 1994, found Rebecca Hossack, cultural development officer at the Australian High Commission,

> relishing the task of enriching Britain with the vast array of film, literature, performance and visual art that has always been prolific in Australia. She says she is amazed at the number of expat Australians who are doing 'amazing things in the UK. It's brilliant — this isn't an easy country and they're everywhere you go. I think that coming from such a country with wonderful space gives you a lack of angst and a sense that anything is possible.

It could just as easily be 1964. To be quite sure this report is genuine, one has to check from the accompanying snap that the putative Ms Hossack is not sporting a mauve wig and diamante spectacle-frames with a wicked arabesque twist. She isn't. It's a tall willowy Nordic blonde that stares out at you here.[21]

It is hard not to catch her enthusiasm after all. While many Australians might view, with justified concern, the continuing 'expat' exodus, they might also pause to reflect on what the wider world is gaining from this haemorrhage of talent and on the enhancement to Australia's international reputation, the tremendous extension of their country's cultural reach, which it involves. The process is too elusive to chart with any precision, but it should not be lightly dismissed. Something of its mystical — and insidious — force is suggested in the experience of the ever-so-English novelist and comedian, Stephen Fry, who found himself stranded and alone one evening in the Polo Lounge of the Beverly Hills Hotel. At one point he heard a familiar voice drifting over to his table, and, as he puts it, 'a healing wave of homesickness swept over me like a moist mountain wind. I forgot America and its billion-dollar entertainment industry … and suddenly I knew I was English and could never be anything else'.[22] It was the voice of Rolf Harris.

'When you're alone in the Polo Lounge', Fry concludes his account of these magical transports, 'the fluting tones of Australia's greatest son beckon you home like a lighthouse'.

Notes

1 Word Children

1 These four figures, or at least three out of the four (in varying combinations), are discussed together in the following publications or broadcasts: Phillip Adams, interview with Robert Hughes on *Late Night Live,* ABC Radio, 26 July 1996; Stephen Alomes, 'The British Press and Australia: Post-Imperial Fantasy in the Contemporary Media', *Meanjin,* Melbourne, vol. 46, no. 2, 1987, pp. 179–80; Bruce Bennett, 'Expatriate Voices', *Voices,* Canberra, vol. IV, no. 3, 1994, pp. 64–6; Mike Carlton, 'Coming up from down under', *Age,* Melbourne, 20 February 1993; Anne Coombs, *Sex and Anarchy. The Life and Death of the Sydney Push,* Ringwood, Victoria, 1996, p. x; John Lahr, cited in Michael Davie, 'Humphries from backstage', *Age,* 2 November 1991; Geoffrey Dutton, *Out in the Open,* St Lucia, Queensland, 1994, p. 449; Martin Flanagan, 'The Remaking of Australia. 1964. Wars in the Wings', *Age,* 28 December 1993; John Huxley, 'Poms v Cons', *Sydney Morning Herald,* 27 May 1995 (hereafter *SMH*); Kerryn Goldsworthy, 'Antipodean Landings', *Australian Book Review,* Melbourne, October 1995, p. 10; Daphne Guinness, 'Sophisticated Australians', *SMH,* 16 November 1996; Greg Hywood, 'The thinking man's Rolf Harris bucketed', *Australian Financial Review,* Sydney, 10 July 1981, p. 37; Margaret Jones, *Thatcher's Kingdom,* Sydney, 1984, pp. 230–4; Catharine Lumby, 'The Australian who conquered America', *SMH,* 20 July 1996; Craig McGregor, *Headliners,* St Lucia, Queensland, 1990, p. 1; Andrew Riemer, *Inside Outside. Between Two Worlds,* Pymble, NSW, 1992, pp. 195–8; Nicola Shulman, 'Devilled Sydney', *Harpers and Queen,* London, February 1989, p. 87; Luke Slattery, 'Expatriates on a Pedestal', *Weekend Australian,* Sydney, 1 December 1996. On relationships between the expatriates of this generation, see Clive James, *May Week was in June,* Picador ed., London, 1991, p. 245; McGregor, *Headliners,* p. 14.

2 Barry Humphries, *More Please,* London, 1992, p. xii, and interview by Colin Riess and Rob Hardy, 'At least you can say you've read it', *Lot's Wife,* Melbourne, 16 September 1974, p. 9; Clive James, *The Metropolitan Critic,* 1st ed., London, 1974, pp. 20, 75, 260, *At the Pillars of Hercules,* London, 1979, p. 64,*Charles Charming's Challenges on the Pathway to the Throne,* London, 1981, pp. 48, 51, *Falling Towards England,* Picador ed., London, 1986, p. 161, *Other Passports. Poems 1958–1985,* Picador ed., 1987, p. xi, *Snakecharmers in Texas,* Picador ed., 1989, pp. 34, 48, *Clive James on Television,* Picador ed., 1991, pp. 385, 567, *The Dreaming Swimmer,* Picador ed., 1993, pp. 29, 65, 183, 'The handing on of a copious view', *Times Literary Supplement,* London, (henceforth *TLS*), 5 July 1996, pp. 8–9; Germaine Greer, *The Madwoman's Underclothes,* London, 1986, p. xxvii, 'International Books of the Year', *TLS,* 1 December 1995, p. 12, but cf. her column in the *Guardian,* London, 21 February 1994; Robert Hughes, *The Shock of the New,* 1st ed., London, 1980, pp. 388, 390, *Nothing If Not Critical,* London, 1990, pp. 377–8, *Culture of Complaint. The Fraying of America,* revised ed., London, 1994, pp. 5964, *Sunday Afternoon* interview by Mary Delahunty, ABC TV, 5 November 1995.

3 On their retention of their Australian passports and the difficuties associated with this, see Clive James, *Flying Visits,* Picador ed., London, 1985, p. 49, and *The Dreaming Swimmer,* p. 98; Murray Hedgcock, 'Clive James a laid-back TV hit', *Australian,* Sydney, 23 June 1985; Lynne Bell, 'A prodigal son is home — for a while', *Woman's Day,* Sydney, 22 July 1985, p. 15; Germaine Greer, 'In a state about Australian entry into Europe', *Guardian,* 1 May 1995; Hughes, *Culture of Complaint,* p. ix.

4 Clive James, *Unreliable Memoirs,* Picador ed., London, 1981, p. 173; *The Metropolitan Critic,* p. 248. Cf. Rosalind Reines, 'Clive James likes women but he's not so sure about the Press', *SMH,* 3 September 1983, and my article, 'Desperately Seeking Clive', *24 Hours,* Sydney, October 1996, p. 42.

5 Germaine Greer, interviewed by Clyde Packer, in *No Return Ticket,* North Ryde, NSW, 1984, p. 99; *The Madwoman's Underclothes,* p. 99; *Daddy, we hardly knew you,* Penguin ed., Harmondsworth, Middlesex, 1990, pp. 26–78, 200–31; 'Home is an illusion', *Guardian Weekly,* 24 October 1993; 'In a state about Australian entry into Europe'.

6 James, *Unreliable Memoirs,* p. 165.

7 Packer, p. 2.

8 K.S. Inglis, 'Going Home: Australians in England, 1870–1900' in David Fitzpatrick, ed., *Home or Away? Immigrants in Colonial Australia,* Canberra, 1992, p.105; Ros Pesman, *Duty Free. Australian Women Abroad,* Melbourne, 1996, pp. 4–6; Ray Mathew, 'The Australian Tradition', *London Magazine,* New Series, vol. 2, no. 6, September 1962, p. 62; Geoffrey Blainey, *The Tyranny of Distance,* Melbourne, 1966, pp. 16–21. On distinctions between expatriates and exiles, and some overlaps in meaning, see Mary McCarthy, 'Exiles, Expatriates and Internal Emigrés', *Listener,* London, 25 November 1971, pp. 705–8; Andrew Gurr, *Writers in Exile. The Identity of Home in Modern Literature,* Brighton, Sussex, 1981, pp. 17–21.

9 Hazel King, *Colonial Expatriates. Edward and John Macarthur Junior,* Sydney, 1989, p. 11; *Literary Links between Britain and Australia,* British Council and National Library of Australia travelling exhibition, 1994, sec. 9: 'Dreaming Spires'; Inglis, 'Going Home', pp. 105–6; Pesman, *Duty Free,* pp. 4, 23–4; Ros Pesman,

David Walker, Richard White, eds, *The Oxford Book of Australian Travel Writing*, Melbourne, 1996, pp. ix, xiii, xx.

10 Inglis, 'Going Home', pp. 105–6; Jack Lindsay, 'The Alienated Australian Intellectual', *Meanjin*, vol. xxii, no. 1, 1963, p. 55; John Arnold, 'Jack Lindsay in Australia', in Bernard Smith, ed., *Culture and History. Essays presented to Jack Lindsay*, Sydney, 1984, p. 37; *Official Year Book of the Commonwealth of Australia*, no. 51, Canberra, 1965, p. 288.

11 *Official Year Book*, 1965, p. 286.

12 Lindsay, 'The Alienated Australian Intellectual', p. 55; P.R. Stephensen, *The Foundations of Culture in Australia*, Sydney, 1936, pp. 121–3.

13 Patrick White, 'The Prodigal Son', *Australian Letters*, Adelaide, vol. 1, no. 3, 1958, pp. 38–9; Robin Boyd, *The Australian Ugliness*, Melbourne, 1960, p. 157; Donald Horne, *The Lucky Country*, 1st ed., Ringwood, Victoria, 1964, pp. 16, 209.

14 Horne, *The Lucky Country*, 2nd ed., Ringwood, Victoria, 1966, p. 11; White, 'The Prodigal Son', p. 38; Boyd, p. 129. For a recent critique of the view that Australia is, or was, an 'anti-intellectual' society, see Brian Head, 'Introduction: Intellectuals in Australian Society', in Brian Head and James Walter, eds, *Intellectual Movements and Australian Society*, Melbourne, 1988, pp. 1–33.

15 Hughes, 'The Intellectual in Australia', *London Magazine*, New Series, vol. 4, no. 5, August 1964, p. 71; James, *The Metropolitan Critic*, pp. 246, 250, *Flying Visits*, p. 30.

16 Humphries (compiler), *Punch Down Under*, London, 1984, pp. 6–7; Greer, *Daddy, we hardly knew you*, p. 288, 'A New Introduction' to Henry Handel Richardson, *The Getting of Wisdom*, London, 1981, n.p.

17 Charmian Clift, 'News of Earl's Court — Fifteen Years Ago', in George Johnston and Martin Johnston, eds, *The World of Charmian Clift*, Sydney, 1979, p. 56; Richard White, *Inventing Australia. Images and Identity 1688–1980*, Sydney, 1981, pp. 148–51, 163–5; Stella Lees and June Senyard, *The 1950s ... how Australia became a modern society, and everyone got a house and a car*, Melbourne, 1987, pp.1–6, 16–23, 28–36, 45, 54–68, 74–6, 84–5, 95–103,140–1; Judith Brett, *Robert Menzies' Forgotten People*, Sydney, 1992, pp. 31–73; Janet McCalman, *Journeyings. The Biography of a Middle-Class Generation 1920–1990*, Melbourne, 1993, pp. 218–38; Flanagan, 'The Remaking of Australia. 1954. Corgis and Bess', ' ... 1964. Wars in the Wings', *Age*, 27 & 28 December 1993; Nicholas Brown, *Governing Prosperity. Social Change and Social Analysis in Australia in the 1950s*, Cambridge, 1995, pp. 4, 87–9, 101–26.

18 McCalman, pp. 207–9, 243–9; Brown, pp. 204-5; Kate Darian-Smith, 'War and Australian Society', in Joan Beaumont, *Australia's War 1939–1945*, St Leonards, NSW, 1996, pp. 54–81; Mathew, 'The Australian Tradition', *London Magazine*, 1962, p. 68; Kate Jennings, 'Unaccountable Within Our Hearts. An Interview with Ray Mathew', *Voices*, vol. III, no. 3, Spring 1993, pp. 5–20.

19 James, *The Metropolitan Critic*, p. 250; Anthony Clare, *In the Psychiatrist's Chair*, BBC radio, 30 March 1989; Greer, 'Liszt's Lookalike', in Ken Thomson, ed., *Barry Humphries. Bepraisements on his Birthday*, London, 1994, p. 40.

20 Humphries, *Bizarre*, New York, 1965, p. 7; 'Is Australia Funny?', ABC Radio, 28 October 1971, typescript in Humphries Papers, Performing Arts Museum, Melbourne, pp. 1–2.

21   Hughes, *The Fatal Shore*, London, 1987, p. 359; 'The Intellectual in Australia', p. 71; 'Getting the Goat', *London Magazine*, New Series, vol. 4, no. 2, May 1964, p. 60.

22   R.G. Menzies, 'The Forgotten People', reproduced in Brett, p. 10. Cf. Stuart Macintyre, 'The Legacy of Sir Robert Menzies', *Voices*, vol. V, no. 2, 1995, pp. 7–8.

23   Horne, *The Lucky Country*, 2nd ed., 1966, p. 203; Hughes, *The Art of Australia*, 1st ed., Ringwood, Victoria, 1966, pp. 105–6; Geoffrey Serle, *From Deserts the Prophets Come. The Creative Spirit in Australia 1788–1972*, 1st ed., Melbourne, 1973, pp. 161–3; Humphrey McQueen, *Black Swan of Trespass. The Emergence of Modernist Painting in Australia to 1944*, Sydney, 1979, pp. 26–30;Richard Haese, *Rebels and Precursors. The Revolutionary Years of Australian Art*, Ringwood, Victoria, 1981, pp. 37–46, 51; Brett, pp. 179–87; A.W. Martin, *Robert Menzies: A Life. Volume 1 1894–1943*, Melbourne, 1993, pp. 194–200; Lees and Senyard, p. 118; Brown, pp. 211–12, 229, 234–5; R.G. Menzies, 'Foreword', and J.J. Auchmuty with A.N. Jeffares, 'Australian Universities: The Historical Background', in A. Grenfell Price, *The Humanities in Australia*, Sydney, 1959, pp. xi–xii, 31–3; Hughes, 'The Intellectual in Australia', p. 73.

24   James, *May Week was in June*, p. 184; Greer, 'Liszt's Lookalike', p. 40; David Malouf, 'Listening to the Voice of Tuscany', in Gaetano Prampolini and Marie-Christine Hubert, eds, *An Antipodean Connection. Australian Writers, Artists and Travellers in Tuscany*, Geneva, 1993, p. 85 (Malouf's emphasis).

25   Stephensen, *passim*; A.A. Phillips, 'The Cultural Cringe', in his *The Australian Tradition. Studies in a Colonial Culture*, Melbourne, 1958, pp. 89–95; cf. L.J. Hume, 'Another Look at the Cultural Cringe', *Political Theory Newsletter*, vol. 3, no. 1, 1991, esp. pp. 15–23; James, 'The handing on of a copious view', p. 8. On developments in Australian reading habits and educational curricula, see S.G. Firth, 'Social Values in the New South Wales Primary School 1880–1914: An Analysis of School Texts', in R.J.W. Selleck, ed., *Melbourne Studies in Education 1970*, Melbourne, 1970, pp. 123–59; W.F. Connell, 'British Influence on Australian Education in the Twentieth Century', in A.F. Madden and W.H. Morris-Jones, *Australia and Britain. Studies in a Changing Relationship*, Sydney, 1980, pp. 162–79; Geoffrey Dutton, *Snow on the Saltbush. The Australian Literary Experience*, Ringwood, Victoria, 1984, pp. 47–76; Brenda Niall, *Australia through the Looking Glass. Children's Fiction 1830–1980*, Melbourne, 1984; Ian Donaldson, 'Centres and Circumferences: Australian Studies and the European perspective', in Patricia McLaren-Turner, ed., *British Library Occasional Papers*, no. 4, London, 1988, p. 10; Martin Lyons and Lucy Taska, *Australian Readers Remember. An oral history of reading 1890–1930*, Melbourne, 1992; David Walker, with Julia Horne and Martyn Lyons, ed., *Books, Readers, Reading, Australian Cultural History*, no. 11, 1992, esp. pp. 18, 44, 58–62, 75, 85, 87, 96–9, 100–10, 124–5, 128–30, 135–6; Ian Britain, 'In Pursuit of Englishness. Public School Stories and Australian Culture', *University of Melbourne Library Journal*, vol. 1, no. 4, Spring 1994/Summer 1995, pp. 10–17.

26   Hughes, *Culture of Complaint*, p. 148; Peter Conrad, *Down Home. Revisiting Tasmania*, London, 1988, p. 10; Humphries, interviewed by Hazel De Berg, 12 October 1981, National Library of Australia, De Berg tapes no. 1238, transcript p.

17319 (see below, pp. 32–3); Christopher Koch, *Crossing the Gap*, London, 1987, pp. 28–32, 93–4.

27 Koch, pp. 26–34, 93–4; Peter Porter, 'Forty years on', in his *Millennial Fables*, Oxford, 1994, p. 14; Bruce Bennett, *Spirit in Exile. Peter Porter and his Poetry*, Melbourne, 1991, pp. 39–40; Keneally quoted in Richard Glover, 'World without words', *SMH Good Weekend*, 26 June 1993, p. 40; Shirley Hazzard, *The Transit of Venus*, Penguin ed., Harmondsworth, Middlesex, 1981, p. 37; Stephensen, p. 122; Charles Higham and Michael Wilding, *Australians Abroad*, Melbourne, 1967, pp. x–xi; Serle, p. 126; Laurie Hergenhan and Irmtraud Petersson, *Changing Places. Australian Writers in Europe 1960–1990s*, St Lucia, Queensland, 1994, pp. xiv, xvi, xviii, xxi–xxxiii; *Literary Links between Britain and Australia* exhibition, sec. 11: 'Australians Abroad'; Pesman, *Duty Free, passim*; Pesman, Walker, White, *Oxford Book of Australian Travel Writing*, pp. xx–xxi.

28 See, e.g., McCarthy, 'Expatriates, Exiles and Internal Emigrés', p. 706; Louis Crompton, *Byron and Greek Love*, London, 1985, pp. 86, 111–12, 119–21, 156–237, 241–2, 297–8, 350–71; Elizabeth Jones, 'The Suburban School', *TLS*, 27 October 1995, pp. 14–15; Paul Fussell, *Abroad. British Literary Travelling Between the Wars*, New York, 1980, pp. 9–23, 130–6.

29 On the long legacy of Australian regard for England, and more specifically London, as a cultural and intellectual mecca, see Serle, p. 215; Nicholas Jose, 'Cultural Identity: "I Think I'm Something Else"', in Stephen R. Graubard, *Australia: The Daedalus Symposium*, North Ryde, NSW, 1985, p. 313; John Rickard, *Australia. A Cultural History*, London, 1988, p. 135.

30 Clift, pp. 55–6; cf. p. 11.

31 James, *The Metropolitan Critic*, pp. 15–29, 246; Conrad, *Where I Fell to Earth. A Life in Four Places*, Hogarth Press ed., London, 1991.

32 Koch, pp. 1–2; James, reported in Kristin Williamson, 'A Literary Lion Starts Again — At The Top', *National Times*, Sydney, 14–20 December 1980; *The Metropolitan Critic*, pp. 4, 250. On the receptiveness to Australians and various other non-English writers in the world of literary journalism in London, see also James, *The Improved Version of Peregrine Prykke's Pilgrimage through the London Literary World*, London, 1976, p. 39.

33 Peter Coleman, *The Real Barry Humphries*, London, 1990, p. 108.

34 Humphries, *More Please*, p. xii; James, 'The Voice of America', *New Yorker*, 14 June 1993, p. 81.

35 James, *The Metropolitan Critic*, pp. 259–60; Hanif Kureishi, *The Buddha of Suburbia*, London, 1990, p. 28.

36 James, *Snakecharmers in Texas*, p. 203; *Brmm! Brmm!*, Picador ed., London, 1992, p. 104.

37 James, *The Remake*, Picador ed., London, 1988, p. 208; *Brilliant Creatures*, Picador ed., London, 1984, pp. 172, 174, 271–302.

2 The Camberwell Tales

1 David Lindley, ed., *Court Masques*, Oxford, 1995, p. 36.

2 On Humphries' erudition, see Ian Donaldson below, and Peter O'Shaughnessy, 'How Edna Everage took to the stage', *Age*, 26 January 1985; Roger Lewis, 'Bazza

comes out of the closet', *Weekend Australian*, Sydney, 5–6 December 1987; 'The Bazza Mystique', *Weekend Australian*, 13–14 February 1988. Humphries comments on his own precocious and recondite tastes in his 'My Monday Wash' column in the *Age*, 16 November 1970, and in the interview with him by Hazel De Berg, 12 October 1981, National Library of Australia (henceforth NLA), De Berg Tapes no. 1238, transcript p. 17323.

3 *An Evening's Intercourse with Dame Edna*, 1982; the disembodied voice was that of fellow-Australian expatriate, Charles Osborne: see his 'Barry, Les, and the Dame from Moonee Ponds' in Ken Thomson, ed., *Barry Humphries. Bepraisements on his Birthday*, London, 1994, p. 70. On the audiences for masques and other forms of court theatre, see Stephen Orgel, *The Illusion of Power. Political Theater in the English Renaissance*, Berkeley, 1975, pp. 1, 8, 10, 39–40. On Dame Edna's intimidating her audience, see Rory Bremner and other critics of Humphries, on *J'Accuse*, Independent Television Network (henceforth ITV), London, 1994.

4 Lindley, pp. 202–3.

5 Lindley, pp. 39–40.

6 Lindley, pp. 203–4, 208.

7 Dame Edna Everage, *My Gorgeous Life*, London, 1989, p. 188.

8 'Highett Waltz' in *The Sound of Edna*, London, 1979, n.p., and *A Nice Night's Entertainment. Sketches and Monologues 1956–1981*, Sydney, 1981, pp. 30–1; 'Australian Vitality' in *A Nice Night's Entertainment*, EMI recording, 1962, side 1, track 1; 'Edna's Hymn' in *The Sound of Edna*, n.p., and *Neglected Poems*, Sydney, 1991, p. 105.

9 *A Nice Night's Entertainment*, p. 28; John Lahr, *Dame Edna Everage and the Rise of Western Civilisation. Backstage with Barry Humphries*, London, 1991, p. 82; on Moonee Ponds' mixed social composition, see article by Peter Smark in the *Age*, Melbourne, 17 July 1974.

10 *A Nice Night's Entertainment*, p. 21.

11 Geoffey Blainey, *History of Camberwell*, Melbourne, 1964, pp. 8, 32–3, 48–58; Chris McConville, *Camberwell Conservation Study*, vol. 2, Melbourne, 1991, pp. ix–x, 5, 17, 19, 82, 91–2, 116, 121–2, and 'Conserving Camberwell' in John Rickard & Peter Spearitt, eds, *Packaging the Past? Public Histories*, Melbourne, 1991; Janet McCalman, *Journeyings. The Biography of a Middle-Class Generation 1920–1990*, Melbourne, 1993, pp. 67–8; Barry Humphries, *More Please*, London, 1992, pp. 3–10.

12 *More Please*, pp. 3, 5; Commonwealth Literary Fund application, 4 October 1960, Australian Archives, Canberra, Series A463/37, item 1970/2690.

13 Peter Coleman, *The Real Barry Humphries*, London, 1990, p. 19; Jim Davidson, 'A Fugitive Art. An Interview with Barry Humphries', *Meanjin*, vol. 46, no. 2, June 1986, p. 150; Collin O'Brien, *The Life and Death of Sandy Stone*, Sydney, 1990, p. 10, and see also pp. 166–73, for 'The Polkinghorn Letters' addressed from '36 Stoddart St. Glen Iris'; the Polkinghorns are literary antecedents of Sandy. Cf. Geraldine McFarlane, ed., *Voices of Camberwell*, typescript of oral history project prepared for the Camberwell Heritage Festival Committee, 1993–94, pp. 1–2.

14 *Life and Death of Sandy Stone*, pp. 132–3, 142–4; cf. pp. 95, 129–31, 135, 138–40.

15 Lindley, pp. 44–6, 51–3, 211–12; Orgel, pp.19–20, 37–8, 40, 49–50, 58, 61, 65, 85, 87.

16 Barry Humphries & Bruce Beresford, *Barry McKenzie Holds His Own*, Melbourne, 1974, p. 72. *An Audience with Dame Edna* was inaugurated on London Weekend Television (henceforth LWT), 3 September 1980; there were further English 'Audiences' in 1984 and 1988. *An Aussie Audience with Dame Edna* was first televised on 14 August 1986. For more detailed descriptions of these and other TV chat-shows conducted by Dame Edna, see 'Audience by a Tall Gladdie', interview by Jane Sullivan, *Age Green Guide*, 10 April 1986, pp. 1, 6; Lahr, *Dame Edna*, pp. 187–92; Coleman, pp. 167–8, 185–6.

17 Lahr, *Dame Edna*, p. 24; cf. p. 69.

18 Lahr, *Dame Edna*, p. 111; Davidson, 'A Fugitive Art', p. 154; *More Please*, p. 309.

19 Ian Donaldson, 'Early Snapshots', in Thomson, *Barry Humphries. Bepraisements*, p. 26.

20 On the political circumstances of her 'damehood', see *Dame Edna's Coffee Table Book*, Sydney, 1977, pp. 23, 88; Humphries' interview by 'Tinkerbelle' [Andy Warhol], 'Barry Humphries/ Dame Edna. The Two Faces of Everage', *Interview*, New York, vol. 7, no. 12, December 1977, pp. 26–7; and Davidson, 'A Fugitive Art', p. 154.

21 *More Please*, p. 151, Lahr, *Dame Edna*, pp. 5, 82; interview by Melvyn Bragg, *South Bank Show*, LWT, 1989; cf. interview by Charles Higham, 'On the Black Side', *SMH*, 24 August 1968; interview by Colin Riess & Rob Hardy, 'Barry Humphries. At least you can say you've read it', *Lot's Wife*, Melbourne, 16 September 1974, p. 8; Roger Baker, *Drag*, London, 1994, pp. 222–3.

22 *Oxford English Dictionary*, Compact edition, vol. 1, p. 639; *A Nice Night's Entertainment*, p. 4; *My Gorgeous Life*, p. 29; Walter W. Skeat, ed., *The Complete Works of Geoffrey Chaucer*, Oxford, 1912, pp. 326–48, 569.

23 *The Canterbury Tales: The Prologue*, lines 445–76; *The Wife of Bath's Prologue and Tale*, in *Complete Works of Chaucer*, pp. 424–5, 565–81; *A Nice Night's Entertainment*, EMI recording, side 1, track 1.

24 Baker, pp. 15, 162, 216–23; interview by Lyndal Crisp, 'Dame Edna, megastar, dissects the new society', *National Times*, 30 August–5 September 1985; Humphries as reported in Michael Ryan, 'Bazza's aunt doesn't like the company they make him keep', *Age*, Melbourne, 26 September 1972; 'Is Australia Funny?', ABC Radio, 28 October 1971, p. 6.

25 *More Please*, pp. 99–100. The incongruities of Anglo-Australia provide a recurrent theme for him: see, e.g., 'Is Australia Funny?, p. 2; 'Up Memory Creek', review of *Great Australian Book of Nostalgia* in *TLS*, 9 April 1976, p. 418; 'The Man Within', interview with Joan Bakewell, *Sunday Times Magazine*, London, 16 May 1976, p. 36; Humphries' second address at National Press Club Luncheon, Canberra, 13 July 1981, tape at National Library of Australia (henceforth NLA); Humphries, 'Bazza and the Big F (for fifty)', *Australian Weekend Magazine*, 11–12 February 1984; 'Barry Humphries on the Couch', in Peter Conrad, *Feasting with Panthers*, London, 1994, pp. 278–9.

26 Higham, 'On the Black Side'; De Berg interview, p. 17319.

27 Craig McGregor, *People, Politics and Pop: Australia in the sixties*, Sydney, 1968, p. 39; Phillip Adams, quoted by Robert Drewe in 'Larrikin in the Ascendant', *Australian*, 12 April 1973; Donaldson, 'Early Snapshots', p. 27.

28 *Life and Death of Sandy Stone*, esp. p. 155; *My Gorgeous Life*, pp. 168–9.

29 *More Please*, pp. 13, 162; Lahr, *Dame Edna*, p. 82, and 'Playing Possum', in *New Yorker*, July 1991, p. 57; 'Black Thoughts, Bright Laughter. Barry Humphries between two moods', *Nation*, Sydney, 8 September 1962, p. 12; Higham, 'On the Black Side'; 'Is this the real Humphries or is there another side?', interview by Kevon Kemp, *National Times*, 19–24 April 1971, p. 21; 'Is Australia Funny?', p. 3; O'Shaughnessy, 'How Edna Everage took to the stage'; Davidson, 'A Fugitive Art', pp. 150, 157; Lewis, 'Bazza comes out of the closet'; *Life and Death of Sandy Stone*, pp. xxxix, xli–xlii, 9–10, 165–74; Coleman, pp. 46–7; 'Back down boring Malvern Road', interview by Michael Davie, *Age*, 3 November 1990.

30 Lahr, *Dame Edna*, p. 59. Cf. Baker, p. 219, who also emphasises only the rebellious and vengeful sides of Humphries' relation with his family. On Humphries' alleged anti-suburban or anti-Australian attitudes, see Humphrey McQueen, *Suburbs of the Sacred*, Ringwood, Victoria, 1988, pp. 6–7, 36–7, 48–9, and my article, 'Bazzamataz', *24 Hours*, Sydney, August 1996, pp. 36–41. Perhaps the earliest commentator to recognise that Humphries' attitudes were more ambivalent was D.R. Burns, 'An Everage Review', *Observer*, Sydney, 15 November 1958, p. 627. See subsequently Sue Castrique, 'Suburbia and Australian Intellectuals in the 1950s. A Study of Robin Boyd, Barry Humphries and George Johnston', unpublished BA Honours thesis, Department of History, Australian National University, 1977, p. 41, though cf. p. 43; John Rickard, *Australia. A Cultural History*, London, 1988, p. 258; McConville, 'Conserving Camberwell', p. 100.

31 *More Please*, pp. 3–7, 74, 113–15; De Berg interview, p. 17325; Lahr, *Dame Edna*, p. 68, and 'Playing Possum', pp. 57, 61.

32 *More Please*, pp. 72, 98, 114; Lahr, *Dame Edna*, p. 79.

33 *More Please*, pp. v, 69, 134–5; Georgina Howell, 'Barry's Secret Sorrow', *New Idea*, Melbourne, 13 January 1996, pp. 20, 159–60; Lahr, 'Playing Possum', pp. 56–7.

34 *More Please*, pp. 208, 301–2, 314–15; Lahr, *Dame Edna*, pp. 64–5.

35 Lahr, *Dame Edna*, pp. 60, 211.

36 'Is Australia Funny?', p. 2; *More Please*, p. 11.

37 *More Please*, pp. 11, 76–7; Lahr, *Dame Edna*, p. 105; cf. Humphries in Bragg interview, 1989, on 'the politics of niceness', and Edna's song, 'Niceness', in *The Sound of Edna*, n.p.

38 *More Please*, pp. 77–8, 152, 253; 'My Love Hat Relationships', undated typescript draft in Humphries Papers, Performing Arts Museum, Melbourne (henceforth PAM); Davidson, 'A Fugitive Art', p. 152; Lahr, *Dame Edna*, pp. 82, 193–6.

39 Bragg interview, 1989; Lahr, *Dame Edna*, p. 60; 'Is Australia Funny?', p. 5.

40 *More Please*, p. 76, Humphries' emphasis; cf. Lahr, *Dame Edna*, pp. 66–7.

41 *Women in the Background*, Melbourne, 1995, p. 155.

42 *Life and Death of Sandy Stone*, pp. 2, 104–5, 153–7.

43 Bragg interview, 1989; 'Edna Everage: Olympic Hostess', in *A Nice Night's Entertainment*, p. 5; Davidson, 'A Fugitive Art', p. 151; Neil Clerehan, 'Are Houses Funny?', *Age*, 23 February 1959; on the 'unexplored territory' of suburbia on the Australian stage in the 1950s, see also O'Shaughnessy, 'How Edna Everage took to the stage'.

44 *Dame Edna's Neighbourhood Watch*, nos 1 & 6, Megastar Productions, London, 1992.

45 Higham, 'On the Black Side'; Lahr, *Dame Edna*, pp. 62–3; *More Please*, pp. 5, 7, 61; Blainey, *History of Camberwell*, pp. 88–90, on the effects of the Depression and the War on the building trade.

46 *More Please*, pp. 73–4; Lahr, *Dame Edna*, p. 68; Robin Boyd, *The Australian Ugliness*, Melbourne, 1960, pp. 8, 207, and *Australia's Home*, Melbourne, 1952, pp. 14–15; *Life and Death of Sandy Stone*, p. 2; *Wild Life in Suburbia*, vol. 1, Score POL recordings, Melbourne, 1958. See also Castrique thesis, chs 2, 3; Nicholas Brown, *Governing Prosperity*, Cambridge, 1995, pp. 159–61.

47 Boyd, *Australia's Home*, pp. 214, 273, and *The Australian Ugliness*, p. 94; cf. Geoffrey Serle, *Robin Boyd. A Life*, Melbourne, 1995, pp. 126–7.

48 'Is Australia Funny?', p. 4; Boyd, *Australia's Home*, Preface, n.p., and *The Australian Ugliness*, pp. 158–9; 'An Ode to the City of Camberwell', *Neglected Poems*, pp. 13–15.

49 *More Please*, pp. 25–7; De Berg interview, p. 17314; Bakewell, 'The Man Within', p. 36; cf. Lewis, 'Bazza comes out of the closet'.

50 Lahr, *Dame Edna*, p. 36.

51 *A Nice Night's Entertainment*, p. 36.

52 'Is Australia Funny?', p. 4; 'Satirist, but he sees both sides', interview by Ross Elliot, *News*, Perth, 8 October 1968; *A Nice Night's Entertainment*, pp. 56–9, 88–95, 104–7, 114–19, 167–77, 184–90; Barry Humphries & Ross Fitzgerald, 'Craig Steppenwolf. A Monologue for the Music Hall', *Quadrant*, Sydney, vol. xix, no. 8, November 1975; 'Rod Nunn', typescripts drafts, 1978, in Humphries Papers, PAM; Humphries, 'A Fillup for Phil Philby Films', in *Quadrant*, vol. xxv, no. 7, July 1981, pp. 18–19; *Life and Death of Sandy Stone*, pp. xviii, 8, 32, 72, 87, 105; cf. Davidson, 'A Fugitive Art', pp. 157–8. I respond to various commentators' views of Sandy — notably Manning Clark's insistence on seeing him as a tragic figure — in my article 'Bazzamataz', pp. 38–40, 42.

53 *More Please*, pp. 55, 57, 72–3, 100, 149; De Berg interview, p. 17314.

54 Higham, 'On the Black Side'.

55 Ibid.; Lahr, *Dame Edna*, p. 68; De Berg interview, pp. 173118–19; Humphries, 'My Heart Belongs to Dada', *Age*, 6 March 1993; *More Please*, pp. 62, 100.

56 De Berg interview, p. 17319; Conrad, *Feasting with Panthers*, p. 285.

57 'My Monday Wash' column, *Age*, 14 December 1970; De Berg interview, pp. 17314–15; *More Please*, pp. 13–16.

58 De Berg interview, p. 17315; *More Please*, pp. 15, 48.

59 Humphries Papers, PAM, 'Drawings' box; Bakewell, 'The Man Within', p. 37; Lahr, *Dame Edna*, pp. 44–51, 69, 89–90, 112, 129–30; Coleman, pp. 20, 27–30, 43, 45–6, 106–12; *More Please*, pp. 104–5, 115–21, 158, 165–7, 239; Donaldson, 'Early Snapshots', and Germaine Greer, 'Liszt's Lookalike', in Thomson, *Barry Humphries. Bepraisements*, pp. 26, 41–2; 'Black Thoughts, Bright Laughter'; 'The Confessions of Barry Humphries', *Bulletin*, Sydney, 6 November 1965, pp. 20–1; Davidson, 'A Fugitive Art', p. 150; Humphries, 'My Heart Belongs to Dada'; Richard Huelsenbeck, 'Collective Dada Manifesto' in Robert Motherwell, ed., *The Dada Painters and Poets: An Anthology*, New York, 1951, pp. 242–6; 'Dadalogue' (1952) and 'Dadalogue 1953', catalogues of first and second 'Pan-Australasian' Dada exhibitions, Humphries Papers, PAM; 'Dadadadadadada', and Humphries, 'Let's Talk Sense about Dada', *Farrago*, 25 June 1952, p. 1; D.A.

Kennedy, 'Dada for now', *Farrago*, 9 July 1952, p. 2; *The Art Works of Barry Humphries*, Melbourne, 1958; Alan Hughes, Barry Humphries, & Graeme Hughes, 'The Barry Humphries uni memoirs. A Special Supplement', *Farrago*, 17 April 1970, pp. 9–11; Margaret Plant, *Irreverent Sculpture*, Melbourne, 1985, pp. 8–21; Ted Gott, *BIG. Barry Humphries. Dada Artist*, Canberra, 1993; 'Tid and the Psychiatrist', 'Cruelty Rhymes', 'A Fairly Painful Listen', all recorded in 1950s, and now released as *Dada Days*, Raven Records, Melbourne, 1993, tracks 6–8; 'A Novel called Tid', in *Paston's Melbourne Quarterly*, Spring 1958 et seq. and in *Gambit. Edinburgh University Review*, Spring 1961, pp. 17–20; 'A Note of Exclamation' in *Bizarre*, New York, 1965, p. 7; *Barry McKenzie Holds His Own*, 'Dramatis Personae' & p. 8.

60 *The Art of Dominic Ryan*, Melbourne, 1984; Lahr, *Dame Edna*, pp. 112–13, 129, 144; Clive James, 'Approximately in the Vicinity of Barry Humphries', in *Snakecharmers in Texas*, Picador ed., London, 1989, pp. 39–40. Other commentators who have spotted the monster in Humphries' characters include Leonard Radic, 'Tigress of Trivia kicks up her heels', *Age*, 8 July 1978; R.F. Brissenden in Introduction to *A Nice Night's Entertainment*, p. xvii; Juliet Herd, 'Just a Suburban Boy', *Australian Weekend Magazine*, 16–17 October 1993, p. 14; Bill Mandle, 'Communicating his disgust in comedy', *Canberra Times*, 24 April 1994; Conrad, *Feasting with Panthers*, p. 277.

61 Ian Syme, 'Humph-Bumph — or Whither the Weltschmertz?', in *Contemporary Art Society Broadsheet*, February 1959, p. 10; the defence is Zoe Caldwell's, cited in Lahr, *Dame Edna*, p. 50; for similar comments, see Nicholas Garland, 'A Topsy-Turvy Man', and Greer, 'Liszt's Lookalike', pp. 38, 42.

62 Humphries on White, cited in Coleman, p. 125.

63 *More Please*, pp. 19–22, 48, 65–71; Lahr, *Dame Edna*, p. 61; De Berg interview, pp. 17316–17; Blainey, *History of Camberwell*, p. 71; Coleman, p. 20.

64 De Berg interview, pp. 17317–18; Coleman, p. 21; Lahr, *Dame Edna*, p. 39; *More Please*, pp. 65–8; 'My Heart Belongs to Dada'; Peter Wilmoth, 'Barry Humphries Unplugged', *Sunday Age*, Melbourne, 22 October 1995; lecture by Ian Bow reported in the *Age*, 10 January 1953.

65 De Berg interview, pp. 17321–2; *More Please*, pp. 83–5; Humphries, 'Bazza and the Big F …'; *Dame Edna's Bedside Companion*, London, 1982, p. 144.

66 'Bazza and the Big F …'; *More Please*, p. 85; De Berg interview, p. 17321; Lahr, *Dame Edna*, p. 39; Riess & Hardy, p. 9.

67 Draft programme notes for *A Load of Olde Stuffe*, 1971, Harry M. Miller Papers, NLA.

68 Bakewell, 'The Man Within', p. 36; *Melburnian*, 14 May 1952, p. 8; *Age*, 8 February 1952; cf. *More Please*, p. 108.

69 De Berg interview, pp. 17322–6; F.R. Leavis, *The Great Tradition*, Peregrine ed., Harmondsworth, 1962, p. 38; R.F. Brissenden recalls the dilemma over Humphries' paper in his Introduction to *A Nice Night's Entertainment*, p. xi; for an account of a Chaucer class at Melbourne Grammar by a contemporary of Humphries, see Chester Eagle, *Play Together, Dark Blue Twenty*, Melbourne, 1986, p. 105.

70 De Berg interview, pp. 17323–5; *More Please*, p. 108; 'Black Thoughts, Bright Laughter'.

71 *Melburnian*, 24 August 1949, pp. 116, 122–3; 29 August 1951, p. 131; cf. 25 August

1948, p. 120. See also 'My heart belongs to Dada'; *More Please,* pp. 91, 93, 103–4, 115; Lahr, *Dame Edna,* pp. 44–5; Coleman, pp. 24–5.

72 *Melburnian,* 10 May 1950, pp. 25, 40–1; 'Humphries late for school again', *Australian,* 1 August 1968; Humphries, 'Confessions of a Conder Fan', *Quadrant,* vol. xxi, no. 10, October 1977, pp. 39, 42–3; De Berg interview, p. 17323; Lahr, *Dame Edna,* pp. 40, 42; *More Please,* pp. 88–9, 101–2; 'My Heart Belongs to Dada'; Conrad, *Feasting with Panthers,* p. 281.

73 James, *Snakecharmers in Texas,* pp. 37–8; Bakewell, 'The Man Within', p. 36; Bragg interview, 1989; *More Please,* p. 88. Cf. Britain, 'In Pursuit of Englishness', *University of Melbourne Library Journal,* vol. 1, no. 4, 1994/5, pp. 10–17.

74 Norman H. Olver & Geoffrey Blainey, *The University of Melbourne. A Centenary Portrait,* Melbourne, 1956, pp. 34–5; Blainey, *A Centenary History of the University of Melbourne,* Melbourne, 1957, pp. 9, 14, 50–2, 120–1, 173, 189–90; 'The Confessions of Barry Humphries', pp. 20–1; *More Please,* pp. 108, 126; 'The Barry Humphries uni memoirs', p. 10.

75 On Humphries' conservation concerns, see his 'An Everage City', *Sun,* Melbourne, 8 September 1962; Claudia [Wright], 'The thrip got loose in Toorak', *Herald,* Melbourne, 13 July 1968; Pamela Ruskin, 'The Compleat Humphries', *Walkabout,* Melbourne, December 1968, p. 44, and 'Ba-ha-ha-ha-harry Ha-ha-ha-humphries. Cuckoo in the Nest', *Theatre Australia,* New Lambton Heights, NSW, December 1977, p. 13; Humphries in: *Age,* 2 November 1972, & *Sunday Mail,* Adelaide, 24 December 1972; Riess & Hardy, 'Barry Humphries …', p. 9; 'Up Memory Creek'; Coleman, pp. 127–8. Cf. *Treasury of Australian Kitsch,* Melbourne, 1980, p. 51; Motherwell, p. xiii, 324.

76 Motherwell, pp. xv, xxx; *More Please,* p. 94.

77 'The Confessions of Barry Humphries', p. 24. On reactionary or right-wing tendencies in Humphries' sensibilities and views, see, e.g., McGregor, p. 34; Davidson, 'A Fugitive Art', pp. 154–7; McQueen, p. 6; Phillip Adams, 'How Bazza turned the tide of cultural cringe', *Australian Weekend Review,* 12–13 September 1992; Janet McCalman, 'Suburbia from the Sandpit', *Meanjin,* vol. 53, no. 3, 1994, p. 551.

78 Davidson, 'A Fugitive Art', pp. 154–5; *Barry McKenzie Holds His Own,* p. 39. Daryl Dalkeith made his first stage appearance in *Look at Me When I'm Talking to You* (1993/94); cf. 'Just a Suburban Boy', pp. 17–18; 'Daryl's back with a biggie', interview with Colleen Ryan, *SMH,* 10 January 1994. For Sir Les on his own political provenance and beliefs, see 'Mr Les Patterson's Historic Address to the British', *Quadrant,* vol. xxi, no. 4, 1977, pp. 10–11; 'My Track Record' in *Les Patterson's Australia extolled by Barry Humphries,* Melbourne, 1978, n.p.; 'Les Patterson: Introducing the Yarts' (1978) in *A Nice Night's Entertainment,* p. 180; 'A Word from Sir Leslie Colin Patterson' (1981) in John Allen, ed., *The Humour of Barry Humphries,* Sydney, 1984, p. 119; *The Traveller's Tool,* London, 1985, Coronet ed., 1986, pp. 7, 116, 178. On Edna's political trajectory, see 'Edna Everage Meets Friends Old and New', *A Nice Night's Entertainment,* recording, side 1, track 2; 'Edna's Dreamy Christmas at the Lodge', *Bulletin,* 22 December 1973, p. 22; Humphries' second National Press Club address, 1981, NLA; 'A Letter from Edna Everage', December 1973, in Barry Humphries (compiler), *Punch Down Under,*

London, 1984, pp. 115–16; *Dame Edna's Coffee Table Book,* pp. 96–7; Bragg interview, 1989; Lahr, *Dame Edna,* pp. 184–5; Rory Bremner & Anna Karpf on *J'Accuse.*

79 Humphries, 'Solemn Musings of a Movie Star', *SMH,* 16 January 1974; 'The Mavericks', interview by Doug Aiton, *Age,* 2 February 1974; Davidson, 'A Fugitive Art', pp. 155–6; *Quadrant,* vol. xix, no. 3, June 1975 to vol. xxxi, no. 6, June 1987; Humphries' letter appeared in *Quadrant,* vol. xxvi, no. 10, October 1982, p. 3.

80 *More Please,* pp. 78–9; cf. his second National Press Club address, 1981, NLA, for earlier reservations about an Australian republic.

81 Humphries, 'The Road to Eventville', *Age,* 13 February 1996; cf. his poem, 'The Suburbs in Between', *Herald–Sun,* Melbourne, 21 December 1995.

82 Humphries to editor of the *Age,* 18 April 1995; Edna Everage, 'My 40 gorgeous years in showbiz', *Sunday Age,* 10 December 1995.

83 Humphries, 'Bazza and the Big F...'; 'Dada Manifesto' reprinted in Plant, *Irreverent Sculpture,* p. 8; Dame Edna, interviewed on *Today,* Channel 9 TV network, Australia, 22 April 1996.

84 Humphries quoted in Lahr, *Dame Edna,* p. 48; cf. 'Confessions of Barry Humphries', p. 21; Leonard Radic, 'Melbourne (1968) as seen by Barry Humphries', *Age,* 27 July 1968; Riess & Hardy, p. 9; De Berg interview, p. 17327; *More Please,* pp. 112–13.

85 Alan Hughes in *Farrago,* 17 April 1970, p. 9; Ruskin, 'Ba-ha-ha-ha-harry Ha-ha-ha-humphries', p. 14; Lahr, *Dame Edna,* p. 47; *More Please,* p. 115; Chris Wallace-Crabbe, 'Going up to the Shop', unpublished memoir, 1996; Peter O'Shaughnessy, 'How Edna Everage took to the stage', *Age,* 26 January 1985; cf. Donaldson, 'Early Snapshots', p. 25, and Greer, 'Liszt's Lookalike', pp. 40–1.

86 'The Confessions of Barry Humphries', pp. 20–1; *More Please,* pp. 112–13, 122, 125–7; Humphries, 'Bazza and the Big F ...'; Bakewell, 'The Man Within', p. 36; De Berg interview, pp. 17326–31.

87 De Berg interview, p. 17327.

88 De Berg interview, pp. 17327, 17331; 'Le Bain Vorace', National Film and Sound Archives, Canberra; 'The Barry Humphries uni memoirs', pp. 11–12.

89 One of the offending sketches, 'India Today', is recorded on *Dada Days,* track 4. Cf. De Berg interview, pp. 17329–30; *More Please,* pp. 120–2, 127; 'The Barry Humphries uni memoirs', p. 11; John Sumner, *Recollections at Play,* Melbourne, 1993, p. 38; other 'eyewitness' accounts of *Call Me Madman!* are discussed in Coleman, pp. 31–2.

90 *More Please,* pp. 121, 240–1, 245–7, 313; 'After the Event' in *A Garland for Stephen. Arranged by Barry Humphries,* Edinburgh, 1991, p. 27; Lahr, 'Playing Possum', p. 59.

91 *More Please,* pp. 91, 104–5, 121, 134–6, 148–50, 183; Donaldson, 'Early Snapshots', pp. 25–7; 'Megastar Humphries panned — by critics and first wife', *Canberra Times,* 18 January 1996, reporting interview with Brenda Wright in *Mail on Sunday,* London; Coleman, pp. 34–5.

92 'Megastar Humphries ... '; O'Shaughnessy, 'How Edna Everage took to the stage'; Davidson, 'A Fugitive Art', pp. 149–50; *More Please,* pp. 142–3.

93 *More Please,* pp. 123, 134, 141–52, 195–6, 204, 213–14, 224, 246; Blainey, *History of Camberwell,* pp. 80–1; Patrick White to Geoffrey and Ninette Dutton, 27 December 1970, in David Marr, ed., *Patrick White Letters,* Sydney, 1994, pp. 370–1; 'Megastar Humphries … '.

94 Lahr, *Dame Edna,* pp. 87–9, 131; 'Megastar Humphries … ', *Canberra Times,* 1996; *More Please,* pp. 152, 155–63, 170–3; Ruskin, 'The Compleat Humphries', p. 42; O'Shaughnessy, 'How Edna Everage took to the stage'; Geoffrey Dutton, *The Innovators. The Sydney Alternatives in the rise of modern art, literature and ideas,* Melbourne, 1986, pp. ix–x, xiv, 152–3, 199, quoting Humphries material in his possession; K.S. Inglis, *Nation. The Life of an Independent Journal of Opinion 1958–1972,* Melbourne, 1989, p. 8; Coleman, pp. 40–4, 49–50; June Salter, *A Pinch of Salt,* Pymble, NSW, 1995, pp. 64–5; Anne Coombs, *Sex and Anarchy. The Life and Death of the Sydney Push,* Ringwood, Victoria, 1996, pp. 44–5, 90, 160.

95 Lahr, *Dame Edna,* pp. 87–9, 109, 115, 124–5, 132–8; 'Confessions of Barry Humphries', p. 21; *More Please,* pp. 155, 158, 164–7, 307–8; Coleman, pp. 41–9, 137–8.

96 Lahr, *Dame Edna,* pp. 21, 37, 56, 68, 96, 110; *Life and Death of Sandy Stone,* p. xliv; Humphries, Introduction to Graham McInnes, *Humping my Bluey,* London, 1986, p. 5; *More Please,* pp. 173–5; Coleman, pp. 50–2; 'Public Will Wait Long Time for Godot', *Age,* 4 February 1957; Samuel Beckett, *Waiting for Godot* (1955), Faber edition, London, 1965, p. 80.

97 O'Shaughnessy, 'How Edna Everage took to the stage'; *More Please,* pp. 175, 323; Coleman, pp. 52–3.

98 Programme for *Rock 'n Reel* and poster for Sydney production of *Godot* in Humphries Papers, PAM; O'Shaughnessy, 'How Edna Everage took to the stage'; Plant, *Irreverent Sculpture,* pp. 12–13; Commonwealth Literary Fund application, 1960; 'Black Thoughts, Bright Laughter'; 'The Confessions of Barry Humphries', p. 24; *A Nice Night's Entertainment,* p. 19; *More Please,* pp.176–84; Coleman, pp. 53–5.

99 The Confessions of Barry Humphries', p. 24; 'Barry Humphries' do it yourself executive kit', *Rydges,* Sydney, December 1973, p. 102; 'An Everage City', *Sun,* 8 September 1962.

100 Lahr, *Dame Edna,* pp. 20–1; Davidson, 'A Fugitive Art', p. 161.

101 *More Please,* pp. 181–2; Denison Deasey, 'Barry Humphries', in *Australian Letters,* vol. 2, no. 1, June 1959, p. 25; 'Black Thoughts, Bright Laughter'; 'The Confessions of Barry Humphries', p. 24; Lachlan Strahan, *Australia's China. Changing Perceptions from the 1930s to the 1990s,* Cambridge, 1996, pp. 78–81, 179, 190, 192, 194.

102 *More Please,* p. 182; Simon Kent, 'I still call Australia … sometimes', *Sun-Herald,* Sydney, 4 February 1996; 'Great Big Fish', *Barry Humphries' Savoury Dip,* EMI records, 1971, side 1, track 4.

103 Commonwealth Literary Fund application, 1960; *My Gorgeous Life,* p. 164; *More Please,* pp. 86, 187–8; Lahr, *Dame Edna,* p. 168; 'In Quest of a Stranger. Synopsis', typescript in Humphries Papers, PAM.

104 *More Please,* p. 92; Donaldson cited in Lahr, *Dame Edna,* p. 166.

105 *More Please,* pp. 190–2, 194–5, 197–8, 205–6, 213, 218, 329–30, Lahr, *Dame Edna,*

pp. 95, 97, 164–5, 169; Coleman, pp. 58–63, 65–9, 170; *Age,* 23 February 1959.

106 Lahr, *Dame Edna,* p. 168; 'Mervyn Arrowsmith: tenor' and 'Interview with Eric Ballarate', Humphries Papers, PAM; 'Debbie Thwaite' and 'Buster Thompson' in *A Nice Night's Entertainment,* pp. 40–7; 'Black Thoughts, Bright Laughter', on Lantana Holman and other Australian characters of this time; Commonwealth Literary Fund application, 1960; *More Please,* pp. 198, 205, 207–9; Coleman, pp. 60–3, 65–9.

107 Betjeman, 'A programme note' to *A Nice Night's Entertainment,* 1962, reprinted in *More Please,* p. 331; cf. pp. 198–9, 205.

108 *More Please,* pp. 210–18; *My Gorgeous Life,* pp. 213–18; Lahr, *Dame Edna,* pp. 169–71; Coleman, pp. 69–72.

109 Lahr, *Dame Edna,* p. 168; Ruskin, 'The Compleat Humphries', p. 44; *More Please,* pp. 255–8, 282–5; Coleman, pp. 113–15.

110 *TLS,* 16 September 1965, p. 812 — his emphasis; on the origins of Barry McKenzie, see also Nicholas Garland, 'The Strange Birth of Bazza', *Age,* 12 November 1988; *More Please,* pp. 228–30; Coleman, p. 84 ; Lahr, *Dame Edna,* pp. 171–2.

111 Riess & Hardy, p. 8.

112 Garland, 'The Strange Birth of Bazza'; 'Quartered', review of *The Wonderful World of Barry McKenzie,* in *TLS,* 11 September 1969, p. 995; Bakewell, 'The Man Within', p. 37; *The Complete Barry McKenzie,* London, 1988, pp. 12, 123; *More Please,* pp. 231–5.

113 Humphries, 'The Chundering Herd', *Bulletin,* 20 October 1973, pp. 62–3; Bruce Beresford, 'Getting "The Getting of Wisdom"', *Quadrant,* vol. xxi, no. 10, October 1977; Adams, 'How Bazza turned the tide...; *More Please,* pp. 247, 250–3, 268, 272, 278–9, 297–305; Julian Jebb, 'Barry Humphries', *Listener,* 24 April 1969, and 'Housewife: Superstar!!', *Plays and Players,* London, vol. 23, no. 8, May 1976, pp. 33–4; Coleman, pp. 75–83, 87, 91–5, 149–51; Lahr, *Dame Edna,* p. 195.

114 Lyndall Crisp, 'Dame Edna sure to do her dreaded best on Broadway', *Australian,* 3 August 1977; reviews of *Housewife-Superstar!* by Richard Eder in *New York Times,* 20 October 1977, and, more favourably, by Rex Reed, *Daily News,* New York, 28 October 1977; Graeme Beaton, 'Dame Edna hits New York — and Broadway hits back', *Australian,* 22 October 1977; Warhol, 'Barry Humphries/Dame Edna'; Humphries' first National Press Club address, 27 April 1978; *More Please,* pp. 311–12; Coleman, pp. 151–3; Lahr, *Dame Edna,* pp. 216–18, and cited in Michael Davie, 'Humphries from Backstage', *Age,* 2 November 1991; *Dame Edna's Hollywood,* NBC television network, USA, 1991.

115 Coleman, pp. 160–4, 183–4, for a comprehensive list of Humphries' publications, 1965–90; *The Barry Humphries Book of Innocent Austral Verse,* Melbourne, 1968; Richard Davenport-Hines, 'Ozmotic purger', *TLS,* 27 December 1991, p. 28.

116 Robert Yates, 'Sir Les hits rock bottom', *Guardian Weekly,* 7 July 1996, p. 27.

117 *More Please,* pp. xii, 311, 313; Humphries to Miller, 2 June 1972, Miller Papers, NLA; Aiton, 'The Mavericks'; *Innocent Austral Verse,* p. 11; Humphries, Foreword to Keith Dunstan, ed., *Knockers,* Melbourne, 1972, p. xvi; 'Confessions of a Conder Fan', p. 47; *Punch Down Under,* p. 8; *Life and Death of Sandy Stone,* p. xliv; Humphries to *Age,* 18 February 1995; Humphries' first

National Press Club address; cf. Humphries, 'Australians Abroad' in Clive Turnbull, ed., *Hammond Innes introduces Australia,* London, 1971, pp. 179–87.

118 *More Please,* pp. 207–9, 247, 265–74, 285–303, 313; Bakewell, 'The Man Within', p. 36; 'Bazza and the Big F...'; Lahr, *Dame Edna,* pp. 153, 214; Coleman, pp. 113, 121, 137, 158, 183; Margaret Rice, 'Diane Millstead', *SMH Good Weekend,* 27 September 1986.

119 *More Please,* p. 182; Radic, 'Melbourne (1968) as seen by Barry Humphries'; Riess & Hardy, 'Barry Humphries ...', pp. 8–9; Peter Weiniger, 'Melbourne still keeps Bazza's soul afloat', *Age,* 19 February 1983; Wilmoth, 'Barry Humphries Unplugged'.

120 'Terribly Well' (1972), *Neglected Poems,* p. 111; 'The Latest Trends from Overseas' (1962), *A Nice Night's Entertainment,* p. 67; *Dame Edna's Neighbourhood Watch,* no. 5, 1992.

121 *Waiting for Godot,* pp. 21, 47.

3 The Awkward Sage

1 Clive James, *May Week was in June,* Picador ed., London, 1991, p. 174.

2 James, *The Silver Castle,* London, 1996, p. 261; *The Dreaming Swimmer. Non-fiction 1987–1992,* Picador ed., London, 1993, pp. 78, 115; *Snakecharmers in Texas,* Picador ed., London, 1989, p. 283; *Postcard from Paris,* BBC TV, London, 1989.

3 *Snakecharmers in Texas,* p. 44.

4 James, interview with Goodall on *Now Read On,* BBC Radio 3, 19 October 1971; *The Clive James Interview: Stephen Jay Gould,* BBC TV, 7 April 1991; *Snakecharmers in Texas,* pp. 289–328; cf. *Unreliable Memoirs,* Picador ed., London, 1981, p. 78; *May Week was in June,* p. 118.

5 *May Week was in June,* p. 202; *The Metropolitan Critic,* 1st ed., London, 1974, p. 265.

6 James, 'He Didn't Stifle', *New Statesman,* London, 1 March 1968, p. 273; *Postcard from Miami,* 1990; *Postcard from Bombay,* 1994; *Postcard from Cairo,* 1993.

7 *Fame in the Twentieth Century,* London, 1993, p. 154.

8 *May Week was in June,* pp. 248–9.

9 *Snakecharmers in Texas,* pp. 3–17; *The Dreaming Swimmer,* pp. 61–70; 'Blaming the Germans', *New Yorker,* 22 April 1996, pp. 44–50.

10 *Unreliable Memoirs,* pp. 22–4; *May Week was in June,* pp. 247–8.

11 *Unreliable Memoirs,* pp. 169–70; *The Metropolitan Critic,* p. 5; *Clive James on Television,* Picador ed., London, 1991, p. 624; *Flying Visits,* Picador ed., London, 1985, p. 63; James interviewed by Roy Plomley, *Desert Island Discs,* BBC Radio, 14 June 1980; *Other Passports. Poems 1958–1985,* Picador ed., London, 1987, p. 213; *May Week was in June,* p. 247; *Postcard from Hong Kong,* 1995.

12 *Unreliable Memoirs,* p. 161; *At the Pillars of Hercules,* London, 1979, p. 202.

13 James interviewed by John Tidmarsh, *Outlook,* BBC Radio, 18 June 1981; *Flying Visits,* p. 43; *Other Passports,* p. 116; *May Week was in June,* pp. 244, 246; *Postcard from Rome,* 1990; *Postcard from Los Angeles,* 1990; Craig McGregor, 'Highbrow Lowbrow', *SMH Good Weekend,* 14 October 1989, p. 28.

14 Janet Hawley, 'Close to Vanishing Point', *SMH,* 14 October 1992; *Unreliable Memoirs,* p. 93.

15 *The Dreaming Swimmer,* p. 73.

16 *Other Passports,* p. 124; *Unreliable Memoirs,* p. 29. I owe the suggestion of *This Above All* to Brian McFarlane.

17 James on *Desert Island Discs; Unreliable Memoirs,* p. 23.

18 *Unreliable Memoirs,* pp. 11–12, 25, 29–30, 60–5, 77–81, 85–9, 121–3; *At the Pillars of Hercules,* p. 117; *The Metropolitan Critic,* p. 261; James interviewed by Margaret Throsby, ABC Radio, 1 June 1994; Doug Aiton, 'A postcard from home', *Sunday Age,* 19 November 1995.

19 *The Late Show with Clive James* on 'Christmas', BBC TV, 1988; *The Silver Castle,* pp. 196, 260; *Clive James on Television,* p. 221; *Unreliable Memoirs,* pp. 80–2, 137–9.

20 *Unreliable Memoirs,* pp. 47–9, 119.

21 *Unreliable Memoirs,* pp. 107–10, 137–8.

22 *Unreliable Memoirs,* pp. 71–3, 76–7, 91; on his sexist and womanising reputation, and his flirtatiousness, see 'Television' column in *Australian Financial Review,* Sydney, 22 June 1979, pp. 12, 15; McGregor, 'Highbrow Lowbrow', p. 28; Helen Trinca, 'Clive's home truths', *Australian Weekend Review,* 9–10 April 1994.

23 *Fame in the Twentieth Century,* p. 102; *The Clive James Show,* no. 5, 1995, Carlton TV; *The Remake,* Picador ed., London, 1988, p. 114.

24 *Snakecharmers in Texas,* pp. 82, 233–6; *Brmm! Brmm!,* p. 100; *Brilliant Creatures,* pp. 120–1, 196, 276, 281, 285. See also *Falling Towards England,* Picador ed., London, 1986, pp. 69, 141; *Fame in the Twentieth Century,* p. 42; *The Fate of Felicity Fark in the Land of the Media,* London, 1975, p. 89; *Flying Visits,* p. 52; *May Week was in June,* pp. 108, 154; *The Remake,* pp. 16, 32, 57, 104, 110; *Postcard from Paris.*

25 'No Stranger to Danger', *Age,* 9 April 1994; *Falling Towards England,* p. 160; *Brmm! Brmm!,* p. 100; *The Silver Castle,* pp. 216–17; *Postcard from Rome.*

26 *Brilliant Creatures,* p. 89.

27 *Unreliable Memoirs,* pp. 45, 111; *Fame in the Twentieth Century,* p. 53; *Other Passports,* pp. 12–13.

28 *Fame in the Twentieth Century,* picture section following p. 86; *The Fate of Felicity Fark,* p. 74.

29 McGregor, 'Highbrow Lowbrow', p. 28; *From the Land of Shadows,* London, 1982, p. 84; *Unreliable Memoirs,* p. 132; *May Week was in June,* pp. 70, 100–1, 192; *The Dreaming Swimmer,* p. 91; *Other Passports,* p. 83; *Flying Visits,* pp. 175–6; *Clive James Show,* II & IV, 1995; *Postcard from Rio,* 1989; *Postcard from Miami,* 1990; *Postcard from Sydney,* 1991; *Postcard from London,* 1991; *Postcard from New York,* 1994; *Brmm! Brmm!,* pp. 13–16, 102; *The Silver Castle,* p. 245; *Fame in the Twentieth Century,* picture section following p. 86; *Clive James on Television,* p. 313.

30 *The Fate of Felicity Fark,* p. 93; *At the Pillars of Hercules,* p. 135; *Unreliable Memoirs,* pp. 111–12.

31 *The Dreaming Swimmer,* p. 76; *Unreliable Memoirs,* p. 11.

32 Aiton, 'A Postcard from Home'; *Unreliable Memoirs,* p. 154.

33 *Unreliable Memoirs,* pp. 118, 123, 128–9, 139, 142, 154.

34 *Unreliable Memoirs,* pp. 130–42, 151–2, 155–6, 160, 163–4, 167; on Anderson, see John Docker, *Australian Cultural Elites. Intellectual Traditions in Sydney and Melbourne,* Sydney, 1974, pp. 131–54; Brian Kennedy, *A Passion to Oppose: John Anderson, Philosopher,* Melbourne, 1995; on the Push, see Humphrey McQueen, *Suburbs of the Sacred,* Ringwood, Victoria, 1988, pp. 29–31; Anne Coombs, *Sex*

and Anarchy, Ringwood, Victoria, 1996, esp. pp. 139–42, 157; on Brennan's 'Lilith', see Frank Kermode, 'Christopher Brennan', in Geoffrey Dutton & Max Harris, eds, *The Vital Decade. Ten Years of Australian Art and Letters*, Melbourne, 1968, pp. 13–14; for James on Brennan, see *Snakecharmers in Texas*, pp. 17–29.

35 James, 'George Russell: A Reminiscence', in Gregory Kratzmann & James Simpson, eds, *Medieval English Religious and Ethical Literature*, Cambridge, 1986, p. 16; *Unreliable Memoirs*, pp. 162–4; *Postcard from Cairo*; *Falling Towards England*, pp. 93–5.

36 *The Dreaming Swimmer*, pp. 169–71; *Clive James meets Jane Fonda*, BBC TV, 1989; *Clive James Show*, no. V, 1995; *Other Passports*, pp. 92–8; *From the Land of Shadows*, p. 189; 'Save the Wales', *Age*, 24 November 1993.

37 'Mondo Fellini', *New Yorker*, 21 March 1995, p. 158.

38 *Unreliable Memoirs*, p. 142. On the convergences, as well as divergences, of the categories 'bohemian' and 'bourgeois' in various cultures, see Ephraim Mizruchi, *Regulating Society. Beguines, Bohemians, and Other Marginals*, Chicago, 1983, ch. 4; Jerrold Seigel, *Bohemian Paris: culture, politics, and the boundaries of bourgeois life*, New York, 1986.

39 'The Eternity Man', *London Review of Books*, 20 July 1995, p. 16.

40 *The Remake*, pp. 35–6.

41 *Unreliable Memoirs*, pp. 142, 155–7, 164; *The Late Show with Clive James* on 'Shakespeare', BBC TV, 1989; *From the Land of Shadows*, p. 161; *Clive James on Television*, p. 368; *Snakecharmers in Texas*, pp. 361–2; *The Remake*, p. 51; Julian Barnes, *Letters from London 1990–1995*, London, 1995, p. 279; *At the Pillars of Hercules*, pp. 15–38.

42 *The Dreaming Swimmer*, pp. ix–x, xii–xiii, 83–7; *Snakecharmers in Texas*, pp. 13, 42; *Clive James on Television*, pp. 11, 372, 396–9; *Falling Towards England*, p. 27; *The Metropolitan Critic*, pp. 23, 259; *At the Pillars of Hercules*, pp. 80–90.

43 Kratzmann & Simpson, pp. 16–17; Frederic Raphael , 'Reach for the Stars', *TLS*, 5 November 1987, p. 1191; Lynne Bell, 'A Prodigal Son is home', *Woman's Day*, 22 July 1985, p. 14; *Unreliable Memoirs*, p. 156; *May Week was in June*, p. 155; *Falling Towards England*, p. 79.

44 For his admiration of great scholars, see *At the Pillars of Hercules*, pp. 97–105; *The Dreaming Swimmer*, p. x; *The Metropolitan Critic*, p. 265; *Other Passports*, p. 71; *Snakecharmers in Texas*, pp. 93–5, 104–6, 116–17, 154, 251; 'The Voice of America', p. 90. Cf. James' dedication to Contini in *Britannia Bright's Bewilderment in the Wilderness of Westminster*, London, 1976, and to Russell in *Charles Charming's Challenges on the Pathway to the Throne*, London, 1981; and the acknowledgments to both scholars in Prue Shaw, ed., *Dante, Monarchia*, Cambridge, 1995, p. xi. For James' anti-academic jibes, see 'Kingsley Amis', *New Review*, London, vol. 1, no. 4, July 1974, p. 27; *At the Pillars of Hercules*, pp. 25, 39, 109, 125, 191; *Brilliant Creatures*, pp. 10, 172, 219, 271–302; *The Dreaming Swimmer*, pp. 55, 65, 126; *Fame in the Twentieth Century*, p. 3; *From the Land of Shadows*, pp.19, 82–6, 107, 195, 200, 211–12; *May Week was in June*, pp. 120, 246; *The Metropolitan Critic*, pp. 25, 78, 144–5, 149; *Other Passports*, pp. 72, 92, 204–6; *The Remake*, pp. 58, 62–3, 97.

45 Kratzmann & Simpson, pp. 16–17; *Falling Towards England*, pp. 79–80, 188.

46 *Falling Towards England*, pp. 42–3; *Snakecharmers in Texas*, pp. 219–24; *Clive James on Television*, p. 372; *The Dreaming Swimmer*, p. 97; *May Week was in June*, p. 222; Joyce Grenfell, *In Pleasant Places*, London, 1979, p. 205.

47 *May Week was in June*, p. 108; *Unreliable Memoirs*, pp. 107, 128, 160–2; *Clive James on Television*, p. 535; Gavin Souter, *Sydney Observed*, Sydney, 1968, pp. 116, 118; Peter Spearitt, *Sydney Since the Thirties*, Sydney, 1978, pp. 7, 136; K.S. Inglis, *Nation*, Melbourne, 1989, pp. 13, 25–6; Dutton, *The Innovators*, Melbourne, 1986, p. 154; *Falling Towards England*, p. 21; James on *Desert Island Discs; Postcard from Sydney*.

48 *The Dreaming Swimmer*, pp. 46–7, 57; *Unreliable Memoirs*, p. 156; *Falling Towards England*, p. 161; *Flying Visits*, p. 21; *Snakecharmers in Texas*, pp. 28–30; *The Metropolitan Critic*, p. 246; and above, pp. 13–14.

49 *Flying Visits*, pp. 15, 29–31; cf. Brian McFarlane, *Australian Cinema 1970–1985*, London, 1987, pp. 20–4; Susan Dermody & Elizabeth Jacka, *Screening Australia*, vol. 1, Paddington, NSW, 1987, pp. 53–8.

50 On versions of this myth in relation to female expatriates, see Ros Pesman, *Duty Free*, Melbourne, 1996, pp. 181–2.

51 *Unreliable Memoirs*, p. 173; McGregor, 'Highbrow Lowbrow', p. 26.

52 *The Metropolitan Critic*, p. 250; *Unreliable Memoirs*, p. 23.

53 'The Voice of America', p. 86; Cynthia Ozick, *What Henry James Knew*, London, 1993, pp. 99–133; *At the Pillars of Hercules*, p. 75; *From the Land of Shadows*, p. 156.

54 *Flying Visits*, pp. 111–12; *The Dreaming Swimmer*, p. 58.

55 *Falling Towards England*, pp. 77–9, 189.

56 *May Week was in June*, pp. 128, 237.

57 *May Week was in June*, pp. 22, 25, 33–7, 127–8, 157–8, 160–3, 185–94, 212–17, 220–31, 238; *Snakecharmers in Texas*, pp. 183–91; James on *Desert Island Discs*; see also Robert Hewison, *Footlights! A Hundred Years of Cambridge Comedy*, London, 1983, pp. 134, 149, 153–60, 209–10; *The Dreaming Swimmer*, pp. 79–82.

58 *New Statesman*, 7 July 1967, p. 24, 21 July 1967, p. 25, 11 August 1967, p. 179, 9 February 1968, p. 181; *The Metropolitan Critic*, pp. 182, 194–5, 201, 205, 226, 229.

59 *At the Pillars of Hercules*, pp. 182–8; *Britannia Bright's Bewilderment*, pp. 3–4, 40–1, 61, 65, 81–2, 85–6, 89–94, 98–103, 106–10; *Clive James on Television*, pp. 105–7, 222, 244, 416, 529–30, 584–5, 621–2, 646–7, 662–5; *The Dreaming Swimmer*, pp. xi, 127, 145, 151, 153, 200; *The Fate of Felicity Fark*, p. 78; *Flying Visits*, pp. 137, 146, 149; *Other Passports*, pp. 149–51, 153–6, 173–81, 186–7, 196–200, 218; *Snakecharmers in Texas*, pp. 331–8; Michael Foot, *Another Heart and Other Pulses*, London, 1984, pp. 91, 93; McGregor, 'Highbrow Lowbrow', p. 30; *Brilliant Creatures*, p. 111; *Clive James on 1988*, BBC TV, 1988; *The Late Show with Clive James* on 'Ten Years of Thatcherism', 1989; *Clive James on the Eighties*, BBC TV, 1989; *Clive James on 1993*, BBC TV, 1993; *The Silver Castle*, p. 196. On the Social Democratic Party in England and the range of its appeal, see Ivor Crewe & Anthony King, *SDP: The Birth, Life and Death of the Social Democratic Party*, Oxford, 1995.

60 *Charles Charming's Challenges*, pp. 90, 100–4; Larkin to Robert Conquest, 29 June 1981, in Anthony Thwaite, ed., *The Letters of Philip Larkin*, London, 1992, p. 650; *May Week was in June*, p. 160; Footlights minutes, 6 February 1967, cited in Hewison, p. 155.

61 *The Dreaming Swimmer*, pp. 49, 93–8, 117–18; 'Save the Wales'; Shaw, ed., *Dante, Monarchia*, pp. xv, xvii–xviii.

62 *Fame in the Twentieth Century*, p. 149; Tim Graham, *Diana. HRH The Princess of Wales. Introduced by Clive James*, London, 1988; Bruce Wilson, 'Is Clive James A

Comedian, A Serious Social Commentator, or Just An Expat Aussie Male Bimbo?',
Advertiser, Adelaide, 14 May 1994; Richard Kay, 'Diana's Private Camelot',
Australian Women's Weekly, April 1995, pp. 10–13; James, 'False Alternatives', *New
Statesman,* 9 February 1968, p. 181.

63 McGregor, 'Highbrow Lowbrow', p. 25; *Hamlet … A Personal View by Clive James,*
BBC TV, 1980; James interviewed by Peter Couchman, ABC Radio, 17 October
1996.

64 *May Week was in June,* pp. 106–11, 237–8; Williamson, 'A Literary Lion
Starts Again', p. 29; Shaw, ed., *Dante, Monarchia,* pp. iii, xi; Mary Killen, 'The
Killen Probe No 5: *University Challenge*' in *Harpers and Queen,* London,
February 1992.

65 *May Week was in June,* p. 221; *The Dreaming Swimmer,* p. 113; *Unreliable
Memoirs,* p. 45.

66 *The Dreaming Swimmer,* p. 81; Rowan Ayers, 'Clive stoops to wiggling for a laugh',
SMH, 14 September 1985; James on *Desert Island Discs;* 'Television' column,
Australian Financial Review, 22 June 1979, p. 12.

67 Catalogue of BBC Sound Archive, James file, pp. 1–3; *The Dreaming Swimmer,* p.
142.

68 Tidmarsh interview with James, *Outlook;* Kilmartin cited in 'Television' column,
Australian Financial Review, 22 June 1979.

69 *The Remake,* p. 26.

70 James on *Desert Island Discs;* Peter Conrad, 'The all-absorbing box', *TLS,* 8 May
1981, p. 511; *Clive James on Television,* pp. 320, 327, 590.

71 *The Dreaming Swimmer,* pp. 101–62; 'IQ beats autocue', *Observer Review,*
London, 17 September 1995; James interviewed by Jim Schembri, 'King of Live',
Age Green Guide, Melbourne, 20 June 1996, p. 1.

72 'Kangaroo Culture Time', *New Statesman,* 26 January 1968, p. 112; *Falling Towards
England,* p. 128; *Clive James Show,* no. IV, 1995; cf. McGregor's criticism of James'
Saturday Night shows in 'Highbrow Lowbrow', p. 26, and my own criticisms in
'Desperately seeking Clive', *24 Hours,* October 1996, p. 43.

73 *The Dreaming Swimmer,* p. xiii; *The Remake,* p. 114.

74 *The Talk Show with Clive James* on 'Culture and the Twentieth Century', BBC TV,
1990.

4 The Return of the Captive

1 Norman & Jeanne MacKenzie, eds, *The Diary of Beatrice Webb,* vol. 1, London,
1986, p. 223. On Greer as 'high priestess', see, e.g., Graham Eccles, 'Giant
Raspberry from Germaine', *Advertiser,* Adelaide, 7 February 1975; Hilary Roots,
'Germaine Greer: "Why I want a baby"', *Australian Women's Weekly,* 14 January
1976, p. 2.

2 *Sex and Destiny,* London, 1984, pp. 135, 259, 299, 303, 306–7, 317.

3 *Slip-Shod Sibyls. Recognition, Rejection and the Woman Poet,* London, 1995, p. 115.

4 Margaret Anne Doody, 'Poxy Doxies', *London Review of Books,* 14 December 1995,
p. 14

5 *Sex and Destiny,* p. 217; 'Mixed reaction to Greer at Frankfurt fair', *Canberra
Times,* 31 October 1984; Susan Faludi, *Backlash. The Undeclared War Against*

Women, London, 1991, p. 353; *Slip-Shod Sibyls,* pp. 412–13, 418–19, 421–2.

6 On the marriage, see Greer, *The Female Eunuch,* Paladin ed., London, 1971, p. 180; Paul Du Feu, 'A Few Words from Mr. Greer', *Bulletin,* 12 June 1971, pp. 35–6, 'The Trouble with Marriage', *Pix,* Sydney, 6 July 1972, p. 36, *Let's Hear It for the Long-Legged Women,* London, 1974, pp. 111–43; John Wasiliev, '"Germaine and I were doomed to fail" — husband', *Herald,* Melbourne, 28 June 1973. On previous and subsequent relationships, see, e.g., Jennifer Dabbs, *Beyond Redemption,* Melbourne, 1987, pp. 113–85; Kate Legge, 'The Greer revolution, 25 years on' and 'Screaming mother ended romantic interludes with schoolgirl lover', *Weekend Australian,* 7 October 1995; Clyde Packer, *No Return Ticket,* Pymble, NSW, 1984, pp. 90, 93, 95; Anne Coombs, *Sex and Anarchy,* Ringwood, Victoria, 1996, pp. 113–15; Greer, 'Liszt's Lookalike', in Ken Thomson, ed., *Barry Humphries. Bepraisements on his Birthday,* London, 1994, pp. 40–1; John Cunningham, 'Second Thoughts', *Weekend Australian Magazine,* 18–19 August 1979; 'Germaine sports a new beau', *Herald,* Melbourne, 29 August 1979. On the advertising for a sire, see David Plante, *Difficult Women. A Memoir of Three,* Futura ed., London, 1984, p. 155. On the alleged hysterectomy, and the controversy caused by the allegations, see Richard Neville, *Hippie Hippie Shake,* Melbourne, 1995, p. 71, and 'The pain in Spain was mainly Germaine', *SMH,* 22 July 1995; 'Londoners' Diary': 'So why no child for the female eunuch?', *Evening Standard,* London, 6 May 1995; 'Greer resigns as feminist war breaks out', *Evening Standard,* 16 May 1995; 'Venom flows in Greer's spat with feminist', *Age,* 18 May 1995; 'Feminist fallout in age of dissent', *Age,* 20 May 1995; Greer, 'We shall not be neutered', *Spectator,* 20 May 1995, p. 54; Andrew Alderson, 'Girl Talk', *Australian,* 24 May 1995; Nicci Gerrard, 'Greer lets fly over an unsisterly slight', *Guardian Weekly,* 28 May 1995; Greer interviewed by Jana Wendt, *60 Minutes,* Channel 9 TV network, Australia, 16 July 1995. For Greer on her biological history, see, e.g., Roots, 'Germaine Greer: "Why I want a baby"'; Patricia Morgan, 'Germaine "fights" for a baby', *Advertiser,* 21 December 1977; Lyndall Hobbs, 'You'll Never Believe It', *Woman's Day,* 1 January 1979, p. 19; Greer, *The Madwoman's Underclothes,* London, 1986, p. 114; 'It's been a struggle, says Greer', *Australian,* 8 November 1995.

7 Russell Davies, ed., *The Kenneth Williams Diaries,* London, 1993, p. 689; David Malouf, interviewed by Phillip Adams, *Late Night Live,* ABC radio, 7 October 1996.

8 Interview by Anthony Clare, *In the Psychiatrist's Chair,* BBC Radio 4, 30 March 1989.

9 Clare interview; Liz Hickson, 'Could this really be Germaine Greer?', *Australian Women's Weekly,* February 1992, p. 61; John McGregor, 'An Agonising Obsession', *Advertiser,* Adelaide, 8 April 1989.

10 Greer, Introduction to Henry Handel Richardson, *The Getting of Wisdom,* Virago ed., 1981, pages unnumbered.

11 *Daddy, we hardly knew you,* Penguin, Harmondsworth, Middlesex, 1990, pp. 127–46, 153–94, 219, 302; Greer, 'We, the protected generation', *Guardian,* 16 May 1994; Clare interview; *Slip-Shod Sibyls,* p. 383; Greer quoted in Kay Keavney, 'The Liberating of Germaine Greer', *Australian Women's Weekly,* 2 February 1972, p. 4.

12 Joan Cahill, quoted in Anthony Dennis, ed., 'Fast Foreword', *SMH Good Weekend,* 20 April 1991, p. 5; Greer, in Jackie Bennett & Rosemary Forgan, eds, *There's Something About A Convent Girl,* London, 1991, pp. 88–9; 'Shock tactics remembered', *Woman's Day,* 5 July 1971; Dabbs, pp. 145, 149.

13 Packer, pp. 88–90, 95; *Daddy, we hardly knew you*, p. 288; *Farrago*, 17 March 1959, p. 7, 19 May 1959, p. 9, 4 August 1959, p. 4; *The Madwoman's Underclothes*, p. xxiv.

14 Blundell quoted in Fiona Harari, 'Great moments in Feminism', *Weekend Australian*, 7 October 1995; Clive James, *May Week was in June*, Picador ed., London, 1990, pp. 23, 41, *Snakecharmers in Texas*, Picador ed., London, 1989, p. 188; Robert Hewison, *Footlights!*, London, 1983, pp. 134, 151, 209–10.

15 Neville, *Hippie Hippie Shake*, pp. 145–7; Greer, *The Madwoman's Underclothes*, p. 16 (this book also republishes a number of her other pieces in *Oz*).

16 Kathleen Tynan, *The Life of Kenneth Tynan*, Methuen ed., London, 1988, p. 302; Kathleen Tynan, ed., *Kenneth Tynan Letters*, London, 1994, pp. 480–1; Greer, 'A Whore in Every Home', in programme for *Mrs Warren's Profession*, National Theatre, London, n.d.; 'Shanghai Express', *Granta*, vol. 50, p. 245.

17 'Play dropped', *West Australian*, 3 August 1973; Tynan, *Life*, pp. 269, 300–1, 351, *Letters*, pp. 555, 577.

18 Justin Wintle, ed., *Makers of Modern Culture*, London, 1981, p. 206; *Who's Who 1993*.

19 James, *Snakecharmers in Texas*, p. 55; *May Week was in June*, pp. 81–2, 153–5, 230.

20 Jordan Bonfante, 'A talent devoted to the cause of women', *Canberra Times*, 5 June 1971; Neville, 'Intellectuals' Playmate of the Year', *Bulletin*, 27 February 1971, p. 42, and *Hippie Hippie Shake*, p. 70; Sir Les Patterson, *The Traveller's Tool*, Coronet ed., London, 1986, p. 71.

21 Neville, *Hippie Hippie Shake*, p. 187; Du Feu, interviewed by Rosemary Munday, 'My Life with Germaine', *National Times*, 10–15 January 1972, pp. 20–1, and *Let's Hear It …*, blurb and pp. 22–4, 42–3, 102–3, 121, 149, 153, 204, 232; *The Female Eunuch*, p. 180.

22 Greer, 'The Ethic of Love and Marriage in Shakespeare's Early Comedies', unpublished PhD thesis, University of Cambridge, 1967, p. ii; Greer interviewed by Duncan Fallowell in 'Greer: a woman of substance', *Times on Sunday*, 24 January 1988; Greer on *Desert Island Discs*, BBC Radio 4, 25 October 1988; Angela Levin, 'Betrayed', *Courier-Mail*, 25 March 1989.

23 Greer, 'The Ethic of Love and Marriage … ', pp. 35, 191–202; cf. *The Female Eunuch*, pp. 208–9.

24 Du Feu, *Let's Hear It … *, p. 126, 'The Trouble with Marriage', p. 36; Nat Lehrman, 'Playboy Interview: Germaine Greer. A candid conversation with the ballsy author of The Female Eunuch', *Playboy*, vol. 19, no. 1, January 1972, pp. 63, 68; Packer, pp. 96, 98; Plante, p. 141.

25 Du Feu, *Let's Hear It … *, pp. 113, 116, 118, 127; Lehrman, 'Playboy Interview', p. 63.

26 Lehrman, 'Playboy Interview', p. 62; Packer, p. 98; Carmen Callil, 'The Book, the Chief, the Hype and the Other Cover', *Weekend Australian*, 7 October 1995.

27 *The Madwoman's Underclothes*, pp. 30–5; E.P. Thompson, *Warwick University Ltd: Industry, Management and the Universities*, Harmondsworth, Middlesex, 1970, pp. 13–18, 42–59, 66–70, 79–87, 95–103, 146–66.

28 *The Female Eunuch*, pp. 315–31; Lehrman, 'Playboy Interview', pp. 74, 76.

29 *The Female Eunuch*, pp. 18–19.

30 Lehrman, 'Playboy Interview', p. 62; *The Madwoman's Underclothes*, p. 25; *The Female Eunuch*, p. 297. For some recent assessments of Greer's influence in popularising feminism, see Polly Toynbee, 'Fatal Myths, Failed Ideals', *Weekend*

Australian Review, 21–22 September 1991; Leslie White, 'The Problem with being Germaine', *Weekend Australian Review,* 12–13 October 1991; Helen Trinca, 'Still stirring after all these years', *Weekend Australian* ('Focus'), 25–26 March 1995; 'Germaine Greer. Feminist guru, or tarnished old icon?', *Observer,* 26 March 1995; Stephanie Bunbury, 'The greatness of Dr Germaine Greer', *Age,* 20 September 1996; Michael Visontay, ed., 'The Female Eunuch. 25 Years On', supplement in *Weekend Australian,* 7 October 1996.

31 *The Female Eunuch,* p. 296.

32 Callil, 'The Book, the Chief, the Hype and the Other Cover'; Mary Spongberg, 'If She's So Great, How Come So Many Pigs Dig Her? Germaine Greer and the malestream press', in *Women's History Review,* Wallingford, Oxfordshire, vol. 2, no. 3, 1993, pp. 407–19; Max Harris, 'How Germaine Greer became Mrs Miniver', *Bulletin,* 31 August 1982, p. 42.

33 *The Female Eunuch,* pp. 301–2, 308–10, 318–19, 330; *The Madwoman's Underclothes,* pp. 25–9.

34 'The Female Eunuch', *Newsweek,* New York, 22 March 1971, p. 50; Lehrman, 'Playboy Interview', p. 62; *The Madwoman's Underclothes,* p. 80.

35 *Town Bloody Hall,* Pennebaker Inc., New York, 1979; *The Madwoman's Underclothes,* p. 86.

36 *Town Bloody Hall; Village Voice,* cited in Lehrman, 'Playboy Interview', p. 62.

37 *Town Bloody Hall;* cf. *Slip-Shod Sibyls,* pp. 390–424. See also Greer, 'On Viewing Paula Rego', in *Paula Rego. Tales from the National Gallery,* London, 1991, p. 34.

38 Catalogue of BBC Sound Archive, Greer file, 30 December 1970 ff; Greer, 'Vanity Bag', 'Germaine Greer on wit and witlessness', 'Germaine Greer on the pornography of food', in *Spectator,* 12 December 1970, pp. 768–9, 13 February 1971, pp. 233-4, 10 April 1971, p. 502; articles from *Suck* and *Sunday Times* reprinted in *The Madwoman's Underclothes,* pp. 51–9, 62–77, 90–116, 120–5, 146–51, 169–71.

39 On her Calabrian sojourn, see *The Madwoman's Underclothes,* pp. ix–xxiii; *Sex and Destiny,* pp. 95–6. On her mother's origins, see *Daddy, we hardly knew you,* p. 112. For details of her Tuscan retreat (location, atmosphere, her motives for going there, and her activities, including gardening), see: Lehrman, 'Playboy Interview', p. 62; Greer interviewed by John Hale, *Voices from Tuscany,* BBC Radio 3, 18 December 1974; Susan Chitty & Thomas Hinde, *The Great Donkey Walk,* London, 1977, pp. 226–7; Tiziana Zeroni, 'Germaine Greer: her heart is in Tuscany', *Northern Territory News,* Darwin, 3 April 1982; Plante, pp. 95–7, 105–15; Julie Herd, 'Greer is merely besotted', *Australian Weekend Magazine,* 4–5 October 1986; *Daddy, we hardly knew you,* p. 15; Jeffrey Smart, *Not Quite Straight. A Memoir,* Melbourne, 1996, pp. 419–21, 445–6.

40 *The Revolting Garden,* London, 1979, pages unnumbered.

41 Plante, p. 112; Lehrman, 'Playboy Interview', p. 82. Her reports on conferences and conventions are republished in *The Madwoman's Underclothes,* pp. 126–45, 195–203.

42 *The Obstacle Race,* London, 1979, p. 335.

43 Andrea Chambers, 'Greer, the good ole girl', *Age,* 21 March 1980.

44 *The Obstacle Race,* p. 189; *Slip-Shod Sibyls,* p. 412.

45 Lehrman, 'Playboy Interview', pp. 64, 76.

46 *The Obstacle Race,* p. 210; *Sex and Destiny,* p. 256; *The Madwoman's Underclothes,* pp. 80–1; *The Uncollected Verse of Aphra Behn,* Stump Cross, Essex, 1989, p. 192;

The Change. Women, Ageing and the Menopause, Penguin ed., Harmondsworth, Middlesex, 1992, pp. 276, 414; *Slip-Shod Sibyls,* pp. 399–400.

47 'The Ethic of Love and Marriage', p. 185; *The Female Eunuch,* p. 130.

48 Keavney, 'The Liberating of Germaine Greer'; Packer, p. 99; Greer, Foreword to Peter Quartermaine, *Jeffrey Smart,* South Yarra, Victoria, 1983, p. 7; Greer, 'Why Germaine took flight', *SMH,* 28 November 1987; *The Madwoman's Underclothes,* p. 149; *Daddy, we hardly knew you,* pp. 68, 79, 112, 153, 232–6; 'Germaine Greer: a home of my own', *Big Issue,* London, no. 63, 25–31 January 1994, p. 4; 'Liszt's Lookalike', p. 40.

49 'Liszt's Lookalike', p. 40; Chambers, 'Greer, the good ole girl'; 'Shock tactics remembered'.

50 Reprinted in *The Madwoman's Underclothes,* pp. 149-51.

51 Greer in *There's Something About A Convent Girl,* pp. 87–90; *Daddy, we hardly knew you,* pp. 7–10, 112, 118, 276, 285–6, 288; Packer, p. 86.

52 Greer in *There's Something About A Convent Girl,* pp. 88, 93; *The Madwoman's Underclothes,* pp. xiv, 36–7, 85–6, 111–12, 163, 225–6, 239, 241, 248.

53 *Daddy, we hardly knew you,* pp. 68–70.

54 'Home is an illusion', *Guardian Weekly,* 24 October 1993; *Daddy, we hardly knew you,* p. 70 (my emphasis). On the Greer/Neville/ Moore controversy, see references in note 6 above.

55 Packer, pp. 89, 94.

56 *Daddy, we hardly knew you,* p. 195; Packer, pp. 90, 93.

57 *Sex and Destiny,* p. 95; *There's Something About A Convent Girl,* pp. 90–1, 93.

58 Greer in *Guardian,* 20 March 1995; for reports and commentary on the article, see, e.g., Peter Ellingsen, 'Germaine Greer: I was rape victim at 19', *Age,* 22 March 1995; Helen Trinca, 'Raped Greer calls for attackers to be outed', *Australian,* 22 March 1995; Caroline Davies, 'Greer tells: I was raped by footballer', and Bruce Wilson, 'Greer's bad memory', *Herald-Sun,* Melbourne, 22 March 1995; Debra Jopson, 'Activists reject call for register of rapists', *SMH,* 23 March 1995; 'Germaine Greer. Feminist guru, or tarnished old icon?', *Observer,* 26 March 1995.

59 Padraic P. McGuiness, 'When making rape accusations is a source of power', *Age,* 24 March 1995; Beatrice Faust, 'An Unwelcome Distraction' and 'Old Wounds reopened for Greer', *Australian,* 25 26 March and 27–28 May 1995; Lehrman, 'Playboy Interview', p. 66; Packer, pp. 92–3; *The Madwoman's Underclothes,* p. 74.

60 Packer, pp. 94–5; Chris Wallace-Crabbe, cited in John Poynter and Carolyn Rasmussen, *A Place Apart. The University of Melbourne: Decades of Challenge,* Melbourne, 1996, pp. 234–5. On Goldberg's ideas and intellectual influence in Australia, see John Docker, *Australia's Cultural Elites,* Sydney, 1974, pp. 130, 156, and *In a Critical Tradition,* Ringwood, Victoria, 1984, pp. 2, 5–10; Richard Freadman, 'The Quest for the Classical Temper: The Literary Criticism of S.L. Goldberg', *Critical Review,* Canberra, no. 32, 1992, pp. 65–6.

61 Packer, pp. 94–5; Coombs, pp. 80–1, 109, 111, 113–15.

62 Packer, p. 95; Poynter & Rasmussen, pp. 235–6; Coombs, pp. 135–6, 182–3, 197; *Who's Who 1993.*

63 *The Change,* p. 25; 'The Development of Byron's Satiric Mode', unpublished MA thesis, University of Sydney, 1962, pp. 4, 266. See also Greer's Preface to Catherine Reilly, ed., *Winged Words. Victorian Poetry and Women's Verse,* London, 1994, p. xv.

64 Mary McCarthy, *Memories of a Catholic Girlhood,* Penguin ed., Harmondsworth, Middlesex, 1963, p. 83; F. R. Leavis, *Revaluations,* Penguin ed., Harmondsworth, Middlesex, 1964, pp. 126–7; Greer, 'The Development of Byron's Satiric Mode', chs III–VI.

65 *Germaine Greer's Sydney,* John McGreevey Productions, New York, 1980; Ben Sandilands, 'Physical Sydney, as seen by Germaine Greer', *Australian,* 30 December 1978. See also *The Madwoman's Underclothes,* pp. 99–101; *The Revolting Garden,* section on 'Australia'; 'Germaine Greer Writes on Australia Revisited', *Bulletin,* 17 August 1982, p. 64.

66 Wintle, p. 206; Packer, p. 95; S. L. Goldberg, *An Essay on King Lear,* Cambridge, 1970.

67 Packer, p. 96; *The Female Eunuch,* pp. 294–5.

68 *The Madwoman's Underclothes,* pp. ix, xxiii.

69 *The Female Eunuch,* p. 113.

70 *The Madwoman's Underclothes,* pp. xxiv, 87; *The Female Eunuch,* p. 308; *The Change,* p. 433.

71 *The Female Eunuch,* p. 150.

72 Camille Paglia, 'Crisis in the Universities', in her *Sex, Art, and American Culture,* New York, 1992, p. 274.

73 Paglia interviewed by Jana Wendt on the Greer/Moore fight, *60 Minutes,* Channel 9 network, 16 July 1995; Paglia, 'Loose Canons', *Observer Review,* 8 October 1995; Faludi, pp. 352–3; Greer, 'We shall not be neutered'. Cf. Greer's attack on militant feminists twenty-five years earlier, reprinted in *The Madwoman's Underclothes,* pp. 27–8. See also references in note 6 above.

74 *Sex and Destiny,* pp. 105, 198–9, 203–5, 217.

75 *Sex and Destiny,* pp. ix–x, 95–7, 207–8, 219, 227; *The Madwoman's Underclothes,* p. xxiii; *The Female Eunuch,* pp. 235–6.

76 *Daddy, we hardly knew you,* p. 235; Hickson, 'Could this really be Germaine?'

77 Faludi, p. 354; *The Female Eunuch,* pp. 236, 282, 287–8.

78 On her Tuscan household, see references in note 39 above, and Susan Chitty, letter in *Spectator,* 3 June 1995, p. 36. On her invitation to the homeless in England, and the reactions to it, see 'Germaine Greer: a home of my own', *Big Issue,* 25–31 January 1994; 'I smelt a rat, but I didn't realise he'd be such a stinker', *Guardian,* 7 February 1994; Martin Henessey in *Mail on Sunday,* London, 6 February 1994, and in John Hind, 'The jury's out on Germaine Greer', *Cosmopolitan,* Sydney, July 1995, p. 51; Lisa O'Kelley & Isobel Hunt, 'Gimme Shelter but leave me dignity. Plain generous or gesture politics?', *Observer,* 6 February 1994.

79 *Daddy, we hardly knew you,* pp. 102, 128, 133, 141, 177, 180–2, 193, 246, 248, 250–1, 271, 291, 296–7, 307, 311. For her comments on what she might have inherited from her mother, see Clare interview, and Hickson, 'Could this really be Germaine?'

80 *The Uncollected Verse of Aphra Behn,* pp. 4, 6, 10; Greer & R. Little, eds, *The Collected Works of Katherine Philips, the Matchless Orinda … Vol. iii, The Translations,* textual notes and commentary, *passim;* 'How to invent a poet', *TLS,* 25 June 1993, p. 7; *Slip-Shod Sibyls,* pp. xvi–xvii, 103, 107, 116, 130, 154, 172, 196.

81 *Daddy, we hardly knew you,* p. 247; *The Madwoman's Underclothes,* p. 88; *The Change,* pp. 45, 433; Alderson, 'Girl Talk'.

82 Hobbs, 'You'll Never Believe It'; *The Madwoman's Underclothes,* p. 101; 'Home is

an illusion'; 'Malouf returns to the native stereotype', *Guardian Weekly,* 7 November 1993. Cf. Duncan Graham, 'A prophet in her own land', *Age,* 15 January 1988; Michele Field, 'Defiant Greer', *Bulletin,* 11 April 1989, p. 26, and 'Remarks Germaine to the republican debate', *Australian,* 14 June 1993.

83 Plante, p. 118; Smart, p. 446.

84 *The Female Eunuch,* pp. 34–5; *Sex and Destiny,* pp. 95, 101; *The Madwoman's Underclothes,* pp. 90, 101, 102, 108, 181–5, 274, 289; *Daddy, we hardly knew you,* pp. 28, 64, 66, 73, 75, 84, 97, 107, 171, 210, 217–19, 222, 237, 307; 'Shanghai Express', pp. 236–8; Plante, pp. 111, 123, 170.

85 *Shakespeare,* Past Masters series, Oxford, 1986, p. 100; 'Grave New World' *Marxism Today,* London, December 1991/January 1992, p. 49. For her continuing ambivalence about communism, see Barbara Amiel, 'Greer. Facing up to life at the turning point', *Australian Weekend Review,* 1–2 April 1989; Greer, 'Shanghai Express', pp. 231–2, 237–8, 244–5.

86 *Shakespeare,* p. 125; Rod Usher, 'Germaine Greer and the fatherless generation', *Age,* 19 December 1986; *The Change,* p. 34; *Paula Rego,* BBC TV, 1992.

87 Andrea Lofthouse & Vivienne Smith, eds, *Who's Who of Australian Women,* Sydney, 1982, p. 213; Chambers, 'Greer, the good ole girl'; Plante, p. 126; Tina Brown, 'Germaine is still battling to get away from mum', *SMH,* 11 February 1984.Greer was founding editor of *Tulsa Studies in Women's Literature,* Tulsa, Oklahoma, 1982. Her work at Tulsa is also represented in the volume she co-edited with Susan Hastings, Jeslyn Medoff and Melinda Sansone: *Kissing the Rod. An Anthology of Seventeenth-Century Women's Verse,* New York 1988. On her (non-academic) experiences in Oklahoma, see Greer, 'If Women Ruled … ', *Australian Weekend Review,* 13–14 April 1996.

88 *Daddy, we hardly knew you,* p. 151; *Sex and Destiny,* p. 37; James Cockington, 'Today's People', *SMH,* 30 April 1991; 'On the Oxford short list', *Sun-Herald,* 7 June 1992; Eva Cox, reported in 'The War between the Women', *Weekend Australian Review,* 24–25 June 1995; Paul Johnson, 'The feminist world war has begun', *Spectator,* 10 June 1995, p. 30.

89 French in *Guardian,* 7 May 1994; Greer in *The Times Magazine,* London, 3 June 1995, 'Diary', p. 4.

90 *The Obstacle Race,* pp. 62–3, 151, 154; *The Change,* pp. 102, 439–40; *There's Something About A Convent Girl,* p. 95; Plante, pp. 145, 150.

91 Phillip Adams, 'Germaine Greer growing old disgracefully', *21-C: previews of a changing world,* Crows Nest, NSW, Autumn 1992, p. 65; Simon Kent, 'Our Germaine finds religion', *Sun-Herald,* 10 May 1992; *There's Something About a Convent Girl,* pp. 93, 95.

92 Neville, *Hippie Hippie Shake,* p. 52.

93 Leavis, p. 128; 'The Ethic of Love and Marriage', p. iii; *Shakespeare,* pp. 17–18, 84–6, 108.

94 *Shakespeare,* p. 5; Greer, 'Diary', *The Times Magazine;* Peter Ellingsen, 'Germs' warfare on biographer', *Age,* 7 June 1996.

95 *Sex and Destiny,* pp. ix–x; cf. *Slip-Shod Sibyls,* p. 116. Gibbons' speech is in Act III, scene iii of *This Happy Breed,* in Noël Coward, *Plays: Four,* Methuen ed., London, 1979, p. 371.

96 Reprinted in *The Madwoman's Underclothes,* p. 16.

5 The Nostalgia of the Critic

1 'The Glory of the Lord Shone Around Them', *Time*, 28 December 1970, pp. 30–5; 'Out of the Junkyard', *Time*, 4 January 1971, p. 37.

2 Robert Hughes, *Nothing If Not Critical*, London, 1990, pp. 295, 367; and *The Shock of the New*, 1st ed., London, 1980, p. 375 (all subsequent references to this edition, unless otherwise stated). I discuss these matters, with differing emphases, in an earlier version of this essay, 'The Nostalgia of the Critic: Postmodernism and the Unbalancing of Robert Hughes', *Thesis Eleven*, Cambridge, Mass., no. 34, 1993, pp. 67–88.

3 *Culture of Complaint. The Fraying of America*, revised ed., London, 1994, p. 108; Ralph Broom, 'Oh, brother! That critic in the Minister's family', *Courier-Mail*, Brisbane, 26 February 1971; 'Artist is mellower, but no less critical', *SMH*, 4 July 1972; Sandra McGrath, 'Robert Hughes and the Convict Experience', *Australian*, 13–14 August 1977; interview with Hughes in Clyde Packer, *No Return Ticket*, North Ryde, NSW, 1984, pp. 9, 16, 24; 'Heaven meets hell on fatal shore', *Australian*, 21–22 February 1987; Richard Neville, *Hippie Hippie Shake*, Melbourne, 1995, p. 195; Luke Slattery, 'The Art of being Robert Hughes', *Australian Magazine*, Sydney, 12–13 August 1995, p. 22.

4 Derryn Hinch, 'Robert Hughes rampant', *SMH*, 1 July 1972; Michael Heyward, 'Fatal core of the Big Apple', *Advertiser*, Adelaide, 1 March 1990; 'The Shock of the Hughes', *Vanity Fair*, New York, November 1990, p. 224; Alex McGregor, 'What makes Barcelona great (Despite the Olympics)', *Age*, 12 April 1992; Bill Wyndham, 'The fatal charmer', *Sunday Age*, 29 October 1995.

5 Bill Grundy in *Evening Standard*, October 1980, cited in: Sandra McGrath, 'Hughes: I'm a fat old enfant', *Australian*, 27 November 1980; 'Harsh Words', *Canberra Times*, 18 October 1980; Packer, p. 18. The more recent English commentators are Henry Porter in *Guardian*, 1993 (reprinted as 'Robert Hughes Exorcises America', in *SMH*, 8 May 1993), and Lynne Truss, 'Big opinions in a small box', *The Times*, 31 October 1996. On Hughes' accent, see also Slattery, 'The Art of being Robert Hughes', p. 16; Catharine Lumby, 'The Australian who conquered America', *SMH*, 20 July 1996. For comparisons with Clark, see Elwyn Lynn, 'Cadavers in a Landscape. A Critique of Robert Hughes', *Quadrant*, vol. xix, no. 5, August 1975, pp. 19–23; McGrath, 'I'm a fat old enfant'; Michael McNay, 'Hughes Who in Modern Art', *Australian Weekend Magazine*, 27–28 September 1980; 'Civilisation, Aussie style', *Bulletin*, 7 October 1980; 'Critics liked Hughes's show but winced at his accent', *Canberra Times*, 9 November 1980; Peter Craven, 'Stuck in the middle with Hughes', *Age*, 8 May 1993.

6 'Court player with snarl of a tiger', *SMH*, 25 May 1985; Andrew Riemer, *Inside Outside*, Pymble, NSW, 1992, p. 196; Gavin Souter, 'Tom Hughes, the Third', *SMH*, 18 September 1970; Tony Stephens, 'Tom Hughes … ', *SMH*, 16 July 1994.

7 For Hughes' family background, see Souter, 'Tom Hughes'; Elisabeth Wynhausen, 'The feverish world of Robert Hughes …', *National Times*, 16–22 November 1980; Janet Hawley, 'The World's Most Influential Art Critic?', *Age*, 29 November 1980; 'Shock of the Hughes', *Australian Weekend Magazine*, 10–11 January 1987; *Who's Who 1993*, p. 941; *Australian Dictionary of Biography*, vol. 9, Melbourne, 1983, pp. 391–3. Cf. Hughes, 'Flying the Black Mamba. A Sydney Boyhood', *London Magazine*, New Series, vol. 9, no. 8, pp. 7–8.

8 Hughes, 'Flying the Black Mamba', p. 7; Malcolm Turnbull, 'From Silk to Riches', *Bulletin,* 21 February 1978, pp. 40, 42; *Who's Who in Australia, 1980,* p. 438; 'Court player'; Stephens, 'Tom Hughes'; Slattery, 'The Art of being Robert Hughes', p. 23.

9 Geoffrey Dutton quoted in Judith White, 'The Painted Word', *Sun-Herald,* 9 December 1990.

10 'The Shock of the Hughes', *Vanity Fair,* November 1990, p. 225; Hughes, 'The Vice of Writing', *University of Melbourne Gazette,* Autumn 1996, p. 17; Wynhausen, 'Feverish world'; Rita Erlich, 'The entertaining Robert Hughes', *Age,* 24 March 1981; *Landscape with Figures. The Art of Australia,* ABC TV, 1975, ep. 4; Hughes, 'Why Watch It, Anyway?', *New York Review of Books,* 16 February 1995, p. 37; *Culture of Complaint,* pp. 89, 92; 'Doric columns, domes and vaults. Robert Hughes', an interview in Geoffrey De Groen, *Some Other Dream: The Artist, the Artworld and the Expatriate,* Sydney, 1984, pp. 120–2.

11 See, e.g., Hughes, 'Dog Eats Dog', *Nation,* 26 January 1963, reprinted in K.S. Inglis, ed., *Nation,* Melbourne, 1989, p. 108; 'Irrational Imagery in Australian Painting', in *Art and Australia,* Sydney, November 1963, pp. 150–9; *Landscape with Figures,* ep. 3; De Groen, pp. 132, 147–9; *Nothing If Not Critical,* pp. 169–70, 287–8, 291, 293; Hughes, 'Matisse still a teacher for our century', *Guardian Weekly,* 11 October 1992, p. 26; Wyndham, 'Fatal charmer'; Mary Delahunty, *Sunday Afternoon:* interview with Hughes, ABC TV, 5 November 1995; Hughes, 'The Case for Elitist Do-Gooders', *New Yorker,* 27 May 1996, p. 34.

12 John Ruskin, *The Stones of Venice,* vol. II, ch. viii, section 135, in E. T. Cook and A. Wedderburn, eds, *The Works of John Ruskin,* London, 1903–12, vol. X, p. 434; 'Inaugural Address at the Cambridge School of Art', 1858, *Works,* vol. XIX, pp. 177–81.

13 De Groen, p. 130; White cited in David Marr, *Patrick White. A Life,* Vintage ed., Milsons Point, NSW, 1992, p. 223.

14 'The Shock of the Hughes', *Vanity Fair,* 1990, p. 225; notes by Hughes supplied for and published in Geoffrey Dutton, *The Innovators,* Melbourne, 1986 p. 189.

15 Dutton, *The Innovators,* pp. 188–9; Hawley, 'World's Most Influential Art Critic?'; Hughes, 'The Vice of Writing', p. 17; Cyril Connolly, *The Unquiet Grave* (1944), revised ed., London, 1945, pp. xii, 1, 32, 35, 44–54. Cf. also *Landscape with Figures,* ep. 7, for Hughes' comments on the attractions of Connolly's nostalgia for pre-war Europe in *The Unquiet Grave.*

16 'Flying the Black Mamba', pp. 10, 13–15; *Culture of Complaint,* pp. 47–8; 'Images of pain and pleasure', *Australian,* 13–14 August 1977; McGrath, 'Heaven meets hell on fatal shore'; *The Shock of the New,* p. 366, and cf. p. 212.

17 *Culture of Complaint,* p. 32; 'Flying the Black Mamba', p. 5; Elisabeth Wynhausen, 'A convict race with roots in a living jail', *SMH,* 17 January 1987.

18 Gerard Windsor, 'Friends and Sometime Scholars: A History of St Ignatius College, Riverview' (unpublished), National Library of Australia MS. 6920, n.d. [*c.* 1975–77], p. 378; 'The Shock of the Hughes', *Vanity Fair,* 1990, p. 225; Wynhausen, 'Feverish world'; Erlich, 'The entertaining Robert Hughes'; Hughes, 'Dolls and Discontents', *Time,* 6 December 1993, p. 88.

19 Windsor, p. 393; De Groen, pp. 22–3; 'Flying the Black Mamba', pp. 10, 13; *Heaven and Hell in Western Art,* London, 1968, p. 35; *The Shock of the New,* p. 56; 'Shock of the Hughes', *Australian Weekend Magazine,* 1987.

20 *The Shock of the New,* pp. 7, 213; 'Flying the Black Mamba', pp. 15–17; De Groen, p. 129.

21 'Flying the Black Mamba', pp. 14–15; Hughes, 'The Well-wrought Ern', Introduction to Michael Heyward, *The Ern Malley Affair,* St Lucia, Queensland, 1993, p. xx, and p. 34 of main text; G. Dutton & M. Harris, eds, *The Vital Decade,* Melbourne, 1986, p. 208; cf. Hughes on McAuley in 'The Intellectual in Australia', *London Magazine,* vol. 4, New Series, no. 5, August 1964, p. 74.

22 Packer, pp. 8, 12. For other comments by Hughes on the abiding influence of his Catholic background on his style of rhetoric and other things, see De Groen, p. 129; Slattery, 'The Art of being Robert Hughes', pp. 22–3.

23 'Flying the Black Mamba', p. 8; Michael Gawenda, 'Hughes, QC, on rights, politics and the coming McCarthyism', *SMH,* 8 November 1984; Souter, 'Tom Hughes'; Turnbull, 'From Silk to Riches', p. 40.

24 De Groen, pp. 123, 130; *Landscape with Figures,* ep. 10; 'Flying the Black Mamba', p. 12.

25 Windsor, p. 390; *The Art of Australia,* revised ed., Harmondsworth, Middlesex, 1970, p. 1; 'Flying the Black Mamba', p. 17; 'The Vice of Writing', p. 17. Cf. De Groen, p. 123.

26 *The Shock of the New,* pp. 180–4; *Barcelona,* London, 1992, pp. 143–53, 343–6; *American Visions,* ep. 6.

27 Dutton, *The Innovators,* p. 205, and *Out in the Open,* St Lucia, Queensland, 1994, pp. 243–4, 250; Inglis, p. 126; Judy Cassab, *Diaries* (31 March 1962), Sydney, 1995, p. 145; 'The Vice of Writing', p. 17; De Groen, pp. 127–8. Details of the destruction of the original printed edition of *The Art of Australia* are still confused, and the alleged reasons for this equally so; for various accounts, see revised edition, p. 19; Muriel Colville, 'Chairing the experts at 28', *Canberra Times,* 27 August 1966; Daniel Thomas, 'The long wait for Hughes book ends', *Sunday Telegraph,* Sydney, 20 December 1970; G.R. Lansell, 'Yesterday's contemporary', *Nation,* 6 February 1971; Broom, 'Oh, brother! … '; Dutton, *Out in the Open,* p. 275, and the slightly different version in Dutton's *A Rare Bird. Penguin Books in Australia 1946–96,* Ringwood, Victoria, 1996, pp. 56–7, 67–71; Christopher Heathcote, *A Quiet Revolution,* Melbourne, 1995, p. 182.

28 Dutton, *The Innovators,* pp. 138–41, 154; Packer, p. 6; De Groen, pp. 125–6; 'Shock of the Hughes', *Australian Weekend Magazine,* 1987; biographical note on Hughes in the original edition of *The Art of Australia,* Penguin Books, 1965, printed at the Griffin Press, Adelaide, p. i; Colville, 'Chairing the experts'; Inglis, pp. 77, 81.

29 James, *Snakecharmers in Texas,* Picador ed., London, 1989, p. 10, and *Unreliable Memoirs,* Picador ed., London, 1980, pp. 132, 161; Humphrey McQueen, *Suburbs of the Sacred,* Ringwood, Victoria, 1988, p. 169; *The Art of Australia,* original ed., p. 64; *Landscape with Figures,* ep. 7; De Groen, p. 123; Heathcote, p. 137.

30 'Robert Hughes Replies', *Quadrant,* vol. xix, no. 6, October 1975, p. 54; Anne Coombs, *Sex and Anarchy,* Ringwood, Victoria, 1996, pp. 158–9.

31 De Groen, pp. 123–4; 'Shock of the Hughes', *Australian Weekend Magazine,* 1987; 'The Shock of the Hughes', *Vanity Fair,* 1990, p. 225; Peter Craven, 'The Dazzling Robert Hughes', *Age,* 9 December 1990; Janet Hawley, 'Art and Nothing But', *SMH Good Weekend,* 2 March 1991, p. 19; 'The Vice of Writing', p. 17; Packer, p. 6; Andrew Riemer, pp. 196–7.

32 *The Art of Australia,* original ed., pp. i, 291–2; Cassab, p. 146 (11 May 1962); Hughes, 'Irrational Imagery in Australian Painting'; *Landscape with Figures,* ep.

10; Hughes, 'Introduction' to *Colin Lanceley,* Sydney, 1987; Hughes, 'Birdman of Toorak. Encounters with Major Rubin', *Nation,* 18 April 1964, reprinted in Inglis, pp. 146–50; cf. Inglis, p. 77, for Elwyn Lynne's review of Hughes' Sydney exhibition; Bill Wannan, 'Warm Landscapes', *Bulletin,* 29 June 1963; Packer, p. 6. On the dominance of abstract landscapes in Australian painting in the 1940s and 1950s, see *Landscape with Figures,* ep. 9.

33 *The Art of Australia,* original ed., pp. 274, 295, & revised ed., p. 315; Hughes, 'The Well-wrought Ern', p. xix; *Landscape with Figures,* eps 2, 10.

34 Reg MacDonald, 'Moment of Truth', *Herald,* Melbourne, 17 December 1966.

35 Michael Shelden, *Friends of Promise. Cyril Connolly and the World of Horizon,* London, 1990, pp. 42–7, 157–9; Paul Fussell, *Wartime. Understanding and Behaviour in the Second World War,* New York, 1989, pp. 209–22; Craven, 'The Dazzling Robert Hughes'; Hawley, 'Art and Nothing But', p. 19; Isabel Lucas, '25 years late, but it's here', *SMH,* 8 February 1984.

36 'Dog Eats Dog', *Nation,* 1963, in Inglis, p. 107; *The Art of Australia,* original ed., p. 295.

37 De Groen, pp. 123–4; McGrath, 'I'm a fat old enfant'; Judy Ruenitz, 'Tiger! Tiger! burning bright', *Vogue Australia,* Sydney, March 1975, p. 93; Dutton, *The Innovators,* pp. 149, 156; *Landscape with Figures,* ep. 10; 'Civilisation, Aussie style'; Packer, p. 15. Cf. McQueen, pp. 168–9. On his attitudes to academics, see, e.g., his Foreword to Anne Robertson, *Treasures of the State Library of New South Wales. The Australiana Collections,* Sydney 1988, p. viii; Michael Shmith, 'Cheerful critic turns on himself', *Age,* 10 March 1990; *Barcelona,* pp. 188–9; *Culture of Complaint,* pp. 23–7, 50–70, 99, 111, 117; Porter, 'Hughes exorcises America'; Craven, 'Stuck in the middle'; Delahunty interview, ABC TV, 1995; Lumby, 'Australian who conquered America'.

38 Packer, p. 20; John Lahr, *Dame Edna Everage and the Rise of Western Civilisation,* Flamingo ed., London, 1992, p. 59. On attitudes to and relations with Smith, see 'Dog Eats Dog', in Inglis, p. 107; *The Art of Australia,* original ed., pp. ix, 2, 66, 120, 130, 224–7, 272, and revised ed., pp. 19, 21, 247–9; Thomas, 'The long wait'; Lansell, 'Yesterday's contemporary'; *Landscape with Figures,* eps 8, 10; Dutton, *The Innovators,* pp. 148–9; McQueen, p. 168; Lumby, 'Australian who conquered America'.

39 *Nation,* 19 December 1959; De Groen, p. 120; Dutton, *The Innovators,* pp. 183–4; *Landscape with Figures,* ep. 2

40 *Landscape with Figures,* ep. 6; cf. ep. 9. On the inadequacies of galleries in Australia before the 1970s, see also Packer, p. 13.

41 *Nothing If Not Critical,* p. 4, and cf. p. 14; 'What's A Museum For?', National Gallery of Australia, Canberra, 25 October 1992; 'Masterpiece Theater', *New York Review of Books,* 4 March 1993, p. 12. For similar statements, see *The Art of Australia,* revised ed., p. 313; Elisabeth Wynhausen, 'Robert Hughes, in grey suit … ', *National Times,* 13–18 January 1975; *The Shock of the New,* p. 7; De Groen, pp. 126, 128; *Culture of Complaint,* p. 148.

42 Hughes, *Frank Auerbach,* London, 1991, p. 7; *The Shock of the New,* p. 257; *Nothing If Not Critical,* p. 224; *American Visions,* ep. 7; *Barcelona,* pp. 479–80; *The Art of Australia,* revised ed., chs 4, 9; *Landscape with Figures,* eps 4, 8, 9; Heathcote, pp. 146–7. Cf. Bernard Smith, 'The Myth of Isolation', in his *The Death of the Artist as Hero,* Melbourne, 1988, pp. 217–29.

43 Broom, 'Oh, brother! … '; De Groen, p. 128; *The Art of Australia,* original ed., pp. 258–9; Dennis Minogue, 'Hughes attacks our myths', *Age,* 7 December 1974; Wynhausen, 'Robert Hughes'.

44 Inglis, p. 124; Packer, pp. 6–7; James, *Snakecharmers in Texas,* p. 11; De Groen, pp. 127, 130, 141–2. Cf. Hughes, 'The Vice of Writing', p. 17.

45 Tom Pocock, *Alan Moorehead,* Pimlico ed., London, 1991, pp. 7–8, 20–6, 220–1, 268–72; Slattery, 'The Art of being Robert Hughes', p. 19; De Groen, p. 127; Packer, pp. 6–7.

46 Hughes, 'Art in a world without angles', *Australian,* 22 August 1964.

47 *Donald Friend,* Sydney, 1965, p. 44.

48 Packer, p. 7; *American Visions,* ep. 1; 'What's A Museum For?'.

49 De Groen, p. 128; Packer, p. 12; 'The Shock of the Hughes', *Vanity Fair,* 1990, p. 226.

50 Packer, p. 8; Erlich, 'The entertaining Robert Hughes'; De Groen, p. 135; Wyndham, 'Fatal charmer'.

51 Wynhausen, 'A convict race'; Packer, pp. 7–10, 15; *The Fatal Shore,* London, 1987, p. vii; biographical note on Hughes in *The Art of Australia,* original ed., p. i; De Groen, p. 131; Hughes, 'The golden virgin of little Siena', *Age,* 19 February 1966; 'The devil in the cemetery', *SMH,* 19 February 1966; 'The first Bohemian', *SMH,* 5 March 1966.

52 'What's A Museum For?'; Slattery, 'Art of being Robert Hughes'; *Barcelona,* pp. 4, 266; Heyward, 'Fatal core'; 'What makes Barcelona great', *Age,* 12 April 1992.

53 Packer, pp. 7–8.

54 'Flying the Black Mamba', p. 5; McGrath: 'I'm a fat old enfant'; Colville, 'Chairing the experts'; MacDonald, 'Moment of truth'; De Groen, pp. 131, 133; Jane Perlez, 'Enfant terrible of art returns to the fray', *Australian,* 28 November 1970; Elizabeth Riddell, 'Robert Hughes returns', *Australian,* 4 July 1972; Packer, pp. 22–3; 'The Shock of the Hughes', *Vanity Fair,* 1990, p. 226; 'Shock of the Hughes', *Australian Weekend Magazine,* 1987; Broom, 'Oh, brother! … '; Wynhausen, 'Robert Hughes'; Sandra McGrath, 'The man who can speak the language of the brush', *Weekend Australian,* 20 August 1977.

55 'The Shock of the Hughes', *Vanity Fair,* 1990, p. 226; Packer, pp. 12–13; Neville, p. 28; Riddell, 'Robert Hughes returns'; 'Artist is mellower', *SMH,* 4 July 1972.

56 Neville, pp. 28, 163, 203, 323; Clive James, *The Metropolitan Critic,* 1st ed., London, 1974, pp. 205–7.

57 White, 'The Painted Word'; *Heaven and Hell in Western Art,* p. 105; *The Art of Australia,* revised ed., p. 20.

58 Neville, pp. 195–6; Gawenda, 'Hughes, QC'; 'Dossier. On the man students love to hate', *Australian,* 2 October 1970.

59 Broom, 'Oh, brother! … '; *Culture of Complaint,* p. 75.

60 *Who's Who 1993,* p. 941; *Who's Who in Australia 1994,* p. 768; Packer, p. 10; Margaret Smith, 'The Rebel's Return', *SMH,* 6 July 1972.

61 Smith, 'The Rebel's Return'; Neville, pp. 84, 104, 215, 221, 241; Packer, p. 23; Greer, *The Madwoman's Underclothes,* London, 1986, pp. 51–9; 'Artist is mellower'. For the later fortunes of Danne and Danton, see Neville, p. 364; Slattery, 'The Art of being Robert Hughes', p. 19; 'Title deeds', *SMH,* 11 April 1992.

62 'Shock of the Hughes', *Australian Weekend Magazine,* 1987; Packer, pp. 11–12.

63 Ruskin, *Fors Clavigera,* 1.4, 7.2, 10.2, in his *Works,* vol. XXVII, pp. 14, 114, 167;

Slattery, 'The Art of being Robert Hughes', pp. 22–3; Wynhausen, 'Robert Hughes'; Hughes, *Culture of Complaint*, pp. 15, 19, 26–8, 32, 60, 90, 128, 162–3; Craven, 'Stuck in the middle'; Lumby, 'Australian who conquered America'; 'Why Watch It, Anyway?', p. 42; *American Visions*, eps 1 & 7.

64 *American Visions*, ep .1.
65 Don Riseborough, 'What ever happened to Robert Hughes?', *SMH*, 13 November 1971; Slattery, 'Art of being Robert Hughes', p. 18; Terry Tacon, 'Top art critic. Hilarious start to task', *Mercury*, Hobart, 7 December 1974; De Groen, p. 132; Packer, pp. 14, 23–7.
66 Shock of the Hughes', *Australian*, 1987; Wynhausen, 'Feverish world'; Packer, p. 27.
67 Erlich, 'The entertaining Robert Hughes'; Riseborough, 'What ever happened …'; Packer, p. 25; 'Shock of the Hughes', *Australian Weekend Magazine*, 1987.
68 Packer, p. 25; Peter Cochrane, 'Brickbats, broadsides and buckshot: Robert Hughes hits town', *SMH*, 10 March 1990; Slattery, 'Art of being Robert Hughes', p. 18.
69 Packer, p. 15; *Culture of Complaint*, p. 83.
70 *American Visions*, ep. 5; Packer, p. 13; Slattery, 'The Art of being Robert Hughes', p. 18; Hawley, 'World's Most Influential Art Critic?'; Trish Evans, '"Shock" is hailed as a masterpiece', *Australian*, 20 March 1981; Ruenitz, 'Tiger! Tiger!', p. 94.
71 *American Visions*, eps 1, 2, 5.
72 *American Visions*, eps 1 & 2; 'Art and Identity', Melbourne Festival of the Arts lecture (in question-time), Melbourne Town Hall, 31 October 1995; *Culture of Complaint*, pp. 147–9.
73 *American Visions*, eps 4 & 5.
74 Riseborough, 'What ever happened … '; *American Visions*, eps 7 & 8.
75 Riseborough, 'What ever happened … '; Hinch, 'Robert Hughes rampant'.
76 Sandra McGrath, 'The Return of Robert Hughes'; Riseborough, 'What ever happened … '; Hughes, 'Dog Eats Dog', in Inglis, pp. 106–8; though for a later, more adverse, view of Greenberg, see De Groen, pp. 133–4, 140.
77 Riseborough, 'What ever happened … '; Wyndham, 'Fatal charmer'; Lumby, 'Australian who conquered America'; *Nothing If Not Critical*, p. 17; Hinch, 'Robert Hughes rampant'. The introductory shots in his *Landscape with Figures* series (ep. 1) show him surveying SoHo from his loft and talking about its rapid development as an artists' community in the years since he had moved there.
78 Cassab, p. 211 (1 July 1972); Keith Looby, 'An Australian holiday for Robert Hughes', *National Times*, 24–29 July 1972; Broom, 'Oh, brother! … '; Riseborough, 'What ever happened … '; 'Shock of the Hughes', *Australian Weekend Magazine*, 1987; 'Guest of Honour', ABC Radio, 30 July 1972, reported in Terry Ingram, 'The high cost of chauvinism', *Australian Financial Review*, 31 July 1972, and 'Aust flavour "hopeless" in art', *SMH*, 31 July 1972.
79 Dennis Minogue, 'Hughes attacks our myths'; Tacon, 'Top art critic'; Wynhausen, 'Robert Hughes'; Nancy Borlase, 'Critic pulls no punches', *Bulletin*, 12 April 1975; De Groen, p. 148; Packer, p. 13: *Landscape with Figures*, ep. 10.
80 *The Fatal Shore*, pp. xi–xv; Packer, p. 15; Riseborough, 'What ever happened … '; McGrath, 'Robert Hughes and the Convict Experience'.
81 'The Shock of the Hughes', *Vanity Fair*, p. 226; 'Images of pain and pleasure'.

82 *The Fatal Shore*, pp. xiii–xiv, 3–4, 76, 92, 299, 317–18, 339, 358, 398–414, 441–2, 457, 460–84, 534, 558, 576, 583–6. Reviews and review articles on the book include: Alan Frost, 'Fatal ambivalence towards our past', *Australian Weekend Magazine*, 21–22 February 1987; Stuart Macintyre, 'Hughes and the Historians', *Meanjin*, Melbourne, vol. 46 , no. 2, 1987, pp. 243–8; Portia Robinson, 'The Shock of the Old', *Age Monthly Review*, June 1987, pp. 3–5; Marian Aveling in *Australian Historical Studies*, vol. 23, no. 90, April 1980, pp. 127–8.

83 Packer, p. 18; 'The Shock of the Hughes', *Vanity Fair*, 1990, p. 226; Richard Guilliat, '"Gulag Australia": Robert Hughes's grisly story of a British invention', *Times on Sunday*, Sydney, 4 January 1987; *The Fatal Shore*, pp. 158, 325.

84 *The Fatal Shore*, p. xiv; Packer, p. 18; McGrath, 'Robert Hughes and the Convict Experience'; Hughes to Dutton, in Dutton, *The Innovators*, p. 188; *Landscape with Figures*, ep. 7.

85 'The Shock of the Hughes', *Vanity Fair*, 1990, p. 224; Slattery, 'The Art of being Robert Hughes', p. 19; 'Shock of the Hughes', *Australian Weekend Magazine*, 1987.

86 McGrath, 'I'm a fat old enfant'; Packer, p. 21; Wynhausen, 'A convict race'; Slattery, 'The Art of being Robert Hughes', p. 19; Hughes, *Culture of Complaint*, p. 131; Gawenda, 'Hughes, QC'; Turnbull, 'From Silk to Riches', p. 41; 'Court player'; Stephens, 'Tom Hughes'.

87 *The Shock of the New*, p. 6.

88 *The Shock of the New*, pp. 97, 99, 134, 184, 318, 364, 369, 389.

89 *The Shock of the New*, p. 375; Elwyn Lynn, 'The Shock of the Hughes', *Quadrant*, vol. xxv, no. 6, June 1981, p. 50; *The Art of Australia*, revised ed., 1970, p. 171. Cf. Bernard Smith's 1981 radio review of *The Shock of the New*, published in his *The Critic as Advocate*, Oxford University Press, Melbourne, 1989, p. 307.

90 *Nothing If Not Critical*, pp. 161, 164. De Chirico's 'La Nostalgie du Poète' (*c.* 1914) hangs in the Peggy Guggenheim collection in Venice.

91 *The Shock of the New*, 'Updated and enlarged edition', London, 1991, pp. 376, 425. Cf. his similar pronouncements on *The Talk Show with Clive James* on 'Culture in the Twentieth Century', BBC TV, 1990.

92 *Nothing If Not Critical*, pp. 6, 237, 327; *Culture of Complaint*, pp. 158–9. Cf. his 'The Case for Elitist Do-gooders', p. 34.

93 Hughes, *Lucian Freud paintings*, London, 1987, pp. 7–8; *Colin Lanceley*, pp. 9, 15, 17; *Frank Auerbach*, pp. 9, 11, 19, 214; *Landscape with Figures*, ep. 10; *Nothing If Not Critical*, esp. pp. 6–8, 15–23, 243–56, 299–312; *The Shock of the New*, 1991 ed., pp. 365, 376, 422–3; *Culture of Complaint*, pp. 158–9, 163, 166–7; 'A Fiesta of Whining', *Time*, 22 March 1993, p. 68; Slattery, 'The Art of being Robert Hughes', p. 22. At the beginning of the 1980s Hughes was already describing himself as a 'mildly conservative art journalist now' (McGrath, 'I'm a fat old enfant'). On Hughes' position *vis-à-vis* other 'obituarists' of the avant-garde, see Paul Mann, *The Theory-Death of the Avant-Garde*, Bloomington, Indiana, 1991, pp. 31–41.

94 *Nothing If Not Critical*, pp. 375–87; *Culture of Complaint*, pp. 63–4.

95 *Nothing If Not Critical*, pp. 54, 196, 386; Heyward, 'Fatal core'. Cf. *Culture of Complaint*, pp. 28, 128; Craven, 'Stuck in the middle'.

96 Riseborough, 'Whatever happened … '; Wynhausen, 'Feverish world'; *The Shock of the New*, 1991 ed., p. 376.

97 *Nothing If Not Critical,* pp. 142, 251, 255–6, 303; cf. *Culture of Complaint,* p. 35; *American Visions,* eps 7 & 8.

98 *Nothing If Not Critical,* pp. 14, 18, 303; *Culture of Complaint,* pp. 136, 150.

99 'The Shock of the Hughes', *Vanity Fair,* 1990, p. 224; *Nothing If Not Critical,* pp. 299–300.

100 'What's A Museum For?'; *Culture of Complaint,* pp. 7, 10–11, 24–6, 30–1, 46–8, 60, 133–4, 140, 146–55, 169–71; Phillip Adams, 'Robert Hughes takes on the Complaints Department', interview, ABC Radio, printed in *24 Hours,* August 1993, p. 56; 'Masterpiece Theater', p. 14; 'Dolls and Discontents', p. 85. On sectarian division in twentieth-century Australia, see Patrick O'Farrell, *The Catholic Church and Community. An Australian History,* Kensington, NSW, 1985, pp. 334–40, 393–401; Naomi Turner, *Catholics in Australia. A Social History,* vol. 2, North Blackburn, Victoria, 1992, pp. 53, 57, 93, 96, 170–82.

101 Slattery, 'The Art of Being Robert Hughes', p. 22; *American Visions,* ep. 8.

102 *Barcelona,* p. 171.

103 *Nothing If Not Critical,* pp. 18–19, 27–8.

104 'Why Watch It, Anyway?', p. 40; *Culture of Complaint,* pp. 73, 84; 'Art in a world without angles'; *Nothing If Not Critical,* pp. 202–6; 'Wilfredo Lam', *Time,* 22 February 1993, p. 68; *The Shock of the New,* p. 108; Hughes quoted in Joanna Mendelssohn, 'Scourge of zealots and whingers', *Bulletin,* 10 November 1992, p. 56.

105 See Guy Brett, *Transcontinental. Nine Latin American Artists,* London, 1990; Santiago Colas, *Postmodernity in Latin America,* Durham, North Carolina, 1995.

106 *Culture of Complaint,* p. 82; *Barcelona,* pp. 45–52, cf. pp. 16–17.

107 *Nothing If Not Critical,* p. 28; Peter Craven, 'Vibrant Hughes of our history', *Australian,* 8 February 1995.

108 Wyndham, 'The Fatal Charmer'; Hughes, Introduction to Malcolm Turnbull, *The Reluctant Republic,* Melbourne, 1993, pp. xv–xxi; 'A Robert Hughes Republic', *Weekend Australian,* 4–5 November 1995; Ebru Yaman, 'Hughes highlights culture's fatal flaw', *Australian,* 31 October 1995; Hughes interviewed by Kerry O'Brien, *7.30 Report,* ABC TV, 26 November 1996; Luke Slattery, 'Hughes blasts "uncaring" PM on race debate', *Australian,* 27 November 1996; Hughes, 'Republican push turns to shove', *Age,* 2 December 1996; *Culture of Complaint,* p. 74.

109 'What's a Museum For?'; De Groen, pp. 136, 140–1; Slattery, 'The Art of being Robert Hughes', pp. 18, 22.

110 Wynhausen, 'Feverish world'; Hawley, 'World's Most Influential Art Critic?'. Cf. De Groen, pp. 137–9.

111 Packer, p. 18; 'Shock of the Hughes', *Australian Weekend Magazine*; *Othello,* II, i, 251–3; Cochrane, 'Brickbats, broadsides and buckshot'; Shmith, 'Cheerful critic'; 'The Shock of the Hughes', *Vanity Fair,* p. 190.

112 Lumby, 'Australian who conquered America'.

6 After-word

1 Patricia Harewood, 'The Birth of Edna', in Ken Thomson, ed., *Barry Humphries. Bepraisements on his Birthday,* London, 1994, p. 45.

2 Richard White, 'Passing Through: Tuscany and the Australian Tourist', in Gaetano

Prampolini and Marie-Christine Hubert, *An Antipodean Connection,* Geneva, 1993, p. 172.

3 For the historical background on these forces, see Geoffrey Blainey, *The Tyranny of Distance. How Distance Shaped Australian History,* Melbourne, 1966, pp. 328–39.

4 John Lack and Jacqueline Templeton, *Bold Experiments. A Documentary History of Australian Immigration since 1945,* Melbourne, 1995, pp. xiii–xvi, 2–5, 12–13, 74–5, 150–2, 160; Sean Carney, 'Out of Empire', *Age,* Melbourne, 19 March 1994; Robert Hughes, *Culture of Complaint,* revised ed., London, 1994, p. 77.

5 David Marr, *Patrick White. A Life,* Vintage ed., Milsons Point, NSW, 1992, pp. 255, 326–9, 382, 387–91, 395, 455; Phillip Adams, 'How Bazza turned the tide of cultural cringe', *Australian Weekend Review,* 12–13 September 1992; Brian McFarlane, *Australian Cinema 1970–1985,* London, 1987, pp. 8–11, 21; John Rickard, *Australia. A Cultural History,* London, 1988, pp. 184–5, 262; Geoffrey Serle, *From Deserts the Prophets Come,* 1st ed., Melbourne, 1973, pp. 218–19, and revised ed.: *The Creative Spirit in Australia. A Cultural History,* Richmond, Victoria, 1987, pp. 218–19.

6 Clive James, *Unreliable Memoirs,* Picador ed., London, 1981, p. 173; cf. Geoffrey Dutton, *Out in the Open,* St Lucia, Queensland, 1994, pp. 362–3; Serle, *The Creative Spirit in Australia,* pp. 187, 215–16, 220–1.

7 A.A. Phillips, *The Australian Tradition,* Melbourne, 1958, p. 91; Geoffrey Thurley, *The American Moment,* London, 1977, p. 5.

8 Hughes, *Landscape with Figures,* 1975, ep. 1, and 'Critic finds sour core to New York art', *Australian,* 13 March 1990; John Lahr, 'Playing Possum', *New Yorker,* 1 July 1991, p. 62.

9 Nicholas Jose, 'Cultural Identity: I Think I'm Something Else', in Stephen Graubard, *Australia: The Daedelus Symposium,* North Ryde, NSW, 1985, pp. 313–15; Serle, *The Creative Spirit in Australia,* pp. 326–7. There were a few Australian commentators who were questioning the assumptions of England's or Europe's centrality from the 1950s and 1960s; see, e.g., Manning Clark, 'Rewriting Australian History', in T. A. G. Hungerford, *Australian Signpost,* Melbourne, 1956, p. 132; Jack Lindsay, 'The Alienated Australian Intellectual', *Meanjin,* vol. 22, no. 1, 1963, pp. 55–6.

10 James, 'The Idea of a National Culture', Melbourne Town Hall, 16 October 1996; interview by Kerry O'Brien, *7.30 Report,* ABC TV, 14 October 1996; interview by Andrea Stretton, *Stretton on Saturday,* SBS TV, 19 October 1996; Phillips, p. 90.

11 Charles Osborne, 'Introduction', *London Magazine,* New Series, vol. II, no. 6, September 1962, p. 5.

12 *Official Year Book of the Commonwealth of Australia,* no. 51, 1965, p. 289; James, *Flying Visits,* Picador ed., London, 1985, pp. 3–4, 7; Christopher Koch, *Crossing the Gap,* London, 1987, p. 116; John Stevens, 'The Age of posh coming to an end', *Age,* 25 February 1972.

13 Koch, pp. 2–3.

14 Frank Moorhouse, *Days of Wine and Rage,* Ringwood, Victoria, 1980, p. 184; Ros Pesman, *Duty Free,* Melbourne, 1996, p. 220; *The Talk Show with Clive James* on 'Britishness', BBC TV, 11 February 1990; Germaine Greer, 'In a state about Australian entry into Europe', *Guardian,* 1 May 1995.

15 J.H. Davidson, 'Notes on a Nationalist: Donald Horne's "The Next Australia"',

Meanjin, vol. 30, no. 4, December 1971; 'Home Thoughts from Abroad. The New Metropolis', *Meanjin,* vol. 32, no. 1, 1973, p. 17; 'The De-Dominionisation of Australia', *Meanjin,* vol. 38, no. 2, 1979, p. 144.

16 Serle, *From Deserts the Prophets Come,* p. 219.

17 Frank Moorhouse, 'Regionalism, Provincialism and Australian Anxieties', *Westerly,* Perth, vol. 23, no. 4, December 1978, p. 61, and *Days of Wine and Rage,* p. 181; Laurie Hergenhan & Irmtraud Petersson, *Changing Places,* St Lucia, Queensland, 1994, pp. xv, xxi.

18 Rickard, p. 262; Pesman, pp. 221–2.

19 Peter Logue, reporting Professor Geoffrey Brennan, 'Bureaucracy could kill Australia's intellectual life ...', *ANU Reporter,* vol. 23, no. 10, 8 July 1992, p. 1.

20 *Year Book Australia,* no. 73, 1990, p. 141; no. 78, 1996, p. 108: Australian Bureau of Statistics, Canberra (the last figures given in this source are for 1994).

21 Jane Cornwell, 'Dream time', *Age,* 12 November 1994.

22 Stephen Fry, *Paperweight,* Mandarin ed., London, 1993, pp. 259–61.

Index